Odin's Wife:
Mother Earth in Germanic Mythology

William P. Reaves

Frontispiece:
Frigga by Sarah Powers Bradish, 1900
after Johannes Gehrts.

Cover Art by Howard David Johnson

Maps by Sharron Puryear

Hardcover ISBN 978-0-578-43084-3

Dedicated to Carla O'Harris
A woman after my own heart
Thank You

"As with any pre-literate mythology belonging to peoples spread over a considerable geographical expanse, and sustained for many centuries, variegation in detail both minor and major is to be expected, and subsequent mythographies bear witness to inconsistencies. Significant patterns nonetheless emerge from extant texts that can be analysed to reveal the underlying mythological understandings they express, expressions that cannot, of course, be taken as hard evidence of actual pre-Christian beliefs."

—Judy Quinn,
"What Frigg Knew: The Goddess as Prophetess," (2015).

CONTENTS

Odin and Frigg on Hlidskjalf
R.E. Kepler, 1902

Introduction

"Any wise commentator on Norse mythology ought to begin by acknowledging frankly that we know rather little about it. Many modern descriptions rely heavily on the *Prose Edda* of Snorri Sturluson, and especially on the fluent and persuasive account of the gods in *Gylfaginning*, its first major section. But Snorri was writing in the 1220s, when Iceland had been a Christian country for two centuries, and his *Prologus* begins with an unambiguous authorial statement of the Christian view of creation."
— John McKinnell, *Both One and Many* (1994), p.13.

A wide range of sources gathered from across Northern Europe from the emergence of the Germanic tribes in the historic record to the close of the heathen era and beyond attest that the Germanic people widely venerated a goddess personifying the Earth under a variety of names. A closer examination of these scattered accounts unveils many common threads which demonstrate the continuity of her character for over a millennium, indicating that these sources speak of one figure known by many different designations. Under whatever local title she appears, this goddess is most often identified as Odin's wife and, as far as the records allow us to know, the mother of other prominent members of the Germanic pantheon. A broader comparison across the Indo-European diaspora demonstrates that this Germanic Earth-Mother bears much in common with her Indo-European counterparts, indicating that her persona and associated mythology have ancient pre-Germanic roots. This is not to suggest in any way that this thoroughly Germanic figure is identical to or even an aspect of the so-called prehistoric Divine Feminine, Universal Great Goddess or Mother Goddess figure widely acknowledged in scholarship today. Such speculation is beyond the scope of this investigation. *To be clear, the present study is concerned only with the presence of a personified Earth-Mother within the historic Germanic territories.*

3

Today, many scholars recognize the importance in popular primitive belief of *hieros gamos* or "sacred marriage," a cosmic coupling in which a masculine Heaven mates with a feminine Earth, commonly exemplified in the Greek myth of Ouranos and Gaia.[1] From the union of a male god and a female earth comes the harvest of fertility of the cosmos.[2] It is most often seen as a natural and common development in many agrarian societies, where, in a very real sense, the Earth is the source of all life. Flora and fauna alike appear to emerge from her womb, and all life is dependent upon her for its existence. The sky is then imagined as a husband and father, whose vital warmth and fluids are required to fertilize his wife, the earth, and create new life. At times the symbolism is overt, as in the Greek myth of Zeus and Danae, where he seduces her in the form of golden rain. In some traditions, the god may be replaced by his representative on earth, often the king. In a Sumerian poem, the earth imagery is clear: "Great Lady, the king will plow your vulva, I, Dumuzi the king, will plow your vulva."[3] As Mircea Eliade has shown, versions of this myth are prominent in Oceania from Indonesia to Micronesia, as well as in Asia, Africa, and the Americas.[4] Other scholars have detected similar patterns in Near Eastern and Old European mythologies,[5] demonstrating that *hieros gamos* played an important role in many indigenous religions across the globe. Within the Germanic sphere, Thomas DuBois observes:

> "Tacitus's description of the Nerthus cult in the first century
> A.D. depicts a ritual possibly related to the *hieros gamos* tradition: the
> goddess Nerthus is paraded through the vicinity in a wagon

---

[1] Erich Segal, *The Death of Comedy* (2001), p. 13.

[2] Thomas DuBois, *Nordic Religions in the Viking Age* (1999), p. 55-56.

[3] Diane Wolkstein and Samuel Noah Cramer, *The Courtship of Dumuzi and Inanna,' Inanna, Queen of Heaven and Earth*, (1983), p. 37.

[4] See *The Sacred and the Profane*, tr. Willard Trask (1959), pp. 147-151 and *Patterns in Comparative Religion*, tr. Rosemary Sheed (1958), pp. 239 - 262.

[5] Such as T. H. Gaster, *Thespis: Ritual Myth and Drama in the Ancient Near East* (1961), pp. 62–64; Sir James Frazer, *Folklore in the Old Testament* (1919-1925); and Marija Gimbutas, *The Gods and Goddesses of Old Europe*, (1982).

accompanied by her priest. ...Skaldic poets of the Viking Age also describe Óðinn as the bridegroom of Jorð (Earth), a fact which would tie him to the *hieros gamos* complex as well."

Nor is this understanding recent. As early as 1829, Finnur Magnússon, wrote:

"Ultimately most pagan people came to imagine the sky as the Earth's husband, as it seems to rest upon the earth and fertilize it with 'Warmth.'[6] This presumably literal god of heaven was assumed to be the creative Principle of Nature with the Earth as its receiver. ...Thus for example, with us Odin (who owed his existence to the Universal or Supreme God) was considered the world's All-father, and Frigga or Earth as All-mother."[7]

In 1873, Edward B. Tylor in his classic work, *Primitive Culture*, noted that "the idea of the earth as a mother is more simple and obvious, and no doubt for that reason more common in the world, than the idea of heaven as a father." Underlying Tylor's argument was the principle of evolution applied to the development of human culture, a common theoretical perspective during the last half of the nineteenth century. While Tylor likely had no intention of establishing Mother Earth as a major figure in primitive world religion, this however, was the effect of his work, particularly in studies of Native American belief.[8] Albrecht Dietrich's *Mutter Erde* (1905) helped to popularize this argument, "bringing the Mother Earth figure into the arena of the worldwide study of religion and culture,"[9] thereby influencing such later scholars as E.O. James and Mircea Eliade.[10]

---

[6] *Varmestoffet*, lit. "warm-stuff", an invisible substance that creates heat according to a now obsolete scientific theory, comparable to radiation today.

[7] *Den förste November, den förste August*, p. 129. Translated from Danish.

[8] Sam D. Gill, *Mother Earth: An American Story* (1987), pp. 107 ff.

[9] Gill, ibid., 110.

[10] Olof Pettersson, *Mother Earth: An Analysis of the Mother Earth Concepts According to Albrecht Dietrich* (1967).

As the science of comparative mythology gained steam in the latter half of the nineteenth century, others expanded upon these simple observations, at first confined to European and Near Eastern religions, but now with an eye to the whole world, expounding evolutionary theories to explain how, when and where the concept of an Earth-Mother first emerged. For this purpose, so-called primitive religions with no discernible connections to the ancient religions of Europe and the Near East were brought to bear. Such scholars left the fertile fields of Indo-European mythology and ventured far into the darker realms of mythogony, the origins of mythology, a much more speculative branch of human psychology. Fixated on the supposed origin and development of religion itself, the scope of their arguments soon turned from the historic character of attested goddesses to the universal nature of a Divine Feminine— in other words from the study of actual mythology to theoretical mythogony, the error of the nature mythologists who saw all gods and goddesses narrowly as personifications of natural and psychological phenomena. What was actually attested in Indo-European and Near Eastern mythologies was thus extrapolated backwards and applied to times and places it was not; gods and goddesses of disparate natures were seen as hypostases of a single universal Sky-Father and Earth-Mother. All deities were forced into this mold, regardless of their culture of origin. Unfortunately, this premise still underlies much scholarship into Germanic mythology today.

From Tylor's general insight, a parallel theory took root concerning the very rise of religion itself. In 1955, Erich Neumann, influenced by the work of psychologist Carl Jung, advanced the concept of a universal "Great Mother" goddess, who reigned as the dominant religious force before the concept of a supreme male deity had developed.[11] E. O. James, author of *The Cult of the Mother Goddess* (1959), expanded upon this, stating that only when the function of the male became apparent in the physiological process of procreation was the primordial Mother Goddess assigned a male companion.

---

[11] Hilda Davidson, *Roles of the Northern Goddess* (1997), p. 2

Other prominent scholars soon accepted the theory and argued that recurring symbols in early prehistoric art were associated with her cult.[12] Archaeologist Marija Gimbutas, who drew heavily on Neumann's study, went further locating this goddess in a concrete cultural context, suggesting that the late Paleolithic period was dominated by matriarchal societies who venerated powerful mother goddesses.[13] She assembled a wealth of evidence, primarily female figurines and decorative patterns, in support of her theory, outlining the basis for it in this manner:

> "It was the sovereign mystery and creative power of the female as the source of life that developed into the first religious experiences. The Great Mother Goddess who gives birth to all creation out of the holy darkness of her womb became the metaphor for Nature herself."[14]

Over the course of her career, Gimbutas developed this argument further, placing increasing emphasis on a unified Goddess, more powerful than any male god, who dominated Paleolithic and Neolithic religion prior to a series of invasions by Indo-European tribes with their patriarchal institutions.[15] In time, individual goddesses of various cultures came to be seen as emanations of this single, universal Great Goddess, whose womb generated all life. In the Germanic field, Hilda Ellis Davidson, Carolyne Larrington and Richard North, among others, have espoused this theory. Christopher R. Fee with David Leeming in *Gods, Heroes, & Kings: The Battle for Mythic Britain* (2001), p. 82, state the case quite plainly:

> "Tacitus reported the existence of an earth-mother called Nerthus, a mysterious goddess associated specifically with fertility. In fact, it seems very likely that the chief deity among the early

---

[12] Davidson, ibid.

[13] Sandra Billington and Miranda Green, editors. *The Concept of the Goddess* (1996), p. 19.

[14] *The Civilization of the Goddess,* (1991), p. 222.

[15] Billington and Green, ibid., p. 19.

Germanic people was none other than the great earth-mother—
the great goddess known in almost every civilization throughout
the world— echoes of whom in her various manifestations make
up the bulk of the later Norse goddesses. Frigg, Freya, Sif, Idun,
and even the primordial Jörd are simply aspects of the same great
goddess. As war-gods replaced nature goddesses as chief among
the pantheon, the great goddess seems to have been split up into
lesser component parts."

In its most mature form, the theory holds that the Great Goddess
ruled over a balanced matristic society until, in the course of time,
powerful empires arose in the Middle East and in Southern Europe,
whose warring rulers invaded and conquered their agrarian neighbors.
Then such groups as the Indo-Europeans, with their militant male
deities and their dominant Sky-Father, were said to have engulfed and
subjugated the peaceful cult of the Great Mother Goddess. These
were people who literally worshiped "the lethal power of the blade"
as Gimbutas wrote— the power to take life rather than create it.[16]

In the last few decades, modern feminism has provided the
context for study and attempted to redefine or 'rebalance' the
relationship between male/female aspects of deity. Typical of the
more radical expressions of this theology is the belief that the Divine
Feminine was somehow lost or deliberately repressed by institutional
religions dominated by patriarchal male deities.[17] Evidence from
many cultures around the world has been brought to bear in support
of this theory, but all too often continuity was taken for granted
without paying sufficient attention to the background and context of
the material.[18] In regard to her seminal work *When God Was a Woman*
(1976), a book which "sought to reclaim deity as female" now seen as
instrumental in the rise of modern feminist theology in the 1970s and
80s, sculptor and art historian Merlin Stone, freely admitted "when I

---

[16] Riane Eisler, "Reclaiming our Goddess Heritage" in *The Goddess Reawakening* (1989), p. 30.

[17] Dawne McCance (1990), *Understandings of 'The Goddess' in Contemporary Feminist Scholarship*, pp. 167-73.

[18] Davidson, ibid., p. 4-12.

first began seriously researching and writing *When God Was a Woman*, in the late sixties, …my goal was to show how narrow and binding our society's images of women were."[19] — a goal more apparent in the book's original title, *The Paradise Papers: The Suppression of Women's Rites*, when it first saw print in the United Kingdom. Of such works, Lotte Motz in *Faces of the Goddess* (1997) remarked: "One gains the impression that the scholars set out in their endeavor with an already fixed belief in the existence of a primordial, maternal, all-encompassing and sovereign deity." She added, "the claims concerning the glory and decline of the goddess cannot be substantiated. Many of the assertions are speculative. Documentation is sparse; references frequently limited to authors who share the vision." Motz concluded:

> "Since the 'Goddess' appears to satisfy the needs of many modern women, it might be inferred that the concept was constructed for just this purpose in modern times. The idea of an archetypical Great Mother, however, was extant before the era of the modern women's liberation movement," (pp. 184-5).

Juliette Wood, sums up this view in *The Concept of the Goddess* (1996) saying, "the Goddess is only the latest manifestation of a view of culture which suggests a Golden Age, whose real meaning was suppressed by some powerful, restrictive force." Thus we not only have cause to doubt the validity of this theory of the universal origin of human religion, but the very existence of the "Great Goddess" herself. As Lotte Motz ably illustrates in her study of prominent goddesses across the globe, the worship of a Great Mother Goddess representing the Earth, now widely accepted in popular culture, was by no means a universal phenomenon. This fact, however, does not preclude the existence of such figures in individual cultures, as Motz

---

[19] Shirley Nicholson, compiler. *The Goddess Re-Awakening* (1989), p. 1.

demonstrated in her own studies into northern European paganism.[20]

Within ancient Germanic studies today, several scholars have acknowledged the existence of an Earth-Mother figure, thereby proving that it is possible to identify such a goddess in the Old Germanic religion without presuming that her worship was universal in nature. While we find an actual goddess who personifies the earth in Old Norse mythology in the form of Thor's mother *Jörð*, many believe her origins are deeper still. For example, Rudolf Simek states: "In the late heathen period, as recorded in our oldest literary sources, Jörð appears to have only been known as Thor's mother, and she plays no further role as an earth-goddess — as she certainly once was."[21] Among recent scholars, there is little doubt that a goddess representing the Earth played an important role in the Indo-European religious tradition, from which the Germanic religion developed. In *The Oxford Companion to Proto-Indo-European and the Proto-Indo-European World* (2006), J.P. Mallory and D.Q. Adams state:

> "The sky god or 'father sky' is lexically the most secure deity and heads the pantheon of Greece and Rome. …Other than ruling the gods in respective pantheons, and serving as father to several other Indo-European deities, the sky god is also seen (at least in some traditions) to unite with 'mother earth.'"

In support of this, the authors point out that "Heaven and Earth" regularly appear as a pair in the lists of deities invoked as witnesses to Hittite treaties; in the Vedic tradition, Dyaus the father is paired with Prthivi, the mother, who represent heaven and earth; in Greece, Zeus is "the father of the gods" and Gaia is "the mother of the gods" but they do not make a couple. Instead Zeus is portrayed as the standard consort of Demeter (*Ge-meter*, "Earth-mother") and Semele, the mortal mother of Dionysus by Zeus, who are likely

---

[20] For example, John McKinnell in *Meeting the Other in Old Norse Myth and Legend*, (2005), p. 204, writes: "Lotte Motz argues that *Svipdagsmál* is a ritual induction of the young hero into a mother-goddess cult."

[21] *Dictionary of Northern Mythology* (1984), p. 179.

manifestations of the Indo-European Earth-Mother in origin. In union with Zeus, Demeter gives birth to Persephone who is intimately associated with the growth of crops and Semele gives birth to Dionysus, a deity of wine and vineyards. According to Herodotus (4, 59), the Scythians conceived of Earth as Zeus' wife. Scholars of comparative mythology believe these figures have a bearing on the study of the ancient Germanic religion, whose origins are assumed to lie in the murky Proto-Indo-European past. James C. Russell in *The Germanization of Early Medieval Christianity*, (1994) holds:

> "The study of Germanic religiosity has always suffered from a paucity of reliable extant sources. However, the work of Georges Dumézil in the field of comparative mythology provides a framework through which this deficiency may be compensated in certain instances. Dumézil's comparative model of Indo-European societies posits the existence of a fundamental similarity in the ideological and sometimes the social structure among the ancient societies of India, Persia, Greece, Rome, and pre-Christian northern Europe. This association permits the careful application of evidence regarding a fundamental ideological concept or 'mythologem' found in one or more Indo-European societies to that mythologem as it exists in another Indo-European society. Through such a process of analogy, one may enhance the understanding of that mythologem in the latter society, for which the currently available documentation may be scanty or inconclusive. When Dumezil's model is applied to pre-Christian Germanic religiosity, various aspects of form and structure hitherto interpreted solely as local, Germanic phenomena, acquire a new dimension, derived from their association with the greater Indo-European family of peoples." (p. 107).

As Martin L. West demonstrates in *Indo-European Poetry and Myth* (2007), among the Indo-Europeans the Earth-goddess is widely celebrated with the title of "mother," providing numerous examples from across the Indo-European spectrum.[22] As we shall see in the

---

[22] Martin L. West, *Indo-European Poetry and Myth* (2007), p. 175ff.

following chapters, a wealth of documented evidence proves that this same figure not only survived, but thrived, in the religious traditions of its West Germanic branch— the branch attested by such languages as Old Norse, Old English, Old High German (OHG), Old Saxon, and Old Frisian, which are the forebears of modern Danish, Swedish and Norwegian, as well as the English, German, Low German (or *Plattdeutsch*), Dutch, and Frisian languages.[23] There Earth is frequently associated with powerful sky gods, particularly in the Old Icelandic literature which provides the best evidence for the pre-Christian faith in the region. That said, it bears repeating that the current work is *not* an effort to identify *any* Germanic goddess with a universal Mother Goddess, or to prove the existence of an Earth-Mother in the Proto-Indo-European era, nor to reduce the known Germanic goddesses into a single figure. This investigation solely seeks to examine the evidence for the prolonged veneration of a native Germanic goddess personifying the Earth. In Northern Europe, she is found under a number of familiar names, but most commonly identified as Odin's wife, allowing us to recognize her. Owing to Earth's close connection with her consort the Sky-Father in many Indo-European pantheons, her origins probably lie in the pre-Germanic era. The evidence, of course, must speak for itself.

Lady with the Mead Cup
Birka, Uppland, Sweden, 10th century

---

[23] A Companion to Old Norse-Icelandic Literature and Culture, Rory McTurk ed. (2005), Ch. 10: Language, pp.173-189, by Michael Barnes, who adds that the "more distant relatives" of this branch "are languages descended from Latin — French, Italian, Portuguese, Romanian, Spanish, etc; Greek; the Celtic tongues —Irish, Scottish, Gaelic, Welsh and Breton; Russian and other Slavic languages; and Sanskrit."

I. The Prehistoric Context

"We have to be content with an imperfect and patchy understanding of the old [Norse] religion. But this does not entitle us to assume that the religion itself was correspondingly primitive or incomplete. We must bear in mind that no extensive direct information about the pagan religion was recorded until fully two centuries after the conversion to Christianity, and the generations which had come and gone meanwhile were, or were supposed to be, hostile to these pagan heresies."

—Jónas Kristjánsson, *Icelandic Manuscripts* (1996), p. 27.

It is widely held that a considerable continuity exists in both the archaeological and physical anthropological records of northern Europe, from the earliest appearance of the Germanic tribes back into the Bronze Age.[24] Within these records, we occasionally catch glimpses of the religious practices of the Germanic peoples. While few concrete conclusions can be drawn from the available evidence of the pre-literate period, we can discern some common themes which recur in later heathen texts that establish the longevity and conservation of the associated religious motifs.

The Germanic people first entered the historic record in the work of the Greek explorer Pytheas, who travelled to Northern Europe, sailing as far as the Arctic Circle, making observations about the peoples he encountered as well as their lands around 325 BC. Departing from the port city of Marseilles (Massilia), he was the first Mediterranean to reach Britain and the first explorer to describe features of northern Europe. To keep foreign ships from reaching the Atlantic islands which were rich sources of tin, copper and gold, the Carthaginians blockaded the Straits of Gibraltar, forcing the merchants of Marseilles to finance the expedition in search of alternative trade routes through northern Europe. Previously,

---

[24] J.P. Mallory and D.Q. Adams, *Encyclopedia of Indo-European Culture* (1997), p. 223.

Marseilles had trading posts as far north as the lower Rhine, but no traveler had reached Germany by ship before Pytheas. Although lost to the modern era, his work *"On the Ocean"* was widely influential in the ancient world, being cited by geographers, historians and ethnographers for centuries after. It is best known from citations in Strabo's *Geographica*, Pliny's *Natural History* and Diodorus of Sicily's *Bibliotheca Historica* which often quote him in disbelief. Strabo for instance, writing three hundred years later, says that Pytheas, who gave an account of "what lies beyond the Rhine as far as Scythia, …has been found, upon scrutiny, to be an arch-falsifier," (I, 4.3). Despite this, his observations have proven substantially correct. For example, he was the first to distinguish the 'Germanoï' of northern and central Europe from the 'Keltoï' dwelling further west.

Which routes Pytheas took and where he landed cannot be determined exactly from the surviving passages, but he must have crossed Gaul following the Rhone and the Loire into the Atlantic. Once there, he circumnavigated Britain, which he described as roughly triangular in shape, making estimates of its sides and naming its three corners. The people there, he said, were great in number and ruled by chieftains who employed horse-drawn chariots in warfare. They tattooed their skins blue[25] and lived in homes made of logs and thatch, suitable to their damp climate. They threshed their grain indoors and stored it in cellars. He sighted Ierne (Ireland), an island said to be inhabited by wild savages, but found the people of Cornwall more civilized in his estimation because of their contact with foreign traders. They skillfully mined tin ore and transported it in boats made of hide to an island called Ictis. The tin was then shipped to Gaul and carried on horseback to Marseilles. He also mentions a remote island named Thule —a six-day sail north of Britain and one day from the 'congealed' or 'frozen' sea— by which he may have meant the Shetland Islands, Norway or Iceland, even if

---

[25] The same is said of the Scandinavian Rus in the tenth century by the Arab writer Ibn Fadhlan in his *Ruslia*: "Each man, from the tip of his toes to his neck, is covered in dark-green lines, pictures and such like."

he had not travelled there himself. Pytheas wrote of northern lands where fauna was scarce and wild fruits, vegetables and roots were the only flora. He observed how the days lengthened as he sailed north and recorded the heights of the sun at different locations, from which later astronomers would calculate latitudes. He also noted that no star stood directly over the North Pole. Before heading home, Pytheas desired to know the origin of amber, a prized substance that came from northern Europe. In this regard, he was the first to mention a people known as the Gutones, thought to be Goths, who lived on an island and along the shores of a sizable estuary near the ocean, where this precious 'gemstone' washed ashore in abundance each spring. The Gutones, who used amber as fuel, collected it and sold it to their neighbors the Teutones, by which it made its way to Greece. To judge by the few surviving clues, the island of the Gutones which Pytheas named Abalus, may have been Heligoland or Zealand, which were rich sources of amber historically. Nothing more is known of his journey home. We cannot trace Pytheas' route past the Elbe. Pliny says that Timaeus (born c. 350 BC) believed Pytheas' story of the origin of amber, but later writers made it clear that, in their opinion, Pytheas was a liar when he described fertile, agricultural lands situated farther north than where the frozen wastes were supposed to begin. No doubt elements of his journey did seem fantastic. Pytheas undertook a bold journey of discovery into the northern regions and came as far as the Arctic Circle, where he said he saw the night-camp of the sun as she rested aglow on the horizon at midnight. He observed the sea freeze along the coastline and long needles of ice hanging there, as well as sailed through a gelatinous mass teaming with "sea-lungs," now thought to mean jellyfish.

Classical sources record the names of ancient Germanic tribes as parties to war as early as the third century BC. Macedonian kings are cited as having conscripted a tribe known as the Bastarnae in 201–202 BC and again in 171–168 BC to fight against the Romans during the Second and Third Macedonian Wars. In the late second century BC, Roman authors speak of armed conflicts between the

Republic and migrating Germanic tribes of Gaul, Italy and Hispania. In his *Commentaries on the Gallic Wars* (*Commentarii de Bello Gallico*, 58– 49 BC), Caesar writes that a tribe known as the Cimbri entered into Norticum (modern Austria) in search of land and food, where they vanquished a Roman army in 113 BC. In 109 and 105 BC, the Cimbri were joined by the Teutoni, originating from Jutland in modern Denmark, defeating additional forces sent by Rome. Another incursion in 101 BC was beaten back at Vercellae, Italy. From the Roman viewpoint, a growing threat from the North had been identified and the Germanic people, as a whole, emerged in history as a formidable enemy of the Empire around the first century, occupying the northern European plain from Flanders in the west to the Vistula river in the east, as well as parts of southern Scandinavia.[26]

By the turn of the first century, the so-called "barbarians" to the North began to make serious inroads, pushing against the borders of the empire. The Battle of the Teutoburg Forest, described by Roman historians as the Varian Disaster (*Clades Variana*), took place in the modern German state of Lower Saxony, where an alliance of Germanic tribes ambushed and destroyed three Roman legions and their auxiliaries, led by Publius Quinctilius Varus, in the year 9 AD. Hermann, a.k.a. Arminius, a Germanic officer in the Roman auxiliaries, led the revolt. The victory of his alliance over Rome's legions in the Teutoburg Forest would have far-reaching consequences for the history of the ancient Germanic peoples and the Roman Empire. Generally regarded as Rome's greatest military defeat, Arminius' victory over Varus has been considered one of the most decisive battles in history, since the rediscovery of Roman sources in the fifteenth century, all of which stress the completeness of the Roman defeat. Though the shock was great, the Romans immediately began preparations to avenge the loss and reconquer the territory. In 14 AD, upon the accession of Tiberius to the Roman throne, the new emperor's nephew, Germanicus, led a massive campaign into Germania. After a few successful skirmishes in the

---

[26] Mallory and Adams, (2006), ibid., p. 19.

summer of 15 AD, including the capture of Arminius' wife, Thusnelda, the army arrived at the site of the fateful battle. According to Tacitus, they found heaps of bleached bones and severed skulls nailed to trees, which they buried as if they were brothers. In boggy lowlands near the Ems river, Arminius' troops ambushed the Roman camp initially catching Germanicus' cavalry in a trap, until Roman infantry arrived to rout them. Unable to achieve a decisive victory, Germanicus' forces withdrew and returned to the Rhine. After a few subsequent raids across the Rhine, resulting in the recovery of two of the three legions' eagles lost in the Teutoburg Forest, Tiberius withdraw his forces and summoned Germanicus back to Rome, where he was reassigned. Tacitus held that Tiberius' decision to recall Germanicus was driven by jealousy, and that another campaign the following summer would have reestablished Roman control of the territories between the Rhine and the Elbe. Despite some successful campaigns in subsequent years, the Romans never again attempted to conquer the Germanic territories east of the Rhine. Nevertheless, Roman incursions into Germania continued unabated, intended less for conquest and more to force the Germanic peoples into political structures compliant to Rome.

The Roman Iron Age in Northern Europe, extending from the first to the fourth centuries, followed by the Germanic Iron Age, lasting from roughly c. 400 – c. 800 AD, was a period of mass migrations and armed conflicts as the Roman Empire sought to gain control over the region. Although accounts from this period emphasize the military might and prowess of the Germanic tribes, Caesar provided the first details concerning the religious practices and beliefs of the Northern European population (VI, 13-16). Whether he described the customs of the Germanic or Celtic tribes remains a moot point, but in his report, we find much in agreement with the ancient Germanic culture. Among the Gauls, Caesar speaks of a common assembly where all legal matters are settled, the shunning of convicted criminals, and public human sacrifice. As their god, the Gauls worship Mercury in particular and have many images of him, whom they regard as the inventor of all arts, the guide of their expeditions, and patron of all commercial transactions. Next to him they worship Apollo, Mars, Jupiter, and Minerva. "They have practically the same view of these gods as other nations do"; Apollo averts disease, Minerva imparts the art of invention, Jupiter possesses heavenly power, and Mars presides over war. The Gauls assert that Father Dis is their progenitor. In contrast Caesar says the Germans worship only the sun, moon and fire— a statement which finds some support in the Anglo-Saxon transliteration of the Roman names of the days of the week, which begins with Sun-day and Moon-day, placing the deities Sun and Moon alongside such gods as Odin, Thor and Frigg. Caesar says the Gauls, like the Germans, compute time by nights instead of days, believing that day follows night. Upon death, they hold that their souls do not perish, but pass from one body to another, and thus are "exceedingly excited to valor, the fear of death being disregarded." Their funerals are magnificent and costly, for they cast into the fire all things which the deceased held dear in life, including human beings. Beloved slaves and dependents were burnt together with their master. Caesar says that throughout Gaul there are two orders of men of any rank and dignity: knights (*equitum*) and druids (*druidum*). The knights, distinguished by birth and resources, are all engaged in war. Those with the greatest number of vassals and dependents wield the most power. The druids, on the other hand, preside over all things sacred, conduct public and the private sacrifices, and interpret all matters of religion. The druids do not go to war or pay tribute like the rest. They are said to commit to memory a large number of verses, which they regard as unlawful to put down in writing. Likewise, they impart sacred knowledge to their youth, respecting the stars and their motion, the extent of the world, the nature of things, as well as the power and the majesty of their gods. In 98 AD, the historian Tacitus gave the first surviving comprehensive account of the Germanic tribes, their customs and lands in his *Germania*, compiled from eyewitness reports and secondhand intelligence, as well as previous literary works. Pliny's voluminous *Bella Germaniae*, no longer preserved, may with some confidence be classed among the authorities utilized by Tacitus.[27] He cites this work as one of his sources in *Annales* I, 69. Tacitus' *Germania* is best described as a military manual, giving an account of Rome's greatest threat to the north. From him, we learn the first name of a Germanic deity, "Nerthus, that is, Mother Earth." He provides additional insight into specific religious practices of the people and alludes to their native mythology, which we will have an opportunity to examine in the next chapter.

By the third century, various German tribal confederations were gathered along the borders of the Roman Empire, east of the Rhine and north of the Danube and Black Sea. During great social upheavals in the fourth to sixth centuries known as *Völkerwanderung* or the Age of Migrations, Germanic tribes moved freely throughout Western Europe. Characterized by the decline of the Roman Empire, the Age of Migrations, known as the Barbarian Invasions from the Roman perspective, saw mass movements of peoples within and into Europe, most notably the Germans, the Slavs, and the Huns. The Germanic Iron Age, marked by the rise of Celtic and Germanic kingdoms in Western Europe, began with the decline of the Roman Empire and the lessening of its grip on the North. In 476 AD, the last Roman emperor in the West was overthrown by Odoacer, the first German to rule in Rome. After the collapse of the Empire, two great powers emerged in Europe during the fifth century. In the West, the Merovingian kingdom, which inherited much of Rome's wealth, power and institutions, ruled over territory largely corresponding to ancient Gaul. While in Eastern Europe and the Balkans, Slavic princedoms reigned, leaving traces of their occupation as far as Oldenburg in the West, before and within the sixth century. The Catholic Church, a third power, also began to expand its reach. Pope Leo III crowned the Frankish king Charlemagne as emperor in 800 AD, reviving the title in Western

---

[27]Gudeman, Alfred. "The Sources of the Germania of Tacitus," *Transactions and Proceedings of the American Philological Association*, Volume 31 (1900).

Europe after more than three centuries, thus establishing the Holy
Roman Empire under the auspices of Christianity which actively
sought to drive the old gods out of Europe in the coming centuries.
In Scandinavia, a place which Tacitus described as the home of tribes
rich in weapons, men and fleets, heathenism held out the longest.
There, the Vendel Period reigned from 550-800 AD, followed by the
Viking Age extending from 793 until 1066 AD, the date of the
Norman Conquest of England. Well-preserved ship graves at
Valsgärde and Vendel, for which the Vendel period is named, yield
finds that show Uppland was a powerful cultural center during this
era, consistent with the accounts of later Icelandic sagas. We have
several historical documents and considerably more artifacts for
study from these periods which serve as windows into native
Germanic belief.

First Rome and then later Romanesque cultures, such as that
of the Merovingians, projected significant political and cultural
influence northward into Denmark and southern Scandinavia during
the historic period.[28] As the Iron Age progressed, the core of the
Roman army came to be recruited from free Germania, and after
their service ended, these young men returned home filled with
knowledge of Roman culture, military organization, strategies and
tactics. As a result, Scandinavian society began to stratify under a new
form of leadership, as warrior kings supported by military retinues
based in part on the Roman model, began their rise to power. During
the end of the Roman Iron Age, archaeologists have detected a shift
in religion in Scandinavian society extending into the Migration and
Vendel periods, involving a significant change in ritual location,
turning away from natural sites such as wetlands and open-air spaces
which formerly had been the focus of sacrality, to the residences of
the newly-established ruling elite, which became the central focus of
cult activity. This shift in both location and artifacts deposited
appears to indicate a change in what the people perceived as sacred
and seems to be reflected in the cosmology and social norms

[28] Rood, pp. 24-26.

20

expressed in Germanic myths and rituals recorded during the literary period, which place less emphasis on natural cycles and more on social hierarchies and their interactions. Rather than a change in the religion itself, this can best be described as a necessary development, parallel to the developments taking place in the social structure of Germanic societies during this period, away from agrarian communities and into organized kingdoms.

Evidence for the Germanic tribes prior to Greek and Roman histories is sparse, and more difficult to decipher. It is generally accepted that Scandinavian prehistory began after the last Ice Age when nomadic tribes moved into the region sometime prior to 7000 BC as the glacial ice sheets retreated. Although it is not known what languages early Scandinavians spoke, DNA studies suggest that a people genetically related to the Yamnaya culture from the Eurasian steppes, which lived a nomadic life out of wagons herding cattle and other livestock (c. 4000–2500 BC), began to arrive in Europe around 2800 B.C, genetically displacing a Neolithic people in north-central Europe identified by archaeologists as the Funnelbeaker culture (c. 4300 BC–2800 BC). Studies suggest that around the time genes associated with the Funnelbeaker culture became less common, migrants from the Yamnaya culture, mainly men, mixed with Neolithic European peoples to form the Corded Ware culture. In the earliest Corded Ware burials from the Jutland peninsula, constituting modern-day Denmark and part of Northern Germany, ninety percent of the bodies are male and derive at least seventy-five percent of their ancestry from the Yamnaya culture of the steppes. The range of the resulting Corded Ware culture came to encompass most of continental northern Europe from the Rhine on the west to the Volga in the east, including most of modern-day Germany, the Netherlands, Denmark, as well as coastal Norway and the southern portions of Sweden and Finland, Poland, Lithuania, Latvia, Estonia, Belarus, the Czech Republic, Slovakia, Switzerland, northwestern Romania, northern Ukraine, and the European part of Russia. Its wide distribution indicates rapid expansion around the time the Indo-

European languages were assumed to have dispersed. According to J.P. Mallory, however, the Corded Ware culture cannot account for the Greek, Illyrian, Thracian and East Italic branches, which may be derived from Southeast Europe,[29] so the origins of the Proto-Indo-European or PIE language must lie further back still. Thus, the Kurgan model, first proposed by Marija Gimbutas in *The Prehistory of Eastern Europe*, Part 1 (1956), is currently the most widely accepted explanation of the origins and spread of the Indo-European languages.

The Kurgan model identifies the Pontic-Caspian steppe as the PIE *urheimat* or "original homeland" and assumes that a variety of PIE dialects were spoken across the region, which gradually expanded until they encompassed the entire Pontic-Caspian steppe, identifying Kurgan IV with the Yamna culture around 3000 BC. Three genetic studies in 2015 lend support to this theory. The Corded Ware culture, which shows genetic affinity with the later Sintashta culture thought to have originated the Proto-Indo-Iranian language, may have disseminated the Proto-Germanic and Proto-Balto-Slavic branches of the Indo-European language in Northern and Central Europe. As the Yamnaya culture (also known as the Pit Grave culture) entered Neolithic Northern Europe during the late Copper Age and early Bronze Age, the same agricultural practices continued, but the introduction of metal changed the social system, characterized by collective megalithic graves with a large number of sacrifices, to a system of individual graves with individual sacrifices. A series of late Neolithic communities of the third millennium BC in southern Scandinavia, Northern Germany, and the Netherlands share the practice of single burial, usually accompanied by a battle-axe, amber beads, and pottery. By the end of the third millennium BC, these tribes, designated as the Battle-Axe or the Boat Axe Culture dominated the region from Scania to Uppland and Trøndelag. Known from about 3,000 grave sites distributed all over Scandinavia, this culture shows strong continuity in stonecraft with earlier cultures

---

[29] *In Search of the Indo-Europeans* (1989), p. 108.

of the region and very few signs of any kind of mass migration. Small, separate farmsteads without defensive protection indicate that these people did not fear invaders. Numerous, widely disseminated petroglyphs (pictures carved on rocks) from this era, which prominently feature ships, indicate that the coastal regions of Scandinavia and the Baltic were united by a vigorous maritime economy, permitting a closer cultural unity than interior continental cultures spread over a similar geographical range could attain. In 1993, the excavation of a so-called "death house" in Turinge, in Södermanland from the last period of this culture, revealed the earliest sign of cremation in Scandinavia, yielding the burnt remains of at least six people, about twenty clay vessels, six work axes and a battle axe, which show close contacts with Central Europe.

Despite the rarity of reliable references prior to the birth of Christ, archaeological data suggests that most of Eurasia had transitioned to the Bronze Age by 2000 BC. In 1991, atop the Ötztal Alps near the Austrian–Italian border, the unprecedented find of a copper axe-head among the personal possessions of Ötzi the Ice-man, Europe's oldest known naturally preserved mummy, proved that metallurgy was in use there as early as 3300 BC, five hundred years earlier than previously estimated. Thus, all following dates are approximate and largely dependent on archaeological finds. The Nordic Bronze Age, which followed the Late Neolithic period when nomadic hunter gatherer societies began to domesticate plants and animals and settle into fixed agrarian communities, is a period of Scandinavian history roughly dated from 1700-500 BC. Of interest to the present investigation, Bronze Age cultures in northern Germany, Denmark, Sweden and Norway produced a wide variety of distinct artistic works including solar discs, helmets, blowing horns known as *lurer*, and an array of ornamental items, all suggestive of ceremonial use and practices. Among these are the Trundholm Sun Chariot found at Sjælland, Denmark dated from about 1800 to 1600 BC which established the use of horse drawn wagons in the region from an early time, and whose markings may have served as a seasonal calculator; the Nebra sky disk c. 1600 BC, currently the world's oldest known realistic representation of the sky, unearthed in the German state of Saxony-Anhalt in 1999, most often interpreted as a device to coordinate the lunar and solar calendars; and four mysterious conical "Gold hats" or *Goldhüte* c. 1400-900 BC, decorated with symbols which appear to have functioned as complex calendrical devices.

The Sky-Disk of Nebra

Avanton Gold Hat

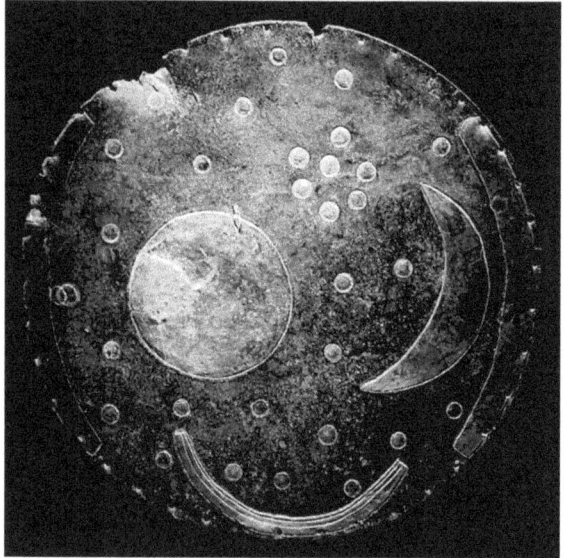

Trundholm Sun Chariot

The closely related symbols and manufacturing techniques of these pointed hats testify to a coherent culture spread over a wide-ranging territory in eastern France and southwestern Germany in the Late Bronze Age. The depiction of an object resembling such a hat on a stone slab in the King's Grave at Kivik in Southern Sweden, which bears much in common with the imagery on the contemporary *hällristningar* (literally "rock-carvings") found across Scandinavia, suggests an association with later Germanic cultic activities

These artifacts, all considered to be religious in nature, demonstrate the importance and sophistication in the observation of celestial cycles throughout the European Bronze Age. The ability to predict pivotal seasonal markers such as the summer and winter solstices, as well as significant solar, lunar and astral events, would have had a tremendous impact on the agricultural activities of the Bronze Age peoples of Northern and Central Europe, and naturally would have taken on religious significance. Nowhere is this more evident conceptually than in early verses of the eddic poem *Völuspá*, composed around 1000 AD, which directly ties the origin of plant-life to the appearance and motion of the sun and other celestial bodies.

Sól skein sunnan	"The sun shone from the south
á salar steina,	on the stones' hall:
þá var grund gróin	then the ground was overgrown
grœnum lauki.	with green leeks.
Sól varp sunnan,	"The sun from the south
sinni mána,	— moon's companion—
hendi inni hægri	threw her right hand
um himinjóðyr;	around the heavenly horse-deer;
sól þat né vissi,	Sun did not know
hvar hon sali átti,	where she had her halls,
stjörnur þat né vissu	the stars did not know
hvar þær staði áttu,	where their stations were,
máni þat né vissi,	moon did not know
hvat hann megins átti,	what might he had.

Þá gengu regin öll	"Then all the Powers went
á rökstóla,	to their judgement seats,
ginnheilög goð,	the high-holy gods,
ok um þat gættusk;	and contemplated this;
nótt ok niðjum	To Night and her offspring,
nöfn of gáfu,	they gave names,
morgin hétu	morning they designated
ok miðjan dag,	and mid-day,
undorn ok aftan,	afternoon and evening,
árum at telja.	to count the years."

During the Bronze Age, trade routes opened between Scandinavia and southern Europe, allowing for the influx of foreign goods, especially metals, into the region. As a result, the previously communal agrarian societies began to stratify, as groups who controlled trade, wealth production and distribution emerged and expanded their control locally and regionally. Religion during this era is often described as solar in nature and religious symbols reflected in artifacts of the period appear to be concerned with the motion of the sun and the cycles of birth, death and rebirth. Bronze instruments, ceremonial ornaments and headgear appear to have been used in rituals, and specialists must have spent considerable amounts of time etching sacred images into rock. In the Nordic Bronze Age, evidence exists for votive offerings, dependent on agricultural surplus and the importation of foreign goods, consisting of ceremonial weapons and jewelry being sacrificed by the social elite. In the latter half of the first millennium BC, however, a change occurred as the climate cooled and trade with southern Europe slowed. Scandinavia appears to have become poorer during this period as Central and Southern Europe entered the Iron Age and the flow of bronze to the North dwindled. This marked the beginning of the Pre-Roman Iron Age, extending from roughly 500 BC to the first century AD in Scandinavia and the Northern European Plain, which developed in close contact with the Hallstatt culture in Central Europe, causing the old Scandinavian elites to lose their grip on power as the iron trade developed and a new class of elite emerged. Around the same time, human bodies, animal bones and pottery began to be deposited in bogs at ritual sites, many of which would maintain their continuity for up to a thousand years. In the Danish region, Lotte Hedeager's landmark archaeological study demonstrated that "in the earliest part of the Iron Age, ritual activities were normally a continuation of later Bronze Age practice."[30] Thus we frequently find similar sets of imagery and symbols across time within the region, suggesting a continuity of religious thought and practice. In this regard, it bears noting that the Scandinavians themselves referred to their own religious practices during the heathen era as *forn siðr* or "ancient customs." This is not to imply that these customs did not change over time, however, for, as Catherine Bell, author of *Ritual Theory, Ritual Practice* (2009) observes, even if adherents believe that their religious traditions are unchanging, in reality they are continually being recreated through the process of ritual, which of necessity adopts new elements and discards old ones as the society evolves. She writes, "Ritual systems do not function to regulate or control the systems of social relations. They are the system, and an expedient rather than a perfectly ordered one at that."[31]

While modern linguists estimate that an early PIE dialect, sometimes designated as pre-Proto-Germanic, was introduced into the region prior to 2000 BC, the earliest examples of the Germanic language are found in runic inscriptions that date from 300 AD onward.[32] As mentioned above, Indo-European speakers are now thought to have arrived in southern Scandinavia with the Corded Ware culture by the middle of the third millennium BC, becoming the Nordic Bronze Age cultures by the early second millennium BC. Proto-Germanic, the last common ancestor of the Germanic branch

---

[30] *Iron Age Societies* (1992), pp. 72 ff.

[31] Bell, 2009 p. 130, as quoted by Joshua Rood in *Ascending the Steps to Hliðskjálf* (2017), p. 19.

[32] Mallory and Adams, (2006), ibid., p. 22.

of the Indo-European family of languages, thus most likely developed in southern Scandinavia, the original home of the Germanic tribes, characterized as a "hive" or "womb of nations" from which the Gothic people "are said to have come *long ago*,"[33] by their sixth century historian Jordanes. Although we find no examples of the written language from the Bronze Age, linguists typically date the first Germanic sound-shifts, making the dialect distinct from its PIE predecessor, to 500 BC. Named for Jacob Grimm, Grimm's Law, also known as the First Germanic Sound Shift, describes in a series of three statements how the inherited PIE stop consonants developed into their Proto-Germanic forms during the first millennium BC.[34] Remarkably, Proto-Norse from the second century AD, which shares other common innovations separating Germanic from PIE, is closely comparable to reconstructed Proto-Germanic, suggesting a common history of pre-Proto-Germanic speakers during the Nordic Bronze Age. Along with a common language, the people would have also possessed a common set of cultural practices, rituals, and a store of sacred knowledge, inherited from their forebears, which gave meaning to the world and their place in it. The common threads that connect distant Indo-European languages and mythologies with those of Northern Europe bear witness to this fact. Considered sacred and necessary for the survival of society, religious ideas are typically among the oldest preserved by a literate culture and the slowest to change.

With respect to the Indo-Europeans as a whole, scholars of comparative religion widely accept that one of the oldest known

---

[33] *Getica* IV, 25: *Ex hac igitur Scandia insula quasi officina gentium aut certe velut vagina nationum cum rege suo nomine Berig, Gothi quondam memorantur egressi,* "Now from this island of Scandza, as from a hive of races or a womb of nations, the Goths are said to have come forth long ago under their king, Berig by name." Charles C. Mierow translation.

[34] Inspired by Rasmus Rask's formulation of sound correspondences in Indo-European languages (1818), Grimm was the first to recognize the significance of systematic sound changes as evidence of relationship, which proved to be a turning point in the development of linguistic research. The Handbook of Linguistics (2008), edited by Mark Aronoff, p. 90-91.

myths was the mating of the Earth and Sky at the beginning of time.[35] Among the West Germanic branch, images symbolizing this *hieros gamos* or "sacred marriage" are present in the earliest artworks. Bronze Age petroglyphs known as *hällristningar* from the southern and middle provinces of Scandinavia, dating from at least 1200 until around 500 BC, are among the earliest evidence of cult activity in northern Europe. These ancient stone carvings, difficult to interpret, clearly contain figures and symbols depicting ritual activity. In them, ship scenes, dance scenes, hunting and farming scenes, as well as evidence of ritual processions can be discerned. The religion which these carvings embody seems to have been primarily concerned with the fundamental principle of life.[36] Among these images are found couples locked in an embrace— one of the pair sporting an erect phallus directed toward the other—most often interpreted as the sexual union of man and woman. They are sometimes associated with agricultural symbols, such as the wheel and plow. The ancient belief that it is possible to influence the fertility of the land through ritual sexual intercourse is well-documented.[37] As late as 1868, when faced with the threat of a catastrophic drought and impending crop failure, the people of a town in Dalsland, Sweden fell back on an old superstition that "there was only one way to achieve the desired result, namely to carry out certain prescribed ceremonies and have a couple copulate on the petroglyphs at Tisselskog, where the images of several mating couples had been carved." This account demonstrates that the belief in the efficacy of ritual marriage survived down to recent times.[38]

At Bohuslän, one petroglyph portrays an embracing couple engaged in a kiss overshadowed by a larger figure wielding an axe.[39]

---

[35] Ursula Dronke, *The Poetic Edda, Vol. II*, p. 396.

[36] Gelling and Davidson, *The Chariot of the Sun* (1969), p. 79.

[37] Gelling and Davidson, ibid., p. 68; see also Terry Gunnell, *The Origins of Drama in Scandinavia*, (1995), pp. 135-140.

[38] Fred Gudnitz, *Broncealderens monumentalkunst* (1962), p. 70; cited and translated by Gunnell, ibid., p. 138.

[39] Reproduced in *The Chariot of the Sun*, p. 66.

We can be fairly confident that the axe-bearer had a name and a myth, although we can never be sure what they were.[40] This figure is most frequently interpreted as a god consecrating the couple on the belief that at that moment, malignant spirits might attempt to blight the beneficent influence of this ceremony. His task, therefore, would be to keep them at bay.[41]

Petroglyph of an axe-wielding god blessing a couple

In the eddic poem *Þrymskviða*, we find a functional analog. Thor the giant-killer is said to customarily consecrate marriages with his hammer, and when it is stolen by a giant who demands the goddess Freyja as wife for its ransom, Thor must impersonate her and agree to wed the giant or risk losing this weapon forever. At the end of the mock ceremony, the hammer is laid in the lap of the bride (i.e. Thor) according to custom. Once again, hammer in hand, the Thunder-god strikes the giants dead. When laid in a bride's lap, the short-handled hammer is an obvious phallic symbol. This, the source of Thor's virility, thus insures the prosperity and protection of gods and men alike. The mighty Thor, an earth-born god with ancient Indo-European origins, is thus styled as Asgard's defender and the protector of Midgard and it inhabitants.

---

[40] McKinnell, ibid., p. 48.
[41] Gelling and Davidson, ibid., p. 68.

Further evidence of ritual activity in the Swedish Bronze Age occurs in images on the Kivik King's Grave Stones from southeast Skåne. Of particular interest is the appearance of eight "female" figures in long robes on either side of what seems to be a cauldron. Immediately above, a group of musicians, characterized by recognizable musical instruments, perform.

Two of the eight Kivik King's Grave stones

Similar figures in procession appear on the Oseberg tapestry (c. 834 AD) in poses that suggest they are dancing. Hooded figures in procession also occur on the Garde Bote Picture Stone from Gotland. These figures have what has been characterized as bird heads. The appearance of a number of winged and beaked human "bird" figures in the petroglyphs near Bohuslän, Sweden suggests that this motif was not uncommon in the religious processions of the time.[42] Again, we find functional analogs in Old Norse myth and legend. In *Þrymskviða*, the goddess Freyja lends Loki her falcon guise and *Skáldskaparmál* informs us that Frigg has one too. In the poem *Völundarkviða*, the elf-smith Völund and his brothers wed swan-

---

[42] Gunnell, ibid., p. 47.

maidens who wear feather dresses allowing them to fly. Near the poem's conclusion, Völund himself takes flight in a device of his own making. Elsewhere, Odin dons the form of an eagle when fleeing with the stolen mead of poetry.

Garde Bote Picture Stone from Gotland

While some scholars have suggested that the scenes described above represent mythical or otherworldly activity, it seems obvious that these images are based on contemporary religious activities.[43] This is made evident by the inclusion of *lurer*, Bronze Age musical instruments that have been discovered in Norway and Denmark in large numbers.[44] In other words, the artists are likely representing actual ritual activities. Such instruments are sometimes depicted as played by horned and possibly tailed figures, implying that costumed actors played an active part in these ceremonies. The prominent horns and exaggerated calves of these figures have led some scholars to suggest they are disguised as goats.[45] We find such costumed processions still occurring well into the Middle Ages and beyond across Northern Europe [See Chapter IV: The Frau Holle Legends].

---

[43] Gunnell, ibid p. 39.

[44] At least one hundred Bronze Age horns like those depicted in the petroglyphs, many of them occurring in pairs, have been recovered in Demark and Norway alone (Gunnell, ibid., p. 41).

[45] Gunnell, ibid., p. 41, cp. Gelling and Davidson, ibid., p. 112-113.

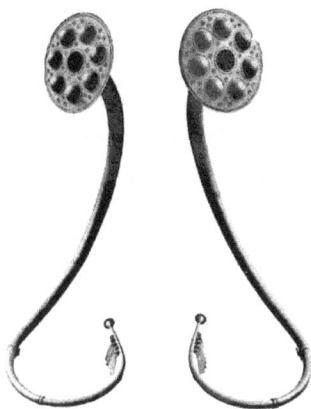

Bronze Lurer, Brudevælte, Denmark

Goat-men playing Lurer

Horned god on a ship

Petroglyph of a ship ceremony from Tanum, Bohuslän

Another recurring feature in these Bronze Age rock carvings is the ship, often filled with human figures. Images of a large figure in a ship among smaller figures are thought to represent giant effigies constructed to represent the god.[46] These lively ship scenes often include sun wheels, processions with wheeled vehicles, horned-, winged- and phallic-figures dancing or playing instruments, all indicative of ritual activity. Sometimes acrobatic figures appear above them as if leaping and tumbling as part of the ceremony.[47] Such a figure was found at Grevensvænge in Zealand Denmark in 1779, depicted in mid-leap along with three others wielding axes, dated to 600 BC, cast in bronze and associated with a ceremonial model ship. The *hieros gamos* is frequently depicted as taking place onboard such a vessel, sometimes with figures waving axes or weapons overhead.[48] Sometimes the ship is carried by a giant horned figure thought to represent a god, which may suggest that models of ships and other cult vehicles were used in these ritual activities.[49] Examples of such model ships and chariots have been discovered, the most famous being the gold boats from the fourth century found in a burial mound at Nors in Thy, North Jutland and the Bronze Age Trundholm Sun Chariot, mentioned earlier. Further support is found in the detailed description of a ship procession by land from Aachen to St. Trond in the twelfth century, quite obviously pagan in nature and so condemned by the Church. Mythic examples include a procession of the gods, preserved in the poem *Húsdrapa*. Some mounted and some in vehicles, they ride to Baldur's funeral pyre set aboard his ship Hringhorn, presumably a vessel with a ringed prow

---

[46] cp. The wicker images used by the Gauls for human sacrifice (Caesar, IV, 16).
[47] Grimm notes, ibid pp. 1241-1242, that the culture of flax is not without its ceremonies. "In some places, at sowing time, the mistress of the house used to get on the table and dance, then jump off backwards: the higher she made the leap, the higher the flax would grow." Gelling and Davidson suggest a similar meaning for the leaping figures.
[48] Gelling and Davidson, ibid., p. 49.
[49] Such figures occur on petroglyphs from Öster-Röd, Kville, Bohuslän and Brandskogen, Boglösa, Uppland. Pictures in Gunnell's *Origins of Drama in Scandinavia*, p. 40.

of the same type interred at Oseberg. Likewise Skidbladnir, the sailing ship of the harvest god Freyr, was large enough to hold all the gods and their horses equipped for war, and yet could be folded up like a napkin and placed in one's pocket. Said to be crafted by dwarves in a contest judged by the gods, the collapsible ship is directly linked to other fertility symbols such as Sif's golden hair, which Loki cut off (a sign of adultery among the Germans according to Tacitus), and Odin's ring Draupnir, which reproduces eight identical copies of itself every ninth night. The same ring is said to have been burnt on Baldur's breast, and is returned to his father in heaven by the messenger Hermod.

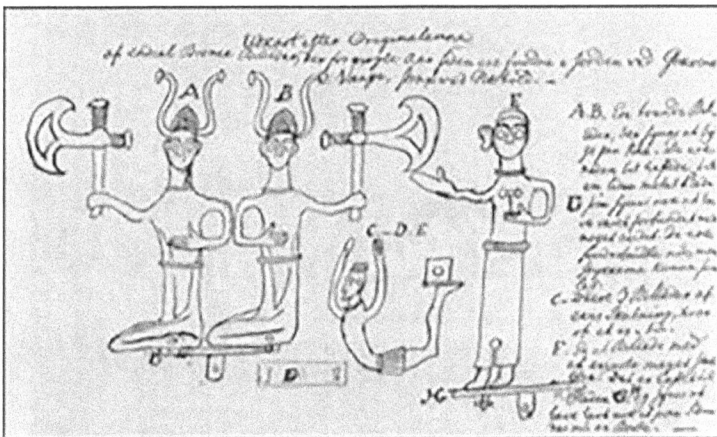

Drawing of the Grevensvænge Figures, 1779

Viksø Horned Helmets

Grevensvænge Figures

Petroglyph of Axe-wielding men from Tanum, Bohuslän

Petroglyph of an Acrobat on a ship from Högsby

The consistency of such motifs through time across the northern European region is remarkable. Two of the four Bronze Age figurines found in Grevensvænge wore horned helmets and carried axes like those pictured in the petroglyphs. One thousand years later, horned helmets of the same kind appear on one of the Torslunda helmet matrices and in other Iron Age pictorial works such as the Oseberg tapestry.[50] In addition, images of horned and apparently masked figures with close parallels to the earlier Bronze

---

[50] Gunnell, ibid., p. 43.

Age rock carvings, appear in images on the Gallehus horns (c. 400 AD), including that of a horn-bearing woman so often encountered in later Scandinavian art. The idea that horned headgear was associated with religious activity finds further support in a bronze and gold horned headdress found deposited in a bog near Hagendrup in northwest Sjælland. The headdress is too small for an adult and therefore may have been placed on an idol.[51] A pair of wooden figures, one male and one female, found near Eutin in Schleswig-Holstein confirm that such images were made.[52] The Maltegård urn lid (c. 600 BC) shares many similarities with Swedish petroglyphs depicting the *hieros gamos*. This round stone with a drilled hole in the center depicts a stick figure of a man with outstretched arms and an erect phallus directed toward the hole. A female figure stands facing him, her arms extended to join his, with the additional motif of a plant or ear of corn placed behind her. This motif occasionally accompanies the more common image of an embracing couple on the minute gold foils known as *Goldgubbar* found in Sweden, Norway and Denmark from 500 AD to the early Viking period. One from Hauge, Klepp in Rogaland, Norway shows the female figure of the couple holding a plant between them. The recurrence of these motifs over such a great expanse of space and time indicates the longevity and conservatism of heathen religious iconography in northern Europe.[53] While no firm conclusions can be drawn about the beliefs and religion of the artists, all that can be stated is that this religion is probably Indo-European in origin.[54] Thus we may justly seek parallels with other Indo-European branches, especially those which migrated into Western Europe.

Organized agriculture has existed in northern Europe since late Neolithic times and archaeological evidence of agricultural activity is found throughout Bronze Age Scandinavia. Because the

---

[51] Gunnell, ibid., p. 43.
[52] Gelling and Davidson, ibid., pp. 55-56.
[53] Gunnell, ibid., p. 49.
[54] Gunnell, ibid., p. 39.

survival of a farming community often depended on the productivity of the land, superstitions naturally rose up around cultivation. Agricultural motifs recur from the earliest iconographical evidence, indicating its religious significance to the people residing there. Prior to the invention of the modern plow which turns soil over, a digging implement known as an ard was used to cut furrows for sowing seed. An ard has a spike that cuts a single furrow as it is pulled along. Primitive societies throughout the world still use it. It can be drawn by a human or by animals. In northern Europe, the ard was first tipped with stone or bone, and later fitted with a metal cap.[55] Its use continued in northern Europe until the Middle Ages. The earliest known European ard, recovered from a bog near Horslev, Denmark, is dated to around 1500 BC[56] and evidence of the ritual burial of ards exists in the British Isles, Denmark, and northern Germany.[57] An ard was also found in a series of unmarked graves at Sutton Hoo, Suffolk, dated to the seventh or eighth century AD. In Vindumhede, Denmark, hair plaits found alongside an ard suggest a link with a women's cult.[58] In a group of petroglyphs from Bohuslän, Sweden, two ards drawn by cattle are associated with a large group of figures accompanied by sun-discs. Although the scene is difficult to interpret, it appears as if a sun-disc is erected at the edge of a cultivated field, where an ard pulled by two animals cuts a furrow to the lively acclamation of gathered bystanders.[59] Another image from

---

[55] Davidson, *Roles of the Northern Goddess*, p. 59.
[56] *The Agrarian History of England and Wales*: Volume 1, edited by Stuart Piggott, Joan Thirsk (1981), "Later History" by P.J. Fowler, p. 215.
[57] Davidson, ibid., p. 60.
[58] P.V. Glob, *Ard og Plov in Nordens Oldtid*, (Aarhus University Press, 1951), p 105. Widespread traditions across the Indo-European horizon dictate that shorn hair be buried. This practice may be explained by an Indo-European cosmogonical motif, which identifies parts of the human body as alloforms of natural phenomena, e.g. breath becomes wind and hair becomes plants. Conversely, traditional IE treatments for baldness often involve the application of plants, as an alloform of hair. See J.P. Mallory and D.Q. Adams, *Encyclopedia of Indo-European Culture*, s.v. "Cosmogony," p. 129. Grass and trees are frequently described as the tresses of the Earth-goddess.
[59] Gelling and Davidson, ibid., p. 80.

Litsleby in West Sweden depicts a man with an erect penis driving a plow pulled by two horned draught animals.[60] In one hand he holds a budding branch or a small tree and in the other an undefined object which may be a hammer or a seedbag. Two furrows are indicated by horizontal lines at the bottom of the picture and the man is clearly shown at the beginning of a third.[61]

Petroglyph of a Plowman from Litsleby, Bohuslän, Sweden

Hilda Ellis Davidson compares this Bronze Age scene with a nineteenth century custom recorded in Uppland of plowing three special furrows on the first day of spring. She writes:

"[Oscar] Almgren (1927, p. 301) …describes how the sod had to be turned up in the direction of the sun, and some of the earth rubbed on the forelocks of the horses, while the plowman was given bread which had been baked at Yule and stored in the corn-bin. A branch from a fruit-bearing tree was carried by the plowman or fixed on the horses reins; this custom was known in Småland and Scania up to 1921."[62]

The scene Almgren describes is remarkably similar to the one depicted on the petroglyph above and consistent with later tilling

---

[60] The image is reproduced on page 59 of Davidson's *Roles of the Northern Goddess* and Gelling and Davidson, ibid., p. 74.
[61] Gelling and Davidson, ibid., p. 79.
[62] Davidson, *Roles of the Northern Goddess*, p. 59

customs recorded in England and Germany.

In the Celtic and Roman Iron Age, the ard was replaced by the plow in farms across Northern Europe. A plow may be fitted with a wheeled carriage to prevent it from tipping over on turns. Powerful animals were needed to draw this heavier and more efficient implement. Oxen continued to be used because they are slow and strong, and the more docile cows were preferred over the males, as they were easier to train.[63] Many customs and superstitions —some of them quite odd sounding today— developed around this activity and were recorded in the late nineteenth century by such scholars as Jacob Grimm and Wilhelm Mannhardt. According to German ordinances known as *Weisthümer*[64] recorded by Grimm, a loaf must be stuck on the axle of the plow before cutting the first furrow; if a plow breaks a wheel, the plowman must provide a loaf "*baked from every kind of grain the plow doth win*"— a commonly recurring motif[65] —and another such ordinance dictates that the loaf must be as large as the plow-wheel itself. Grimm saw these "curious regulations" as vague recollections of earlier sacrificial loaves laid in the first furrow.[66]

Classically trained scholar Sir James Frazer noted a parallel from southern Europe. He explains that in Thesmophoria, it was customary to throw pigs, cakes of dough, and pine branches into caverns sacred to Demeter and Persephone. During the next annual festival, women who had been ritually purified for three days descended into the caverns to retrieve the decayed remains of the pigs, the cakes, and the pine-branches and brought them to an altar. The decayed matter was then sown with the grain to ensure a good crop. This ancient ritual was explained by a legend that held that when Pluto carried off Demeter's daughter Persephone, a swineherd

---

[63] P.J. Reynolds, *Iron Age Farm: The Butser Experiment*, (1979), p. 50.

[64] J. Grimm, *Weisthümer*, 7 volumes (1840-1872).

[65] cp. a loaf "of *the grain that the farm beareth and the mill breaketh*," "*a cake of all grain that the mill grinds*." Grimm, *Deutsche Mythologie*, (Stalleybrass tr), p. 1240-1241.

[66] Grimm, ibid., p. 1240.

named Eubuleus happened to be herding swine on the spot and his herd thus vanished along with Persephone. Frazer draws attention to analogues in the folk-customs of northern Europe, particularly the practice in Hesse and Meiningen of roasting a pig on Ash Wednesday or Candlemas (Feburary 2ⁿᵈ) and keeping the bones till sowing-time, when they are put into the field or mixed with the seed. The corn from the last sheaf is often kept until Christmas and made into a boar-shaped cake. In the spring it is broken and mixed with the seed.[67] In Scania, a salted pig's head from the Yule feast was kept and given to the plowman and his horses to eat on the first day of plowing in the spring.[68] In North Germany, a plow was found buried accompanied by human skulls and animal bones, suggesting a sacrifice.[69] In Sjælland, an incomplete plow was buried with parts of a wagon and the bones of cattle, sheep and pigs. Despite Frazer's simplistic interpretations of them, the northern European harvest customs cataloged by him clearly have elements in common with the Greek traditions concerning Demeter and thus, as Hilda Ellis Davidson believed, deserve fresh consideration.[70] In this regard, the association of harvest cakes with swine should not be overlooked.

Besides their capacity for breeding, wild pigs have long snouts and tusks and their ability to turn over soil when foraging may account for their association with agriculture. In northern European iconography, the use of the boar emblem is pervasive. In one of the earliest accounts of Germanic pagan customs, Tacitus speaks of a Germanic tribe known as the Aestii whose language resembles that of the British (*Germania*, ch. 45). They worship the *Mother of the Gods* and wear the figure of a wild boar as the emblem of her cult. Here the boar is connected not only with a Mother goddess but with agricultural activity. Tacitus says that the Aestii prefer clubs to iron weapons and cultivate grain and other crops with a perseverance

---

[67] *The Golden Bough*, chs. 48-49.
[68] Davidson, ibid., p. 64.
[69] Davidson, ibid., pp. 60-61.
[70] Davidson, ibid., p. 69.

unusual among the Germans. A close connection between the boar and agriculture survived for many centuries. Grimm cites an early Latin commentary by Verelius (seventeenth century) on *Hervararsaga* which says that Swedish peasants, after baking a cake known as the *jula-galt*,[71] dry some of it and keep it until spring. They then grate a portion of it and feed it to the plow-horses and another part to the plow-men. In the popular belief of Thuringia, whoever abstained from eating until dinnertime on Christmas, would catch sight of *a golden pig*.[72] In practical terms, this may have been the last and finest course of the meal, since a Laueterbach *weisthum* of 1589 decrees that a *goldferch*, a hog gelded before it is weaned, be led around the benches on Three Kings' Day (therefore Yule), probably before it was slaughtered.

Freyr drives Gullinsbursti to the Wood Barri
Charles E. Brock, 1930

In the same region, when the wind sets the corn stalks in motion, they sometimes say, "The Boar is rushing through the corn." In the Netherlands, "Derk with the boar" makes his rounds and

[71] *jula-galt* , literally "Yule-boar," a loaf or cake baked in the shape of a boar; Grimm, ibid., p. 51, probably related to the *sonargaltr,* sacrificial boar dedicated to Freyr annually.
[72] Grimm, ibid., p. 51.

looks after the plows.[73] In the same vein, when Freyr rides to Baldur's funeral in Snorri's *Edda*, he is said to drive in a cart drawn by his shining boar, *Gullinbursti* ("Golden-bristles). Freyr's connection with grain is made clear in *Lokasenna* 45-46, where his servant is named *Byggvir*, derived from *bygg*, "barley."[74] He is expressly associated with ale, made from barley, and his job is to "distribute food among men," *deila með mönnom mat*. In *Skáldskaparmál* 14, Freyr is called *árguð*, harvest god. *Gylfaginning* 24 confirms this, saying *hann ræðr fyrir regni ok skini sólar ok þar með ávexti jarðar, ok á hann er gott at heita til árs ok friðar*, "he is ruler of rain and sunshine, and thus of the produce of the earth, and it is good to pray to him for prosperity and peace." From all this, it is evident that a long history of agricultural customs associated with ritual and ceremony with close affinities to those of other Indo-European peoples have existed in northern Europe since the prehistoric era. On this fertile ground, our search for the Germanic Earth-Mother in the historic record commences.

The Bronze Age
Nils Asplund, 1938

---

[73] Grimm, ibid., p. 268.
[74] Ursula Dronke, *The Poetic Edda* Vol. II, p. 368.

The Cult Wagon of Strettweg, c. 600 BC
Depicting a goddess surrounded by people and animals
Discovered near Strettweg, Austria, 1851

II. Nerthus, that is, Mother Earth

"Tacitus' much-quoted account in *Germania* ch. 40 of the ceremonies related to the goddess Nerthus in the area around Schleswig-Holstein or Jylland is of particular interest here for several reasons. First of all, it suggests that the images of the Bronze Age petroglyphs depicting the *hieros gamos* and processions related to a fertility deity had parallels in southern Scandinavia as late as AD 100, when Tacitus wrote his account. Secondly, it provides the first reliable evidence that the ceremonies were now associated with a *named* goddess, who must therefore have had her own mythology and background. This in turn implies that enacted rituals to do with the goddess probably had a mythological parallel."

—Terry Gunnell,
The Origins of Drama in Scandinavia, (1995), p.53.

In literature, *Terra Mater* (Mother Earth) first appears as a distinct figure of the old heathen religion in the *Germania*. Despite intense scholarly debate over the motivations of its author, *Germania*, written by the Roman historian Tacitus around 98 AD, was probably intended as an accurate account of the customs and conditions of the Germanic tribes who posed a threat on the northern border of the Roman Empire for several hundred years. While his moral observations of the Germanic tribes in contrast to the Roman way of life have led some scholars to propose that this was his chief aim in writing it, this is not sufficient as a general interpretation of the text.[75] Not only does Tacitus criticize the Germanic way of life almost as often as he praises it, but much of the material has nothing to do with moral issues and cannot be explained simply as filler. J.B. Rives remarks that "to use the *Germania* as a historical source, then, requires careful evaluation and a willingness to acknowledge uncertainty. Yet it remains for all that a tremendously important source."[76] In commenting on Tacitus' claim that "ancient lays" (*carmina antiqua*) constitute the only record of their history, among the Germans,

---

[75] J.B. Rives, Tacitus *Germania*, (1999), p. 51.
[76] Rives, ibid., p. 66.

Rives observes:

> "That the early Germanic people had a rich tradition of oral
> poetry is suggested by the remains of early English, German, and
> Norse literature. Although very little of the extant material
> antedates the eighth century AD, it contains clear indications of
> earlier origins. First of all these traditions employ the same basic
> form: a line split into two halves by a strong caesura and linked by
> alliteration, each half-line normally having two primary stresses and
> a variable number of weaker stresses. The common tradition
> suggests that this form was established before there was much
> cleavage between the Scandinavian and continental Germanic
> cultures. Moreover, alliterative runic inscriptions date back to the
> fourth century AD (Lehmann, 1968). Secondly, several texts refer
> to historical figures of the sixth, fifth, and even fourth centuries
> AD. Attila for instance, appears in one of the lays of the *Poetic
> Edda*, the *Atlaqviða*, and is also mentioned in the English poems
> Widsith and Waldere; Widsith is also said to have visited
> Eormanric, a Gothic king of the fourth century. We can thus trace
> the tradition of early Germanic poetry, in both form and content,
> as far back as the fourth century AD, and there is no reason to
> doubt that it also existed in the time of Tacitus, especially if we
> compare the strong tradition of oral poetry among other Indo-
> European speakers."[77]

The *Germania* is divided into two halves. The first discusses
the common customs of the Germanic people *en masse*. The second
speaks of individual tribes leading the reader on, so to speak, a tour
of Germania. While the first half of *Germania* (ch. 1-27) deals with the
Germani as a whole, defining their boundaries, describing their origins,
and detailing their customs, the organization of the second half is
markedly different, providing specific information about distinct
groups, beginning with those residing beyond the Rhine (chapters 28-
37), then moving to those dwelling beyond the Danube (ch. 38-45)
and lastly to those of unknown ethnicity, living on the outskirts of

---

[77] Rives, ibid., p. 109.

the known world (ch. 46). At least some of the information in the later chapters relates to the northernmost tribes whose religion had much in common with that of the those from which the various Scandinavian nation-states emerged.[78] In chapter 40 of this all too brief work, Tacitus provides the first detailed account of a heathen ritual recorded in the Germanic territories. Serious scholars scarcely neglect it when discussing Germanic pagan beliefs and practices.[79]

Nerthus, that is, Mother Earth
An Abridged History of England, **1840**

Tacitus begins his account by telling of the *Langobardi* (Lombards), a tribe distinguished by their boldness in battle, who despite their small number, retained their independence in the midst of mighty neighbors made up of seven tribes, including the *Anglii,* the ancestors of the English Angles. Tacitus writes:

"The Langobardi are distinguished by being few in number.

---

[78] *A Companion to Old Norse-Icelandic Literature and Culture,* Rory McTurk ed. (2005). Chapter 17: *Pagan Myth and Religion,* by Peter Orton, p. 303.
[79] Orton, ibid., p. 303.

Surrounded by many mighty peoples they have protected themselves not by submissiveness, but by battle and boldness. Next to them come the Reudigni, Aviones, Anglii, Varini, Eudoses, Suarines and Huitones protected by rivers and forests. There is nothing especially noteworthy about these states individually, but they are distinguished by a common worship of Nerthus, that is, Mother Earth, and believe she intervenes in human affairs and rides through their peoples. There is a sacred grove on an island of the Ocean, in which there is a consecrated chariot draped with a cloth, which the priest alone may touch. He perceives the presence of the goddess in the innermost shrine and with great reverence escorts her in her chariot, which is drawn by female cattle. There are days of rejoicing then and the countryside celebrates the festival, wherever she deigns to visit and to accept hospitality. No one goes to war, no one takes up arms. All objects of iron are locked away then and only then do they exercise peace and quiet, only then do they prize them, until the goddess has had her fill of society, and the priest brings her back to the temple. Afterwards the chariot, the cloth, and if one may believe it, the deity herself are washed in a hidden lake. The slaves who perform this office are immediately afterwards swallowed up in the same lake. Hence arises dread of the mysterious, and piety, which keeps them ignorant of what only those who are about to perish may see."[80]

While some scholars have disputed various aspects of the Nerthus cult, from her very name to her status as a genuine Germanic earth goddess, none of these arguments has proven particularly effective in light of a comprehensive and careful examination of the evidence. Most often doubted is the name Nerthus itself. Tacitus writes, *Nerthum, id est Terram matrem,* "Nerthus, that is, Mother Earth." Nerthus is only one of three divine names of ethnic origin in *Germania,* demonstrating that Tacitus probably had a Germanic source for it. Some scholars have disputed the certainty of this reading because of variant forms of the name found in the manuscripts, all of which date from the fifteenth century or later.

---

[80] A.R. Birley, translator; Tacitus, *Agricola and Germany* (1999), p. 58.

These variant readings are: *Nerthum, Nertum, Neithum, Nehertum, Necthum, Herthum,* and *Verthum.*[81] Jacob Grimm himself addressed this point as early as 1835. Rather than any nationalistic desire to connect German folklore to Old Norse mythology, as some have suggested, the authority behind Grimm's Law relied on his skills as a linguist, clearly stating that "the manuscripts collated have this reading." Nor was this his preference: "I should prefer *Nertus* to *Nerthus,* because no other German words in Tacitus have TH, except Gothini and Vuithones." He rejects the reading Herthus, "though the aspirate in *herda* might seem to plead for it, the termination *–us* is against it."[82] Thus, the assertion by Lotte Motz that Grimm selected the name "*because* it coincides phonetically with Njörðr" is without foundation.[83] Modern scholars, knowledgeable of linguistics, support the reading *Nerthum.* John McKinnell, compelled to respond to the growing chorus of late twentieth century critics, explains the correctness of this reading:

> "The usually accepted stemma has three families, and readings shared by the best manuscripts of any two of them are thought likely to be correct. The best X group manuscripts (Vatican, Cod. Vat. 1862, Leiden UL XVIII Periz.Q.21) read *Neithum;* the best y manuscripts (Cod. Vat. 1518, Codex Neapolitanus) have *Nerthum,* and the best Z manuscript (Iesi, Æsinas Lat. 8) reads *Nertum.* The sound /th/ did not exist in classical Latin, though the spelling is found in words derived from Greek or the Germanic languages (such as *thesaurus* 'treasure', or the name *Theodoricus*). Tacitus would therefore be unlikely to introduce the spelling *th* gratuitously. In the fifteenth century, the Italian scribes who produced most of the earliest surviving manuscripts (including the Iesi manuscript) would have a natural tendency to replace *th* with *t*, as was consistently done in their native language (see Italian *tesoro, Teodorico*), but would be very unlikely to do the reverse. *Nerthum* is therefore more

---

[81] John McKinnell, *Meeting the Other in Old Norse Myth and Legend*, p. 50.
[82] Grimm, ibid., p. 251.
[83] Lotte Motz, *The King, The Champion and the Sorcerer* (1996), pg. 116. Emphasis by Motz.

probably correct than *Nertum*. If both Y and Z should read *Nerthum*, that reading must be preferred. A different stemma, proposed by Robinson, has only two groups, and the best manuscripts in both read *Nerthum*. Whichever stemma is correct, *Nerthum* therefore seems the likeliest reading, although it could represent either a grammatically masculine *Nerthus* or a grammatically neuter *Nerthum*."[84]

The form *Hertha* is a false reading of comparatively modern origin. In 1519, Rhenanus, the pious scholar who published Tacitus, wrote *Herthum* for *Nerthum*, manifestly the same as the Old High German *Herda*, earth. Based on his authority, the text of Tacitus was uniformly given as *Herthum* up until 1817, when editors such as Franz Passow restored *Nerthum* to the Latin text.[85] That the name Nerthus is grammatically masculine in form has led some critics such as Klaus von See[86] to conclude that Tacitus had no genuine information about the cult of Nerthus other than this name, and therefore based his account of the Germanic 'god' on the Roman cult of *Magna Mater* (the Great Mother), a cult in which Tacitus was himself entitled to participate.[87] Therefore, the most frequent objections to the authenticity of the Nerthus cult are based upon superficial comparisons to its Roman reflection, almost always ignoring their sharp contrasts.[88] Besides the superficial similarity of the designations *Terra Mater* and *Magna Mater*, or more properly *magna deum mater*, "great mother of the gods,"[89] scholars prone to compare the two point out the fact that both cults included a public procession which

---

[84] McKinnell, ibid., p. 51.

[85] *Gentleman's Magazine* (Feb. 1856), p. 143 in "Heligoland" by William Bell.

[86] *"Der Germane als Barbar"*, *Jahrbuch für Internationale Germanistik*, 13, (1981): pp.42-72.

[87] Alternately, Richard North has suggested that Nerthus was originally a male deity in the company of the female *Terra Mater*, and that Tacitus misunderstood his source. *Heathen Gods in Old English Literature*, ch. 2 (1997).

[88] cp. McKinnell, p. 51 ff.: Grimm, ibid., p. 255, first brought these connections to light, identifying an Indian analog in Bhavani, wife of Shiva. His quoting the sources at length made it unnecessary to highlight their obvious differences.

[89] Grimm, ibid., p. 254 citing Lucretius 2, 597.

terminated with the ritual washing of the idol in a lake. The differences between these cults, however, are not insignificant, and thus there is little reason to suspect that Tacitus drew on his knowledge of the Roman cult in his description of the Germanic Earth-Mother. Tacitus describes the goddess in question as *Terra Mater*, not *Magna Mater*. The Romans knew a *Tellus* or *Terra Mater*, who had a different ceremony than the one attributed to Nerthus; cattle were sacrificed to her on the 14th of April.[90] The worship of Cybele, *the great mother of the gods*, spread from its chief sanctuary, Pessinus in Phrygia, to Greece by the early fourth century and then on to Egypt and Italy. Heeding the counsel of the Sibylline oracle concerning the threat of foreign invaders, the Roman senate brought her worship to Rome in 204 BC as the first officially sanctioned Eastern cult. Lucretius provides one of the best descriptions of her festival,[91] considered decadent even by Roman standards, as it was celebrated around the time of Julius Caesar.[92] In one telling of her story, the goddess was born a hermaphrodite and was castrated at birth, leaving her female. Attis, her consort, was the child of a nymph, impregnated by the goddess' discarded member. Cybele fell in love with Attis, but grew jealous of him after he was unfaithful to her and so drove him insane. He died from blood-loss after castrating himself. This myth was reenacted during the festival. In her train, men, known as Galli, castrated themselves in devotion to her, following the example of Attis. Since this practice was outlawed among the Romans, the Galli were all recruited from outside of Rome. Once a year, decked out in their exotic feminine garments, long hair and amulets, these self-mutilated eunuchs were allowed to parade a statue of the goddess, seated in a chariot pulled by wild lions, through the streets accompanied by the clatter of cymbals and the sounds of tambourines. Gathered spectators threw flower petals and coins before them. Bulls were ritually slaughtered at her

---

[90] North, ibid., p. 21.
[91] *De Rerum Natura*, Book 2, 600 ff.
[92] cp. Cattulus, Poem 63.

increasingly elaborate feasts.[93] During the rest of the year, the Senate confined the Galli to an enclosed sanctuary and declared that no citizen had the right to enter the annexes occupied by them or take part in their frenzied orgies. In detail, this cult is quite unlike the peaceful public procession of Nerthus, in which all iron objects were locked away. Instead of wild lions, her car was drawn by domestic cattle.[94] A single priest, rather than a motley crew, attended her and only he was allowed to touch her sacred vehicle.

The Nerthus Procession
Carl Emil Doepler Jr., 1905

Although some scholars have pointed out possible foreign models for Tacitus' account of the Nerthus cult, it is more probable that he based his account on native Scandinavian tradition.[95] A

---

[93] Source: http://abacus.bates.edu/~mimber/Rciv/Megalesiaci.htm (last viewed 1/2/2011).

[94] "In the *Rigveda,* which contains a proliferation of bovine imagery, the cow is associated with the earth, while the bull represents the sky. In Greek mythology, Zeus sometimes takes the form of a bull, and his partner that of a cow. According to Homer, Zeus' wife Hera has the strange-epithet 'cow-faced.' In Hittite mythology, the storm-god is also represented as a bull." (West, p. 185).

[95] E.O.G. Turville-Petre, 'Fertility of Beast and Soil' in *Old Norse Literature and Mythology: A Symposium,* ed. Edgar Polemé, (1969), pp. 249-252.

divinity in a wagon is well-known in Germanic lore, thus there is little need to speculate that Tacitus borrowed the idea from Roman sources. According to Snorri's *Edda*, Thor drives a wagon drawn by goats, Freyr arrives at Baldur's funeral in a cart led by a boar, and Freyja rides in a car pulled by cats. Njörd too is known as "god of the wagon" in a skaldic strophe cited in the primary manuscript of Snorri's *Edda*; where other manuscripts have *Vana guð* ('god of the Vanir'), *Codex Regius* has *vagna guð*.[96] The Big Dipper (Ursa Major) was commonly known as the *Wain* or wagon. In skaldic poetry, Odin is known as *runni vagna*, "mover of wagons"; *vinr vagna*, "friend of wagons"; *vári vagna* "protector of wagons"; and *valdr vagnbrautar*, "ruler of the wagon-road." The sky itself, home of the gods, is known as "the land of wagons (*land vagna*)," indicating that the constellations were imagined as the gods circling the heavens in their cars.[97]

Other Germanic literary sources also support the procession of an idol in a wagon among the northern European tribes. In the latter half of the fourth century, the Church historian Sozomen (c. 400–450 AD), writing of the dangers that beset Ulphilas [Wulfias] among the heathen Goths, recounts how Athanaric, chieftain of the Thervingians, appointed Winguric (Wingureiks), a *goði*, to eradicate the Christian faith from the land. He placed a *xoanon* (wooden idol) in an *armamaxa* (covered carriage) and ordered it conveyed to the homes of those suspected of practicing Christianity. If they refused to fall down and sacrifice (evidently to the deity represented by the statue), their tents were set ablaze.[98] Sozomen says:

> "[Ulphilas] exposed himself to innumerable perils in defense of the faith, during the period that the aforesaid barbarians were abandoned to paganism. He taught them the use of letters, and

---

[96] North, ibid., p. 24.
[97] *Skáldskaparmál* 31: *Hvernig skal kenna himin? Svá at kalla ...land sólar ok tungls ok himintungla, vagna ok veðra, "How shall the heaven be named?* It shall be named ...land of sun, of moon, of planets, of wagons, of winds." Anthony Faulkes translates the word *vagna* as "constellations," see Faulkes, *Edda Snorri Sturluson*, (Everyman, reprinted 1997), p. 88.
[98] North, ibid., p. 147.

translated the sacred scriptures into their own language. …Athanaric resented the change in religion that had been effected by Ulphilas; and irritated because his subjects had abandoned the superstition of their fathers, he imposed cruel punishments on many individuals; some he put to death after they had been dragged before tribunals and had nobly confessed the faith, and others were slain without being permitted to utter a single word in their own defense. It is said that the officers appointed by Athanaric to execute his cruel mandates, caused a statue to be constructed, which they placed on a chariot, and had it conveyed to the tents of those who were suspected of having embraced Christianity, and who were therefore commanded to worship the statue and offer sacrifice: if they refused to do so, they were burnt alive in their tents. But I have heard that an outrage of still greater atrocity was perpetrated at this period. Men, women, and children, who were compelled to offer sacrifice, fled from their tents and sought refuge in a church, whither also they carried the infants at the breast; the pagans set fire to the church and consumed it, with all who were therein."[99]

In Crimea, Winguric paraded the idol before a tent used by Christians for their church service. Those who honored the idol were spared, and the rest were burned alive in their place of worship around the year 375 AD. A total of 308 people died in the fire, of which twenty-one are known by name, written with multiple variants in manuscript. A woman called Baren or Beride, also recorded as Larisa, led the congregation in a hymn as the fire consumed them. The so-called "26 Gothic Martyrs" linked to this incident are commemorated on March 26 in the Christian Orthodox calendar and on October 29 in the Gothic calendar fragment, "in remembrance of the martyrs who with Werekas the priest and Batwin the *bilaif* (minister?) were burned in a crowded church among the Goths," *gaminþi marwtre þize bi Werekan papan jah Batwin bilaif aikklesjons fullaizos*

---

[99] *Historia Ecclesiastica* VI, 37, translated by Edward Walford as *The Ecclesiastical History of Sozomen* (1855), pp. 306-7.

ana Gutþiudai gabrannidai.[100] It is noteworthy that Athanaric did not persecute Christians in general, but primarily members of his own community who had converted. Since the purpose of the procession seems to be to promote prosperity, Carla O'Harris has suggested that Anthanaric's true motivation in persecuting the coverts may have been their unwillingness to participate in the time-honored rituals that would insure the well-being of the land, and therefore the community at large. His chosen means of execution, death by fire, may indicate that Athanaric saw the Christians as practitioners of witchcraft, whose religious rites would offend the gods and thereby blight the land.

In the late sixth century, Gregory of Tours recounted what has been described as the "very last Western evidence of a ritual precisely described as dedicated to the Mother of the Gods."[101] In an anecdote marking the end of the old religion, he described the procession of a goddess called Berecynthia (probably a Roman interpretation of a local goddess), as she was drawn through fields and vineyards in a wheeled vehicle known as a *carpentum* (carriage) or *plaustrum* (wagon) "according to the wretched custom of the pagans" in order to ensure their prosperity, while the people sang and danced before her.[102] During her festival at Augustodunum near Lyon, Simplicius, the bishop of Autun (d. 418), saw the peasants conveying her white-veiled statue around the newly-sown fields and prayed for its destruction. Straightaway, the statue fell from its cart and broke.[103] According to local recensions of the *Passion of St. Symphorianus* of

---

[100] George W. S. Friedrichsen, 'Notes on the Gothic Calendar (Cod. Ambros. A)', *Modern Language Review* 22 (1927); The 'twenty-six' martyrs include the twenty-one who are named, Batwin's four children, and an anonymous man who ran up to confess his faith as the tent began to burn.

[101] Philippe Borgeaud, *Mother of the Gods,* (2004), p. 122.

[102] *Liber in Gloria Confessorum* 77 cited by H.E. Davidson in *The Lost Beliefs of Northern Europe* (1993), p. 133, partially translated in North, ibid., p. 22.

[103] Pamela Berger, after Harmening's *Superstitio*, pp. 43-48 notes "a majority of the hundreds of mother goddess statues uncovered in modern times in the areas that make up Gaul and Germania either have their head struck off or bear other evidence of purposeful disfigurement," *The Goddess Obscured* (1985), p. 37.

Autun from the early fifth century, Symphorian, the son of a senator named Faustus, was beheaded around the year 180 AD, during the reign of Marcus Aurelius for refusing to worship the goddess. Autun is described as a city of many temples filled with idols. Berecynthia, Apollo and Diana were especially venerated. On a certain day, rustic people performed "unholy" ceremonies dedicated to Berecynthia, "the mother of demons" (*matris daemonum*). They conveyed her statue in a cart, followed by a multitude of people gathered together in procession. Symphorian refused to adore the statue and so was taken to the local authorities. When asked by the Roman consul why he refused to worship the idol, he responded that, as a Christian, he would not adore the statue of a demon. For this offense, he was martyred. That such processions were a familiar sight in Roman Gaul is made evident in chapter 12 of the *Life of Saint Martin of Tours* (c. 316-397) by Sulpitius Severus, who wrote:

> "While Martin was going a journey, he met the body of a certain heathen, which was being carried to the tomb with superstitious funeral rites. Perceiving from a distance the crowd that was approaching, and being ignorant as to what was going on, he stood still for a little while. For there was a distance of nearly half a mile between him and the crowd, so that it was difficult to discover what the spectacle he beheld really was. Nevertheless, because he saw it was a rustic gathering, and when the linen clothes spread over the body were blown about by the action of the wind, he believed that some profane rites of sacrifice (*profanes sacrificiorum ritus*) were being performed. This thought occurred to him, because it was the custom of the Gallic rustics in their wretched folly to carry about through the fields the images of demons veiled with a white covering."

Upon closer inspection, he discovered that "they were simply a band of peasants celebrating funeral rites, and not sacrifices to the gods."[104] Along the same lines, the conveyance among his people of

---

[104] Translated by Alexander Roberts. *From Nicene and Post-Nicene Fathers, Second Series*, Vol. 11. (1894).

King Frotho III's body in a wagon for three years after his death as told by Saxo Grammaticus in *Gesta Danorum* at the end of chapter 5 is sometimes cited as another example of such a procession. Germanic kings were also known to do this on occasion while alive. Like Nerthus who rode in a wagon drawn by cows, the Carolinian historian Einhard tells us that once a year, the ruler of the Merovingian dynasty drove an "old fashioned" cart pulled by bulls through the countryside.[105] The bulls that pulled the cart were considered special, like the kings they transported. Hence, the theft of those beasts would impose a sanction two and a half times higher than that of a gelded ox. Although the purpose of the procession is not stated, the metal head of a bull bearing a solar disk was recovered from the tomb of Meroveus' son, Childeric I, at Tournai (now in Belgium) in 1653, suggesting a link to a fertility cult.[106]

Procession of a Merovingian King
Alphonse de Neuville, 1875

This connection between the bull, a fertility god and the Merovingians is perhaps best understood by consideration of a myth

---

[105] *Einhardi Vita Caroli Magni*, 1. In MHG, *Scriptores rerum Sangallensium. Annales, chronica et historiae aevi Saxonici*, Hannover, (1829).
[106] Gelling and Davidson, ibid., p. 163-164, which shows a sketch of the artifact, now lost.

preserved by the seventh century historian known as pseudo-Fredegar. Interpolating the work of Gregory of Tours, he tells a story about the conception of Merovech, the eponymous founder of the dynasty. According to him, the Frankish king Chlodio, known as the long-haired king, was taking a summer bath with his wife, when she was attacked by a creature from the sea, which Fredegar calls a *Quinotaur*, Latin for "bull with five horns." The text describes the creature as *bestea Neptuni,* "a beast of Neptune." When she bore a son, it was unknown whether the boy was conceived by the man, Chlodio, or the beast from the sea. At its very foundation, the Merovingian dynasty was associated with a fertility cult involving cattle and the sea. In Greek mythology, the Minotaur was conceived in a similar fashion. Minos, king of the island of Crete prayed to Poseidon to send him a pure white bull as a sign of support. The sea-god granted his wish expecting Minos to sacrifice the creature to him, but upon seeing the magnificent bull Minos decided to keep it for himself, and sacrificed another instead. To punish him, Poseidon filled Minos's wife, Pasiphaë, with lust for the creature. She secretly had the artisan Daedalus craft a cow guise for her in order to mate with the white bull from the sea. Their offspring was the terrible Minotaur.

Other relevant examples of ritual processions cited by scholars include the description of Thor's chariot at a temple in *Ólafs saga Tyrggvasonar,* the moving image of Thor kept on an island in the north of Norway as told in *Rögnvalds þáttr ok Rauðs,* and the account in *Hauks þáttr hábrókar* of an otherwise unknown god named Lytir, who traveled to a sacrifice at Uppsala in a special wagon that awaited his arrival for three nights. However, the most frequently cited and the strongest parallel confirming the details of the seasonal circuit made by Nerthus in *Germania* remains the Icelandic *Gunnars þáttr helmings.*[107] The tale, dating from the late thirteenth or early fourteenth century, is a religious parody recounting the plight of a man named Gunnar who flees from Norway to Sweden in the first year of Ólaf's

---

[107] Preserved in the *Flateyjarbók,* it forms the second half of *Ogmundar þáttr dytts* in *Óláfs saga Tryggvasonar in mesta.*

reign (995 AD), taking refuge there with a priestess of Frey. He accompanies her as she travels among her people giving *arbót* ("help with the crops").[108]

Freyr and Skirnir
Alexander Zick, 1901

In this procession, Freyr and his bride, represented by a wooden idol accompanied by a priestess, ride in a horse-drawn wagon through the countryside, just as the goddess Nerthus rode in a

---

[108] *með okkur Freyr þá er hann skal gera mönnum árbót,* "drive with Freyr and he shall give help with crops," cp. Freyr's designation *árguð* in *Skáldskaparmál* 14 and Chapter III: The Anglo-Saxon *Æcerbót.*

covered wagon drawn by cattle attended by a male priest nine hundred years earlier. The time of the procession is marked by peace and feasting. Gunnar bravely leads the horse through a blizzard, but when he requires rest and enters the wagon, Freyr attacks him. As they wrestle, Gunnar vows to return to King Ólaf and the Christian faith should he survive. At once, "the devil" exits the wooden idol and takes flight allowing Gunnar to smash the statue to pieces. Impersonating Frey, Gunnar impregnates the priestess before returning to Norway and Christianity. When the pregnancy of the priestess is revealed, the Swedes take Freyr to be the father, saying: *uar ok uedratta blid ok allir hlutir suo aruœnir at eeuaü madr munde sligt*, "the weather looked balmy and everything gave such hope of a good season that no man could have done such a thing."[109] Here too, good harvests are attributed to the god.

Intended to make light of the pagan past, this story instead confirms many of the details of the Nerthus cult as described by Tacitus: an idol is drawn through the countryside in a wagon attended by a priest of the opposite sex; only the priest can sense the presence of the god and touch the idol; during the procession, peace reigns. The Latin and Norse narratives describing the ritual processions of Nerthus and Freyr show no direct signs of literary borrowing from one another, and the authors could not have known the Dejbjerg wagon from Jylland, Denmark (1st century BC) or the Oseberg wagon (834 AD), both of which are believed to have served a ritual purpose. Whether the story in *Gunnars þáttr helmings* was factually true or not is unimportant. What matters most here, according to Terry Gunnell, is that people believed it to have some foundation in reality. Thus, it appears "to have firm roots in oral tradition, just like the numerous local legends recorded in Sweden and Denmark (including Dejbjerg) telling of golden wagons hidden in lakes that the Swedish folklorist Bengt af Klintberg (1998) has compiled."[110] At the very least, this tale

---

[109] As cited by North, ibid., p. 24.
[110] "Blótgyðjur, Goðar, Mimi, Incest and Wagons," in *Norse Mythology—Comparative Perspectives*, edited by Pernille Hermann, et al, 2017, p. 125-126.

provides evidence that people in the early fourteenth century accepted the idea that religious processions conveying effigies of heathen gods through the countryside were still taking place during the reign of Ólaf Tryggvasson.[111]

The wintertime procession of Freyr's idol may be related to the *hieros gamos* of Freyr and Gerd described in the eddic poem *Skírnismál*. While Freyr is the god of harvests who once carried a sword which shines like the sun, his wife, the giantess Gerd, is often interpreted as the frozen earth, initially unreceptive to his penetrating and fertilizing warmth. The phrases *myrkt er úti*, "it is dark outside" (st. 10) and *long er nótt*, "one night is long" (st. 42), can hardly apply to the summer months in Scandinavia when the days are long and the nights barely existent.[112] The poem's movement from a civilized, male, inside space to a wild, female, outside space, represented by *Gerð* (literally "field"), who is separated from the world by a ring of fire, also contains "a strong element of the processional"; its action link a central place inhabited by gods to a sacred space on the periphery, which may have had a basis in fifth- or sixth century reality when sacrificial practices in Sweden appear to have been transitioning from outdoor spaces with close connections to female deities (cp. *Völuspá* 33 and *Grímnismál* 7) to the indoor spaces of the male ruler.[113] The action begins with Freyr enthroned on Hlidskjalf and ends with an agreement for him to meet his bride in "the wood Barri." As Gunnell demonstrates, a wide range of Yuletide pairing games and mock-marriage traditions, often with elements of the processional, are found all over Scandinavia.[114] These traditions flourished despite Church prohibitions in Scandinavia against the celebration of real marriages at any time during the Christmas season. Conversely, in Shetland, all marriages were to be celebrated during the three winter months. Such regulations may have had their roots in an association

---

[111] Gunnell, *The Origins of Drama in Scandinavia* (1995), p. 54.
[112] Gunnell, ibid., p. 57.
[113] Gunnell (2017), ibid. p. 127.
[114] Gunnell (1995), ibid., 133-135. For examples, see Chapter IV. The Frau Holle Legends.

between marriage ceremonies and heathen winter festivals. In Scandinavia, mock-marriages and bridal figures were long associated with both the winter and the summer solstices.[115] In the costumed traditions of the Northern nations, we frequently find pairs of actors, one of each sex. Thus the emphasis on gender in these accounts is probably significant.

Nerthus is most often identified as one of the Vanir. It has long been recognized that the name *Nerthus* is an etymon of *Njörðr*, the most senior of the named Vanir gods, and father of Freyr and Freyja.[116] Grimm himself noted that the name Nerthus was identical to the later Old Norse name Njörðr, an "identity as obvious as that of Freyr to Freyja."[117] According to John McKinnell (2005), the development would be "Nerthus > *Njarðuz (breaking) > *Njörðuz (u-mutation) > Njörðr (synscope)."[118] Much has been made of this apparent gender gap. Over the years, scholars have suggested that the deity described by Tacitus was actually male or had changed gender over time, reflecting the reduction in the status of women between the times of Tacitus and Saxo.[119] The competing theory that Nerthus was a hermaphrodite received some attention when it was first proposed, but is now generally rejected. Such interpretations, however, are unwarranted since a number of wooden idols recovered from the peat mosses of Denmark and Schleswig-Holstein demonstrate that the deity could be of either sex. As we shall see, those from Foerlev Nymølle and Rebild skovhuse are female, while those from Broddenbjerg, Spangeholm and Rude Eskildstrup are male. The site at Aurkemper Mose, Braak, Holstein produced one of each gender, suggesting a cult in which a god and goddess were worshiped as siblings and marital partners.[120] The difference of sex between Njörd and Nerthus is less of a problem than some imagine,

---

[115] Gunnell (1995), ibid., pp. 135-140.
[116] At least as far back as Jacob Grimm in *Deutsche Mythologie*, ch. 13.
[117] *Deutsche Mythologie*, ch. 10.
[118] McKinnell, ibid., p. 50.
[119] McKinnell, ibid., p. 52, citing North pp. 1-25.
[120] McKinnell ibid., p. 55

for among the gods most commonly associated with such processions, we find other gender-reflexive names such as Freyr and Freyja, who are siblings; as well as Fjörgynr and Fjörgynn, which designate the earth-goddess and the father of Odin's wife respectively.[121] Thus, it is not inconceivable that Njörd and Nerthus represent siblings or a couple.[122] This is all the more likely since in *Lokasenna* 36, Njörd is said to have fathered Freyr with his own sister, who remains unnamed in the fragmentary accounts left for study.[123] Nerthus' temple *in insula Oceani* (on an island in the Ocean) also may point in this direction, since Njörd is a sea-god and *Oceanus* is a proper name derived from Greek mythology. Therefore, it may be significant that Tacitus chose the word *Oceanus* rather than Latin *mare* to describe her island home.[124] Despite the great age separating these sources, Richard North observes:

"The formal relationship between two divine names, between *Nerthus* of the Anglii and *Njörðr* of the Norsemen, is evidence of a cultural continuity in this period sufficient to permit further comparison between Tacitus' *Germania* and pagan poems in the Old Norse-Icelandic vernacular. In these ways, Icelandic literature may be read uniquely, or in combination with Tacitus and later Latinate and even Hellenistic sources to interpret the literary traces of heathen gods in Old English literature."[125]

Besides associating the Earth-Mother with the Ocean in his text, Tacitus describes Nerthus' mode of transportation ambiguously, calling it a *vehiculum*, leaving room for speculation regarding its form.[126] Some have suggested the wagon was outfitted as a ship. In support of this, the late eddic poem *Solarljóð* contains a curious

---

[121] *Fjörgynn*, a masculine name, attested in *Lokasenna* 26 and *Gylfaginning* 9; *Fjörgynr,* a feminine name, attested in *Hárbarðsljóð* 56, *Völuspá* 56, etc. See John Lindow, *Handbook of Norse Mythology*, (2001), pp. 117-118.
[122] Orton, ibid., p. 304.
[123] *Við systur þinni gaztu slíkan mög ok er-a þó vánu verr.*
[124] North, ibid., p. 29.
[125] North, ibid., p. 11.
[126] M.J. Rudwin, *The Origin of the German Carnival Comedy* (1920), p. 9.

passage which states that "Odin's wife", a common kenning for the earth, "rows in earth's ship," *Óðins kván rær á jarðar skipi* (st. 77), adding that she is "eager after pleasures" and "her sails are hung on the ropes of desire." Thus, another possible parallel may be found in the description of a protracted ship procession that traveled by land and water from Aachen, the westernmost city in Germany, to the Belgian town of St. Trond (Sint-Truiden), in the year 1133, according to *Gestorum Abbatum Trudonensium* written by Rodulf, the Abbot of St. Trond (c. 1070–1138).[127] Hilda Ellis Davidson (1998) summarizes his account:

> "It tells how a man from near Aachen got permission to build a ship, which he had put on wheels and had drawn by weavers. They took it to Aachen, Maesdricht (where it was given a mast and sail), Tongres, Borgloon, and finally to Trond. Here the abbot warned the townspeople against it, and the weavers had to guard it day and night, but nonetheless it was welcomed with riotous delight by the townspeople; in the evening half-naked women are said to have rushed to the ship and danced around it. At midnight the dance ended and a great shouting took place, but sadly no words were recorded. This went on for twelve nights, and when more sober citizens wanted to burn the ship, there was such an outcry that it departed unharmed to Louvain, although the gates of the town were closed against it."[128]

Jacob Grimm, who provided an excerpt of the text in Latin,[129] notes that despite the earnest objections of the Christian clergy, the secular authorities sanctioned the procession and protected it, that it rested within the authority of several townships whether to grant admission to or refuse the approaching vessel, and that the popular sentiment seemed to be that it would have been considered uncouth

---

[127] *A History of the Abbey of St. Trond*, Book XII. chapters 11-13.
[128] *The Roles of the Northern Goddess*, p. 112.
[129] *Teutonic Mythology*, Vol I., pp. 259-260.

not to welcome it and forward it on its way.[130] The ceremony has a decidedly heathen tone. A large procession of people of both sexes (*utriusque sexus processione*) accompanied the ship along its route. When a reception was demanded for it and refused, a heated argument broke out which could only be settled by open conflict. For this reason, Rodulf calls the ship a Trojan Horse (*Troiani equum*). It was built in the forest of Inda in Ripuaria, a region in western Germany whose chief city was Cologne, by weavers, "which the common folk hold to be wanton and proud above all other handiworkers." They drew the ship along by ropes tied to their shoulders and prevented the great throng of revelers from coming too close to it, taking oaths and tributes from those who did, suggesting the ship was considered sacred. The abbot's primary objection to the procession was that the vessel, in his opinion, was "the abode of evil spirits" (*malignorum spirituum domicilium*), so that it could justly be called "a ship of Bacchus, Venus, Neptune or Mars." Rodulf remarks that it was "strange to me that I was not compelled to offer up a sacrifice to Neptune in front of the boat (*ante navim Neptuno hostias immolare*) as they were accustomed." He describes droves of scantily clad women with their hair loose, shamelessly dancing around the earth-ship (*terrae navis*). Wherever it stopped, the country folk (*pauper rusticus*) gave joyful shouts, sang songs of triumph, and danced around the vessel. Between moonrise and sunrise crowds of women "leapt from their beds with hair yet disheveled, some half-naked and others clad only in a cloak, and burst impudently in to mingle with those who were dancing around the ship." Men and women alike, a thousand at any time, celebrated in this manner long into the night —behavior immediately reminiscent of the joyous ship-scenes featured in the Bronze Age petroglyphs. Remarkably, one petroglyph from Norrköping, Östergötland shows such a ship being dragged by four-footed beasts, possibly horses. Grimm wrote that although heathen worship had been "checked and circumscribed" in the region for

---

[130] Printed in full in *Patrologiae Cursus Completus*, Volume 173, edited by Leo Marsicanus, (1854), p. 181-184.

centuries that some memory of ancient heathen rites must have survived in the memory of the common people there, which is not unlikely since at the time this happened Sweden was not yet fully converted to Christianity; Adam of Bremen had described the heathen temple at Uppsala in his *Gesta Hammaburgensis ecclesiae pontificum* (1073-1076) less than sixty years before; Saxo Grammaticus had not yet penned his *Histories* in Denmark (c. 1185), and Snorri Sturluson had not yet written the *Prose Edda* in Iceland (c. 1220), which clearly demonstrates that heathen lore was still circulating orally in the North at the time. In this context, a guild of weavers constructed a wheeled-ship, which they pulled from town to town in Western Germany and Belgium, causing the rural people to revel. Occurring almost three centuries before the literary tradition of *Das Narrenschiff* (The Ship of Fools) began in 1494, there is no reason to connect the two traditions.

Flora's Ship of Fools
Hendrick G. Pot, 1637

Originating in the heathen era, the land-ship remained a feature of seasonal processions in Northern Europe throughout the

Middle Ages. A record of the Lübeck Carnival procession of 1458 in Schleswig-Holstein reports that sixteen women and eight men were aboard a ship-cart when it accidentally capsized. In Nuremburg, a procession of maskers known as *Schembartlauf*, (analogous to the *Perchtanlauf*) drew a ship-car occupied by revelers from 1475 onward. Traces of such annual processions can still be found in ordinances issued by the town-council of Ulm in Swabia, the seat of the Suevi, dated 1524, 1531 and 1532 prohibiting people from going about with plows or ships on *Fastnacht* (Jan 6th) in disguise, blackening their faces or making themselves otherwise unrecognizable, with a penalty of one gulden.[131] In the year 1527, however, such lawlessness prevailed and so the council permitted "dancing and drumming and whistling in the streets at night" dressed in *Fastnacht*-disguises and visiting the neighbors— an edict they rescinded in subsequent years.

Prominent scholars such as Hilda Ellis Davidson have long compared Rodulf's account of the Low German ship procession by land to the wagon procession of the Nerthus cult. The theory that the *vehiculum* of Nerthus was a ship-cart finds some support in the fact that her procession set out from a sacred grove located on an island in the ocean. Jacob Grimm, on the other hand, considered the land-ship to be the vehicle of a different Germanic goddess described by Tacitus. In *Germania* chapter 9, the Roman historian states that part of the Suevi sacrificed to Isis. Although he could not ascertain the origin of this "foreign rite", he believed that her emblem, "fashioned in the form of a light warship, proves that the cult is imported." Even so, there is no evidence that Isis worship ever extended into Northern Europe. Therefore, it seems probable that the Swabian deity identified as her by Tacitus was a native Germanic goddess. J.B. Rives notes that this was more of a case of mistaken identity than *interpretatio Romana* since Tacitus actually believed the Suevi had adopted foreign rites. Since the cult of Isis was widespread throughout the Roman Empire at the time and promulgated primarily through Roman influence, it is highly unlikely that a Germanic tribe

---

[131] Carl Jäger, *Schwäbisches Städtewesen des Mittelalters*, Vol I, p. 525-256.

outside of the empire would have adopted it. Consequently, most scholars agree that Tacitus (or more likely his source) identified a native goddess as Isis, because of similar rituals associated with them involving ship processions by land.[132] When searching for the identity of Isis of the Suevi, it should be noted that the Greco-Egyptian goddess, like the Nordic Freyja, was a sensual fertility goddess who wandered the world weeping in search of her lost husband. In Egypt, Greece and Rome, votaries of Isis pulled a ship as part of a procession in her honor. In the North, Freyja's family, the Vanir were closely associated with ships. Her father Njörd resides in *Noatún*, the "Ship-yard" and her brother Freyr possesses a vessel large enough to transport all the gods equipped for war which could be folded up like a napkin and placed in one's pocket. Its name, *Skíðblaðnir*, means "assembled from pieces of thin wood," fitting for a cult-ship built for the duration of the festivities.[133]

Moreover, dozens of votive images dating to the second and third centuries AD, mainly from the Netherlands, depict a Low German goddess named Nehalennia often depicted with a boat or holding an oar. She was first attested on twenty-eight inscriptions discovered near Domburg on the island of Walcheren, after a storm eroded sand dunes there in 1645 and again in 1870, exposing the remains of a presumably Roman temple devoted to her. Almost as many more were discovered in the town of Colijnsplaat on the shore of the Oosterschelde in the early 1970s and two others were found near Cologne, Germany, east of Aachen, the city where the ship procession described by Rodulf of St. Trond commenced. In these images, Nehalennia commonly appears seated, accompanied by a dog, and carrying a basket of apples or baked loaves. While she cannot be convincingly identified with any later Germanic goddesses, her emblems suggest a connection to the Earth-Mother. In some images, she is shown with two other goddesses, associating her with the threefold Matronae of Central Europe. A sea-god sometimes

---

[132] Rives, *Germania* p. 162.
[133] Rudolf Simek, *Dictionary of Northern Mythology* (1984), p. 289.

appears on the sides of her altar or separately, carrying a dolphin and armed with a trident like his Greek counterpart Poseidon.

Altar of Nehalennia beside drawing from L.J.F. Janssen's
De Romeinsche Beelden en Gedenksteenen van Zeeland, 1845

According to Wolfgang Golther (1895), Roman merchants were accustomed to offering sacrifices to the native deities on the coasts where they traded. If a Roman subject were to meet a goddess which seemed familiar to him on a strange shore, he would erect a stone altar to her, employing their common attributes. The local name of the deity was typically inscribed on the monument in Latinized form or else the name of the corresponding Roman god with a Germanic qualifier, for example: *Marti Thingsus*, *Mercurio Channini*, *Herculi Magusano*, etc. The pictorial representation was thus dependent on *interpretatio Romana*, and not wholly convertible back into its Germanic form. Therefore, behind the Roman Nehalennia may stand a native Germanic goddess whose emblem was a ship. Presumably, like the Vanir, she was associated with shipping, trade and commerce.

The Nerthus procession, which ends with a sacrifice in a lake, can further be confirmed by ceremonial objects recovered from bogs and wetlands. The term *xoanon*, used by the fifth century historian Sozomen for the idol seen riding in a cart, is supported by archaeological evidence. The word refers to a rough-hewn or barely worked piece of wood, as opposed to the elaborately carved idols of the Classical world, which corresponds conceptually to the Old Norse term for god, *áss*, the singular of —thought to be derived from the Germanic root **ans*, **ansuz*, recorded for Gothic as the Latin plural *Anses* by Jordanes— which has an Old Icelandic homonym meaning "wooden pole or beam." In a tenth century account of Vikings on the Volga river, the Arab diplomat Ahmad ibn Fadlan, who was sent by the Abbasid caliph al-Muqtadir to the court of the Bulghar king, describes a group of wooden poles set up near a harbor consisting of a tall pillar with the face of a man carved in it, surrounded by smaller figures made in the same fashion, representing the family of gods. During his journey of about 4000 km, Ibn Fadlan described the peoples he encountered, devoting about a fifth of his work to the Rūsiyyah, Scandinavian traders living on the river banks near the camps of the Volga Bulghars. He writes that as soon as they arrived on shore, his heathen host brought food and an alcoholic beverage to the wooden idols as an offering, before prostrating himself in prayer before them.

A similar arrangement was found around the sacrificial bog (Opfermoor) near Oberdorla, the largest known Iron Age cult site in Central Europe. The bog, which includes a shallow marshy pool, in the municipality of Vogtei, formerly known as Oberdorla in Thuringia, has yielded a rich variety of such idols. The site was a regional cult center from the Hallstatt Period (sixth century BC) to the Migration Age (fifth century AD). Among the idols recovered are rough-hewn poles or posts, sometimes equipped with a phallus; several forked sticks with a head carved on the top, all female; broad planks cut in silhouette with blank faces representing males with rectangular bodies and females with slanted cuts indicating breasts, broad hips and vulvas, similar to the male and female figures found along the Wittemoor Timber Trackway in Berne, Lower Saxony; and finally one carved from a squared piece of wood with an inclined head and a base. An impressive pair of idols made from elongated branches was also recovered at Braak near Hamburg dated from the second to third centuries BC. The male, which stands ten feet tall, and the slightly shorter female both have emphasized sexual organs.

The Broddenbjerg Freyr   **The Freyja of Rebild**

The famous male idol from Broddenbjerg, fashioned from a forked tree limb, measures about 40 inches tall and was set on a cairn built at the center of a bog, where it was surrounded by offerings. A rough face was carved on one end to give it a human appearance. The natural form of the wood lent itself to depicting a man with an erection, akin to the idol of Fricco in the eleventh century temple at

Uppsala described by Adam of Bremen. A rough-hewn birch idol, measuring approximately 1.05m tall, recovered in late June 1946 at Rebild skovhuse in Denmark was wrapped in textiles which may have clothed her. Dubbed the "Freyja of Rebild," the gender of the figure is clearly indicated by an emphasized bosom and vulva scored with a deep cut in the trunk. A more detailed wooden idol of undetermined gender and age, since destroyed, was found in 1859 at Possendorf near Weimar in Thuringia with up-raised arms, including carved hands and fingers, attached to the wooden body. Such finds provide valuable clues to religious practices in Northern Europe during the heathen era.

In support of Tacitus' account of the Nerthus procession, several ceremonial wagons have also been recovered. Two Iron Age wagons from the first century BC, one with an alder wood stool probably used as a seat, were found near Dejbjerg in Jutland, Denmark, along with two more partially recovered from Danish cremation graves, conceivably may have been used for ritual processions.[134] Richly ornamented with bronze fittings in the typical La Tène style, indicating Celtic manufacture, both of the wagons from Dejbjerg are four-wheeled vehicles with a relatively low compartment, approximately 1.8 meters in length with a central pole extending another 1.8 meters in front. The elaborate bronze details suggest they were reserved for ceremonial use, while their circumstances indicate a ritual deposit. Found in a bog, both wagons were carefully dismantled and surrounded by an enclosure of stakes as if they had been deliberately sacrificed.[135]

In 1904, a remarkable archaeological discovery was unearthed at Oseberg, Norway, consisting of a well-preserved Viking ship that contained the remains of two women along with a rich array of grave goods. Widely celebrated as perhaps the finest find of the Viking Age, the magnificent ship was completely covered by a mound or

---

[134] McKinnell, ibid., 52; Hilda Ellis Davidson, *The Lost Beliefs of Northern Europe* (1993), p. 133.
[135] Rives, ibid., pp. 292-293.

haugr, measuring approximately 40m wide and 6.5m high. Constructed from oak planks, the vessel measured 21.4m long by 5.1m wide and contained 15 pairs of oar holes, meaning up to thirty men could row the ship. Its stern and ringed bow were carved with elaborate engravings. While seaworthy, the ship was relatively light and thus thought to have been used for coastal voyages only. Dendrochronological analysis of timbers in the grave mound dates the burial to the Autumn of 834 AD. The damp conditions within the mound allowed the ship and its contents to survive nearly intact for over a thousand years.

The remains of two women were placed in a specially built wooden tent located at the center of the mound. One of the women, aged 75-80 years old, wore a luxurious red dress made of wool woven with a lozenge twill pattern and a fine white linen veil with a gauze weave. The second woman, in her early fifties, wore a plainer blue wool dress with a wool veil, possibly indicating stratification in their social status. The connection between the two remains unclear. Some believe the women were related, others have interpreted them as Queen Asa and her handmaiden. It is plausible that the two represent a noble woman interred with her sacrificed slave. An analysis of the find by archaeologist Anne Stine Ingstad connects the two to a heathen cult and interprets the older woman as a völva or priestess. Other skeletal remains found on the ship included thirteen horses, two oxen, and four dogs, perhaps intended to accompany or assist the women on their voyage to the underworld.

The details of the Oseberg find largely agree with an account of just such a burial witnessed by Ibn Fadlan, who attended the funeral of a Scandinavian chieftain along the Volga river in Russia around 921 AD. According to him, the man's slaves were asked by the family of the deceased whether any of them would accompany their master to paradise, and so the chieftain was joined in death by a willing slave girl, who was ritually slain for the occasion. During the ceremony, animal sacrifices were also cut up and thrown onto the ship. Ibn Fadhlan says that, after outfitting the corpse in luxury items,

"They carried him inside the pavilion on the ship and laid him to rest on the quilt, propping him up with cushions. Then they brought alcohol, fruit and herbs and placed them beside him. Next they brought bread, meat and onions, which they cast in front of him, a dog, which they cut in two and which they threw onto the ship, and all of his weaponry, which they placed beside him. They then brought two mounts, made them gallop until they began to sweat, cut them up into pieces and threw the flesh onto the ship. They next fetched two cows, which they also cut up into pieces and threw on board, and a cock and a hen, which they slaughtered and cast onto it."[136]

The Oseberg Ship and Wagon
© 2017 Kulturhistorisk Museum, UiO / CC BY-SA 4.0

The Oseberg grave had been opened in antiquity and so no objects of precious metals, if ever present, were found. Still a remarkable collection of wooden and textile artifacts were left behind. The furniture included a richly carved wooden wagon, four elaborately decorated sleighs, three beds as well as a number of

[136] James Montgomery translation.

wooden chests. A bedpost shows one of the few examples of what has been dubbed the valknut symbol. Five zoomorphic posts fashioned from maple wood, all of similar size and carved with animal heads, were laid in the grave. The exact function of these posts remains unknown. They each contain slots for handles so that they could be carried, suggesting they may have had some sort of religious significance. More mundane items, such as agricultural and household implements were also recovered. These include farming equipment, looms and needlework tools, regular household items such as vats, barrels, a hand grinder, and crockery, as well as the so-called "Buddha bucket" named for two brass and cloisonné enamel ornaments on the handle in the shape of a seated figure with crossed legs. Although often compared to depictions of the Buddha in the lotus posture, a more immediate connection exists between these two ornaments and Insular or Hiberno-Saxon illuminations of the Gospels from the British Isles such the Book of Durrow.

The Oseberg burial is one of the few sources of Viking age textiles, and the wooden wagon is the only complete Viking age cart found to date. The elaborately carved four-wheeled wagon appears to have been incapable of turning corners, and thus likely was limited to ceremonial use. The cart is composed of parts made from different types of wood. The frame is made of oak and its two shafts of ash, joined by a short iron chain. The cart was probably pulled by two horses, one on each side of the shafts. It could be disassembled for transport. The back of the cart is decorated with cats, calling to mind the team that drew Freyja's chariot. The front end of the cart shows a man lying on his back surrounded by serpents, possibly representing Gunnar in the snakepit. These familiar scenes may have had significance to the ceremony. A tapestry buried with the Oseberg wagon, of which several fragments survive, offers further insight. It is one of a series of textile remains recovered from the Oseberg ship, including woolen garments, imported silks, rolled rugs, decorative tapestries and curtains, which vary widely in respect to quality, weaving techniques and materials. Among them we find imported silk cloth, embroideries using silk thread, tablet bands and woolen fabrics for a variety of uses.

The burial chamber was constructed immediately behind the ship's mast. Inside, the two women were laid under a wood-frame tent on a bed made up with linen. Long, narrow, woven tapestries, perhaps hung as a frieze on the wall, lined the chamber. The main fragment of one such tapestry depicts a religious procession involving three wagons. The lead wagon holds two figures; at least one is female. The other two wagons are covered, and it has been plausibly suggested that they held holy objects of some kind. Of this pictorial representation of a heathen religious procession, Terry Gunnell (1995) writes:

> "The images contained in the Oseberg tapestry are often extremely unclear and enigmatic, but nonetheless clear enough to suggest that what is being portrayed in the pictures should be viewed in a ritual context. This is evident not only from the wagon processions but also from the row of dancing female figures, and the line of celebrants who have a stance similar to that often depicted on the Bronze Age petroglyphs. *(footnote:* The fact that several magical swastika symbols appear between the dancers lends credence to the idea of the dance having religious connotations to do with fertility). Finally, and perhaps most telling, is the image of the sacrificial tree bedecked with a number of human corpses, thus supporting Adam of Bremen's later description of the sacrificial grove near the heathen temple at Uppsala."[137]

The Oseberg tapestry, as it is known, is embroidered with mythological and battle scenes, stylistically similar to the Bayeux tapestry. One of its fragments features a scene showing two black birds in flight, hovering above a rider on horseback. Anne Stine Ingstad, who discovered the remains of a Viking settlement at L'Anse aux Meadows in 1960, has interpreted these birds as Huginn and Muninn flying over an image of Odin. Another fragment of the

---

[137] ibid., p. 60.

tapestry contains a group of boar-headed women bearing shields, which may represent valkyries.[138] Another depicts a female figure clad as a bird of prey, standing in front of what has been described as a temple. Yet another contains an image of an armed man, clad in an animal skin, approaching a figure wearing a horned helmet and carrying a pair of crossed spears, like those on the Torslunda helmet plates. A horned figure also heads the wagon procession. While his helmet appears somewhat indistinct in the surviving fragment, both Björn Haugen and Mary Storm, who did the actual reconstruction of the tapestry under his direction, assured that the motif was "that of a man wearing a helmet with horns."[139] One can speculate that this figure represents a god, as its scale suggests no ordinary mortal. It is by far the largest figure depicted on the tapestry. Due to the fantastic nature of the imagery, it is probable that at least some its scenes have a mythological context.[140] Many of the postures, helmets and equipment depicted occur elsewhere in Germanic material from the Bronze Age petroglyphs forward, once again, pointing to the continuation of an almost homogeneous religious tradition with very ancient roots.[141] As we have seen, the ritual wagon procession was a well-established part of that tradition in northern Europe during the heathen period. This practice may be seen as continuing into the Christian era when statues of the Virgin Mary and other saints were carried around to bless the fields.[142]

---

[138] Gunnell, ibid, p. 61, states "Regarding the boar-headed figures, it is worth noting that Tacitus writes of the Aestii (from the area around the coast of Lithuania) as bearing 'boar figures', or according to Mattingly, 'boar masks,' (*insigne superstitionis formas aprorum gestant*) as an emblem of the mother of the gods whom they worshipped."

[139] Ruth Mellinkoff, *The Horned Moses in Medieval Art and Thought* (1970), p. 157, note to page 45.

[140] Gunnell, ibid., 63. See also E.O.G. Turville-Petre, *Myth and Religion of the North* (1964), p. 57.

[141] Gunnell, ibid., p. 60.

[142] Davidson, ibid.

Scenes from the Oseberg Tapestry c. 834 AD

Drawings by Mary Storm, 1940

Ritual Wagon Procession

Dancing Women

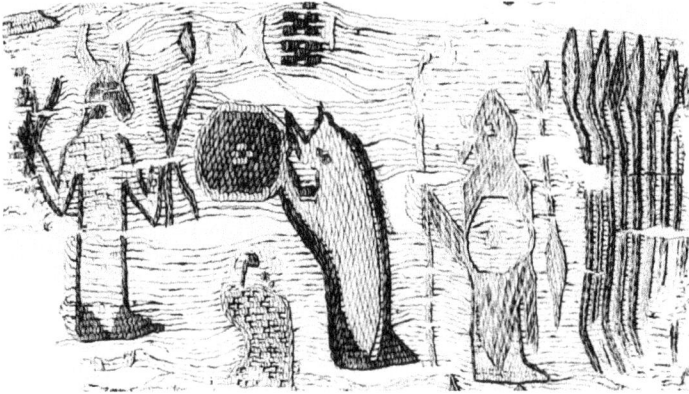

Horned Warrior and Boar-headed Woman

Bird-headed Woman

Sacrificial Tree

Outline of Horned Man Leading the Procession

**Costumed Procession led by Horned Man (top row, left)
Detail of the Oseberg Tapestry c. 834 AD**

III. The Anglo-Saxon *Æcerbót*

"Æcerbót is Christian for the most part, but has passages (often quoted) that almost certainly go back to heathen times. Thus the line *eorðan ic bidde and upheofan* 'I pray to earth and to high heaven,' has a strongly Christian context but nevertheless is unmistakably heathen. The famous line *Erce, Erce, Erce eorþan modor,* whatever it means, surely appeals to mother earth."

—Albert C. Baugh, *The Literary History of England* (2003)

Among the Germanic tribes that worship Nerthus, "that is Mother Earth," in the first century, Tacitus identifies the Longobardi (Lombards) and the Anglii (Angles, ancestors of the English). Therefore, it should come as no surprise when we find evidence of just such a procession in the earliest Old English records demonstrating that this practice survived among them into Christian times. The Anglo-Saxon *Æcerbót,* an elaborate eleventh century ritual intended to remedy unproductive land, is a mixture of prose directives and alliterative verse, probably intended for community performance.[143] The text includes four metrical prayers. After Tacitus' report on Nerthus, these superficially Christian but substantially pagan prayers are one of the clearest traces of Mother Earth in a Germanic source.[144] The character of the ritual indicates a pagan communal procession honoring the earth goddess, and is supported by both literary and archaeological evidence across the Germanic-speaking regions.

As recorded, the *Æcerbót* begins before sunrise with the removal of four pieces of sod, one from each side of a field. Oil, honey, and yeast are gathered, along with milk from every kind of animal, wood from every kind of tree except hardwood, and a piece

---

[143] Preserved in the *Exeter Book.* A full transcript of the ritual is provided in Appendix A.
[144] M.L. West, *Indo-European Poetry and Myth,* (2007), p. 177.

of every herb, except burr, found on the land. These are sprinkled with holy water, which is allowed to drip on the clods, with the words: "Grow and multiply and fill the earth. In the name of the Father and the Son and the Holy Spirit be blessed." They are then brought into a church, placed greenside toward the altar, and four masses are sung over them. Before sunset of the same day, the clods are then carried back to the field; four small wooden crosses each bearing the names of the four evangelists are laid into the holes left by the removal of the sod. The saints' names are invoked and the turf is replaced, accompanied by additional prayers repeated nine times.

The Goddess Ceres from Heinrich Steinhöwel's translation of Giovanni Boccaccio's *De mulieribus claris*, 1474

After bowing humbly nine times toward the east, the farmer utters an additional prayer to "earth and sky, and to the true Saint Mary." Further prayers and gestures follow; then the farmer blesses seed obtained from an almsman given twice as much in return, and ritually prepares the plowing equipment by boring a hole in the beam of the plow, and filling it with incense, fennel, hallowed soap and hallowed salt. He then sets the seed on the plow and intones a prayer, clearly conscious of the *heiros gamos*, which begins:

Erce, Erce, Erce,	"Erce, Erce, Erce,
eorþan modor,	Mother of Earth,[145]
Geunne þe se	May the Almighty,
alwalda ece drihten,	eternal Lord grant you
Æcera wexendra	fields growing
and wridendra	and flourishing,
Eaciniendra and elniendra, etc	increasing and strengthening, etc.

The plowman then cuts the first furrow, reciting another prayer which began with these words, *Hal wes þu, folde, fira modor:* "May you be well, Earth, Mother of men! May you be growing in the Embrace of God, filled with food for the benefit of men."[146] He then takes a loaf made from *ælces cynnes melo,* "every kind of grain" grown on the land, kneaded with milk and holy water, and places it in the first furrow continuing to pray. The ritual ends with the recitation of the Lord's Prayer three times, with an appeal to God that every seed sown may sprout.

In the Anglo-Saxon agricultural system, the lord of the manor and not the individual landholder was of central importance from the earliest times. By the eleventh century (the date of the text), the growth of large secular and ecclesiastic estates made the rise of feudalism possible. Under this system, agriculture was essentially a communal enterprise. No fences or hedges separated one man's plot from another. As a rule, each man's holdings were in the form of narrow plow strips, so that no one farmer had a monopoly on the good land. The arable land was thus plowed in common and sown by common agreement. The only person who could have thus demarcated his land by taking sods from all four corners of the field as instructed in the *Æcerbót* ritual was the lord of the manor, who as a patron of the parish church could have arranged for a priest to sing masses over the sods, effecting a blessing for the entire community at once. In regard to this elaborate ritual, John D. Niles (1980) observes:

---

[145] Night is the mother of *Jörð* (Earth) in *Gylfaginning* 10. Here, a goddess governing the Earth must be meant, according to the context.
[146] Richard North translation.

"The rite would have been so dramatic a visual and auditory experience, from sunup to sundown, with the processions from the fields to the church and from the church to the fields, with the singing of the masses and the chanting of the prayers, that the attention of an entire community would have been riveted on the act of opening the fields."[147]

Such a thing is not easily forgotten through the generations, and may well have ancient origins. The prayer itself seems to have an Indo-European pedigree. A Greek version of such a hymn recorded by Hesiod in *Works and Days* reads: "Pray to Zeus of the Earth and pure Demeter, for Demeter's holy grain to ripen heavy."[148] Here again, the earth-goddess is coupled with the sky-god. In the Anglo-Saxon *Æcerbót*, the Christian God takes the place of the old Indo-European Sky-Father. The Earth is exhorted to become pregnant in his embrace. Both *eorpan modor* and *folde fira modor* resemble *Terra Mater*, the earth-goddess Nerthus, whom Tacitus reports the continental Anglii worshiped in the first century AD.[149] The term *folde fira modor*, "earth, mother of men," should be compared further with *Germania* 2 where he states that the Germanic tribes descend from Tuisto, *dues terra editus*, "a god born from the earth." This implies that at least one of Tacitus' German informants believed that all the Germanic tribes descended from the earth.[150] From this and other evidence, Richard North concludes:

"...although a connection between the farming cultures represented in *Germania* and *Æcerbót* may seem less likely than an influence of the charm from this or another ecclesiastical source, the conception of the *folde fira modor* in this charm as lying *godes fæpme* ("in the embrace of God") is not part of Christian doctrine

---

[147] "The Æcerbot Ritual in Context" in *Old English Literature in Context,* p. 56.
[148] *Opera et Dies,* ll. 465-9 as quoted by West, ibid., p. 183.
[149] North, ibid., 251.
[150] North, ibid., p. 46; cp. the *Prologue* to Snorri's *Edda* which says "They reasoned the earth was alive....For this reason they gave it a name and traced their ancestry to it."

and brings *Æcerbót* closer to *Skírnismál* and to other pre-Christian poems that reflect a common Germanic tradition of the earth."

Hilda Ellis Davidson, writing in *Roles of the Northern Goddesss* (1998), affirms this view, stating:

"From references to Earth (*folde*), Mother of men, and to earth bringing forth in God's embrace, together with appeals to St. Mary and the god of high heaven, it seems probable that this was originally addressed to a goddess who caused grain to sprout and grow, with a call to the sky god to send the necessary rain." (p. 62)

It is evident to scholars that the Nordic oral tradition has a close relationship in both form and content to that recorded in related non-Scandinavian compositions like the Old English *Widsith*, *Doer,* and *Beowulf,* and the Old High German *Hildebrandslied*, which date back to the ninth or tenth centuries.[151] That the contents of the Old English metrical charms are conceptually connected to the Old Norse religion is generally taken for granted by scholars such as Ursula Dronke who, in commenting on the use of the alliterative terms *ásom* and *alfar* (Aesir and Elves) in *Völuspá* 49, remarks: "The antiquity of this formula is suggested by an echo of it in an Old English Charm."[152] Based on the evidence, one may reasonably conclude that the veneration of the Earth-Mother is equally ancient. The formula *Erce, Erce, Erce* may contain her name, although some have questioned whether Erce is a name at all. If so, it may mean "bright" or "pure" from OHG *erchan*, Gothic *airkns*,[153] and is probably related to the name of a legendary figure found chiefly in Low Saxon districts, a divine dame known as Frau Herke or Harke who flies through the country between Christmas and Twelfth-Day dispensing prosperity. In the traditions of the Altmark, she either scratches the maids who have not spun off all their flax or befouls

---

[151] *A Companion to Old Norse-Icelandic Literature and Culture*, Rory McTurk ed.; Terry Gunnell, Ch. 5: "Eddic Poetry," p. 93.
[152] *The Poetic Edda*, Vol. II (1997), p. 147.
[153] M.L. West, *Indo-European Poetry and Myth* (2007), p. 177.

their spindles. Stories concerning her must have once been more numerous.[154] More commonly called Frau Holle, her byname Harke or Herke, can be traced with some certainty to around 1406, when the German historian Gobelin Person of Paderborn, located in the German state of North Rhine-Westphalia, wrote in his *Cosmidromius* (ch. 38) that, from antiquity, the common folk there had revered the goddess Hera, also called Juno and Ceres, who flew through the air bestowing earthly abundance between the feasts of the Nativity and the Epiphany (Dec 25th to January 6th).[155] The locals called her Frau Here (*vrowe here*), a name he equates with Hera, the wife of Zeus. Her name and annual activity, however, clearly connect her to Odin's wife, the native Frau Holle or Herka, who was still called *Frau Har(r)e* until relatively recent times around Halle, toward Potsdam, and in the Prignitz.[156]

As early as 1851, Benjamin Thorpe observed that, since Gobelin's account points to a Low Saxon Earth goddess, "there seems to be no doubt" that the Erce, invoked as *eorþan modor* in an Anglo-Saxon spell for the fertilizing of the land, is identical to her.[157] With less certainty, the *Æcerbót's eorþan modor* can be related to an obscure goddess named by the tenth century Anglo-Saxon historian, Venerable Bede. In his *De Temporum Ratione,* Bede wrote that the month of March was called *Rhedamonath* by his people, after "Rheda to whom they sacrificed."[158] The name may be compared to Hertha, a variant of Nerthus, because Dutch, German and English all show evidence of metathesis, a phenomenon in which consonants reverse positions within words without changing their meaning, thus

---

[154] Thorpe, *Northern Mythology* (1851), p. 280.

[155] Erika Timm, *Frau Holle, Frau Percht und verwandte Gestalten*: 160 Jahre nach Jacob Grimm aus germanistischer Sicht betrachtet, (2003), p. 56, 58.

[156] Wachnitius, p. 109, Graesse (1868) 1, p. 116f, Weitland 1911: 5, cited by Timm, ibid., p. 56.

[157] Thorpe, *Northern Mythology* Vol. I, (1851), p. 280, citing Müller, p. 127.

[158] The name is recorded as *Redimonat* (March) in a rhymed Chronicle of Appenzell in Switzerland in the 1600s and as *Retmonat* in Chorion's *Ehrenkranz der Teutschen Sprach* published at Strassburg in 1644, supporting Bede's statement.

rendering *Herthum* as *Rhedum*, or *Hertha* as *Rheda*.[159] So despite lingering doubts regarding the significance of the word *Erce* in the Old English *Æcerbót*, the charm itself unquestionably refers to a pre-Christian earth-goddess, conceptually connected to parallel figures within the Germanic realm.

Herthe, the Earth-Mother
Trogillus Arnkiel's
The Cimbric Heathen-Religion, 1691

---

[159] Gardenstone, "Nerthus, Mother Earth," (2012).

THE DISTRIBUTION OF THE LEGENDS OF
FRAU HOLLE, FRAU PERCHT
AND RELATED FIGURES
Based on the Research of Dr. Erika Timm, 2003.

© 2018 William P. Reaves

BALTIC SEA

Flensburg

The Nerthus Procession, 98 AD

NORTH SEA

Kiel
Rostock
Schleswig-Holstein

THE WILD HUNT
LED BY ODIN

East Frisian Islands

West Frisian Islands

Hamburg
Schwerin
Mecklenburg-Western Pomerania

Frau Gode, Wode, etc.

Bremen

Beetgum

Oldenburg

Frau Frekka, Frick, etc.

THE WILD HUNT

Hludana

Lower Saxony

NORTH EUROPEAN PLAIN

Frau Herke, Harke, etc.

Hanover

Potsdam
Berlin

NETHERLANDS

Magdeburg

Brandenburg

North Rhine-Westphalia

Saxony-Anhalt
Wittenberg

Nehalennia

Paderborn
Heresburg

Halle

Ship Procession by Land, 1133 AD

Kassel

Merseberg
Saxony

Maesdricht
Cologne

Thuringia

Dresden

Trond
Aachen

Zwickau

BELGIUM

Hesse

Koblenz

VOGTLAND

Vrouw Vreke

Frau Holle, Holda, etc.

Hof

Frau Werra of the Vogtland

Rhineland-Palatinate
Mainz

CZECH
REPUBLIC

LUX.
Trier

Würzburg
Bayreuth

FRANCONIA

Saarland

Nuremberg

Heidelberg

FRANCE

Bavaria

Stuttgart

Baden-Württemberg
Ulm

Frau Percht, Bercht, etc.

SWABIA

Augsburg

Munich

Constance

Salzburg

SWITZERLAND

Tyrol

Pongau
Pinzgau

THE ALPS

AUSTRIA

IV. The Frau Holle Legends

"Deities, by their very nature, frequently attract numerous epithets and bynames, e.g. 'Lord', 'deliverer', 'almighty'; as these will suffer differential survival among sister groups or replace existing names, references to what were once the same deity may be lost over time."

— J.P. Mallory and D.Q. Adams, *The Oxford Introduction to Proto-Indo-European and the PIE World*, (2006), p. 423.

Of the seven nations named by Tacitus as votaries of Nerthus, only two can be placed with some certainty into a geographic region, according to Lotte Motz. They are the Varini, probably living near the river Warnow in present-day Pomerania, and the Anglii, probably dwelling in Anglia on the shores of the Baltic Sea. It is clear, however, that these tribes were situated in the North of the European continent and on the peninsula of Jutland near the Baltic or the North Sea.[160] With one cult spread across at least seven northern European nations, the scale of *Terra Mater*'s worship in the first century must have been massive.[161] Thus we must take notice when we discover a parallel figure with a congruous range recorded in medieval German folklore and surviving in popular legends down to the beginning of the twenty-first century. Across Germany, Austria, and Switzerland are found a closely related group of popular legends involving a faded heathen goddess associated with both the plow and the spinning wheel.[162] She appears under such names as Frau Holle, Holda, Percht, Bercht, Herke, Harke, Herra and Werra, among many others. Further north, the same figure is known as Frau Frekka or Frick, as well as Frau Wode or Gode, who accompanies her husband Wodan as he heads the Wild Hunt. Despite the wide

---

[160] Lotte Motz, "The Goddess Nerthus; A New Approach" (1992).
[161] Richard North, *Heathen Gods in Old English Literature*, p. 20.
[162] Hilda Davidson, *The Lost Beliefs of Northern Europe*, p. 115.

variations in her name, she always has the same character, visiting homes during the Twelve Nights, dispensing rewards and punishments, paying particular attention to spinning and domestic order. She comes as a beauty or a hag. Those who know her both love and fear her. In the early nineteenth century, Jacob Grimm recognized these legends collectively as the remnant memory of a pre-Christian goddess.[163] In the early twentieth century, Viktor Waschnitius published a rich collection of tales and traditions involving her.[164] Most recently Erika Timm, a professor of Yiddish studies at the University of Triers, has thoroughly cataloged her history, producing a vivid color map which details the distribution of her documentation.[165] For the most part, Dr. Timm's findings support those of Jacob Grimm. In regard to his critics, she asks rhetorically how it is possible for the scholars to have such differing theories regarding Frau Holle's origin, if they all were using the same sources.[166] Because of the obvious resemblance of their attributes and stories, scholars generally agree that these figures represent a single being. Noting the "striking similarity" between Frau Göja (Fru Go, Fru Gude) of Northern Germany and "the great ladies of the wintertime of the provinces of Germany — of whom the most important are Frau Holle and Frau Perchta," Lotte Motz concluded:

"Though many names are encountered, the creatures show such strong resemblances to one another that we may be sure of one basic configuration; she is a spirit of the woodland, a visitor to human dwellings in the winter season. She may inspect the order of the household, check on the behavior of children, and receive the offered gifts. She may punish or ordain fortune or misfortune for the coming year."[167]

---

[163] Grimm, ibid., ch. 13.4.
[164] *Perht, Holde und verwandte Gestalten* (1913).
[165] At http://germanicmythology.com/original/FRAUHOLLE_TIMM.html originally published in *Frau Holle, Frau Percht und verwandte Gestalten*, S. Hirzel Verlag Stuttgart (2003).
[166] Timm, ibid., p. 13.
[167] Lotte Motz, *The Beauty and the Hag*, (1993), pp. 78-79, 124.

Motz argued that this figure represents an earlier Germanic goddess of winter because of her association with Christmas and New Year's.[168] But Hilda Ellis Davidson countered that Motz's supposition is not supported by the evidence, since in the stories collected by Waschnitius her two main functions, spinning and plowing, are not predominantly winter activities. Davidson, however, did not dispute the origin of this divine dame in the pre-Christian religion, and aptly compared her to the Earth Mother Nerthus, who was said to go around the fields, making them fruitful.[169] In 1982, Eugen Drewermann and Ingritt Neuhaus drew a similar conclusion:

> "Frau Holle is none other than the Germanic goddess Hulda (or Berchta). In her, the figure of Mother Earth lives on. …She is also the queen of the heavens, whose bed-feathers fall to the earth as snow."[170]

Although not confined to Germany, this demoted goddess is best known there. Legends of Frau Holle or Holda are especially prominent in the states of Thuringia and Hesse, while those of her counterparts Frau Percht or Bercht are concentrated in the Alpine regions; those of Frau Werra in the Vogtland; those of Frau Herke and Frau Gode in Lower Saxony and Saxony-Anhalt to the North, and those of Frau Frekka in Mecklenburg and Pomarania bordering the Baltic Sea.[171] She is sometimes known as the White Lady, as well as by other local names. A close comparison reveals little distinction among them; they are evidently one figure. Their identity is most

---

[168] Lotte Motz, (1984) *"The Winter Goddess: Percht, Holde, and Related Figures," Folklore* 95, 151-166; *The Beauty and the Hag* (1993), pp. 124-131.
[169] Davidson, ibid., p. 116.
[170] Frau *Holle: Marchen Nr. 24 aus der Grimmschen Sammlung. Freiburg im Breisgau,* 1982, quoted in translation in *Frau Holle: In the Marchen and Beyond* by Kerby Lynn Boschee, (2006).
[171] Lotte Motz, ibid., (1993) see esp. chapter VI2.1: *The Great Goddess of the Countryside,* p. 124-125, cp. the map of the Frau Holle legends in Erika Timm's *Frau Holle, Frau Percht und verwandte Gestalten* (2003).

plain in that they all make their rounds at the same time, during the Twelve-Nights including Christmas and New Years.[172] Her image in the popular imagination ranges from matronly or saintly to terrible and frightening. According to some legends she appears as a beautiful, spectral figure dressed in flowing white robes with a veil concealing her face, and in others as an ugly, old wizened witch with wildly disheveled hair, burning eyes and a fiery tongue. In stories of Frau Holle, her good nature shines forth, while in tales of Frau Percht, her bad nature predominates.

In Grimm's fairy-tales, Frau Holle appears as a spinner and rewarder of good deeds. Once when an industrious girl named Goldmarie accidentally dropped her spindle into a well, her angry stepmother forced her to retrieve it. Terrified, the girl jumped into the well and lost her senses. When she awoke, she found herself in a beautiful sunlit meadow. As she walked along, she came upon an oven filled with fresh loaves of bread, which cried out to her to remove them before they could burn. She did so and soon after came upon a tree full of apples, which cried out to her to pick them. She shook the tree vigorously until none were left hanging and gathered them up into a neat pile before moving on. Soon she happened upon a small cottage. Inside an old woman with long teeth named Frau Holle asked her to help with the housework. In spite of her appearance, the old woman spoke so kindly, the girl agreed and helped her shake her bed until feathers filled the air, and so, as they say in Hesse, it began to snow in the world. Day after day, the girl took care of everything to Frau Holle's satisfaction, so she enjoyed the good life, dining on roasted meat with the old woman every night. In time, the girl grew homesick and asked to return home. So Frau Holle led the girl to a gate where she showered her with gold, returned her lost spindle, and sent her on her way. When the gate closed, the girl found herself above the earth again and returned home with her newly acquired wealth for which she was warmly received.

---

[172] Grimm, ibid., p. 273.

Grimm's Household Tales
Walter Crane, 1882

Woodcut published
in *Wonder-World*, 1875

Once her stepmother learned how Goldmarie had gotten the gold, she sent her own daughter Pitchmarie, who was slow and lazy, down the well, hoping to repeat the same fortune. She too awoke in a beautiful meadow and walked along the same path. Coming upon an oven full of loaves of baking bread, she refused to remove them lest she get dirty. When she came upon a tree full of ripe apples, she refused to shake it lest one fall on her head. When she arrived at Frau Holle's house, she was not afraid of the old woman and went straight to work, thinking of the gold she would receive as her wages. But soon, the lazy girl returned to her old ways and did less and less each day, hardly wanting to get up in the morning. Even then, she never made the bed as Frau Holle requested. Soon tired of this behavior, Frau Holle soon dismissed her from her duties. Secretly happy, the girl eagerly awaited the anticipated shower of gold. But when Frau Holle led her to the gate to go home, a kettle of pitch fell on her instead, which would not wash off as long as she lived. In variants of the story, the lazy girl passes through the gate into a foggy swamp filled with snakes and toads or ends up dunked in muddy water.

In another of Grimm's household tales, when a crippled boy

named Jacob is driven from home by his older brother, who refused to care for him despite having promised their dying father to be good to him "as a brother should", Frau Holle appeared to the distraught child as an old woman, sitting on a stone in the forest at work on a spinning wheel. The boy had broken his leg as a child and limped ever since, thus everyone called him Crooked Jacob. Frau Holle took pity on him and brought the boy into her own cottage for a time, putting him to work watering her rosemary bushes, feeding her cats and tending her flax fields. In the winter he cut wood. In the spring, they bore their goods to market on their backs. She carried his load when it was too heavy for his lame leg. Afterwards, she took him back home, employing her spindle as a walking stick as they went. The boy had once lived in a castle which stood on the Schellenberg in Lower Franconia. In its courtyard stood a mighty linden tree. It was said that as long as the linden flourished, the castle would stand and its occupants would thrive. Despite the old woman's earnest pleas to honor his oath to care for his brother, the selfish man refused to share the rich inheritance their father had left. As he drove them both away, Frau Holle cursed the great linden tree, which started to wither, and in due time the whole estate fell into ruin. As the tree died, the castle crumbled. The selfish brother met his fate when it collapsed onto the condemned castle, crushing him inside with his treasure. Frau Holle returned to divide the wealth and give Jacob his rightful half. She instructed him to purchase a farm, which she promised to bless as long as he lived. He dutifully obeyed her command. Although he never saw Frau Holle again, no scourge ever befell his livestock, no vermin plagued his orchards and no hail fell in his fields. When the harvest was more work than his men could handle, they would find the bales already bound and stacked for them to haul away each morning. Frau Holle richly blessed him all the days of his life.

Commonly manifested as a superior being with a helpful disposition, who is never cross unless she discovers disorder in domestic affairs, Frau Holle (also called Holda, Hulda, Hülli, and

Holl) is well known in popular legends and fairy-tales distributed extensively throughout Thuringia and Hesse. Today, Thuringia is a free state (*Bundesland*) in central Germany, bordered by the German states of Lower Saxony, Saxony-Anhalt, Saxony, Bavaria, and Hesse. The eastern part of Thuringia is a vast lowland plain cut through by the Saale river, flowing northward from its headwaters in Bavaria. Thuringia's most prominent geographical feature is a mountain chain in the southwest known as the Thuringian Forest (*Thüringer Wald*), famous for Wartburg Castle where the Catholic Reformer Martin Luther stayed for some time in exile. Merseburg, one of Germany's oldest towns is located upstream along the Saale in Saxony-Anhalt, ten miles south of Halle, the home of thriving Bronze Age- and Iron Age settlements centered around the salt mines there. The biggest part of Saxony-Anhalt consists of rich plains used primarily for agriculture. These areas have long proven to be fertile grounds for the preservation of pre-Christian seasonal rituals, which the Church tried in vain to stamp out for centuries. So widespread is the folk-belief in Frau Holle there, it is probably rooted in the ancient pagan religion of the region.

The greatest degree of familiarity with these legends occurs in the Meissner region located within sight of Kassel, the site where these fairy tales were first written down. In the same region, a lake known as *Frau Holle Teich* or "Frau Holle's Pond", sits between twin peaks of the Meissner Mountains at an elevation of 620m.[173] There, one can now see a statue dedicated to the goddess.[174] This place was mentioned for the first time as *Frau Hollen Bad*, "Frau Holle's Bath", in 1641 by Landgraf Hermann (1607-1658), who described it as a "large pond or lake, which was mostly cloudy," noting that old reports say a female spirit bathes in it at noon and disappears afterwards.[175] Travelers have flocked to the area since at least 1724 as

---

[173] Located between the Kasseler Kuppe, 750m, and the Kalbe, 720m.
[174] Standing over 3 meters tall, this wooden sculpture was carved by Viktor Donhauser and his son Ilia in 2004.
[175] In *Niederfürstentums Hessen*, a regional geography of Hesse.

a tribute to her enduring legend. Gold coins from the reign of the Roman Emperor Domitian (81 AD to 96 AD) unearthed there suggest that *Frau Holle Teich* was already a cult site nearly two thousand years ago. Although small, it is the highest body of standing water in those mountains, and rumored to be infinitely deep. The pond itself is said to be the entrance to Frau Holle's underwater domain, which consists of a silver castle and lush gardens filled with flowers, fruits and vegetables, which she generously distributes to women and girls. The fairy tale Goldmarie and Pitchmarie is localized here. According to local folklore, women wishing to become mothers come to bathe here, and storks deliver newborns from its waters; children born on a Sunday can hear bells ringing there, a tradition which probably arose due to the presence of bell-frogs.

Holda by F.W. Heine, 1882

Frau Holle, in her many forms, loves to lurk in lakes and ponds. She is sometimes seen as a fair White Lady bathing in such waters before disappearing, a trait in which she resembles Nerthus.[176] The same figure is said to bathe between the hours of eleven and noon in *Frau Hulli's Badeplatz*, a pool near the river Main in Lower Franconia, alone or with two equally beautiful maidens. In 1838, while out working in the pastures, a young shepherd named Bernard of Hasloch grew weary in the heat, because his family, who usually brought him lunch, did not arrive as expected. He waited for hours and got so overheated that he finally took the path down to a lush river valley. Exhausted and cooled by the fresh moist air, he soon fell asleep. He had not slept long, when he was awoken by a noise and saw bathers in the water before him beyond some brush. Astonished, he peered over the bushes and saw three beautiful women playing in the shallow water. He hoped to see more and crept closer, but broke one of the branches he was bending to see. When the twig snapped unexpectedly, he looked around in vain, for the women had vanished. He leapt into the water, but there was nothing left to see.[177]

Frau Holle is represented as a being of the earth girdling the sky. She operates both above and below the clouds, and is especially tied to the weather. A rolling fog is said to be the smoke from her hearth. When she bakes bread, the whole sky turns red. As she flies through the air on stormy nights, bolts of lightning known as *Hollenzopf*, "Holle's braids," reveal her own long, tangled strands of white hair.[178] Jacob Grimm remarks: "to have travelled with Holle," is said of someone whose hair is a mess or standing on end. During the cold winter months, she shakes out her down pillows and bedcovers, filling the air with feathers, causing it to snow. The comparison of snowflakes to feathers is very old. According to Herodotus, the Scythians pronounced the regions north of them inaccessible,

---

[176] Grimm, ibid., 268.

[177] A. Fries in *Zeitschrift für deutsche Mythologie und Sittenkunde,* Vol 1, (1853), p. 23-29.

[178] Sonja Rüttner-Cova, *Frau Holle: Die Gesturzte Gottin. Marchen, Mythen,* (1988), p. 103.

because they were filled with feathers.[179] Throughout Germany, people are familiar with these beliefs. The first snowfall of the year brings joy to the children, who go out to frolic in it. That this event is associated with Frau Holle increases her popularity with them.

Frau Holle
Alexander Zick, 1901

She is more generally a figure of reward and punishment to children. If their toys are not picked up and if they don't do what they are told, then Frau Holle will come and punish them. Daily chores and routines are within her jurisdiction. Abiding by or neglecting the simple tasks she assigns will result in a due reward. It is not yet forgotten in Hesse that Frau Holle visits villages during Christmas time, inspecting homes and handing out gifts from her garden and kitchen— the fruits of the earth, nuts and apples, and

---

[179] *History* IV, 7: "With respect to the feathers which are said by the Scythians to fill the air, and to prevent persons from penetrating into the remoter parts of the continent, ...the Scythians, with their neighbours, call snow-flakes feathers because, I think, of the likeness which they bear to them," (G. Rawlinson tr.).

plenty of freshly baked cookies and cakes. For ill-behaved children, she brings coal and switches. Her annual appearance falls between the Twelves, the twelve nights between December 25th and January 6th —Christmas and Epiphany— Twelfth-Night being the last of these, followed by Twelfth-Day. The Twelves are considered the time between the old and the new year.[180] The long, dreary nights and short, gray days of winter with their threatening storms and violent winds give the goddess mysterious qualities.

Frau Holle is foremost a spinster. The cultivation of flax is assigned to her. As the overseer of the *Spinnstubbe* ("spinning room") in times past, she checked the diligence of spinners. When she toured the country at Christmas, the distaffs were well-stocked and left standing for her inspection.[181] If she found everything as it should be, she pronounced her blessing, and if not, her curse. She presented industrious maids with new spindles and magically filled their reels overnight. She would set a lazy spinner's distaff on fire or spoil the thread. In Thuringia, the grey-haired Frau Holle would leave a gift by the distaff on New Year's Eve, but in the villages of Franconia, she smeared the distaffs of slovenly girls with dung.[182] One of her favorite punishments for lazy spinners was to take their unspun flax and tie it up in knots which could not be untangled. Such spoiled balls of yarn were also called Holle's braids. The common tradition of baking Christmas bread in the form of a braid may be traced to her cult. Thought of as a fair and kind taskmaster, Frau Holle is also widely associated with a day of rest when no work may be done. This work ban ensured a day of rest, fostering reflection and gratitude toward the eternal creative powers. Love and reverence toward the Earth-Mother are expressed in the sanctity of her Sabbath (Saturday), celebrated as Holle's Day. In the Rhön mountains, farmwork was forbidden on Hulla's Saturday. No one is permitted to hoe, spread

---

[180] Rüttner-Cova, ibid., p. 119.
[181] Grimm, ibid., p. 269-270.
[182] Wachnitius, p. 80.

manure, or "drive the team afield."[183] Consequently, all work must be diligently completed in the days leading up to this day of rest. The demands of the goddess vary by region. At certain times such as on Saturday night, all day Sunday, and other holy days such as Twelfth-Night, no flax may be worked or Frau Holle will come.[184]

In nearly identical legends from High German regions including Swabia, Alsace, Switzerland, Bavaria, and the Austrian Alps, the names Frau Perchta or Berchta, sometimes shortened to Percht and Bercht, are most common. Although her name suggests a benign being — *percht* means "magnificent" or "splendid" and *bercht* means "bright" —she is rarely represented as such. She is more often described as an old hag with long teeth, who also had oversight of spinners. Like Frau Holle, she too makes her rounds between Christmas and New Year's Day. In times past, whatever spinning she found unfinished on the last day of the year, she spoiled. In the Tyrol, Perchta would visit and provide young brides with thread or yarn; they had to complete their spinning by Christmas or risk incurring her wrath. Most often, she spoiled their distaffs. Of a distaff in state of disorder, it was said: *da nistet die Perchta drin*, "Perchta nests within."[185] If angered, she might visit the spinning room on Twelfth-Night, tossing empty reels in through the window, demanding that they all be filled in short order. If her demands were not met, she broke and befouled the flax. From Langendembach in the Thuringian Forest comes such a tale that tells of an old woman who refused to quit working on Twelfth-Night, complaining "Frau Percht brings me no shirts, I must spin them myself." At that, the window blew open and Frau Perchta threw several empty reels into the room demanding that they all be spun full in an hour's time. Terrified, the spinster spun a few rounds on each and tossed them all into a nearby brook. With this, Perchta was appeased.[186]

---

[183] Grimm, ibid., p. 270.
[184] Davidson, ibid., p. 115, cp. Grimm.
[185] Wachnitius, ibid., p. 33.
[186] Grimm, ibid., pp. 275-276.

Her legend lives on in the Austrian Duchy of Salzburg and parts of the Tyrol, where she appears during the Twelve Nights from Christmas Eve to *Perchtentag* ("Perchta's Day"), the 6th of January. In Salzburg, she sometimes takes on the appearance of a bright, lovely woman, who floats through the air in shining robes. She is often imagined as surrounded by a crowd of small children, protectively wrapped in her electric blue cloak. Just how splendid she appears is attested by the local name for the atmospheric phenomenon known elsewhere as St. Elmo's fire, which manifests as small light blue or purple flames, creating a coronal discharge around pointed objects during a thunderstorm or a combination of heavy snowfall and high winds. In the mountains of Salzburg, they call it *Perchtenfeuer,* "Perchta's fire." According to local legend the bright lady may be seen wandering around the great fortress of Salzburg in the dead of night. She has a dual nature, sometimes filled with goodness and charity toward mankind, and at other times full of hate and malice. Near the start of each year, she lurks at crossroads, waiting for travelers in the guise of a tiny old crone with gleaming eyes, a long hooked nose, and wildly tangled hair. When people approach her, she greets them with a friendly smile and holds out a black cloth. If a person accepts it, he will not survive the year, but if he brings out a crucifix and says, "Frau Percht, Frau Percht, throw your cloth to the earth," then joy and blessing will be bestowed on him and his household. If she shows herself in a stable, sickness and death are sure to strike the sheep and cattle unless one hangs a bunch of consecrated St. John's wort on the crossbeam. On Walpurgis Night (the night before May Day), two sticks in the form of a cross had to be placed on the stable door lest she enter. Her train of followers share their mistress' dual nature, the *Schön Perchten* ("Beautiful Perchten") being kind, benevolent creatures and the *Schlacht Perchten* ("Wild Perchten") being frightful, malicious things. In swarms the latter come among men with their weird shrieks and laughter. They enjoy drawing men into danger with alluring sounds and spells, exposing and punishing their hidden sins.

Frau Perchta has redeeming traits as well. She rewards children who have worked diligently and learned their lessons well with nuts and sugar plums. When a fog floats over the fields, they see her gliding along, wrapped in a flowing white mantle. Her presence makes the farmers' fields fruitful and causes their cattle to thrive. In the 1800s and early 1900s, on the evening of Twelfth-Night, the superstitious would leave their dinner scraps on the table for her and her companions. When they had gone to bed and all was quiet in the house, she would come in the form of a little, wizened old woman with a crowd of children and feast on the leftovers. But woe to the prying eye who peeped through the key-hole just then! Many a man, it was said, had been blinded for a whole year as a punishment for his curiosity. More often, Frau Perchta came in her frightening form, riding a gale, with tangled hair and a long, hooked nose, in order to punish slothful spinners and naughty children. On Lake Zürich, she was called *de Chungere,* because she put knots (*chungel*) in the yarn of lazy girls. In the Vogtland, they call her Frau Werra, a name probably derived from *"gewirrt"*, describing tangled or unkempt hair. She performed a strict inspection on New Year's Eve to determine whether all the distaffs had been spun off. If not, she defiled them. In a tale recorded in the Carinthian town of Gailtal during the nineteenth century, a person who found himself outside on the eve of *Perchtentag* heard a cow-bell in the distance, fast approaching. Frightened, he ran inside the nearest house. He scarcely had time to slam the door, when he heard violent rapping and scratching from outside. "It is Percht," he said, and the next morning discovered the door was scarred with deep scratches from top to bottom.[187] Other tales from Thuringia tell of peasants who encountered Perchta as they travelled between towns on *Perchtennacht,* ("Perchta's Night").[188] At a crossroads at night, she appeared to them as a tall stately woman all dressed in white beside a broken plow or cart surrounded by

---

[187] Mrs Herbert Vivian, *"The Perchtan Dancers of Salzburg"*, *Wide World Magazine,* Volume 21, (1908).

[188] In Hesse, the Thursday before Christmas is called *Hollenabend,* Holle's Eve.

weeping children. She commonly requested some service of the passerby, typically aid in repairing her broken plow or wagon, and insisted he take some wood shavings left over from the mending as payment. The unsuspecting helper typically disdained the offer, but took a small amount to appear polite. He soon discovered to his delight and chagrin that however many pieces he accepted had now become solid gold. When he returned to the spot to search for more, he could find no trace of her.

The White Lady by Wilhelm Strumpf
Max Geißler's *Das Buch von der Frau Holle*, 1903

Clearly related to these legends are folktales of a White Lady or White Woman who appears in the mountains. Such stories are heard everywhere in Germany.[189] On the Launberg in Upper Hesse, she appears at sunrise sitting on the hillside with her spinning wheel, wheat spread out to dry beside her on a white cloth. A baker passing

---

[189] Grimm, ibid., p. 962-965.

by took some of the grains with him and at home found nothing but gold. The same was told of a peasant near Friedigerode. On the Boyneburg, a poor shepherd once saw a snow-white maiden sitting in the sunlight beside the castle door. On a white cloth spread before her lay uncracked pods of flax. He picked up and admired the pods, while unbeknownst to him a few of the seeds fell into his shoe. The maiden smiled at him, but said nothing. As the shepherd returned home, one of his feet began to bother him and when he removed his shoe, six grains of gold rolled out into his hand. On the Otomannsberg near Geismar, a maiden dressed in snow-white garments, holding a bunch of keys is said to appear every seven years.[190] Similarly, legend holds that a treasure is buried beneath the castle at Wolfartsweiler, where every seventh year, when white lilies are in bloom, a white maiden with plaited black hair appears, wearing a golden girdle and holding a bunch of keys on her belt or in her hand. She shows herself to children and is said to leave them gifts of food or gold. On a hill near Langensteinbach, a white woman is said to appear in the forest near the long-ruined Church of St. Barbara at leap-year. Dressed in a white gown and green shoes with a bunch of keys at her side, she once beckoned to a young girl from the abandoned church choir. Her hands and face were white as snow and her hair raven black. She held a bouquet of blue flowers in her hand. Terrified, the girl ran to fetch her father and brothers working outside, but when they arrived, the white maiden was gone. At Osterrode, every Easter before sunrise, a white maiden appears at the old castle there, washing a large set of keys in the brook. Once she led a poor weaver into the ruins and picked three white lilies for him, one of which he placed in his cap. When he returned home, the lily in his cap had become pure gold and silver, which he traded to the Duke for a pension. The Duke placed the flower in his princely coat of arms. Three lilies also appear on the right side of the coat of arms of Fulda in Hesse. As the ancestoress of kings and protectress of their castles, this *Weisse Frau* or *Dame Blanche*, "White Lady,"

---

[190] Keys are kept by the lady of the house, cp. *Þrymskviða* 16, 19; *Rígsþula* 23.

sometimes named Berthe, was often represented as a radiant woman with one swan-foot, flat-foot, oversized-foot or club-foot, a characteristic which alludes to the mythic swan-maidens and feather guises of the goddesses in eddic mythology.

Among Germanic nobility, the white-robed goddess was transformed into a spectral woman in white, whose appearance foretold the coming of great events or served as a sign of an impending royal death for generations. Sometimes she was tied to a specific ancestoress or event, but more often appeared as a spectral harbinger of death. The earliest accounts of the apparition date back to the late fifteenth century, gaining in popularity as the years passed. Such a legend can be found in almost every significant castle in Northern Europe. In the Berlin Palace, she first appeared on New Year's Day 1598 to Johann Georg, the Prince-elector of Brandenburg, eight days before his demise, and was seen again before the deaths of Johann Sigismund in 1619, Frederick I in 1713 and that of Frederick Wilhelm II in 1797. Throughout the eighteenth and nineteenth centuries, whenever there was a death in the imperial family, some of the German newspapers were sure to report that watchmen on guard at the palace in Berlin or in Potsdam saw this apparition and were scared out of their minds. When Katherine, the wife of King William of Würtemberg, a sister of the Emperor Nicolas, was on her deathbed, the door of her chamber flew open, as if driven by a blast of wind. Her nurse got up and closed the door, but when she turned to go back to her seat, she saw the White Lady in her chair beside the bed. Two days later, on the 9th of January 1819, the queen was dead. On the eve of January 20th 1834, while the people of Stuttgart slept, a carriage with six horses came rattling down the road and pulled up before the palace. Its steps were lowered in the sight of the sentinels and the White Lady stepped out. The gates did not open for her, yet she continued on, passing through them as though walking through a veil of fog. With stately bearing, she paced along the great gallery for a time, then vanished. The next morning Duke Ferdinand of Würtemberg, the king's uncle, was found dead. Well documented cases in Berlin of the same apparition occurred in 1840 before the death of Frederick William III and again in 1861 prior to the death of Frederick William IV. The Vicomte d'Arlincourt reported that he heard from the lips of the Arch-Duchess Marie Louise, the widow of Napoleon, that the White Lady never failed to appear in the imperial palace at Vienna before the death of one of the House of Austria.

Like the White Lady, Frau Perchta and Berchta, Frau Holle was also connected with prophecy, although on a more domestic level. Near Hörselberg in Thuringia, maidens would place new fiber on their distaffs on Christmas Eve before Frau Holle began her rounds. A local rhyme ensured for every thread, one good year would follow: *So manches Haar, so manches gutes Jahr*, "As many strands, as many good years." The work had to be finished by Epiphany when she returned, with nothing left unspun, or else, the rhyme continues: *So manches Haar, so manches böses Jahr*, "As many strands (leftover), as many bad years."[191] On Christmas Eve or Christmas Day, a bowl of cream with spoons crossed over it was left out for her. When the members of the household woke up, the position of the spoons foretold the family's fortune for the coming year.[192] If the spoons had been moved or dipped in the cream, it meant she and her children had eaten and so accepted the offering, ensuring blessings in the new year. That this custom is ancient is evident by the early references to it. *Aberglaubensverzeichnis*, a dictionary of superstitions believed to have been written by Rudolf, a Cistercian monk, between the years 1236 and 1250, observes:

> *In nocte nativitatis Christi ponunt regine celi, quam dominam Holdam vulgus appelat, ut eas ipsa adiuvet.*

> "On the night of Christ's nativity, they set the table for the Queen of Heaven (*regine celi*), whom the common people call Frau Holda, so that she might help them."

---

[191] Washinitius, ibid., p. 105.
[192] Waschintius, ibid., pp. 36, 48.

In agreement with this, *The Life of St. Eligius* (588-660 AD), who served as the chief counsellor to the Merovingian King Dagobert I, warns the newly converted people of Flanders, "nothing is ominous about the Calends of January. ...[Do not] set tables at night or exchange New Years' gifts or supply superfluous drinks." Throughout the Middle Ages, the Church, of course, railed against such customs as "preparing a table for Perchta" and participating in processions, going about with "incense, cheese, a rope, and mallets" on "the eighth day of the Nativity of our Lord."[193]

In some traditions, special foods had to be eaten on her feast-day. One record from 1760 specifies that no leguminous plants may be consumed when Frau Holle makes her rounds during the Twelve-Nights. In folk-tales of Orlagau near the Saale, if Frau Perchta finds anyone who has not eaten *zemmede*, a cake made of milk and flour, on the night before Twelfth-Day, she will cut him open, remove any other food she finds inside, and replace it with handfuls of straw before sewing him up with a plowshare as her needle. On the last day of the year, the Thuringians serve dumplings and herring. On that evening in the Vogtland, everyone must eat *polse*, a thick pap of flour and water prepared in a particular way. If anyone omits this dish, Frau Werra will rip his stomach open.[194] Similarly, Perchta's Day must be kept with a traditional meal of gruel and fish. If anyone partakes of another dish on that day, she cuts open his belly and sews up the wound using a plowshare as her needle. In Bavaria, greasy cakes are eaten on the eve of the Epiphany so, if Frau Berchta attempts to slice anyone open, her knife will slide off.[195] At Christmas-time a spoonful of every dish must be placed on a gate or fence outside the house as an offering to appease this dreaded lady.

There is no question that Frau Holle is an ancient figure. The name *Hludana*, etymologically derived from the same stem as *hlöd*

---

[193] Hermann Usener, *Religionsgeschichtliche Undersuchungen*, 1889, cited by Pierre Daniel Chantepie de la Saussaye, *The Religion of the Teutons*, p. 274.
[194] This and the preceding examples are found in Grimm, ibid., p. 272-274.
[195] Grimm, ibid.,277.

("pile of earth"),[196] is found in five Latin inscriptions: three from the lower Rhine towns of Nijmegen, Birten (near Xanten), and Kalkar, in North Rhine-Westphalia (CIL XIII 8611, 8723, 8661), one from Iversheim, a part of Bad Münstereifel in the very south of North Rhine-Westphalia, west of modern Bonn (CIL XIII 7944) and one from Beetgum, Frisia (CIL XIII 8830) all dating from 197- 235 AD. Many attempts have been made to interpret this name. The most steadfast connections are with Frau Holle and Hulda on one hand, and the Old Norse Hloðyn, a name for Thor's mother, the Earth, on the other.[197] The earliest direct reference to Holda occurs in a eulogy by Walafrid Strabo (808-849 AD) for King Louis the Pious' wife Judith, the daughter of Count Welf. Her mother was a Saxon and her father a Bavarian, one of the peoples allied with the Lombards. In his tribute to Judith, Walifrid sings: "Oh, if eloquent Sappho or Holda should visit us to dance," *O si Sappho loquax vel nos inviseret Holda, ludere jam pedibus.* As a holdover from the old heathen religion, Holda was demonized by the new faith. Christian religious texts often state that she flies through the air with witches in her train. The ninth century *Canon Episcopi* censors women who claim to have ridden by night in just such a "crowd of demons."[198] Burchard, the bishop of Worms (c. 950–1025) and a native of Hesse, expands on this in a later recension of the same work included as part of his twenty volume compilation of Church law known as the *Decretum*. In the nineteenth book, titled *de Paenitentia* (*Penitential* or "Corrector") under *De arte magica*, Burchard writes:

> "Have you believed there is some female, whom the stupid vulgar call Holda [*Holdam*] who is able to do a certain thing, such that those deceived by the devil affirm themselves by necessity and by command to be required to do, that is, with a crowd of demons

[196] Britt-Mari Näsström, *Freyja—the Great Goddess of the North* (1995), p. 50, citing J. Sahlgren "Forbjudna Namn" *Namn och Bygd* 6 (1918), pp. 22-27.
[197] Rudolph Simek, *The Dictionary of Northern Mythology*, sv. Hludana, pp. 154-155.
[198] As quoted by Lotte Motz in *The Beauty and the Hag*, p. 128.

transformed into the likeness of women, on fixed nights to be required to ride upon certain beasts, and to themselves be numbered in their company? If you have performed participation in this unbelief, you are required to do penance for one year on designated fast-days."[199]

In this passage, the word *holdam* can be understood as a proper name or an epithet meaning "generous," "propitious" or "lovely." A minority of the manuscripts, roughly one in seven, clarify this with the addition of the word *striga*, reading instead *strigam holdam*, "the witch Holda" or the "lovely witch." In 1858, Dr. Adolf Helffrich discovered a single manuscript in Madrid which had instead *Friga holdam*, "the lovely Frigga." Later copyists of Burchard's *Penitential* on occasion replaced the word *holdam* with the unflattering *unholdam*, perhaps because *holda* was considered inappropriate to describe such a being. Ulphilas, the translator of the Gothic Bible (ca. 311–383 AD), used both the feminine *unhulþo* and the masculine *unhulþa* for the notion of a malignant being. Holda of German legend is a kind, merciful goddess or lady, originally from *hold* (grace, mercy), Gothic *hulþs* (*Luke* 18:13). The term *holde* must have been known and commonly used in MHG for supernatural beings. Notker in his *Capella* 81 translates *verus genius* (true spirit) as *min ware holdo*. Albrecht of Halberstadt, in his translation of Ovid's *Metamorphoses*, uses *ivazzerholde* for nymph. The philologist Claude Lecouteux who examined early and high medieval glosses to such texts, associated *holda* with fairy lore, concluding that the addition of the negative prefix *un-* was part of the process of demonization, where the good "*holden*" became the "*unholden*" in Christian interpretation. Along the same lines, Grimm notes that Frau Holle is sometimes seen as the queen or leader of elves and *hulde-folk*, her name being extended to her entire troop, who appear as *die guten holden, guedeholden, holderchen, holdeken*, etc, terms synonymous with "good elves" in Germanic fairy tales and legends.

That the various names of this figure were formed from adjectives describing her attributes— *Holda*, "the lovely"; *Perchta*, "the magnificent"; *Berchta*, "the bright" and *Frekka* or *Frigga*, "the beloved"— demonstrates that she appeared to her people as a

---

[199] Burchard of Worms*; Canon Episcopi*; Book 19, ch. 5, Question 70 (Migne, P.L., vol 140, p. 962).

benevolent deity of radiant beauty and grace. As such, her role as the White Lady was assumed by the Virgin Mary in Christian times. Just as when snow flew it was said that Frau Holda is making her bed and when rain fell that she was washing her veil, the same was said of the Virgin Mary, who was especially invoked for rain during the Middle Ages. A chronicle in Liège for the year 1240 describes a procession of priests and people calling on the saints for rain. Their efforts were in vain, however, because they had forgotten to include the Mother of God so that when the saints laid their petition before Him, *Mary opposed.* The constellation called "Orion's Belt" in English is known as "Frigg's Distaff" (*Friggerock*) in Scandinavia. Similarly, the constellation the Swedes knew as *Friggerock, Fröjas rock* or *Frejerock,* all meaning "Frigg's Spindle", the Danes called *Mariärock* or *Marirock,* "Mary's spindle."[200] From the northern viewpoint, the constellation falls on the celestial equator and so the stars rotating in the night sky were associated with her spinning wheel.

Frigg Spinning the Clouds
J.C. Dollman, 1908

While Frau Holda's helpful attributes were assigned to the Virgin Mary, she continued to be demonized in Christian texts. The Codex of Ausburg from the fifteenth century states: "Diana who is commonly known as *Fraw Percht* is in the habit of wandering through

---

[200] Citations by Grimm, ibid., p. 302.

the night with a host of women." In 1550, Alberus Erasmus, in the nineteenth fable of his satirical *Buch von der Tugend und Weisheit* ("Book of Virtue and Wisdom") wrote: "To this host also came an army of women carrying sickles in their hands, Frau Hulda had sent them."[201] Thomas Reinesius in the seventeenth century spoke of Werra of the Vogtland and her "crowd of maenads."[202] And in 1630, a man was convicted at a witch trial in Hesse for having ridden in the Wild Hunt of Frau Holle. She is sometimes expressly identified as a goddess of the old religion. In 1494, Stephanus von Lanzkrana in *Die Hymelstrass*, admonishes those who believe in *"frawn percht, frawn hold, herodyasis* or *dyana,* the heathen goddess."[203] Martin of Amberg says that meat and drink are left standing for her as an offering. The Catholic Reformer Martin Luther mentioned her in a number of his writings, beginning from 1517 through the late 1520s, when referring to common superstitions. His references to her reveal the extent to which she belonged to the local popular belief.[204] Frau Holle's association with the "Diana of Würzburg" indicates just how old her veneration may be. The *Passio Minor* of the *Passion of St. Kilian,* written sometime between 788 and 800 AD, describes the saint's attempts to convert the people of Würzburg to Christianity and some of the opposition he faced. The worship of Diana was one practice to which the people were particularly attached. As the author reports: *volumus servire magnae Dianae, sicut et anteriores nostril fecerunt patres, et prosperatisunt in eo usque in praesens*, "We want to serve the great Diana, as our fathers did and in doing so, have prospered well to this day." Although the statement was written by a Christian, it must be remembered that St. Boniface, who felled the Oak of Jove [Thor], had only founded the diocese of Würzburg in 741/742, so the author's parents had grown up practicing the pre-Christian customs of that area. Considering the importance placed on the transmission of traditions from the old to the young in Germanic societies, the scribe most certainly would have had firsthand knowledge of her worship. Erika Timm rules out this being a reference to the actual Diana, since the adoration of the Roman goddess never reached that far north. She notes that in five

[201] Waschnitius, p. 87.
[202] Motz, *The Beauty and the Hag*, ibid., p. 128.
[203] Waschnitius, p. 47.
[204] Elizabeth Wylie-Ernst, *"Frau Holle and the Recreation of Myth."* Dissertation, University of Pittsburgh, 1995.

of the eleven sources pertaining to Frau Holle prior to 1500 AD, she and Diana are equated with one another.[205] Not only does Timm agree with Grimm's assertion that the Diana of Würzburg is none other than Frau Holle, she also supports his conclusion that the deity worshipped at Würzburg, as described in the *Passio Minor*, represents Odin's wife, *Frija*.[206]

Costumed Christmas traditions are quite common throughout northern Europe, as well as in England and Scandinavia. In some regions, Holda, Percht and Bercht play a prominent part in them. Indeed, vivid visual descriptions of her may allude to a popular portrayal, perhaps as part of a seasonal festival or holiday drama. In 1522, in *The Exposition of the Epistles* at Basel, Martin Luther writes:

> "Here cometh up Dame Hulde with the snout, to wit, nature, and goeth about to gainstay her God and give him the lie, hangeth her old ragfair about her, the straw-harness; then falls to work and scrapes it featly on her fiddle."

Frau Perchta, Woodcut
Hans Vintler, 1486

According to Oberlin, Luther compared Nature rebelling against God to the heathenish Hulda "with the frightful nose."[207] Martin of Amberg called her Percht *mit der eisen nasen*, "with the iron

---

[205] Timm, ibid., pp. 15-17.
[206] Timm, ibid., p. 304.
[207] Quoted from Grimm, ibid., p. 269.

nose."[208] Hans Vintler, a late medieval Tyrolean poet, called her Frau Perchta with the long nose and a MHG manuscript refers to her as *Berchten mit der langen nas*. She is called *Trempe*, the trampling one, and *Stempe*, the stamping one, indicating that she and her train were expected to make a racket. In Pinzgau, her followers are known as *Perchten* and roamed the village in disguise carrying cow-bells and cracking whips to drive the witches out. On *Perchten nacht*, the night before Epiphany, the young men of Salzburg dressed up in fantastic garb and leapt wildly in the fields, shouting in her honor. The higher the leap, the higher next year's crop would grow. This behavior, called *Perchtenlauf*, "Perchta running," was also customary in Tyrol.[209] The raucous rabble of maskers marched along with jingling bells and resounding whip-cracks, entering houses, dancing and drinking, winding from village to village like the Wild Hunt itself. Such tumultuous masquerades were thought to be beneficial to the crops; a bad harvest would be attributed to omission of the Perchten. Whether the way was wet or pitch black, the procession went forward with flaring lights, the men leaping along with the help of long poles, waking the slumbering valley with their merrymaking. Such behavior is immediately reminiscent of the acrobats depicted on Bronze Age petroglyphs in Scandinavia and a bronze figure found at Grevensvænge, Zealand in 1779, dating roughly between 800 BC and 500 BC. Likewise, some of Perchta's followers, known as *Perchten*, personify horned and furry beasts, like those figures from prehistoric petroglyphs thought to represent men dressed as mountain goats, with curved horns and built-up leggings. [See Chapter I: The Prehistoric Context]. The name Percht itself may be related to *perg* or *berg* meaning "mountain."[210] In 1890, Hans Junger, known to be a reliable narrator, described such a party in Salzburg as consisting of twelve men known as the Perchten, who were concealed in black

---

[208] *Gewissensspeigel*, mid-fourteenth century.
[209] cp. Waschnitius, pp. 37, 57.
[210] Motz, *The Beauty and the Hag*, p. 125.

cloaks with hoods.[211] On their heads, they wore carved wooden masks, some with movable parts, with exaggerated features: long teeth, twisted horns, protruding beaks and spiny bristles; all carrying clusters of bells sewn onto broad leather straps, or swinging cast iron cow bells.

Perchten Masks
Salzburg, early 20th century

The train was led by a man with a big drum, followed by lads with peaked hats and carrying lanterns on long poles. Taking up the

---

[211] Ibid., Mrs Herbert Vivian.

rear came the fool "Lapp" and his wife "Lappin," a boy in women's weeds. Some blew horns while others shook bells, making a great deal of noise as they wound though the valley. Sometimes a grotesque image of the local goddess was carried about in effigy.[212] In the Swiss Entlibuch, on the Thursday before Christmas, the people performed a Posterli-hunt, the Posterli being a specter in the shape of an old woman or nanny-goat. In the evening, the young men of one village would draw a representation of her in a sled to another village with loud shouts and clashing tins, blowing alp-horns, ringing cow-bells and cracking whips, where they were greeted in a similar manner. The people of the Tyrolean Alps still observe such customs, performing Perchten dances as part of their regional festivals. In times past, these occurred at irregular intervals—sometimes of twenty years or more. In 1867 there was a display and then nothing until 1892, then again in 1907.

In them, *Schön Perchten* or "Beautiful Perchten" bring the blessings of good fortune and bountiful crops in the New Year, while the *Schlacht Perchen* or "Wild Perchten" ward off harmful spirits. In the nineteenth and early twentieth centuries, the Beautiful Perchten of Pongan near Salzburg dressed in Tyrolean loden —a green tweed coat and breeches— crowning themselves with immense head-dresses constructed of two diamond-shaped boards called *tafel*, altogether some ten or twelve feet high, covered with red velvet. On them were fixed every kind of ornament they could collect— silver chains, pocket watches, mirrors, artificial flowers, jewelry, and coins. At the very top were perched additional objects extending their height such as a moon with a star atop it or a bird with its wings spread. The cost of these cumbersome head-dresses was so high that only the wealthy could afford them. The noblest of the Beautiful Perchten wore bird headdresses, made of large moss-covered boards with every rare bird shot in the neighborhood fixed on them. A huge peacock with outstretched wings and a gigantic tail stood on top.

---

[212] Waschnitius, ibid., pp. 73-74.

Beautiful Perchten Dancers, 1908

Of terrific weight, these immense headdresses were supported by an iron rod fastened at the waist. The backside of the boards were usually covered with canvas and painted with a pastoral scene. Modern versions of these headdresses can still be seen today in festivals throughout the region.[213] In their right hands, the Beautiful Perchten clasped a naked sword and with the other they led their partners — young men skillfully disguised as women, in black patent leather sailor hats and wide white aprons. Accompanied by a band, they proceeded to the town square leading their partners with slow and deliberate steps. The procession would march to the middle of the square, where the Beautiful Perchten, never relaxing their affected pomp, began dancing in measured steps at a pace adapted to their weighty headgear. The Wild Perchten trailed behind them.

In contrast to the Beautiful Perchten, the Wild Perchten comprised a motley crew of peasants in repulsive masks, clad in a

---

[213] A collection of these from Jan 1, 2007 and Jan 4, 2015 can be viewed on the *Altenmarkter Perchtenlauf* site at http://netsh70321.dbdserver.de/

strange collection of tatters, made up as such stock characters as the ragman and his wife (played by a man almost twice his mate's size decked out in drag), a chimneysweep, a postman, a chained bear and his handler, and a cowering village idiot, all darting about, brandishing sticks and sounding particularly penetrating bells. Others dressed as beasts and devils accompanied them. As a rule the Wild Perchten performed their *Perchtenlauf* after dark. In times past, they would make their rounds on the three Thursdays of Advent armed with whips, drums, iron kettles, and a quantity of larger and smaller bells. Some of their masks were extraordinarily grotesque, adorned with long teeth and twisted horns, a long tongue rolling out of the mouth, protruding eyes, deep wrinkles, warts and such, with variations of devil- and animal-masks being the most popular. At first this train affected a certain dignity, as if having no desire to look conspicuous. Thus, according to custom, the spectators would tease and taunt them until they emitted the expected war-cries, whistles, growls and groans.

Wild Perchten Dancers, 1908

Until then, the wild ones kept a calm demeanor, but afterward begin to quarrel amongst themselves. The chimneysweep and the ragman would enter into a violent argument, hurling insults at one another until the chimneysweep made a wild plunge in his direction, nearly knocking over half-a-dozen spectators; and then they would chase each other about, dodging in and out of the gathered crowd, executing acrobatic leaps and bounds. The postman took this opportunity to flirt with the ragman's wife, an affront which could not be tolerated, so the ragman dropped his quarrel with the chimneysweep, rushed to clasp his "darling Eliza" and punch the postman upside the head. All the while, the untamed bear pursued by his master prowled about in a stealthy manner, catching those absorbed in the performance unaware and startling them. Sometimes a group of such Wild Perchten from one village met a band from another village and warfare ensued. On one occasion, four Perchten were killed and buried by the rest near Wagrein in graves marked with stone crosses. These Wild Perchten did not fear the devil, and it was rumored that if a Perchten-runner went for fourteen days before the occasion without praying or making the sign of the cross it would make him more agile than the others. According to a tale told by an old woman of Gastein in the early twentieth century, indeed, one year the spectators were amazed to see one of the Wild Perchten jumping up onto the rooftops of houses, swinging with ease from one gable to another, until they could no longer see him. Something seemed amiss they thought and so hurried off to fetch a priest. The reverend came and began casting blessings to the four winds. Suddenly the missing Percht dropped from the sky and landed at the priest's feet. Barely alive, the dying man managed to utter: "Oh, sir, you might have spared me your blessing. You cannot imagine the heavenly feel of dancing aloft on the clouds. When your reverence came, the devil forsook me and here I am!" With that he drew his last breath.[214]

The traditional Perchten in neighboring towns and valleys vary somewhat. In the Pinzgau region, southwest of Salzburg, their headdresses consist of a round hat in the shape of a crown, adorned with erect white feathers. On either side, wide brilliant-colored

---

[214] Mrs. Herbert Vivian, "The Perchten Dancers of Salzburg" with photographs in The *Wide World Magazine: An Illustrated Monthly of True Narrative* (1908).

ribbons fall below their waists as they dance. Their coats and knickers are embellished with gaudy embroidery and their long white stockings striped and worked with eclectic designs. A specific kind of *Schön Perchten* called *Tresterer* wear bright red and yellow suits with golden crowns adorned with rooster feathers. *Schwegler* or flutists play music to which the *Tresterer* dance. They travel in groups from farm to farm, performing a folk dance to reawaken the fields for a good harvest. *Schlacht Perchten* and a host of folk characters accompany this procession including the Lapp and his Lappin, *Huhnerpercht* (a raven-billed *Perchten*), and *Krapfenschnappers* (wolfish *Perchten*). In the Rauris Valley southwest of Salzburg, *Schnabelperchten*, dressed up as giant bird women, with long beaks protruding from under headscarves, roam about in groups, emitting a piercing "caw-caw" announcing their arrival. They check the cleanliness of the farmhouse, and carry baskets filled with gifts which they distribute in orderly homes. Like Perchta, these bird-women threaten to cut open the stomachs of lazy housewives, stuffing them with whatever mess they find. For this purpose, one of the group carries an oversized set of scissors. In Southern Italy, the Christmas witch, Befana, whose name is thought to derive from *Epifania* (Epiphany), retains much in common with Perchta. She likewise visits homes on Twelfth-Night, bringing gifts for good children and coal or sticks for those who have misbehaved. She arrives, covered in soot, riding on a broom and may sweep the floor before she leaves. In the Austrian town of Bad Mittendorf, southeast of Salzburg, creatures called *Schabmänner* or "Sweeper-men" dressed like straw brooms open the *Perchtenlauf*, clearing the way for St. Nicholas. In Goldegg, a small village in the Pongau region south of Salzburg, the citizens stage a *Krampus* or *Perchten* parade, replete with several folk figures. Besides the *Schlacht Perchten* or more devilish *Krampuses*, there are Frau Percht and her witches, the *Hassergoaß* (a goat figure), a jester with large pointed cap named Hans Wurst, a large group of *Schön Perchten* (men in folk costume with huge symbolic headdresses like those described above), *Zapfenmandl* (a wooly man covered in pine cones), *Werchmandl* (a man covered in fur),

Kaminkehrer (a man in white cap and black face, who brings good luck), as well as the *Baer und Baerentrieber* (bear and his handler), *Schneidermandl* (a tailor caricature), *Puppenweibl* (a man in drag representing a dollmaker), *Korbelweibl* (a caricature of a man and his wife), night watchmen, and the Three Wise Men. Such customs live on in the same regions today, although their appearance has become decidedly more devilish as time has passed. Originally the *Schön Perchten* were seen as the masters or deities of the *Krampuses*, but in modern times the lines between the *Perchten* and *Krampus* has become blurred. Today the Krampus, traveling with or without St. Nicholaus, leads a large troop of hell-raisers known as the *Krampuslauf*. Sometimes as many as four hundred horned, hairy, demonic creatures parade through the remote villages around Salzburg and in Western Austria, particularly in the Ponzau region.

A similar costumed tradition survived among the British until the early twentieth century. In some parts of rural England, the first Sunday and Monday after Twelfth-Day are still known as *Plough Sunday and Plough Monday,* marking the start of the agricultural year with the resumption of farmwork after the Twelve Days of Christmas. These days were the occasion of special ceremonies reminiscent of the *Æcerbót;* the principle purpose of *Plough Sunday* being the blessing of the farmhands in church, dedicating their work to the service of God, so that the people may eat. The primary feature of *Plough Monday* is an annual procession performed by bands of brightly clad young men, dragging a decorated plow from house to house. In northern England, the plow was driven in a procession made up of as many as forty people. Rustic youth called *Plough-stots* (from an old word meaning 'steer' or 'young ox') dragged the plow. They wore white shirts on the outside of their jackets with bright-colored ribbons as sashes across their chests and knotted on their caps. Sometimes they performed a skit or dance, accompanied by fiddle and flute music with the recitation of set verses, which as a rule were little more than introductions of the performers, each given a distinctive name. Regarding Christmas customs in England, John

Brand in his *Observations on Popular Antiquities* (1777) wrote:

"In the North there is another Custom used at or about this Time, which if I mistake not, was antiently observed in the Beginning of Lent: The Fool Plough goes about, a Pageant that consists of a Number of Sword Dancers, dragging a Plough with Music, and one, sometimes two, in a very antic Dress; the Besy, in the grotesque Habit of an old Woman, and the Fool, almost covered with Skins, a hairy Cap on, and the Tail of some Animal hanging from his Back." (p. 176)

Plough Monday—Dance of Bessy and the Fool
Brand's Popular Antiquites, Vol. I (1841)

Recorded verses include up to seven named characters. A man dressed as an old woman known as Bessy, accompanied by a man dressed in animal-skin and tail known as the Tommy or Fool, commonly led the rabble through the town collecting money for drink or charity. These performers, often masked, black-faced or dressed as women, followed the procession. In some versions, the Tom or Fool entered first and drew a circle with his sword. He was then introduced by Bessy who called on the others in turn, each walking round the circle to music; then came an elaborate dance with careful formations, which degenerated into a fight.[215] At Whitby, the formations consisted of six armed men, who began their dance slowly and simply, gradually becoming more rapid and complex, until near the close, a series of well- planned moves resulted in a hexagon of plaited swords at the center of the ring, so firmly interlaced that one of the performers held it aloft without it coming undone.[216] As they danced, masked Toms performed antics for the crowd, while men dressed in women's clothing, called *Madgies*, rattled canisters soliciting money. They paraded from town to town for two or three days in this manner collecting coins. Prior to the Reformation, the aim of the collection was to raise funds for *Plough Lights*, wax candles lit by husbandmen during the *Plough Mass*. Remarkably, John Brand himself adds:

> "With regard to the Plough drawn about on this Occasion; I find the Monday after Twelfth Day, called antiently (as Coles tells us) *Plough Monday*, 'when our northern Plough Men, beg *Plough Money* to drink' ...so in hard Frosts our Watermen drag a Boat about the Streets, begging Money," (p. 178).

In England, as on the Continent, we find such processions associated with both a plow and a ship, the general purpose of which seems to have been to spread agricultural luck insuring a good harvest. According to one nineteenth century observer: "when they are well paid, they raise a *huzza*; where they get nothing they shout 'Hunger and starvation!'" Ceremonies of this kind are recorded throughout the eastern half of England from Norfolk to Northumbria and are best documented in East Anglia and

---

[215] Edmund K. Chambers, Minstrelsy, *The Mediaeval Stage*, Vol. I (1903), pp. 193-194; *Theatre and Drama in the Making: From Antiquity to the Renaissance*, Vol. I, edited by John Gassner and Ralph G. Allen (1964), pp. 145-147, reprints one version from Durham.

[216] G. Young, *History of Whitby* (1817), Vol. II, p. 880.

Lincolnshire.[217] In Cambridgeshire, *Plough Monday* ceremonies known as *Plough Witching* were observed until the early 1900s. References to these traditions date back to the late 1400s and are probably related to the German legends of Frau Holda and Perchta.[218] In *A Compendiouse Treetise Dyalogue of Dives and Pauper,* a folio printed by Richard Pynson in 1493, among superstitions censured at the beginning of the year was the *"ledyng of the Ploughe aboute the Fire as for gode begynnyng of the yere that they shulde fare the better alle the yere followyng."*[219] Morris or Moorish Dancing, which traditionally takes place at Whitsun or Pentecost, the seventh Sunday after Easter, may be related to this tradition. William Hutchinson in *A View of Northumberland* (1778), Vol. II. p. 18, speaking of costumed sword-dancers at Christmas, remarks: "Others, in the same kind of gay attire, draw about a Plough, called the *Stot Plough,* and, when they receive a gift, make the exclamation *Largess!* but if not requited at any house for their appearance, they draw the Plough through the Pavement and raise the ground of the front in furrows. I have seen twenty men in the yoke of one Plough." Some scholars believe these customs were brought into the Danelaw in the ninth century. Likewise, the custom of plowing up the doorposts of those who gave nothing to the plowboys at Shrovetide was practiced in Denmark until the eighteenth century. In the nineteenth and twentieth centuries, the *Plough Festival* featured a good deal of merriment in the form of mumming plays and dancing, particularly the sword dance, but only the *Plough Mass* and *Plough-stotting* "were part of the religious ceremony which was, ostensibly, the nucleus of the celebration, and to which all other customs were merely attendant trappings," according to Geoffrey Ridden, the author of the most detailed study on the subject.[220]

---

[217] John D. Niles, "The Æcerbot Ritual in Context" in *Old English Literature in Context*, 1980.
[218] Davidson, *Roles of the Northern Goddess*, p. 68.
[219] Cited in Brand's *Observations on Popular Antiquities* (1877), Vol. I, p. 396.
[220] Quoted by John D. Niles.

Many of the costumed Christmas visiting traditions of northern Europe involve male and female counterparts, including the well-known St. Lucia tradition, typified by a young girl in white wearing a candle-crown. This decidedly Christian image is countered by the continued use of the term *Lusse långnatt* (Lusse long-night), which suggests an association with the Winter Solstice. In Västergötland and Småland, the Lucia tradition involves men dressing up as old women and women dressing up as old men known as *Lussegubbar* and *Lussegummar* respectively. These figures wear white shirts accented by belts, shoes and leggings made of straw. In western Norway, *Lussia* is regarded as a dangerous female troll who is supposed to visit farms on December 13th, sometimes accompanied by a group of spirits known as *Lussiferd* or the *Lussi*-ride. This was enacted by members of the community dressed in animal skins and horns, who went from house to house demanding food. The most recurrent of these costumed Yuletide visiting traditions is that of the *Julbock* (Yule-buck), often accompanied by a female companion the *Julgeit* (Yule-goat), both wearing fur-skins and horns. These figures travel from house to house at the head of a lively procession singing *Julbock* songs. These processions often include other traditional figures, such as St. Stephan or Helm-Steffan, dressed in straw, who enact short dramas akin to the English Mummer's Plays. A scene in the fourteenth century *Þorleifs þáttr jarlsskálds* may be the first literary reference to this custom. In this tale, Thorleif enters Jarl Hakon's hall at Yule in disguise, seeking revenge. He stumbles in on crutches, giving him the appearance of walking on all fours, wearing a ragged beggar's costume and a goat's beard. He conceals a bag beneath his clothes with the opening hidden under the goat's beard, so that those present believe he has eaten whatever food they give him. He enters the hall in this disguise and causes a commotion. Once he has drawn the attention of the Jarl, he speaks a *nid*-verse and thus exacts his revenge. The wearing of a costume and the delivery of a verse constitute the definition of a public performance. The scene has much in common with known traditions surrounding the *Julbock*. The continued popularity of these widespread traditions is evidenced by the many laws against them. A Danish national law of 1668 forbade the enactment of the *julbock* and a Norwegian law (inclusive of Iceland) passed in 1687 stated that "all frivolous and contemptible games at Christmas" were strictly prohibited and all offenders were to be seriously punished.[221] In Sweden, the tradition is first mentioned in 1555 by Olaus Magnus, and local ordinances against the *julebukkslekn*, "Yulebuck games," appeared in Sweden from 1695 onward. According to a local custom in Setesdal, the animal slaughtered for the Christmas meal was known as the *julebjukke*;[222] it was to be fed the final sheaf of corn from the last harvest. Today a goat made of straw called the *Julbock* is a popular Christmas decoration in Scandinavia and a special kind of Christmas cake cut into the shape of a goat is also known by this name.

Julbock in the *Nordisk Familjebok*, 1910

[221] Gunnell, ibid., p. 116.
[222] Gunnell, ibid., 121.

Might these varied Yuletide processions be the remains of older pagan practices? One thing is certain, evidence of ritual processions can be traced back to the late Bronze Age in petroglyphs found all over Sweden and Denmark, involving what often appear to be horned-, winged- and costumed figures, playing instruments and carrying banners and circular symbols, often identified as sun-wheels [See Chapter I: The Prehistoric Context]. According to Terry Gunnell, while it is beyond doubt that these customs have early roots, they should not be seen as concrete remnants of any ancient tradition, but rather a hodge-podge of earlier customs and beliefs associated with Yule.[223] When considering the origins of these legends, one should note that Norwegian and Danish folktales mention a forest spirit called Hulla, Huldra, or Huldre. Dressed in a blue garment and a white veil, she visits the pastures of herdsman and joins in the dances of men. In the forests, Huldra is seen leading her flock, milkpail in hand. She is mistress of the *huldrefolk* or mountain spirits. In Iceland, these are called the *Huldufolk*, hidden people, akin to the *landvættir*.[224] Known as Gjøa, Gói, or Gjö in Norway (cp. *Frau Goden*), she may be the source of the Icelandic Gryla legend.[225] Gryla and her sons, the *Jólasveinar* (nine or thirteen in number), have a reputation for stealing and eating naughty children in the days leading up to Christmas. Similarly, in the folk belief of Lower Styria, a forested state in southern Austria, children who have not completed their chores by Christmas may disappear from the house altogether. Frau Perchta takes them.

Despite the decidedly devilish nature of many of these popular festivals and traditions, in Germany as a whole, Frau Holle is more often regarded as a helper and protector of women and children. In the village of Hasloch in Lower Franconia, the people call her Frau Hulda, Hulli, or Holla. There she appears as a ghostly beautiful, but benign being, dressed in a long white gown with a veil

---

[223] Gunnell, ibid., pp.99, 112.
[224] Grimm, ibid., pp. 271-272.
[225] Lotz, *The Beauty and the Hag*, p. 79.

completely concealing her face. Although she carries no lantern, she shines brightly, acting as a beacon for travelers on dark nights. She will appear to weary wayfarers to lighten their loads, and assist women and children with farmwork, spinning and domestic chores. At the foot of a low mountain near the Main river, there is a flat stone called *Frauhullistein*, where Frau Hulda always rests when carrying loads of straw or wood for women and children whose burdens have become too heavy to bear. Because she always stops to rest in the same spot, two depressions called *kötzenstollen* can be seen there in the rock.[226] According to Adalbert von Herrlein, who localized the legend to the Schellenberg between Heimbuchenthal and Wintersbach, these footprints first appeared when she stopped there with Crooked Jacob on their way to market. She alone carried two cows. When the bundle the lame boy bore became too much for him to bear, she threw it and the boy on her back. The load was so heavy that when she stopped to rest, her feet sank into the stone.[227]

Although she appears to help those in need, such stories do not end well, if the recipient is ungrateful. Once Klara Behringer, a crone who lived in Hasloch, exhausted herself carrying a heavy load uphill from the lower part of the valley. The old woman made no complaint, but was so worn out she could go no further when Frau Hulda compassionately came out of the mountain to assist her. Being a proud woman, Klara refused, saying: "I've carried my load this far, I can bear it further. I want nothing to do with witches!" At that, Frau Hulda vanished and the old woman no longer knew where she was. She had lost her way. Nothing looked familiar, so she walked in the wrong direction through thick bramble for some time, until her clothes were torn and her skin scratched. When someone yelled "watch where you're going!" she regained her senses. The shout broke the spell, and at once she knew where she was again.[228]

---

[226] Waschnitius, ibid., p. 81-82.
[227] *Sagen des Spessarts* (1851), p. 182.
[228] A. Fries in *Zeitschrift für deutsche Mythologie und Sittenkunde,* Vol 1, (1853) p. 23-29.

Frigg-Holda by Gustav Richter
Neues Museum, Berlin, 1852

In her many forms, Frau Holle is most often associated with children. In some districts, a newborn is said to have been drawn from Frau Holle's pool and delivered to its new home by storks.[229] In the mid-nineteenth century there was such a place most everywhere in Germany, even if it is not named for Frau Holle.[230] In some places, such as Hornhausen, the same was said of certain wells. Children peering at their own reflections in such waters will say that they see Frau Holle's children staring back at them. Young brides who bathe in *Frau Hollen Teich* near Meissner are supposed to become healthy

---

[229] Davidson, ibid., p. 116, cp. Grimm. See also F. Woeste, *Zeitschrift für deutsche Mythologie und Sittenkunde* (1855), Vol 2, pp. 91-2, which lists several locations.
[230] *Zeits. für deutsche Mythologie und Sittenkunde*, Vol 1, (1853), pp. 95-96.

and fertile wives.[231] The White Lady is represented as loving children, and is said to be seen by exhausted young mothers, tending to their newborns, sitting by the cradle rocking and caressing the infant. On one occasion a nurse came into the children's room, and seeing such a woman soothing a child, asked sharply who she was and what right she had to be there. The White Lady replied, "I am not a stranger here like you; and these little ones are not yours, but my children's children." Likewise, Berchta or Berthe, will appear and continue to rock the cradle once the nursemaid has fallen asleep. In 1970, Jungian psychologist Marie-Louise von Franz remarked:

> "In German folklore, there is a belief that the souls of children, before they are born, live as sheep in the realm of Mother Holle — a kind of earth-mother goddess — and those souls of unborn children are identical with what the Germans call *Lammerwolkchen*, in English, 'fleece-clouds.'"[232]

Throughout Germany, this motherly figure is frequently accompanied by a host of small children. When youngsters die before baptism, they are said to return to Frau Holle who keeps and nurtures them, making them part of her entourage. She transforms them into well-mannered, industrious boys and girls who help her with the plowing and watering of the fields. In one tale a young mother who had lost her only child recognized him among Frau Holle's train. When she approached, he plead with her to stop mourning for him, informing his mother that he must work night and day collecting her tears in a jar. In the Saale valley, Perchta is accompanied by *heimchen*, a band of weeping children who water the field while she works underground with her plow.[233] These children complain loudly that they have no home.

---

[231] Waschinitus, ibid., p. 89.
[232] *The Problem of the Puer Aeternus*, p.36. Thanks to Carrla O'Harris for pointing this out.
[233] Grimm, ibid., 275.

Frau Holda by Ludwig Pietsch, 1860

This train of lost souls connects Frau Holle to the Wild Hunt, traditionally led by Odin. [See Chapter VI: The Wild Hunt]. Into this same furious host, according to popular belief, are adopted the souls of infants who have died unbaptized. Not having been christened, they remain heathen and thus are left to heathen gods.[234] As mistress of the Wild Hunt, Frau Holle is alternately known as *Frau Gode, Frau Goden, Frau Gaue, Frau Gauden, Frau Wode* and *Frau Woden,* demonstrating her connection to Woden or Odin. Like Frau Holle, she loves children and gives them gifts so that when youngsters play "Frau Gauden" they sing:

---

[234] Grimm, ibid., p. 269.

Fru Gauden hett mi'n lämmken geven,
darmitt sall ik in freuden leven

"Frau Gauden has given me a little lamb (i.e. a baby),
so that I may live happily."[235]

The name Frau Woden (and its many variants) clearly means
"Mrs. Odin," suggesting the two were seen as a married couple.
Because of this clear connection, Jacob Grimm came to believe that
this folk figure was a late remembrance of Odin's wife, Frigg. In the
third volume of his *Deutsche Mythologie*, Grimm wrote: "I am more and
more convinced that Holda can be nothing but an epithet of the mild
and gracious Fricka; and Berthe, the shining, is identical with her
too."[236] In Lower Saxony, the parts assigned to Frau Holle are played
by Frau Freke, corresponding to Anglo-Saxon *Fricg*, Old High
German *Frikka, Frikkia*, Old Norse *Frigg*.[237] Johann Georg von
Eckhart (1664-1730) in *De origine Germanorum,* p. 398, wrote: "The
common people of the Saxons honor Frau Frekke, who bestows on
them gifts, the same whom the nobles amongst the Saxons reckon as
Holda."[238] In Westphalia, the name of an old convent, Freckenhorst,
Frickenhorst [compare *Frœcinghyrst*] points to a sacred *hurst* or grove
of Frecka (feminine), or of Fricko (masculine). Adalbert Kuhn found
evidence of a Frau Freke in the Uckermark, where she is called
Fruike, which corresponds to Frau Harke in the Mittelmark and Frau
Gode in the Prignitz.[239] A *Vrouwe Vreke* appears in Belgium, where
there is also a Vrekeberg, located near Gelrode in Flemish Brabant,
or over the border into Dutch South Limburg in the countryside near
Maastricht. In a medieval Belgian legend of *trouwen Eckhout* (the
faithful Eckhardt), *Vreke* represents sensual love, as opposed to the
spiritual love of Our Lady.[240] Her servants are Kabauter (Kobalds).

---

[235] Grimm, ibid., p. 927; Translated by Heidi Graw.
[236] Grimm, ibid., pp. 947-948.
[237] Grimm, ibid., p 301.
[238] Translated by Carla O'Harris.
[239] Grimm, ibid., p. 304.
[240] Dr. Coremanns, *L'Année de l'Ancienne Belgique*, (1844), p. 131.

In fact, the further north one travels in Germany, the more Frau Holle's bynames identify her as Odin's wife. From the farthest southern regions of her range traveling north, she is called Frau Holle, Berchta, Perchta in High German lands to the south, and Frau Herke, Harke, Frekka, Frau Gode, and finally Frau Wodan in Low German regions in the north. Still further north of Frekka's (Frigga's) territory lays the greatest concentration of legends identifying Odin as the master of the Wild Hunt. This pattern is immediately evident in the color-coded map graphically illustrating the distribution of the Frau Holle legends throughout Germany first published in *Frau Holle, Frau Percht und Verwandte Gestalten* by Erika Timm (2003). Timm theorizes that the origin of her byname Herka ultimately lies in *La familia Herlekni* (Old French *mesnie Herlequin*), a name for the Wild Hunt recorded by Orderic Vitalis in 1091. Peter of Blois, archdeacon of London and Bath (c. 1135-1204) calls it *milites Herlewini*, the "troop of Herelwini." The word *Herlekini* is thought to be a corruption of the Old English *Herla Cyning* or "Herla King", which is related to the tribal name *Hari'i* recorded by Tacitus (*Germ.* 43), thought to derive from an Indo-Germanic root meaning "host leader," thus referring to Odin. If this is correct, the name Frau Herke, like the name Frau Woden, appears to derive from the Germanic custom of calling married women by their husbands' first name from the late 1400s onward.[241] In regard to Herke, not only does she assume her husband's name, but in some places she is identified as the leader of the Wild Hunt. The names Frau Gauden (Goden, Gode, Gaue, etc) appear to fall into the same category.

German harvest customs throughout the same regions preserve obvious relics of heathenism tying Frau Goden directly to Odin. David Franck records a tradition among old people in Mecklenburg that no one weeds flax on *Wodenstag* (Wednesday) lest Woden's horse tramples the seedlings, and from Christmas to Twelfth-Day, they must not spin nor leave any flax on the distaff, for

---

[241] Timm, ibid., p. 213

"Wode is galloping across."[242] In Lower Saxony, it was customary to leave a clump of grain standing in the field "to Woden for his horse."[243] In Schonen and Blekingen, it was custom for reapers to leave a gift in the field "for Oden's horses." The Swedish scholar Hyltén-Cavallius speaks of a similar custom in the district of Wärend. In the latter half of the eighteenth century, Swedish peasants, when mowing a field, would bend down a few green blades of grass, cover them with moss to prevent them being trampled by cattle, and declare "Odin shall have this for his horses." In the early twentieth century, E. Elgvist recorded a farmer in the same district as saying, "This year the corn grows poorly, for Odin or his servant has taken something from every ear."[244] In northern Germany, the peasants honored a spirit called by various names such as Wod, Wold and Wauden. As early as 1593, Nicolaus Gryse, a Luthern clergyman from the city of Rostock located near the Baltic coast, described the custom. During the rye-harvest, a little strip of grain was left unmowed at the end of each field, where it was plaited together with flowers and sprinkled. The reapers then danced around the bundle, hats off with raised scythes, singing the following verse three times:

Wode, hale dynern Rosse nu Voder,
Nu Distel vnde Dorn,
Thom andern Jhar betr Korn

"Wode, fetch now fodder for thy horse,
Now thistles and thorn,
For another year of better corn!"[245]

Gryse himself believed that this Wode was the heathen god Wodan. In Schaumburg, when the harvesting is done, it is custom for the reapers to plant their scythes in the ground and beat the blade

---

[242] Grimm, ibid., pp. 155-156.
[243] Grimm, ibid., p. 154.
[244] *Folkminnen och Folktankar* XVI (1929), p. 91.
[245] Translation by James Mason, "The Folklore of British Plants" in *Dublin University Magazine*, Vol 83 (Jan 1874).

three times with their strops. Before taking a drink, they spill a sip of it onto the ground, wave their hats in the air and cry aloud "*Wold, Wold, Wold!*" Afterward they march home shouting and singing. If the ceremony is omitted, the next year will bring meagre crops.[246] After harvest in the village of Steinhulde, the men gather at a nearby lake, light bonfires on a hill, wave their hats and shout "*Wauden! Wauden!*" In other Low German districts, this office is turned over to a woman.[247] In Prignitz, they call her *fru Goden* and leave a bunch of grain standing in each field which they call *Vergodendel*, "Fru Goden's portion."[248] In the district of Hameln, it was custom, if a reaper while binding sheaves passed over one, to jeer and call out: "Is that for *fru Gauen?!*"[249] The *Hannoverischen Gelehrten Anzeigen* (1752) records that in remote places of the principality of Calenberg, the country folk gathered around the last sheaf, took off their hats and shouted loudly:

Fru Gaue, hahlet ju Fauer,
dut Jahr up den Wagen,
dat ander Jahr up de Kare,[250]

"Frau Gaue, keep some fodder,
this year on your wagon,
the next year on the cart."

The names *Frau Gode, Goden, Gaue, Gauen,* and *Gauden* directly connect this legendary figure to Odin. In Old Norse, the fourth day of the week is known as *Oðinsdagr*, Odin's day. Etymologically, the names Wode/Gode and Wodan/Goden are the same, as there was a time when the letters G and W were interchangeable.[251] In Swedish and Danish, it is *Onsdag*; in North Frisian, *Winsdei*; in Middle Dutch, *Woensdach*; in Anglo-Saxon, *Wodenes dæg*, but in Westphalia, they call it *Godenstag, Gonstag, Gaunstag, Gunstag*, and in documents from the

---

[246] Grimm, ibid., pp. 156-157.
[247] Grimm, ibid., p. 252.
[248] Timm, ibid., p. 191; *Vergodendeelsstruss.* Grimm, ibid., p. 253
[249] Grimm, ibid., pp. 252-253.
[250] Timm, ibid., p. 191-192.
[251] Timm, ibid., p. 71-72.

Lower Rhine, *Gudestag* and *Gudenstag*. Likewise, in the *Origo Gentis Langobardorum*, the first literary appearance of Odin and his wife, they are known as *Godan* and *Frea*. Grimm observes that a dialect which says *fauer* instead of *foer, foder* ("fodder"), will equally have *Gaue* for *Gode, Guode*.[252] This connection is made more explicit in one version of the ritual recorded in 1910 on Ith, a small mountain range about 12 km east of Hameln and extending 20km south. Once finished with their work, the fieldhands there placed green ash-twigs in the knot of the last bushel. The landowner sat down beside it and every reaper and baler raised a stalk or blade, and shouted together:

Friggöu, Friggöu, Friggöu!
Dütt Jahr up'r Kare,' t andre up'n Wagen!

"Friggöu, Friggöu, Friggöu!
This year on the cart, the next upon the wagon!" [253]

Woman in a Wagon
Levede, Gotland Picture Stone

Then they danced and sang around "the Lord and his *Friggöu.*" As Erika Timm notes, local variants of the same verse were recorded in 1924 and 1931. Here the name Friggöu, which can be

---

[252] Grimm, ibid., p. 253.
[253] Timm, ibid., p. 191, quoting Paul Sartori, *Sitte und Brauch,* vol. III (1914).

none other than a form of Frigg, clearly corresponds to the older Frau Gaue in the parallel rhyme from Calenberg cited above. Thus, in the names *Frau Wode or Woden, Frau Gode, Goden, Gaue, Gauen* and *Gauden, Frau Herka* and *Frau Harke* (cp. Anglo-Sacon *Erce*), German farmers have preserved the memory of a *Mrs. Odin* at work beside her husband in the fields long after the coming of Christianity. When compared to analogous folk figures found across German-speaking regions, it becomes clear that this goddess is one entity known by a variety of names, including Holle, Holda, Percht, Bercht, Berthe, Herke, Harke, Frekka, Frigg, Frick and their many variants.

Frekka by Arthur Rackham, 1911

V. Odin, The All-Father

"The discovery that one and the same person, place or thing is
referred to under many different names should not be surprising. If
our text were skaldic verse we would accept such polyonymy
simply as the poet's method of satisfying the strict metric demands
of his chosen form. But the relatively unrestricted eddic strophe is
far less demanding: such an explanation can not be the only one.
The massive complex of heiti and kenning structures which we are
about to discuss must be the result on the one hand, of a desire to
replace tabu lexemes with noa correspondencies and, on the other,
of a feeling of the need for elevated and esoteric language when
dealing with religious tremendum. The religious decoding of the
relevant textual corpus therefore depends largely on establishing
the identities obscured by polyonymy."

Jere Fleck, "Óðinn's Self-Sacrifice—A New Interpretation. II:
The Ritual Landscape", Scandinavian Studies, (1971).

Historically, Odin is the first recognizable Germanic god called by a
Germanic name, which can be traced through to the late heathen era.
The earliest record of Odin's name occurs in a runic inscription on a
silver-gilt fibula discovered near Ausberg, Baveria in 1843 known as
the Nordendorf Fibula I. Dated to between the mid-sixth century
and the first half of the seventh century, it reads in full *"Logaþore
Wodan Wigiþonar awaleubwinix."* While its overall meaning is debated,
the name Wodan in the inscription "poses no problem."[254] *Wigiþonar*
is commonly thought to refer to Thor, with the prefix *wigi* alluding to
his role in battle or as a consecrator, and the identity of *Logaþore*
remains disputed, but here *Wodan* is a clear cognate of Odin.[255] This
inscription establishes with certitude that Odin conceptually existed
among the Germanic people by the early seventh century, even if it

---

[254] J. McKinnell and R. Simek, *Runes, Magic, and Religion: A Sourcebook*
(2004), pp. 48-49.
[255] Simek, Rudolf, *Dictionary of Northern Mythology*, (2007), pp 235-236.

says next to nothing about what that concept included.

ᛚᛟᚷᚨᚦᛟᚱᛖ·ᚹᛟᛞᚨᚾ·ᚹᛁᚷᛁᚦᛟ ᚾᚨᚱ

The Nordendorf Fibula I
and a transcription of its inscription

Likewise, the earliest physical evidence for Odin in Scandinavia comes from a runic inscription carved on a human skull fragment uncovered in Denmark at Ribe in southern Jutland, dated to about 725 AD. The text appears on the inner portion of the skull, which shows signs of having been exposed to the elements for some time before the inscription was made. The fragment bears two bored holes, which would allow it to be worn as an amulet. Although the inscription is not well understood, its most accepted form reads:

Ulfr auk Uþin auk Hutiur
Hialb buris uiþr
Þaima uiarki auk tuirkunig buur

"Wolf and Odin and High-*týr*
are help for Bur against these:
pain and dwarf-stroke —(carved by) Bur."[256]

[256] Translation after Mindy Macleod and Bernard Mees, *Runic Amulets and Magic Objects* (2006), p. 25 based on the citations of the inscription and its translation by Joshua Rood in *Ascending the Steps to Hliðskjálf, The Cult of Óðinn in Early Scandinavian Aristocracy* (2017), p. 121.

The generally accepted interpretation holds that a man named Bur carved the runes, requesting aid against pain and "dwarf-stroke" (perhaps a shooting pain, akin to "elfshot") from three deities designated as "Wolf, Odin, and High-*týr*." The word *týr* here need not refer to the eddic god *Týr*. As Joshua Rood has pointed out, if the term is understood as the informal noun *týr* ("god"), a parallel with an oath invoking three gods recorded in multiple Icelandic sources emerges: *Hjálpi mér svá nú Freyr ok Njörðr ok hinn almáttki ás,* "so help me Freyr and Njörd and the almighty god." In this context *hutiur* (High-*týr*) and *hinn almáttki ás* essentially mean the same thing. Regardless, the name Odin alone in the inscription is uncontested, conclusively demonstrating that a god by that name was known in the north by the early seventh century. The remainder of evidence for Odin before that time comes from outside sources.

Naturally, when foreign observers such as the Greeks and Roman encountered the people of the North, they spoke of their native gods in familiar terms. Classical historians, almost to a man, agreed that the people of northern Europe held the god "Mercury" in highest esteem. Of the Scythians, Herodotus (c. 425 BC) writes:

> "The gods which they worship are but three, Mars, Bacchus, and Dian. Their kings, however, unlike the rest of the citizens, worship Mercury more than any other god, always swearing by his name, and declaring that they are themselves sprung from him."[257]

In his *Commentaries on the Gallic Wars* (6, 17), Caesar says of the Celts: "Among the gods, they most worship Mercury,"[258] and of the Germans, Tacitus in *Germania* 9 remarks: "Among the gods, Mercury is the one they principally worship."[259] As a token of the superiority of his worship, Pliny the Elder (*Natural History* 34, 18) mentions a gigantic statue of Mercury in the community of the Arverni in Gaul by the sculptor Zenodorus which took ten years to complete. The

---

[257] Herodotus, *Histories,* Book 5, ch. 7; Wordsworth Classics, p. 390.
[258] Translated by H.J. Edwards, (1917).
[259] Translated by A.R. Birley, (1999).

Mercury of the Arverni, located in the Netherlands (Pays Bas), was depicted seated on a throne. Unfortunately its exact location and ultimate fate are unknown. Pliny writes:

> "We see enormously huge statues devised, what are called Colossi, as large as towers. Such is the Apollo on the Capitol, brought over by Marcus Lucullus from Apollonia, a city of Pontus, 45 ft. high, which cost 500 talents to make; or the Jupiter which the Emperor Claudius dedicated in the Campus Martius, which is dwarfed by the proximity of the theatre of Pompey;. ... But all the gigantic statues of this class have been beaten in our period by Zenodorus with the Hermes or Mercury which he made in the community of the Arverni in Gaul; it took him ten years and the sum paid for its making was 40,000,000 sesterces. ...Zenodorus was counted inferior to none of the artists of old in his knowledge of modeling and casting. When he was making the statue for the Arverni, when the governor of the province was Dubius Avitus, he produced facsimiles of two cast cups, the handiwork of Calamis, which Germanicus Caesar had prized highly and had presented to his tutor Cassius Salanus, Avitus's uncle; the copies were so skillfully made that there was scarcely any difference in artistry between them and the originals."

Early references to the veneration of Mercury by the northern peoples are, of course, uncertain evidence for Odin-worship, primarily because the available sources indicate that the concept of Odin as the Germanic equivalent of Mercury might have developed much later within learned Christian circles. While it clearly reflects *interpretatio Romana*, whereby foriegn gods were recorded under Roman names, the actual claim that Mercury is the equivalent of Odin comes via Christian authors, who wrote centuries later.[260] Commonly dated to the fourth century, the adoption of the Roman week among the continental Germanic tribes, which equates Odin

[260] Rood, ibid., p. 117.

with Mercury, has also been called into question.[261] Phillip Shaw has shown that votive stones among Germans living in the Rhine region during the Roman Iron Age equated the names of various local deities with Roman gods such as Mars and Mercury, whose names were associated with Tuesday and Wednesday in the Roman calendar. He concludes that it would be surprising if such heterogenous groups who equated multiple deities with Mercury would be able to settle on one god when naming a weekday; and conversely that it would not be surprising if the theophoric week, which initially developed among the Christian Anglo-Saxons and Franks, had spread to neighboring groups who interacted with them. In a 2014 interview, Shaw elaborates:

> "Although there are several different parallels drawn between a figure with a Germanic name and one or other of these Roman deities, not one of these parallels involves the name of any of the Germanic deities whose names feature in the names of the days of the week. ...These equivalences are first attested in actual manuscripts from the early Middle Ages, where they reflect Anglo-Saxon engagement with classical texts. Based on these observations, I began to re-think the plausibility of the supposed fourth-century translation of the day-names into the Germanic languages. While we are unlikely ever to arrive at absolute certainty on how, when and why this act of translation took place, I think that there are good reasons to doubt the fourth century theory, and good reasons to suspect the hand of the Christian schoolroom in the development of the names for the days of the week that we still employ today."[262]

Even if one cannot be certain when the names of the days of the week were translated from Latin, independent evidence suggests that the Germanic god identified as Mercury in early Roman sources

---

[261] Shaw, "The Origins of the Theophoric Week in the Germanic Languages" in *Early Medieval Europe*. Vol. 15, Issue 4, pp. 386–401 (2007).
[262] http://ethandoylewhite.blogspot.com An Interview with Dr. Philip A. Shaw, 19 December 2014, (last viewed 8/11/2017).

is best understood as Odin, known from later Germanic sources. Although Roman writers frequently refer to Mercury as a prominent figure of worship among the Germans, these deities' rankings in their respective pantheons were certainly not equal. The apparent identification of Mercury with Odin probably had less to do with Mercury's classical role as messenger of the gods and was more focused on his role as psychopomp, guiding souls to the realm of the dead. If we assume that Odin's hat and spear attested in the medieval sources were already attributed to him at this early date, there is an obvious iconographic parallel with the broad-brimmed hat and staff of Mercury.[263] Besides being a wandering god and patron of travelers, Mercury, like Odin in later eddic mythology, was also known as a deceiver and thief. Both gods were responsible for the written word; Mercury invented the alphabet and Odin initiated runic letters. As Shaw demonstrates, Mercury had a number of epithets throughout Gaul and Germania during the Roman period. Among these are multiple inscriptions dedicated to *Mercurius Arvernus* (Mercury of the Averni) in the Rhineland, *Mercurius Cimbrianus* (Mercury of the Cimbri) in Germanic Superior, *Mercurius Cissonius* extending from France and Southern Germany into Switzerland, as well as one off inscriptions to *Mercurius Artaios* in Beaucroissant, *Mercurius Gebrinius* in Bonn, and *Mercurius Visucius* in Stuttgard, among others. While these epithets are commonly interpreted as the names of tribal gods, another plausible explanation is polyonymy, a prominent feature of Germanic poetry, where one god is called by a number of designations. According to the *Eddas*, Odin was known by many epithets, at least one of which may have been etched on such a votive monument. In 1984, a badly fragmented inscription to *Mercurious-Hranno* on the base of a largely destroyed statue was discovered in Bornheim-Hemmerich near Cologne, Germany. An angular object between the severed legs of the statue probably once continued up to its head representing a spear or staff. A cock, whose tail-feathers remain on the left calf, stood on his left foot, resting near a tortoise.

---

[263] Rives, ibid., p. 159.

The right leg bears the weight of the figure. A number of related reliefs and inscriptions in the area dating to the first century AD, indicate that a temple probably existed somewhere in the vicinity. Norbert Wagner points out that the name *Mercurious Hranno* is undoubtedly Germanic, and probably related to *Hrani*, a name meaning "ruffian, troublemaker" employed by Odin in the fourteenth century *Hrolfs saga Kraka* (ch. 23, 30). The name also appears in the dative nominative plural in the Old English poem *Widsith* designating a North Germanic tribe, indicating that it is centuries older than the saga. He concludes:

> "This means that a very remarkable characteristic of the god Odin, previously known only from relatively late sources and only for the far North, is now confirmed by the existing inscription for a far earlier period for the middle-western part of continental Germania for the god Wodan/Mercurius."[264]

Rosmerta and Mercury
Germanic votive images, 2nd and 3rd centuries

---

[264] Norbert Wagner, "*Ein Neugefundener Wodansname,*" *Bonner Jahrbücher* 188 (1988), p. 238-239.

The earliest known monument of a Gallo-Roman Mercury which can convincingly be associated with Odin shows him as the companion of Rosmerta, a Gaulish goddess of prophecy, depicted as the distributor of liquor with attributes of spoon-strainer, mixing bucket, staff and patera (libation bowl).[265] A very popular goddess, her cult was widely established along trade routes from England to Germany. Usually associated with Mercury, she is the female half of a divine couple venerated over much of northwestern Europe, particularly in central and eastern Gaul. Evidence of her worship is found in Germany on both banks of the Rhine, in France along the Rhône, Meuse, and Moselle rivers, as well as among the Dubonni in southwest Britian. There is a substantial amount of evidence which indicates that she had a real personality and was a goddess in her own right.[266] Known from almost twenty-five inscriptions, her name is Gaulish for "great provider," an apt designation for Mother Earth. In a statue from Paris, she holds a cornucopia and a basket of fruit, common attributes of Greco-Roman divinities of agricultural abundance and fertility. In a bas-relief from Eisenberg, she holds a patera in her left hand and purse in her right. A stone bas-relief from Escolives-Sainte-Camille shows her holding both a patera and a cornucopia. In a relief from Autun showing the divine pair seated together, she holds a cornucopia and Mercury holds a patera at her left side. A study of the Rosmerta figures clearly links her to those characteristics typical of the queen and prophetess in the *comitatus*, common to the Celts and Germans.[267] She appears as a distributor of food and drink, is connected with fate and prophecy, and carries a rod or spindle as an attribute. On a relief from Gloucester, the goddess paired with Mercury holds a staff in her right hand, "presumably a symbol of authority." Her ties to fate are shown by her close affinity to Fortuna in *intepretatio Romana*.[268] Such goddesses

---

[265] Michael J. Enright, *Lady with a Mead Cup* (1996), p. 261.
[266] Miranda Green, *Symbol and Image in Celtic Religious Art* (1989), p. 57.
[267] Enright, ibid., p. 242.
[268] Green, ibid., p. 59.

were sometimes accompanied by wheels, like the goddess on the second century BC Gundestrup cauldron, flanked by two spoked wheels and pairs of fantastic beasts, which suggest her idol may have been drawn in a cart.

**Inner Plate B of the Gundestrup cauldron, c. 150 BC
North Jutland, Denmark**

Before leaving the discussion of Rosmerta, it is worth mentioning another Romanized goddess named on several epigraphic stones found in the same area. Inscriptions provide us with various spellings of her name: *Aeracura* or *Aera Cura*, in one or two words.[269] Her name occurs no less than four times in provinces of the Rhine, three times in the provinces of the Danube, once in Austria, once in Great Britain, four times in Upper Italy, twice in Rome, as well as once in a Roman providence in North Africa.[270] Although she is most often identified as a Celtic deity, given the geographic distribution and frequency of attestations, she is more likely a Germanic

---

[269] Several versions of the name occur: Aeraecura at Perugia; Aerecura at Mainz, Xanten, Aquileia and Rosia Montana, Verespatak Romania; Aericura at Sulzbach, Malsch; Eracura in Mautern an der Donau, Austria; Ercura at Fliehburg; Erecura at Cannstatt, Tongerin and Belley (Ain) in Aube; Hercura at Stockstadt am Rhein, Herecura at Cannstatt, Freinsheim and Rottenburg am Neckar where the form Herequra is also found. William Klauser, *The Esoteric Codex: Deities of the Underworld*, (2015).

[270] *Bulletin épigraphique de la Gaule*, Volume 1, (1881), p 119.

goddess. From a Roman outpost within Numidia in present-day Algeria, an inscription on an altar unearthed there reads:

TERRAE MATRI AERECVRAE
MATRI DEVM MAGNAE IDEAE

"Mother Earth, Aerecura,
the Great Mother of the Gods of Ida."

This single distant instance may demonstrate just how far Germanic mercenaries conscripted by the Roman army carried evidence of their beliefs. Like the Germanic Earth-Mother, Aericura is associated with bodies of water. Beyond her geographical associations with the Rhine and the Danube rivers, Aericura was venerated at Cannstatt, Stuttgart in Germany, a place rich with mineral springs believed to cure disease. The Dutch historian Jona Lendering noted the similarity between her iconography and that of Nehalennia. A stone from the town depicts her as a goddess of plenty with a basket of fruit in her lap. Several unmarked reliefs representing a seated goddess, well-dressed with shoes and a basket of fruit have been discovered scattered throughout the region. Epigraphic monuments in Latin, concentrated in central Germany, sometimes identify Aericura as companion to Dis Pater, god of the dead. She appears alongside him in a statue found at Overseebach, Switzerland and in the Baden-Württemberg region of Germany. Agricultural attributes in Aericura's iconography clearly illustrate her role as an earth goddess. Noémie Beck, who sees no significant difference between her attributes and those of the widespread images of the Matres and Matronae, characterizes her as a "land-goddess."[271] The origin of the name Aericura remains obscure, whether it is of Latin, Celtic, or Germanic derivation; all have been proposed. Its first element has been etymologically related to words meaning copper (*aereus*), basket (*aero*), and mistress (*era*)— the last of which connects her name to the Greek goddess Hera, wife of Zeus. Erika Timm and Carla O'Harris have suggested a phonetic connection to the Anglo-Saxon Erce, Mother Earth, and the German Herke, a byname of Frau

---

[271] Noémie Beck, *Goddesses in Celtic Religion—Cult and Mythology: A Comparative Study of Ancient Ireland, Britain and Gaul* (PhD thesis, University College of Dublin).

Holle. Her name has also been linked to that of the Germanic Mercury by Garrett S. Olmsted, who writes:

"From Corbridge, Northumberland comes an inscription to the DEO ARECVRIO, [God Arecurio] possibly an erroneous reading of a cursive MERCVRIO through interpreting the initial M as AR, as suggested by Turner. If the Latinized o-stem Arecurius is correct it may refer to Dis Pater, the companion of Aerecura."[272]

He suggests they constitute a pair of divinities, the god Mercurio or Arecurio and the goddess Arecura, a married couple with reflective names. While Julius Caesar and Tacitus agree that Mercury was the highest of the gods among the Germans, Ceasar in his *Commentaries* writes that the Gauls considered Dis Pater to be their progenitor. Thus, the deities named Dis Pater and Aerecura on epigraphic monuments within Germania, do not necessarily belong to a Celtic cult. The distribution of evidence speaks against it, since their greatest concentration lies in Germanic territory. Like Frigg, Aericura is frequently shown seated alongside her husband Dis Pater, who like Odin descends into Hel at will, rules over the deceased in Valhalla, and speaks with the dead. In addition, Dis Pater, often considered the Celtic Zeus, is sometimes accompanied by a raven or dog. Depicted together with their accompanying attributes, this celestial couple in the Germanic context could just as well represent Odin and Frigg enthroned on Hlidskjalf, via the medium of *interpretatio Romana*. The evidence, unfortunately, is simply too sparse to draw any conclusions. All that can be safely said is that the iconography of Dis Pater and Aericura draws a much closer parallel to that of the Germanic Mercury and Rosmerta, and later to that of Odin and Frigg, than to that of any other Celtic god pair. In regard to the present investigation, votive monuments to Rosmerta and Aecura, both associated with Mercury, occur in regions where legends of Frau Holle and *Vrouw Vreke* (Frau Frekke) predominate, south of the broad area where the Nerthus cult flourished in the first century.

The image of a Saxon idol known as Irminsul, directly associated with both Odin and his Roman counterpart Mercury, first appeared in Sebastian Münster's *Cosmographia,* c. 1590. Depicted as a god of war and commerce, holding a rose-banner and a scale, he

---

[272] *The Gods of the Celts and the Indo-Europeans* (1994), p. 304.

wears a full suit of armor, characteristic for illustrations of Woden at the time, based on a woodcut by Olaus Magnus published in 1555. The inspiration for the drawing seems to be a reference in the twelfth century *Kaiserchronik* concerning the origin of the name Wednesday, and therefore describing Woden, which reads:

> ûf ainer irmensiule
> stuont ain abgot ungehiure,
> daz hiezen si ir choufman.

"On an Irminsul
stands an enormous idol
which they call their merchant."

Irminsul
Sebastian Münster's
Cosmographia (c. 1590)

Commonly considered to be the seat of the ancient Saxon religion located near Heresburg (now Obermarsberg) in Northern Germany, the first reference to Irminsul appeared in the *Annales Regni*

Francorum or *Royal Frankish Annals* (772 AD). During the Saxon wars, Charlemagne repeatedly ordered the idol's destruction. Rudolf of Fulda (865 AD) describes it in his *De Miraculis Sancti Alexandri* ("The Miracles of Saint Alexander"), chapter III, as a great wooden pillar erected and worshipped under the open sky. In some sources, this pillar is personified. Widukind of Corvey in *Deeds of the Saxons* (c. 970) describes such an Irminsul erected to celebrate the Saxon's victory over the Thuringians in 531. He says the Saxons set up an altar to their god of victory, identified as Hirmin or Hermes (Mercury), whom they depicted as a wooden column. In 1605, four decades before the *Codex Regius* came to light, the Irminsul was directly identified with both Mercury and Odin. Richard Verstegan, in his *Restitution of Decayed Intelligence in Antiquities,* writes:

"Whereas Tacitus saith, that of all the Gods the Germans especially honored Mercury find upon certaine dayes offered men unto him in sacrifice, this Idol Ermensewl (Irminsul) is taken to be the same that the Romans interpreted for Mercury, though some others have interpreted him for Mars, and Woden with less reasone for Mercury; for that he was held of the Saxons for their God of war, as Mercury among the Romans never was. And in all likelihood of truth, the Romans for some property which the Germans ascribed to their Idols, might well for the like property ascribed by them unto theirs, take them to be the very same Idols, albeit they were of the Germans called by other names, and made in other manner. And so in like sort hath Thor been of some interpreted for Iupiter, for that among his other marvels he made, and caused, thunder, and was chiefly honoured upon the same day whereon the Romans honoured their Iupiter. Friga is also interpreted for Venus because among other her qualities she was a furtherer of friendship, and that on the very day of her chiefe celebration, the Romans chiefly honoured their amiable Venus."

A much clearer parallel can be seen in an even earlier source, briefly mentioned before, which links the Germanic Mercury to a goddess designated as *Vrowe Here* (Frau Here), said to be worshiped

together with him by the ancient Saxons.[273] As such it is worth
quoting at length. Penned by Gobelin Person (*Gobelinus Persona*, 1358-
1421), a prominent historian and church reformer from the bishopric
of Paderborn in North Rhine-Westphalia, his master work
Cosmidromius, completed in 1418, remains one of the most important
historical works of the fifteenth century. In chapter 38, composed
some time before 1406, speaking of local history and superstition, he
writes:

> "Charles the Great in the year of our Lord 769, took hold of
> the reign in the kingdom of the Franks and ruled for forty-six
> years; of course, three years together with his brother Carlomann
> and the remainder of the years ruled alone. In the second year of
> his reign, the General Assembly of Worms convened to decide
> upon the approach to the Saxon War, and they, without delay,
> advanced altogether with swords and fire to plunder the castle of
> Eresburgh, which presently is called Mount Mars in the Latin
> tongue, and seized the idol which the Saxons call Irminsuel,
> destroyed it and then took it back all the way up to the Weser
> River, and withdrew with twelve Saxon hostages. Understand that
> this idol Irminsuel is Mercury or what the Greeks call Hermes
>
> ...They consecrate the idol or statue in the aforementioned
> place to this god, because Irminsuel is a statue of he who is called
> Hermes. And because in this aforementioned place all men in the
> district assemble in order to sacrifice to the idol out of reverence
> and devote themselves to it, that place is called Eresburgh, the
> Mountain of Reverence. Actually Juno, who, in the writings of the
> Greeks, is called Hera, was worshiped in the same place before
> Hermes or perhaps at the same time, thereupon they call that place
> Heresbergh, which is clearly the Mountain of Hera or Juno, and
> afterwards, once they occupied and fortified that place, called it
> Heresburgh, the Castle of Hera. Moreover, this Hera was
> worshiped by the Saxons, which can be seen by the fact that certain
> of the common people recite what they themselves have heard
> from antiquity, just as I myself have heard, that between the festival

---

[273] Timm, ibid., pp. 56-58, recognizes *Her(r)e* as a form of the name Herke.

of the Birth of Christ and the holiday of the Epiphany of the Lord, Mistress Hera flies through the air, because the pagans assign the air to Juno. And because, whenever they call upon Juno as Ceres and depict her with bells and wings, the common people call her *vrowe here* (Frau Here), or corrupt the name *Vor Here de Vlughet* [of Flight], and believe that she brings abundance at that time."[274]

The significance of this remarkable passage cannot be overstated. Written nearly two decades before the re-discovery of Tacitius' *Germania* in 1425, it clearly identifies a local Saxon god with Mercury, which *Germania* and a handful of other sources also identify as Odin (see further). The author expressly speaks of local belief, recording what "the common people" said they "themselves have heard from antiquity [*or* the elders], just as I myself have heard."[275] Although he travelled widely throughout Italy in the company of Pope Urban VI before being ordained in 1386, Gobelin Person was a native of Paderborn, Germany who was born, bred, and ultimately buried in the vicinity. Although deeply learned, he was in a position to both know and understand local legend. Remarkably, he not only identifies the local Saxon goddess known as Frau Here (*Vrowe Here*) with the Greek goddess Hera, the Queen of the Classical pantheon, but also identifies her with Ceres, the Roman goddess of agriculture, demonstrating that the identification was based on more than just a superficial similarity between the names Here and Hera. Among the Saxons, *Vrowe Here* [*Frau Here*] is thus the Queen of Heaven *and* Mother Earth at the same time. Drawing on ancient local tradition which he himself had heard, he says that the common folk believe she flies through the air between Christmas and New Year's Day bringing abundance, adding the unique details that she was depicted with bells and wings. These last two details directly correspond to what we know of Frau Percht, whose followers, the *Perchten*, frequently sound bells [See Chapter IV: The Frau Holle Legends].

---

[274] Carla O'Harris translation.
[275] *Quod autem Hera colebatur a Saxonibus, videtur ex eo, quod adhuc quidam vulgares recitant se audivisse ab antiquis, prout et ego ipse audivi.*

The same is said of the followers of Freyr, lord of harvests. In the sixth book of his Danish history, Saxo says that the hero Starkad went to Old Uppsala where he saw the Sons of Frey perform on stage at the time of the sacrifices:

> "He went to the land of the Swedes, where he lived at leisure for seven years' space with the sons of Frey ... he was stationed at Uppsala at the time of the sacrifices, he was disgusted by the effeminate gestures and the clapping of mimes on the stage, and by the unmanly clatter of bells. Hence it is clear, how far he kept his soul from lasciviousness, not even enduring to look upon it," (Oliver Elton translation).

Saxo describes the shows from his Christian perspective as lascivious, fitting for a god of fertility. At Uppsala, Freyr was called Fricco and depicted with an immense phallus; he presided over marriages. The name Fricco directly connects him to Frick, Frikka, Frekka, which as we have seen are alternate names of Frau Holle, and to Frigga, the beloved wife of Odin. That she has wings can be confirmed by images in the iconography and mythology of the region which is well-acquainted with prophetic goddesses in the form of birds. According to *Skaldskaparmál* 18, Frigg, like Freyja, owns a falcon guise which Loki borrows. Remarkably, Gobelin couples the veneration of this *"Vrowe Here"* and her local sanctuary with that of the Classical Mercury, who is widely recognized as Odin from other Latin sources. In addition, he precisely pinpoints the time of her flight as taking place between the Feasts of the Nativity and the Epiphany, corresponding to the Twelves, the time of the annual progress of Frau Holle, as well as the ride of Wild Hunt in Northern European tradition, when Odin and his wife flew through the air visiting homes —all this according to local oral legends concerning the old Saxons, which the author himself had heard in the latter part of the fourteenth century as a native of Paderborn, beginning with the Christian invasion of Saxon territory and the destruction of their sacred pillar, the Irminsul, which Gobelin identifies as an idol of Mercury at Eresburg [Heresburgh], now the city of Obermarsberg, south of Paderborn some 650 years earlier.

Throughout Romanized heathen Germania, mostly near Roman settlements or villas in the German provinces, Jupiter, the Roman king of the gods, appeared atop pillars erected in the second and third centuries AD. Some occur in Gaul and Britain as well. In Northern Germany, they commonly depict Jupiter on horseback, trampling a giant, often in the form of a snake; these are known as *Jupitergigantensäulen,* "Jupiter giant-columns." In Southern Germany, he is typically depicted enthroned; these pillars are simply known as *Jupitersäulen,* "Jupiter Columns." A square *Viergötterstein* ("four gods' stone") forms the base of the pillar, depicting Juno, Minerva, Mercury and Hercules on its four sides. Atop it rests a *Wochengötterstein* (a stone depicting the seven weekday gods) which, supports the column crowned with the statue of Jupiter. Both aspects of the god atop these pillars can be associated with Thor, the foe of the Midgard Serpent and the throned counterpart of Jove in the Anglo-Saxon transliteration of the Roman weekdays. The average height of a Jupiter Column is around 4 meters, while the one at Mainz is more than 9 meters high. They were often placed within an enclosure accompanied by an altar. No such monument has survived intact; they are known only from excavations or secondary use, such as spolia in Christian churches. Recent reconstructions of Jupiter Columns have been raised where they were recovered, including Ladenburg, Obernburg, Benningen am Neckar, Sinsheim, Stuttgart, Mainz and near the Saalburg.

In this context, it is worth mentioning that just a few decades before Charlemagne felled the Saxon Irminsul, a Christian missionary named Winifred, later Saint Boniface of Mainz, felled the Holy Oak of Jove about 723 AD in the neighboring state of Hesse, center of the Frau Holle legends. The tree designated as *robor Iovis* (Jove's oak) by Boniface's biographer Willibald could refer to an Oak of Odin, if Jove is understood as the king of the gods, but it is more commonly interpreted as the Oak of Thor, Odin and Earth's son, since Thor is otherwise identified with Jove (aka Jupiter) in the Anglo-Saxon transliteration of the Roman weekdays, where Thor's day corresponds to *Iovis Dies*, Jove's day. Thus, we find a series of interrelated testimonies that refer to a family of gods, corresponding to Odin, his wife the Earth-Mother, and their son the Thunder-god at the time of the Christian conversion in continental Germany. Of interest, Willibald states that the locals openly sacrificed to both trees and springs, the latter of which was a favorite haunt of Odin's wife Frau Holle in her various forms. Willibald wrote:

> "Now at that time many of the Hessians, brought under the Catholic faith …were wont secretly, some openly to sacrifice to trees and springs; some in secret, others openly practiced inspections of victims and divinations, legerdemain and incantations; some turned their attention to auguries and auspices and various sacrificial rites; while others, with sounder minds, abandoned all the profanations of heathenism, and committed none of these things. With the advice and counsel of these last, the saint attempted, in the place called Gaesmere, while the servants of God stood by his side, to fell a certain oak of extraordinary size, which is called, by an old name of the pagans, the Oak of Jupiter [*robor Iovis*]. And when in the strength of his steadfast heart he had cut the lower notch, there was present a great multitude of pagans, who in their souls were earnestly cursing the enemy of their gods. But when the fore side of the tree was notched only a little, suddenly the oak's vast bulk, driven by a blast from above, crashed to the ground, shivering its crown of branches as it fell; and, as if by the gracious compensation of the Most High, it was also burst into four parts, and four trunks of huge size, equal in length."[276]

We find a similar scene in Gaul three centuries earlier. Germanus, the bishop of Auxerre from 418-448, is said to have been the son of wealthy parents, who was educated in the best schools in Gaul, probably at Autun and Lyon "where learning flourished," before traveling to Rome to study and practice law. There, he married a wealthy Roman woman before returning to Auxerre, where he rose

---

[276] George W. Robinson translation, 1916.

to high office, becoming one of the six so-called Dukes of Gaul, each of whom governed a certain number of provinces. Nominally he was a Christian, but a custom prevailed from ancient times of paying reverence to a pear tree at the center of town by hanging trophies of the chase in it. Upon his return from a hunt, Germanus would hang the heads of every beast he killed on this tree, according to the heathen custom of oscillation in which the heads and faces of victims were hung upon trees and dedicated to the gods.[277] The then-current bishop Amator attempted to induce Germanus to abandon this practice, but could not prevail, and so when Germanus was out hunting, Amator cut down the tree and burnt it.[278] When Germanus returned, he was furious with the bishop and drove him out of the city, threatening his life. Amator, however, won respect from him for his courage. He confessed that he was not worthy of martyrdom, and the bishop and the duke soon made peace again.

Among the Anglo-Saxons, the Roman god Mercury was identified with Odin from the earliest times. In the Anglo-Saxon transliteration of the Roman weekdays, Mercury is identified with Odin. The fourth day, *Dies Mercurtius,* Mercury's Day, is rendered as *Wednesday,* Wotan's Day, while the sixth day belongs to that of his wife *Frigg.* Odin's son Thor, representing the fifth day, is placed between them. Evidence suggests that Odin was well-known among the pre-Christian people of England. *UUoden* or Woden is listed as the ancestor of kings in genealogies found in the *Anglo-Saxon Chronicle* for the years 547, 560, and 855. The early Anglo-Saxon Church

[277] Referring to the site of Arminius' victory at the Battle of the Teutoburg Forest six years after the conflict, Tacitus writes: "In the centre of the field were the whitening bones of men, as they had fled, or stood their ground, strewn everywhere or piled in heaps. Near, lay fragments of weapons and limbs of horses, and also human heads, prominently nailed to trunks of trees. In the adjacent groves were the barbarous altars, on which they had immolated tribunes and first-rank centurions." *Annals*, Church and Brodribb tr.
[278] The Germanic peoples, who are said to have worshiped in groves, have a widespread tradition of a "ward-tree", whose health reflects the moral condition of the estate. Destroying such a tree, no doubt, was considered bad luck, and an offense to the local land-wights.

probably tolerated Odin for political reasons, since, as among the Scythians, descent from him defined royal status.[279] Before the end of the eighth century, Woden was acknowledged as the founder of all Anglian and Anglian-dominated tribes.[280] After that time, royal genealogies were extended further back to include Frealaf, Geat, Sceldwas, —the father of Scyld— and eventually the foriegn Noah. In the tenth century, Æthelweard, an Anglo-Saxon nobleman of royal blood, said that the heathen Anglo-Saxons made sacrifices to Wodan, "the king of the barbarians" (*Uuoddan regis barbarorum*) before battle, claiming that Hengst and Horsa, the founders of that nation, were Odin's grandsons (*Chronicorum* IV, 1).

Odin with his Ravens
Bronze Helmet Plate, Vendel Period

A number of place-names primarily in southern England, well outside of the jurisdiction of the Danelaw suggest an early Woden cult in the southern regions of pre-Viking England. These include

---

[279] J. M. Wallace-Hadrill, *Early Germanic Kingship* (1971), pp. 72-97.
[280] Richard North, *Heathen Gods in Old English Literature* (1997), p. 112, citing a survey by Kenneth Sisam.

Woddesgeat (Wiltshire), *Wodnesbeorg* (Wiltshire), *Wodnesdene* (Wiltshire), *Wensley* (Derbyshire), *Wodnesfeld* (Essex), and *Woodnesborough* (Kent). In the tenth century, Ælfric in his condemnation of pagan practices among the Anglo-Saxons in *De Falsis Diis*, ll. 133-135, characterizes the hated god *Mercurius* as *swiðe facenfull and swicol an dædum*, "full of crime and treacherous in his deeds," and the *Exeter Book Maxims* unfavorably compare Woden to the Christian god: *Woden worhte weos, wuldor alwalda, rume roderas*, 'Woden made idols, the Almighty [made] glory, the spacious heavens."

Although the evidence is sparse, among the Anglo-Saxons, Odin seems to have shared at least some of the attributes he had in Icelandic sources. In Bede's account of the last days of seventh-century Anglian paganism, Coifi, the high-priest of Deira (c. 627), declared the old religion a waste of time, rode to his own shrine at Goodmanham and threw a spear at the altar of the gods. Henry Mayr-Harting has suggested that this act may be "a small but highly significant pointer to the cult of Woden and the knowledge of his mythology at the time."[281] In later Icelandic sources, Odin casts his unerring spear Gungnir over his enemies as a sign of war. Woden also appears in a tenth or eleventh century Anglo-Saxon healing charm preserved in the *Lacnunga* (*MS BL Harley 585*), which reads:

Wyrm com snican,	A snake came crawling,
toslat he man;	he wounded nothing.
ða genam Woden	Then Woden took
VIIII wuldortanas,	nine glory-twigs,
sloh ða þa næddran,	Smote the adder
þæt heo on VIIII tofleah.	so that it flew apart into nine.
þær geændade	There apple and poison
æppel and attor,	brought it about
þæt heo næfre ne	That she never would
wolde on hus bugan.	dwell in the house.
Fille and finule,	Chervil and fennel,
felamihtigu twa,	very mighty two

[281] H. Mayr-Harting, *The Coming of Christianity* (1972), pp. 22-30.

þa wyrte gesceop	These herbs he created,
witig drihten,	the wise lord,
halig on heofonum,	holy in heaven,
þa he hongode.	when he hung.[282]

The charm goes on to address each of the nine herbs, naming their attributes and accomplishments. Each are cited as remedies against poisons, implying that Odin, the Hanged God (*Hanga-týr*) himself, created them. However, due to the late date of the charms, Scandinavian influence cannot be ruled out.

We also find early evidence of Odin on the continent. In the seventh century, Jonas of Bobbio records an encounter St. Columban had with the Germanic tribe known as the Suebi, who were preparing a sacrifice to their god:

"Once as he [Columban] was going through this country, he discovered that the natives were going to make a heathen offering. They had a large cask that they called a *cupa*, and that held about twenty-six measures, filled with beer and set in their midst. On Columban's asking what they intended to do with it, they answered that they were making an offering to their god Wodan (whom others call Mercury). When he heard of this abomination, he breathed on the cask, and lo! it broke with a crash and fell in pieces so that all the beer ran out."[283]

In an eighth century citation, Paulus Diaconus, a historian of the Lombards, writes "Wodan indeed, whom by adding a letter they called Godan, is he who among the Romans is called Mercury and worshiped by all peoples of Germany as a god."[284] This document, or more accurately, its anonymous authority, is also significant for introducing Odin's wife *Frea*, whose Anglo-Saxon equivalent *Frig* became the namesake for the modern Friday. Evidence for the worship of Odin is also found in the ninth century Saxon Baptismal

[282] Karen Louise Jolly, *Popular Religion in Late Saxon England, Elf Charms in Context* (1996), p. 126.
[283] Source: http://www.fordham.edu/halsall/basis/columban.html (1/01/15).
[284] William Dudley Foulke tr.

Vow (*Vatican Codex pal.* 577) which compelled the Saxons to renounce Wodan, Thunear, and Saxnot.[285] In the tenth century, we find a reference to Odin, Frigg, and Baldur in the OHG *Second Merseburg Charm*; and an eleventh century reference to the gods Odin, Thor and Fricco in the temple at Uppsala by the historian Adam of Bremen. By the thirteenth century, Odin appears fully developed as the head of the pantheon in the *Eddas* and *Sagas* of Iceland, generally acknowledged to be composed of older material.

Odin's fame extends well beyond the end of the heathen era. He appears yet again in a seventeenth century recording of a medieval Swedish ballad titled *Stolt Herr Alf* (Proud Lord Alf).[286] In stanza 8, King Asmund calls upon him to defeat Lord Alf: "Help now Odin Asagrim, I have need to call upon you." The word *Asagrim,* meaning "Leader of the Æsir" contains the *hápax legómenon*[287] - *grimmr* for "leader, ruler" found on Runestone Sö 126, where it appears as the second element in the title *folksgrimR,* "ruler of the people." Sophus Bugge (*Runverser* 161) noted that skaldic poets used the noun *gramr* to mean "king" or "warrior" and that the related adjective *grimmr* was most likely used in a similar fashion. This preserved word form helps determine the age of the composition. Two different, but almost identically-worded manuscripts of this ballad dating from the seventeenth century are now held in the Royal Swedish Library. These two versions were recorded from several performances by ballad singer Ingierd Gunnarsdotter (1601–1686) and appear in the collection known as *Någre gamble Wijser* (NGW). Recorded between the years 1679-81 near Lyrestad parish in Västergötland, the dialectal language of the ballad indicates that it hails from southwestern Scandinavia. Since only two poems of the

---

[285] *Ec forsacho allum dioboles uuercum and uuordum, Thunaer ende Uuöden ende Saxnote ende allum them unholdum the hira genötas sint* ("I renounce all the words and works of the devil, Thunaer, Wōden and Saxnōt, and all those fiends that are their associates."). Here, Saxnot ("sword-god") may indicate Freyr, the god with the sword.

[286] Thanks to Mark Puryear of the Norroena Society for pointing this out.

[287] A term of which only one instance is recorded.

Poetic Edda had been published in 1665 and the Swedish ballad appears before all printed versions of the related material in Icelandic and Faroese, the popular printed texts of the 1700s cannot be the source of transmission. The ballad was well established in Scandinavia by the 1700s, suggesting it preserves authentic mythological material. That this is possible is evidenced by the various ballad versions of the *Thrymskvida* story in which Thor must dress as a bride to retrieve his stolen hammer. Such versions as *Tord af Havsgaard* and *Tord of Meersburg*, already established before the widespread dissemination of the recently recovered eddic poem, tell essentially the same tale. These late ballads serve as a powerful illustration of the conservation of religious ideas in the oral tradition over time. Long standing narratives, it seems, were slow to change and difficult to wholly stamp out of human memory.

This long chain of evidence for Odin, dating from the earliest appearances of the Germans in the historic record, leaves little doubt that he remained a prominent figure within the Germanic pantheon as far back as the written records allow us to know. Yet Odin is often seen as a late arrival to Scandinavia. Among early eddic scholars, this idea was initially supported by Snorri's statement in the *Prologue* to *Gylfaginning* that Odin was an immigrant to the North. There, Wodan or Odin, a descendant of King Priam of Troy, at the prophetic advice of his wife Frigida or Frigg after the Classical Trojan War, "set off from Turkey and took with him a very great following. ... And did not halt their journey until they came north to the country that is now called Saxony." According to Snorri, he founded a great dynasty ruling over all of France, Germany and Denmark before entering Sweden and establishing his own kingdom there. Although the substance of the theory is little changed, modern scholars no longer rely on Snorri's account, substituting more scientific reasoning. As early as 1904, H.M. Chadwick, in his *The Cult of Othin* concluded:

"If cremation is to be associated in any way with the cult of Othin, it is during the latter part of the first century that we must suppose the cult to have been introduced into Sweden. This hypothesis receives some slight support from a statement in Tacitus (*Germ.* 40). He says that seven northern tribes worshiped the goddess Nerthus, i.e. Mother Earth, 'on an island in the ocean.' There can be no serious doubt that this goddess Nerthus is closely related to the Scandinavian god Njörðr. A rite very similar to that described by Tacitus was practised by the Swedes in connection with the worship of Fro (Freyr) the son of Njörðr. The festival of Nerthus was accompanied by a holy peace; wars were not undertaken, and weapons were put away; 'peace and quiet are then only known and loved' until the goddess returns to her temple. From this description it seems likely enough that the cult of Woden-Othin prevailed among these tribes, but that it was combined to some extent with the older cult of Nerthus-Njörðr. ...The conclusions attained in the course of this discussion may be briefly summarized as follows: —(1) The cult of Othin was in all probability known in the North at the beginning of the sixth century; there is no reason for supposing that it was then new. (2) The cult does not seem to have been practised by the Swedes in the first half-century of the present era. (3) If the adoption of cremation was due to the cult of Othin, the cult can hardly have been introduced into Sweden later than the end of the first century. (p. 64-65)."

More often than not, scholars have been inclined to see Odin as a usurper, who came late to the throne. It has often been argued that Odin is a late import into Scandinavia from continental Germany, owing to his adoption and promotion by an emerging political elite centered around regional kings supported by their military retinues, between the fourth and eighth centuries. Since at least the mid-twentieth century, Odin has almost universally been interpreted as a lesser local god who must have rose to the top of the ranks sometime between the seventh and tenth centuries, when his name first began to appear in literary sources.[288] In 1964, E.O.G.

---

[288] Kevin J. Wanner, "God on the Margins Dislocation and Transience in the Myths of Óðinn", (2007), p. 323; Joshua Rood, *Ascending the Steps to Hliðskjálf* (2017), pp. 154 ff.

Turville-Petre observed, "While there is no compelling evidence that the cult of Óðinn was practiced widely in the west before the Viking Age, there are reasons to believe that it spread and developed during that age."[289] Citing the few indications of cult veneration for Odin in Iceland, the lack of place-names, and the relatively few myths concerning him, Rudolf Simek (1984) wrote: "Since there can be no doubt that Odin was the god of poetry, …the skalds of heathen times, not surprisingly show a particular inclination in favour of the god of their own craft."[290] Richard North (1999) concurs, stating that "the uncritical acceptance of Óðinn's pre-eminence in *Gylfaginning* as typical of his status in the pagan period often obscures rather than clarifies the many problems of Germanic mythology," adding: "It is unlikely that Woden, a god of magic and warfare, was regarded as the 'All-father' in heathen times."[291] In agreement with this view, Thomas DuBois (1999) infers:

> "Tellingly Óðinn's apparent rise to power in the Scandinavian pantheon finds reflection of him as a crafty, usurping, duplicitous deity, lacking in many accounts the unambiguously admirable qualities of Þórr."[292]

Demonstrably, linguistic arguments concerning the name of the Indo-European Sky-Father, reconstructed as *Dyeus Pater*, primarily inform this view since he is typically identified as *Tiwaz* (later Týr) and not Odin in the Germanic sphere. However, when one considers the continuity of Odin, and earlier Mercury, in the historic record and recognizes Odin's character and attributes in those of the proposed Indo-European Sky-Father, there is little reason to doubt that Odin is a direct heir to the mantle of *Dyeus Pater*. Like his Greco-Roman counterparts, Odin is one of three

---

[289] *Myth and Religion of the North*, p. 66.
[290] *Dictionary of Northern Mythology*, p. 243.
[291] *Heathen Gods in Old English Literature*, p. 15.
[292] *Nordic Religions of the Viking Age*, p. 58. For an effective rebuttal of this view, see Wanner (2007), pp. 340-346. I would add that Odin's "crafty" nature is already present in his identification with Mercury, the god of thieves.

brothers, who are the third generation from Chaos. Like them, he surveys the world from his heavenly throne, wields a casting weapon, carries on affairs, and is associated with a goddess representing the earth. Even if their names are not parallel, their attributes are. Comparative mythology within the Indo-European milieu demonstrates that natural phenomena once personified and worshipped, by degrees through epic treatment, becomes gods and goddesses with individual personalities and relationships centuries before being recorded in the oldest mythological documents preserved for study. By their very nature, deities which began as personifications of such things as the sky, the sun, the earth, the thunderbolt, etc, once personified were regarded and revered as actual persons with their own individual fates. In other words, they come to be seen as promoters of those natural phenomena and no longer as express personifications of them. Since the nineteenth century, a wide spectrum of Indo-European scholars has held that the ruler of the Indo-European pantheon was a sky god, designated as *Dyeus Pater*, literally "God the Father" or "Sky-Father." The name, and the theory itself, are based on a comparison of the godhead in several Indo-European mythologies: in Latin *Ju-piter*, in Greek *Zeus*, in Sanskrit *Dyaus*, the first element of his name being a word meaning "God", "Divinity", or "Bright Heaven" joined with the title "Father." In the Germanic languages, this prefix corresponds to the name *Týr*, as well as the common noun *týr* (plural *tívar*), which simply means "god."

Once linguists identified *Dyeus Pater* as the proper name of the Indo-European Sky-Father at the beginning of the nineteenth century, this honor has uniformly been bestowed on Odin's son Tyr, the one-handed god known from the *Eddas*, but *only* because his name corresponds etymologically to that of the Greek *Zeus* and the Indic *Dyaus*.[293] Therefore the evidence for this identification is primarily linguistic, and does not account for a potential change in name. That alone should give us pause.

---

[293] Rudolf Simek in *Early Germanic Literature and Culture*, Vol. I, p. 89.

Odin by Sarah Powers Bradish, 1900
After Johannes Gehrts, 1885

In the other branches, these names are commonly coupled with the title *Pater*, Father, except in the Germanic branch, where Tyr is not only *never* characterized as a father, but is cuckolded by Loki, who declares that Tyr never got "rag nor penny" in compensation for his wife bearing Loki a son (*Lokasenna* 40). Instead, both suffixes regularly appear in epithets of Odin. He is the "All-father" (*Alföðr*) and "Father of men" (*Aldaföðr*) as well as the biological father of prominent gods such as Thor, Baldur, Vidar and Vali. In addition, Odin is known as *Farma-týr* (Cargo god), *Fimbul-týr* (Great god), *Gauta-týr* (God of the Geats), *Geir-týr* (Spear god), *Hanga-týr* (Hanging god), *Her-týr* (God of hosts), *Hropta-týr* (Invoking god), *Reiðar-týr* (God of riders), and *Rúna-týr* (Rune god). In fact, the suffix *týr* is attached to Odin's names more often than any other god. According to the conventions of comparative mythology, Odin should rightly be considered the Germanic analog to the old Indo-European Sky-Father. Like Zeus and Jupiter to the south, he serves as ruler and father to the primary gods, seated on his heavenly throne Hlidskjalf, looking out over the world. Only Odin's proper name, not being a cognate of the reconstructed compound **Dyeus Pater,* has prevented scholars from reaching this rather obvious conclusion.

There is a near consensus that Odin's name derives from a root akin to Old Norse *óðr,* German *wut,* Anglo-Saxon *wōþ,* words meaning "high mental excitement, ecstasy," which calls attention to a common link between his votaries: poets, warriors and sorcerers, whose professional success depended, at least in part, on accessing supernatural power and inducing states of inspiration or frenzy.[294] Adam of Bremen says, *Wodan, id est furor,* "Odin, that is the Furious." More generally, the name Odin (**Wodanaz*) comes from a root meaning "raging, frenzied, spirited," an appropriate designation for a sky-god. So instead of assuming Odin came late to the throne, usurping an earlier Germanic predecessor, we might just as readily conclude that somewhere along the line that one of the Sky-Father's epithets came to stand in for his proper name —that **Dyeus Pater* became **Wodanaz*— perhaps due to a taboo of naming the god directly.[295] Martin L. West explains:

> "More than one factor contributed to the replacement of names. A god's primary name might be avoided for taboo reasons. It might be displaced by familiar epithets or titles, rather as the Christian deity is no longer known as Yahweh or Jehovah, but is mostly just called God, or alternatively the Almighty, the

---

[294] Wanner, ibid., p. 323.
[295] For a detailed explanation of this "Lethe Effect," particularly in northern regions, see Paul T. Barber and Elizabeth Wayland Barber, *When They Severed Earth from Sky,* (2004), p. 19.

Heavenly Father, the Lord, and so forth. ...Gods' names are not invented arbitrarily, like those of aliens in science fiction. Originally, they have a meaning, they express some concept, and sometimes this is still apparent or discoverable."[296]

Peter Flötner, Tuisco, 1543   Richard Verstegan, Tuysco, 1605
THE IDOL OF TUESDAY

Since the early nineteenth century, scholars have identified *Dyeus Pater* with an unattested Germanic "war-god" theoretically called *Tiw* or *Tiwaz*. The name is based on the Anglo-Saxon transliteration of the names of the weekdays, where *Tiwesdaeg* (Tuesday) corresponds to *dies Martis* (Mars' day), making the god *Tiw* an analogue of Mars, the Roman god of war. It should be mentioned that up until that time, the name Tuesday was generally believed to derive from the Germanic god Tuisco, described by Tacitus in *Germania* ch. 2 as "an earth-born" deity, whose son Mannus was the source and founder of the Germanic people. Popularized by British publisher Richard Verstegan in his *Restitution of Decayed Intelligence in*

---

[296] West, ibid., pp. 134-135.

Antiquities (1605), this theory was widely repeated in popular works until the early 1900s.[297] Verstegan, who had artistic precedents for all seven of the so-called Saxon gods,[298] based his image of Tuysco on Peter Flötner's design for Tusico, the eponymous father of the Teutonic race, in silver relief minted between 1537-1543. In 1763, the French scholar Paul Henri Mallet, an early translator of Snorri's *Edda*, first proposed that the English *Tuesday* and the Allemand (OHG) *Dingstag* actually derived from Tyr, a son of Odin in Snorri's *Edda*, and that "this proved that Tyr answered to Mars," *Dies Martis*, in Latin.[299] Mallet wrote:

> "I do not believe that mention is made of him anywhere else, except in the Edda and other Icelandic monuments. And yet it is certain that this God hath been adored by all the northern nations; since in all the different dialects of this people, the name of the third day of the week, which the Romans consecrated to Mars (*Dies Martis*) hath been formed from the name of Tyr."

---

[297] Tuesday is said to be Tuisco's day in: Gaspar Bellerus' *Nederlantsche Antiquiteyten* (1613); Trogillus Arnkiel's *Cimbrische Heyden-Religion* (1691); Jacob von Royen's *Antiquitates Belgicae* (1700); Thomas Mortimer's A *New History of England* (1764); William Derham's *Physico-Theology* (1773); John Henry Brady's *Clavis Calendaria* (1815); Pinnock & Goldsmith's *History of England* (1823); *The Juvenile Every-day Book* (1836); Leopold Ziegelhauser's *Allgemeine Populäre Götterlehre* (1837); *Ladies Garland*, Vol. I (1838); Robert Bigsby's *Old Places Revisited*, Vol. 3 (1851); Peter Parley's *Annual* (1870); Robert Kemp Philp's *The Domestic World* (1872); Andre Addison Crabtre's *The Funny Side of Physic* (1872); Frank Stockton Dobbins' *Gods of Our Saxon Ancestors* (1883); John Hosking's *The Elements of Christian Theology*, etc.; Shobal Vail Clevenger's *The Evolution of Man and His Mind* (1903), George Kunz's *The Curious Lore of Precious Stones*; George Lyman Kittredge's *The Old Farmer and His Almanack* (1920); and numerous others. In Samuel Fallows & Henry W. Ruoff's *Human Interest Library* (1914), Tuesday is attributed to Tyr, showing that this theory had not yet taken root in the popular imagination.
[298] Konrad Bothe published the first images presenting idols of the Moon and Crodo, also called Saetr, in *Cronecken der Sassen*, 1492. Olaus Magnus then published a woodcut representing Woden, Thor and Fricca (Frigg) in *Historia de Gentibus Septentrionalibus*, 1555. An illustration of the Sun idol first saw print in Johannes Pomarius' *Chronika der Sachsen und Niedersachsen*, 1588.
[299] *Introduction a L'histoire de Dannemarc*, p. 81; translated as *Northern Antiquites* (1770) p. 82.

From his initial identification with the eddic god Tyr, the so-called Saxon "war-god" *Tiw*, known only from a comparison of the Roman names of the days of the week, soon acquired additional traits. In the 1830s, Mallet's insight was given a scholarly footing by Jacob Grimm who "safely inferred" the names *Tiw* and *Zio* from the Anglo-Saxon *Tiwesdæg* and the OHG *Ziestac* for Tuesday, which in his opinion was comparable to a multitude of Indo-European cognates belonging to the root *div*, "allowing us to make up a fuller formula *div, tiv, zio*," which yield the meanings "brightness, sky, day, god." "These *intricate etymologies* are not to be avoided," he remarked, for "they *entitle* us to claim a sphere for the Teutonic god *Zio, Tiw, Tyr* which places him on a level with the loftiest deities of antiquity."[300] As support, Grimm pointed out two ninth and tenth century glosses,[301] which designate the Swabians (Suevi) as *Ziuwart*, "men of Zio," or "Men of God" and the city of Augsburg as *Ziesburc* ("City of Zio," "City of God"), which he accepted as evidence for a god named *Zio*, comparable to the Anglo-Saxon *Tiw*, and understood as a cognate to *Dyeus Pater* based solely on the linguistic relationship of these reconstructed terms. The theory was discussed primarily in German language scholarship until the 1880s when Grimm's *Deutsche Mythologie* was translated into English by James Stalleybrass, after which it became widely promulgated. By then, the unattested name *Tiw* had developed into the equally unattested proto-Germanic *Tiwaz*. The reconstructed "primitive form" of the name was now widely regarded as the equivalent of the Vedic *Dyaus*, Greek *Zeus*, Latin *Diespiter* (*Jupiter*), both in name and character, and closely connected to the Indo-European root *deivos* (Sanskrit *devas*, Latin *divus*), meaning "gods." Without embellishment, *Johnson's Universal Cyclopaedia* (1895) summarizes the theory as it was known on the cusp of the twentieth century:

---

[300] Grimm, ibid., vol. I, p. 196 (Stalleybrass tr.), emphasis added.
[301] Probably referring to the same source(s), Peter Buchholz cites a gloss to the Wessobrunn prayer which calls the Alamanni *Cyowari* (worshipers of Cyo) and their capital Augsburg *Ciesburc* in *Perspectives for Historical Research in Germanic Religion, History of Religions*, vol. 8, no. 2 (1968), p. 127.

"Comparative mythology assures the parallel of an old Teutonic god, probably 'the bright one,' *Tiwaz* (Scand. *Tyr*), with Sanskrit *Dyaus*, Greek *Zeus*, Latin *Ju-piter*, god of the shining heaven. Originally supreme god, he became the Teutonic Mars (giving the name to Tuesday, *dies Martis*); a few traces of his worship are found, notably an inscription in England. His supremacy was overthrown by Wodan (Anglo-Saxon *Woden*; Scandinavian *Odin*), the god of wind and storm, *'Mercurius'* in Roman interpretation (hence Wednesday)."[302]

That, at its core, this was a linguistic theory primarily based on the names of the days of the week is made abundantly clear in the *Encyclopædia of Religion and Ethics* (1914), which states:

"We, find among the Teutons three specially prominent gods, who, moreover, are met with in all the different tribes, and must, accordingly, have come down from a period when the Teutons were still an undivided people. These three are *Wôðanaz*, the god of the dead and of the wind; *Þonaraz*, the god of thunder and of the sky; and *Tiwaz*, the god of war. With these is associated a female figure who appears in the OHG sources as Fria, in the ON as Frigg ("the beloved," "the wife"), and is always regarded as the consort of Wodan. Roman writers identify Wodan with Mercury; Donor—in the earlier period—with Hercules, and subsequently with Jupiter; Ziu-Tyr with Mars; and Fria-Frigg with Venus; and thus, when the Roman calendar was introduced among the Teutons, the *dies Martis* was rendered Tuesday, the *dies Mercurii* Wednesday, the *dies Jovis* Thursday (Norse *Thorsdagr*), and the *dies Veneris* Friday."

Along with the names of the weekdays, the only other hard evidence for *Tiwaz* mentioned was the "inscription in England" cited above, which is a Roman epigraph found on the British frontier. Based on it, "the old sky-god" *Tiwaz* was promoted to a god of legal proceedings by the early 1900s. The same source goes on to say:

---

[302] Charles Kendall Adams, Vol. 8, p. 82.

"The third pan-Teutonic god was the war-god—the OHG *Zio*, AS *Tyw*, ON *Tyr*, whose name appears in the OHG *Ziestag*, AS *Tiwesdæg*, ON *Tyrsdagr*. He has often been regarded as a survival of *Tiwaz*, the Teutonic sky-god of pre-historic times, but in our extant sources he is never anything else than the god of war. ...Batavian mercenaries stationed near Hadrian's wall dedicated altars to him as *Mars Thingsus* (*Things* another appellation of *Zio*; cf. *Dien-* in German *Dienstag*, 'Tuesday'), the god of the popular assembly (cf. Danish *Ting*).

The inscription *Mars Thingsus* (*Deo Marti Thincso*) occurs on a single altar from the Roman fort of Vercovicium at Housesteads in Northumberland, dated to the third century. It is thought to have been erected by Frisian mercenaries stationed at Hadrian's Wall. This dedication has been interpreted to mean "Mars of the Assembly" based on the Old Icelandic *Þing* (Thing), "legal assembly." As support, the OHG *Dienstag, Dingstag* for Tuesday was regarded as designating "assembly day" and the old Germanic "sky-god" *Tiwaz*, via his connection to Mars, took on a judicial function for the first time. Edgar Polemé (1996) summarized the theory this way:

"Among the South Germans, *Tiwaz* (= Tyr) was expressed as Mars in the *interpretatio romana*. This Mars, however, also has juridical aspects, as witnessed by inscriptions referring to *Mars Thingsus*, the Mars of the Thing."[303]

In the 1930s, Jan de Vries argued that the priestly role of the Germanic king was originally separate from the military role as reflected in Tacitus' distinction between the Germanic *rex*, "king," chosen for his birth and the *dux*, "war-chief," chosen for his valor (*Germania* ch. 7). He speculated that these two aspects of kingship were originally rooted in the different functions of the gods *Tiwaz*

---

[303] *Indo-European Religion After Dumézil* (1996), p. 63. Note the incorrect use of the plural "inscriptions."

(Tyr) and *Woden*.[304] According to DeVries, the priestly functions, which reflected the sacral aspect of the ruler, were also centered in *Tiwaz*, god of order and law, as evidenced in Tacitus' designations "priest and king" in *Germania* 10:

"Kept at the public expense, in these same woods and groves, are white horses, pure from the taint of earthly labour; these are yoked to a sacred car, and accompanied by the *priest and the king* (*sacerdos ac rex*), or chief of the tribe, who note their neighings and snortings."

On the strength of this rather weak argument, DeVries held that early Germanic kingship was originally priestly in nature and therefore dominated by the highest god *Tiwaz* —his high rank, however, was based solely on a linguistic comparison of his unattested name with the recorded names of the rulers of other Indo-European pantheons, even though *Tiw* was actually equated with Mars! DeVries speculated that Woden must have come to prominence as a war-leader during the early migration period, causing the role of the "priest-king" *Tiwaz* to decline.

Georges Dumézil, recognizing the inherent problem with the linguistic argument in the 1950s, embraced DeVries' tripartite theory, emphasizing the function of gods over their names, thereby equating *Tiwaz* and Odin with the Hindu gods Mitra and Varuna, whom he saw as fulfilling first function roles of lawgiver and king. Dumézil writes:

"As for the consequences of the relative chronology that one deduces from the equation *Dyauh* = *Zeus* = *Jupiter* = *Tiuz* (supposing that equation is exact: there are reasons for deriving *Týr* and *Zio* rather from *deiwo-*, the generic Indo-European name for the gods), these consequences are founded on a simplistic and erroneous interpretation of this equation, and more generally on a false conception of the role and prerogatives of linguistics in such

---

[304] William A. Chaney, *The Cult of Kingship in Anglo-Saxon England* (1970), p. 13

matters. ...The agreeable phonetic conformity of *Zeus, Jupiter,* and *Dyauh*, precious for the linguist, does not carry the mythologist very far. He quickly notices that the first two gods and the third do not in the least do the same things. The Vedic god, who is without great actuality, scarcely goes beyond the materiality of the luminous sky, which taken as a noun, his name signifies. Jupiter and Zeus, on the contrary, are not the sky made divine (which Ouranos, the grandfather of Zeus, onomastically is), but the very real, very personal king of the gods and of men, and the lightning god. ...Under the same conditions, it is therefore possible that the old Indo-European name **Dyeu-* in its supposed Germanic form **Tiuz*, does not apply to the god who is functionally analogous to *Dyauh*, nor even perhaps to *Zeus* and *Jupiter*. The functions of these last two may have been assumed, among the Germanic peoples, by a god bearing another name, a new name, properly Germanic. It is possible by the same reasoning that **Tiuz*, if indeed there was a **Tiuz*, might have co-existed with another god, **Woðanaz*, Indo-European in function and in his position in the tripartite structure, but not in his name," [305]

Dumézil believed that the Indo-Europeans tended to organize their societies and their pantheons in the same manner. He proposed a tripartite system broken down into three primary functions: 1) maintenance of the religious and judicial order, 2) military prowess, and 3) the provision of sustenance. In the Germanic pantheon, he proposed that Odin and Tyr once fulfilled these "first function" roles. Although Tacitus states in *Germania* 11 that legal issues among the Germanic tribes are settled by a gathered group of elite leaders or else by the general assembly, Dumézil made Tyr (**Tiwaz*, which he writes as **Tiuz*) the chief justice, remarking: "In my research Jan de Vries has aided me greatly with his passages devoted to the Germanic god Romanized as Mars." [306]

---

[305] Georges Dumézil, *Gods of the Ancient Northmen*, edited by Einar Haugen, (1973); chapter 2: "Magic, War, and Justice: Odin and Tyr", translated by John Lindow, p. 37.
[306] *Mitra-Varuna: An Essay on Two Indo-European Representations of*

Many of Dumézil's ideas concerning Odin were developed and popularized by subsequent authors, particulary the notion that Odin was an Indo-European god of sovereignty who eventually overshadowed and supplanted *Tiwaz* as the supreme god of the Germans. He suggested that Odin's function as a war-god was an extention of his role as a god of sovereignty, since sovereigns must fight wars, and as such he eventually replaced Tyr, who was the true god of war. He felt this explanation was obvious in regard to Odin, since "in the practices of the Germanic peoples, war invaded all, colored everything," noting that "one could peruse all Scandinavian literature (except the escatology, where as a rule all the gods must fight) without finding a scene where Tyr appears or does anything on a battlefield." Dumézil agreed with DeVries, who concluded "in general, too much emphasis has been placed on the warlike aspects of Tyr, and his significance for the Germanic law has not been sufficiently recognized."[307] Dumézil cites the third century Frisian inscription *Mars Thingsus* and the translation of *Tiwesdaeg* (Tyr's day) as *dingesdach* in Middle Low German and Middle Dutch as *dinxendach*, "Thing day" or "Assembly day", as evidence of this equation, despite the fact that Scandinavian literature also lacks a scene where Tyr appears or does anything at a legal assembly.

Throughout the remainder of the twentieth century, scholars promoted the tenuous theory of the old Germanic sky-god *Tiwaz* as fact. In *Pagan Scandinavia* (1967), Hilda Ellis Davidson wrote: "At the time of Tacitus the Germanic gods are believed to be Tiwaz and Wodan, called Mars and Mercury by the Romans. Tiwaz appears to have been the supreme sky-god, who also ruled the battlefield and established law among men. Wodan was the god of the dead, associated with magic and inspiration." In 1969, she elaborated: "There is some reason to believe that Wodan/Odin, the Germanic god of magic and the dead, took over some of the powers of the

---

Sovereignty (1988), p. 125.

[307] Ibid., p. 44, quoting DeVries.

earlier Tiwaz, the god of the sky who also presided over battle."[308] Unfortunately, she did not state what that reason is. The evidence certainly had not changed, but the theories that took root in it had grown so thick by the 1960s, the resulting bramble today is nearly impregnable. Despite the lack of hard evidence, the belief that Tyr is a displaced sky-god is almost universally accepted. Common wisdom now holds that Tyr the one-handed is the Germanic heir to the mantle of the ancient Indo-European Sky-Father.[309] Yet, outside of linguistic theory, there is no direct evidence to support this claim. The name *Tiwaz remains unattested and Odin/Mercury has held the prominent spot in the Germanic pantheon since the beginning of the historical record.

Even though Tyr is often assumed to have once been a more powerful deity and ruler of the Germanic gods, he remains a relatively obscure figure in the Germanic sources. He first appears as a distinct deity in the Eddas. Tyr sits at the table in Lokasenna, rising to defend Freyr from Loki's abuse, and in Hymiskviða, he accompanies Thor to the giant Hymir's home to fetch a brewing kettle. Although Snorri calls him the son of Odin, the Hymiskviða-poet calls him the son of Hymir, perhaps due to the Germanic tradition of fosterage.[310] In Gylfaginning, Tyr is the only god brave enough to feed the young wolf-pup Fenrir, and the only one daring enough to place a hand in the monster's mouth when it came time to bind him. For this act of valor, he lost his sword-hand. In the end, his sacrifice comes to naught, when the wolf breaks free and swallows Odin whole.

---

[308] Gelling and Davidson, *Chariot of the Sun.*

[309] In some pagan circles, *Tiwaz is given a wife, Zisa, a local Suevian goddess who had a wooden temple in Ausberg, attested in the eleventh century (TM, p. 292). Grimm associates her name with a "supposed" feminine *Ziu,* stating she thus has "all the better right to be placed by our *Zio,*" characterizing his own argument as a "guess," (TM, p. 298).

[310] *Fosterage,* the practice of raising children of a higher social standing, in order to cement political relationships. *Skáldskaparmál* 4 preserves evidence that Thor was fostered by the giants Vingnir and Hlóra, characterized as Loricus, Duke of Thrace, and his wife Lora in the *Prologue to Gylfaginning.*

"Mars or Tyr"
18th century Icelandic manuscript

At its very core, the identification of Tyr with the ancient sky-god is based on nothing more than a comparison of the name Tyr with the names of other Indo-European Sky-Fathers. While it is true that the name Tyr is cognate with *Dyeus*, the first part of *Dyeus Pater*, the god Tyr is not. He is never referred to as father and is not associated with the sky in the Germanic record. He possesses none of the attributes characteristic of the Indo-European Sky-Father. If Tyr ever held such a position, no record of it remains. His name simply means "god" in Old Norse and is closely connected with other words meaning "god" and "divinity" in other Germanic and Indo-European languages. The singular form -*týr* frequently occurs as a suffix in epithets of Odin, as shown above, and the plural form *tívar* applies to

175

the gods collectively. All else is supposition based on assumption. As Rudolf Simek[311] illustrates:

> "The Old Scandinavian name for the Germanic god of the sky, war, and council *Tiwaz* (OHG Ziu) who is the only Germanic god who *was already important* in Indo-European times: Old Indic Dyaus, Greek Zeus, Latin Jupiter ...ON *tívar*, (plural to Týr) are all closely related etymologically to each other. ...*Despite his early importance*, Tyr is a relatively unimportant god in the ON mythology of the Eddas. ...He *must have* played a more important role at some stage as is clear from the plural of his name *tívar* meaning 'gods' as well as the fact that in skaldic poetry his name could be used as the basic word in kennings for other gods, especially for Odin; this proves that his name originally, but still in Viking times, could simply mean 'god.'"

The apparent etymological identity between *Týr* and **Dyeus* and the speculations that followed led early scholars like H.M. Chadwick, who attributed the theory to Henry Petersen (1876), to hypothesize that a local war-god named Odin had usurped Tyr's functions sometime before the sixth century when the name Odin first appeared, and that his cult became pan-Germanic by the Viking Age.[312] Not only is such a rapid spread of a cult extremely unlikely, there is no clear basis for such a major shift in the Germanic religion in the prehistoric past in either the available literary or archaeological records. For this reason, some scholars have begun to back away from this theory. When discussing the one-handed god, Andy Orchard (1997) merely states:

> "Týr's very name, of course, is apt to sow confusion being derived from Germanic **Tiwaz* as a simple noun for 'god' and related to both Greek *Zeus* and Latin *deus*. The singular form of his

---

[311] *Dictionary of Northern Mythology*, s.v. *Týr*.
[312] Chadwick, *The Cult of Othin* (1901), p. 49 cites: H. Petersen *Om Nordboernes Gudekyrelse og Gudetro i Hedenold* (1876); Wolfgang Golther, *Germanische Mythologie,* p. 223; and Eugene Mogk in Paul's *Grundriss der Germanischen Philologie* I, p. 1070.

name often occurs in poetic periphrases or kennings for the other Æsir, while the plural form, *tívar*, simply means 'gods.'"[313]

Avoiding the reconstructed form **Tiwaz* altogether, John Lindow (2001) agrees, stating "Etymologically, Týr's name is related to an Indo-European root meaning 'deity' (e.g. compare the Latin *deus*)."[314] More recently, scholars such as Martin L. West have taken a more circumspect approach, suggesting instead that Odin may have "stepped into an older scheme in which the Sky became father of the gods and men in marriage to the Earth."[315] Ursula Dronke concurs, noting that Odin or his Indo-European ancestor is best interpreted as a solar deity, who, like the sun, had only one eye that sees everything. He travels and visits the homes of men like the sun, and as the originator of life, "like the sun, he is *Alföðr*." His fate, like that of the sun, is to be swallowed by a wolf. Dronke concludes that "this vast background of archaic fragments" helps to explain Odin's place as the foremost god in Germanic mythology, a role he retained beyond the end of the heathen age and into the modern era.[316] Martin L. West writes:

> "A Germanic reflex of the god **Dyeus* is not readily identified, since (as already noted) the Nordic Tyr and his continental cognates seem to derive their names from the generic title **deiwós* and do not resemble **Dyeus* in character. It is possible, however, that Wodan-Odin (proto-Germanic **Woðanaz*) while not being a direct continuation of **Dyeus* took over certain of his features. In Lombardic myth as retailed by Paulus Diaconus (1.8), Wodan was imagined habitually surveying the earth from his window, beginning at sunrise. This corresponds to the position of Odin in the Eddas. He has the highest seat among the gods, and from it surveys all the worlds, rather as Zeus, sitting on the peak of Mt. Ida, can survey not only the Troad, but Thrace and Scythia too.

---

[313] Simek, ibid., p. 168.
[314] *Handbook of Norse Mythology*, p. 299.
[315] *Indo-European Poetry and Myth*, (2007), p. 183.
[316] Dronke, *Poetic Edda*, Vol. II, (1997), p. 126.

Odin also has the distinctive title of father. In the poems he is called *Alföðr*, 'All-father.'"[317]

Why Odin cannot be "a direct continuation of **Dyeus* is left unsaid. The weight of evidence certainly converges on that conclusion. As the first god called by a Germanic name recognizable in later eddic and skaldic poetry, Odin's first appearance in literary sources need not correspond to his actual rise to the head of the pantheon. Because he has clear analogs in related Indo-European mythologies, it is likely Odin was venerated among the Germanic people under other titles before being recorded in historical sources. Odin alone, and not Tyr, exhibits the essential character of the Indo-European Sky-Father in all but name. This is not to suggest that his character remained static from the Indo-European era to the rise of Christianity. Ethnic idols, unlike their revealed counterparts bound by written scriptures, tend to change as the culture of their adherents changes. Therefore, it seems certain that Odin's character evolved over time adapting to the changing cultural realities of his votaries. As Scandinavians developed from a decentralized tribal society into smaller and larger kingdoms, and eventually into nation states, this would naturally be reflected in their mythology. Once the Germanic tongue differentiated from its Proto-Indo-European stem and began to develop independently, the Germanic gods also began to evolve independently, distinguishing themselves from their forebears. In Northern Europe, **Dyeus Pater*, a god of the bright sky with solar associations, appears to have retained his primary characteristics while becoming the one-eyed Odin. His single eye accentuated his role as a sky-god, serving double duty symbolically. Odin's good eye can be interpreted as the sun, the "one eye in the sky", while his missing eye, hidden in Mimir's well, can be seen as the sun's reflection in water. When the sun and moon appear in the sky together, the moon takes on the appearance of a dead or clouded eye, compared to the glowing orb of the sun. The position of Odin's

---

[317] West, ibid., p. 173

throne in Asgard at the apex of heaven, peering down on Creation, marks high noon, just as the geographical sites of the two other two divine tribes, Alfheim in the east and Vanaheim in the west, mark sunrise and sunset. His role as progenitor was emphasized, reflected in such names as *Alföðr*, "All-Father"; *Aldaföðr*, "Father of men"; *Galdraföðr*, "Father of *galdur* (Old English *gealdor*, spell-songs)"; *Herföðr* and *Herjaföðr*, "Father of Hosts"; *Jölfuðr* or *Jölföðr*, "Yule Father"; and *Sigföðr*, "Father of Victory." Less apparent in this regard perhaps is the phallic imagery associated with Odin. Described as the "one-eyed", "hooded" god with a broad hat who hangs headdown from the world-tree,[318] he appears to embody the uncircumcised penis hanging from the male body, represented by the world-tree. In addition, Odin may represent the Tree itself and by extension the male form. In *Völuspá* 17, the first man is named *Askur*, "Ash." Beginning in strophe 29 of *Grímnismál*, the world-tree is designated as *Askur Yggdrassils* seven times. This, its most common designation, appears to be a kenning signifying "the Ash of Ygg's (Odin's) horse" or "the Man (rider) of Odin's horse", i.e. Odin himself, and may be the original designation of Yggdrassil.[319] This conceit is most apparent in the mead myth when Odin enters Gunnlod's cave in the guise of a snake through a bored hole. The phallic imagery is overt. In the end, he escapes as an eagle with the stolen mead of poetry in three vessels with names belonging to the three wells that feed the Tree. To underscore the validity of this interpretation, Yggdrassil is pictured with the serpent Nidhögg gnawing at its roots and an eagle perched atop its crown. This subtle conceit may also explain the

---

[318] In *Hávamál* 139, Odin peers downward into Mimir's well and takes up the runes, suggesting he hung from his feet, the only position that would allow him to do so. See Jere Fleck, "*Óðinn's Self-Sacrifice;* Parts I and II in *Scandinavian Studies*, Vol. 43, Nos. 2 and 4, 1971.

[319] The name Yggdrasil, otherwise attested as *Askur Yggdrasils,* occurs once in all of eddic poetry; It is found in both the *Codex Regius* and *Hauksbók* mss. versions of *Völuspá* 17 which read, *Ask veit ek standa, heitir Yggdrasill*, "I know an ash standing named Yggdrasil." The same verse, cited in the *Codex Regius* mss. of *Gylfaginning* 16 reads, *Ask veit ek ausinn heitir Yggdrasils*, "I know an ash sprinkled named Yggdrasil's", which is a paraphrase of *Askur Yggdrasils*.

phallic shape of several standing runestones, some of which may bear images of Odin.

At the time the eddic songs were composed. Odin clearly held a central place at the head of the Germanic pantheon, as its ruler and progenitor. Likewise, Odin's wife appears to have evolved from an agricultural goddess once firmly rooted in the land to a more domestic goddess overseeing activities of the home, such as spinning, child rearing and household chores. This development would have been a slow organic process, over the course of several generations, barely perceptible to the religion's adherents as Germanic society became less nomadic and more settled. In the same manner, Snorri's *Edda* testifies to how the perception of the old gods had evolved in the twelfth and thirteenth centuries, long after the Christian conversion.

In *Gods of the Ancient Northmen*, George Dumézil raised and refuted the primary arguments against Odin being an ancient Indo-European god. As he saw it, there were three primary objections: 1) the relative rarity of Odinic placenames in Scandinavia and their complete absence in Iceland, 2) the nearly complete parallel absence of Odinic personal names, and 3) the lack of a god corresponding to Odin in the mythology the Saami borrowed from the Scandinavians, which honors Thor, Freyr and Njord. Rather than attribute these facts to the lateness, either of the god or his rank in the Nordic pantheon, Dumézil offered other plausible explanations: If Odin was always the first-function god of chieftains and the great Scandinavian sorcerer, he had no chance of being adopted by the Saami who had their own magic tradition, independent from their neighbors. On the other hand, gods of thunder, fecundity and navigation would be of practical value. In rural areas, it is completely understandable that farmsteads, hamlets and seaports would receive their names from beneficial patron gods, in hopes of receiving their blessings. As the head of statistically small social groups, nobility and skalds, Odin's name naturally would not occur as frequently in such toponymns. The total lack of Odinic placenames in Iceland confirms this view.

Founded as a "veritable republic of rich peasants", its settlers would have had little occasion to name a single place after the god-king. The rarity of personal names containing that of Odin, according to Dumézil, could equally be explained by his character, which in some respects was "disquieting and terrifying." An analogous situation occurs among the Indo-Iranians, who record many proper names which contain the divine names Mithra and Indra, but none containing Varuna, whose correspondence to Odin is striking. Dumézil notes that Oscar Montelius, the famous Swedish archeologist, saw the advent of runic writing, imported from the south during the Christian era, as the *terminus a quo* (earliest possible date) for Odin, the god of runes, but he did not find this argument compelling either, since runes, however recent they may be, would have fallen under the purview of Odin, the highest magician. The word *rúnar* itself derives from an old Germanic root which designated magical secrets. In Gothic, the word *runa* only had the sense of "secret, secret decision", akin to the Old Irish *rūn* "secret, mystery". The Finnish borrowing, *runo*, only refers to epic and magic chants. Thus Odin could have been the master of such secret knowledge long before the word became a technical term for written signs. The sheer number and diversity of the domains in which Odin operates would seem to confirm that he had usurped or grown into at least some of these roles. As the ruler of the gods, their greatest magician, the patron of poets, kings and elite bands of warriors, as well as their host in the afterlife, not to mention his agricultural functions derived from folklore, is it not too much for any single god to play so large a role? According to Dumézil, this too can be explained by his status as a god of the first function, which contains all of the others. In Dumézil's opinion, critics would not have given much credence to such flimsy arguments against Odin's age and function if they had not relied on the linguistic theory placing *Tiwaz* at the head of the Germanic pantheon.

Odin the Wanderer
George von Rosen, 1886

The final barrier barring Odin from being a direct hier to the Indo-European godhead *Dyeus Pater* is his status as a liminal god, often cited as certain evidence for his late rise. By most accounts, Odin was the patron of poets, warriors, kings and sorcerors. Despite being the central figure most closely associated with northern society's cultural and political elite, the primary producers and consumers of the Norse sources, Odin consistently appears to operate at its moral and geographical edges.[320] Examples of this are neither isolated nor idiosyncratic. Although he clearly possesses central places of his own, such as Asgard and Valhalla where his throne is located, Odin seemingly spends little time in the places over

---

[320] The argument and examples that follow reflect those of Kevin J. Wanner in "God on the Margins: Dislocation and Transience in the Myths of Óðinn" in *History of Religions* 46, no. 4 (May 2007): 316-350.

which he reigns. Odin's mythos is characterized by motifs of both social and spatial marginality. To some this indicates his original position as an outsider and a usurper, however, in the Indo-European context, Odin's status as a traveller does not preclude his role as leader. In the known myths, Odin travels to the worlds of men, giants and death, often putting his own life in danger. Many of his names indicate his status as a wanderer between worlds: *Fráríðr* (One Who Rides Forth), *Gangleri* (Travel-Weary), *Váfuðr* (Wayfarer), *Vegtamr* (Way-Tamer), *Gestr* (Guest) and *Gestumblindi* (Blind Guest). Despite occasionally traveling in the company of other gods, he most often journeys alone, in disguise, and with covert intent. He is described as wearing a cloak, a beard and a hat which conceal his face. In whatever guise he chooses, Odin most often appears as an old man with one-eye, a persistant feature by which he can be recognized. This characteristic seems to have developed in the more militaristic Germanic milieu then in constant conflict with the Roman empire, where war-injuries were presumably commonplace among men of a mature age. There is some evidence, however, that this motif may have already been introduced into Proto-Germanic mythology prior to its separation from the PIE stem, since it recurs in both Roman and Celtic sources.[321] As described by Dionysius of Halicarnassus in *Roman Antiquities*, Book 5, ch. 23, during the first war of the Republic, as the Roman army retreated in disorder over the Tiber bridge, Horatius *Cocles* (the "one-eyed") held the attention of the opposing army by casting terrifying looks at it. The author adds, "his miraculous audacity paralyzed the enemy," an attribute shared by Odin according to *Ynglingasaga* 6. As one of three brothers involved in the defense of a fortress with a special bridge, Horatius shows a number of parallels to Odin including once being wounded with a spear and receiving land obtained by ploughing.[322] Described as high-

---

[321] My thanks to Carla O'Harris for drawing my attention to these.
[322] Odin hangs on the world-tree wounded with a spear in *Hávamál* 138, and obtains land by ploughing from King Gylfi through Gefjon, one of the Æsir, before meeting the king in person in the opening chapter of *Gylfaginning*.

born and "of all men, the most remarkable for the fine proportion of his limbs," he exhibits evidence of worship such as having a grove and statue consecrated to him, where gifts including food were offered. Georges Dumézil, who first pointed out this legend when speaking of the relationship between Odin and Tyr, notes that the scope of these parallels is extremely unequal.[323] In Rome Horatius *Cocles* performs illustrious feats with no other interest than that of patriotic propaganda, while in Scandinavia Odin's mutilation is clearly symbolic, creating and manifesting his character as a paralyzing visionary. Drawing a parallel between Tyr and the hero Mucius Scævola (the Left-handed) in chapter 29 of the same source, Dumézil notes that the nature of such rare analogies excludes the possibility that they are independent, and raises the possibility that one derived from the other. Likewise, in the Irish euhemerizations of Celtic mythology, Lug the Long-Handed and Nuadu Silver-Hand (so named because his hand was severed in battle) correspond to Odin and Tyr. Because any blemish disqualified one from being a king in Irish culture, Nuadu is replaced by Lug. Associated with a magic spear, like Odin, Lug is best known for defeating Balor, a giant with one eye which never opened except in battle where it paralyzed hosts. A similar quality is attributed to Odin's eyes in *Hávamál* 150. Since these correspondances were first noticed, scholars have scoured world mythologies seeking the combination of the One-eyed and the One-handed. Only the Irish epic presents something comparable, although noticeably more distant. However, the plots of the Scandinavian and the Roman analogies cited above are too different to suppose a direct or indirect loan from one to the other causing Dumézil to conclude that the only natural explanation was for the Germanic and Romanic peoples to have retained this original pairing from their common origins.[324]

Apart from having numerous aliases tied to his many adventures, some of Odin's epithets refer to his habit of traveling

---

[323] Dumézil, *Mitra-Varuna* (1940).
[324] Dumézil, *Gods of the Ancient Northmen*, pp. 46-47.

incognito: *Fjölnir* (Concealer), *Grímnir* (Masked One), *Hengikeptr* (Hang-Jaw), Löndungr (Shaggy-cloak), and *Síðhöttr* (Longhood). In the *Eddas* and Sagas, he is often depicted clandestinely traveling to the worlds of men, the giants and the dead. He opens *Hávamál* with sage advice to those who would be wayfarers and guests, to watch and be wary, while in *Vafþrúðnismál*, perhaps the most representative story of a disguised Odin, he repeats the refrain, "much have I traveled" seven times. On this occasion, he visits Vafþrúðnir's hall "to contend in ancient staves with that all-wise giant." The contest ends abruptly when Odin poses a question only he can answer: "What words did Odin utter into the ear of his son, before he was placed on the pyre?" Having lost the contest, albeit through a ruse, the giant forfeits his head (st. 19). Most often such disguises permit Odin entry into places controlled by others and give him the tactical advantage required to achieve his goal. His stories are marked by themes of death, fate, and sacrifice, reflecting Odin's primary aims: a perpetual quest for knowledge and the attainment of noble warriors for Valhall. Both are part of the god's preparation for Ragnarök and tied to the general theme of impermanence, characteristic of Germanic lore. This fatalism is evident in the mythology, as well as in legendary sagas such as *Beowulf*, *Völsungasaga*, and the Nibelungen cycle. Odin's journeys into Jötunheim are clearly aimed at gaining knowledge or the means to preserve and transmit it. His quest for such intelligence is most often interpreted as an effort to forestall the foretold fates of both himself and the world or to mitigate their effects. In this context, Odin's seemingly fickle nature, often turning on those he favors, is seen as a positive trait. Rather than being seen as a betrayal of those who serve him, Odin's reception of fallen warriors is frequently described in terms of sacrifice. A subgenre of court poetry trumpets the arrival of slain kings into Valhall. Their reversal in fortune is accepted and justified. Odin's decision that a notable warrior should die in battle was seen as flattering and even necessary, since Odin gathers only the best to fight beside him on the final day, presumably reconciling those facing the real prospect of death and defeat on the battlefield to their fates. Rather than argue that this material represents the common ideology or ethos of the Norse people, Kevin Wanner (2007), the author of this theory, purposes that,

> "What we have, in essence, is a poet's eye view of Norse myth, whether accessible directly in the work of eddic and skaldic composers or at one remove, as in the poetics of Snorri or the sagas and histories that rely heavily and often explicitly on verse traditions. Or, to consider the problem from the side of the consumer, the vast majority of these works we know to have been produced for royal, noble, or other elite patrons." [325]

In the Germanic context, the myths of Odin with their motifs of marginality best reflect the social realities of the poets and their consumers, kings and nobility, who, like Odin, were perpetual travelers and guests. Although known skalds after 900 AD were almost exclusively from Iceland, largely settled by Norwegians who had fled the centralization of power pursued by Harald hárfagri and thus rejected kingship, those who aspired to be court poets, had little choice but to travel to Norway, Denmark, or Sweden and seek patrons among the network of kings and nobles reigning there. Likewise, the custom among Scandinavian kings of not having a fixed place of residence or single center of power can be traced through to the earliest history and likely prehistory of Germanic social organization. This so-called ambulatory or itinerant kingship finds support in both the literary and archaeological record. In the Middle Ages, kings could claim hospitality for themselves, their retinues, and their agents among any of their subjects. The obligation to contribute food and necessities for the royal household as it traveled from place to place constituted one of the earliest forms of taxation. This right was so abused that in the late thirteenth century attempts were made in all three kingdoms to regulate it. The conversion to Christianity legitimized the concentration of power in fixed sites. According to

---

[325] Wanner, ibid., pp. 340-350.

Knut Helle,[326] the conversion-era kingships of Óláfr Tryggvason, Óláfr Haraldsson and Harald harðráði were marked by political and religious unification, as well as a growing awareness of the importance of urban centers. For this reason, later kings' sagas depict Norwegian rulers as active promoters of the first towns. The notion of a capital city as the permanent royal residence, however, was not a heathen ideal and only occurred centuries later in Christian times when it was falsely attributed to Odin in the *Prologue* to the *Prose Edda*. He is portrayed there, not as a god, but as a human immigrant from Asia who arrived with his retinue in Sweden in the aftermath of the Trojan War (c. 1200 BC) and founded a new city, based on the model of Old Asgard, which its Christian author Snorri Sturluson identified as the classical city of Troy in Turkey. Although attributed to the heathen "king" Odin, the idea is clearly a late synthesis of native Scandinavian and Roman Catholic history, which itself was a hybrid of Biblical and Classical Roman history.

Today some scholars[327] equate Snorri's fictive history of Odin and his Asia-men with the so-called Proto-Indo-Europeans, a theoretical tribe of people speaking a single tongue that would ultimately produce the major languages of Europe, Central Asia and the Indian-subcontinent, inferred from a comparative linguistic theory which was not formulated until the late 1700s. Despite having no direct attestation of the PIE language, linguists using the comparative method estimate a datespan from 4,500 to 2,500 BC for the dispersal of the earliest form of the *ur*-language, much too old to be Troy. There is no reason to believe that Snorri or his literary predecessors had any real information about the movements of their ancestors two to three thousand years before their day. This effectively rules out Odin as an actual foreign immigrant to Scandinavia. In reality, he enters the historic record as Mercury, a

---

[326] "The History of the Early Viking Age in Norway" (1998) cited by Wanner.
[327] https://bladehoner.wordpress.com/2017/11/16/snorris-ancestral-stories-about-the-men-from-asia/ "Snorri´s Ancestral Stories about the 'Men from Asia'", November 16, 2017 for example.

native Germanic god called by a Roman name, said to be foremost among deities and worshipped by kings, who trace their genealogies back to him. As Odin, he remained the ruling god of the migrant Germanic tribes who had by then moved into southern Europe long after their Proto-Indo-European forebears had become settled in the North. Thus, we find an unbroken chain of evidence for the All-Father Odin, who first appears by that name in the seventh century, fully recognizable as the Indo-European Sky-Father *Dyeus Pater* by his main attributes, if not by his name. References to the Gaulish, Germanic and Scythian Mercury forge links between the two. The chain can be extended further through the legends of Frau Holle and her husband leading the Wild Hunt from the Middle Ages forward to the present day.

Wotan's Head
Hans Thoma, 1919

VI. The Wild Hunt

"Wodan's name is associated with a spectral host which has been seen at least into the beginning of this century throughout Germania, galloping madly through the night sky over field and forest and through village streets. ...Complicating the picture are variants of the Hunt. In one there is a lone hunter —*der Wilde Jäger* himself— with his hounds, but no hunting party. He is after one of the ghastly witches; when he catches her he flings her over his horse. But there are also several hunts which are led by a Huntress named Fru Gode, Fru Waur, Frau Holda, Berchta and her alpine sister Perchta with her Perchten."

—Kris Kershaw, *The One-Eyed God* (2000), pp. 20-21

Throughout northern Europe, an enormous mass of material in the way of popular tales, legends, folklore and superstitions, depict Odin and his wife leading a Wild Hunt or Furious Host, riding through the skies at year's end. This host is typically called the *wütende her*, the furious host, but also *Wuotunges her*, Wodan's host.[328] In the howling wind of winter storms, people imagined that they heard the Wild Huntsman and his host, all mounted on snorting steeds and accompanied by baying hounds. In the southern parts of Germany, as well as on the borders of the Lower Rhine and in Thuringia, people believed that a host of damned souls wander restlessly until Judgement Day, swept along in the gales. But on the plains of Northern Germany and in Scandinavia, as well as in parts of England and Northern France, popular belief held that a spectral huntsman on horseback leads the pack.[329] Since the Middle Ages, this concept has played an important part in popular belief, where it is commonly known as the *wilde jagd* (Wild Hunt) in northern Germany, *witthendet heer* (the Furious Host) in southern Germany, and by other names, such as the *Asgardreia* (Asgard Ride) in Denmark, the *Herlathing* in

---

[328] Grimm, ibid., p. 919.
[329] Jan de Vries, *Contributions to the Study of Othin, Especially in his Relation to Agricultural Practices in Modern Popular Lore* (1931).

England, and *Mesnée d'Hellequin* in northern France. In Thuringia, Hesse, Franconia, and Swabia, the traditional term is *das wütende heer* (the Furious Host) and it must be of long standing use since Konrad von Heimesfurt, the twelfth century poet of *Diu Urstende* uses the term *daz wuetunde her* to describe the mob who condemned Christ; in *Rolandslied,* c. 1100 AD, Pharaoh's army, which pursued the Hebrews and was drowned in the Red Sea, is designated *sîn wôtigez her,* (204, 16);[330] and in *Reinfried of Brunswick,* a Swiss verse novel composed prior to 1291 AD, an unruly crowd awaiting the arrival of a knight is likewise called *daz wüetende her.*

Despite seemingly wide variations, these stories are uniform in their essential traits. In districts where the custom of sacrificing the last sheaf of grass to Odin's horse is practiced, the Wild Huntsman is commonly identified with the same god. Odin's original role as the leader of the Wild Hunt is established from parallel phrases and folktales across the region. The root of the whole notion is easily discerned in the expression *Wodejaget,* that is, "Wodan hunts" —used in Pomerania and Holstein when a rumbling in the air is heard. On hearing a noise at night, as of horses and carts, the Swedes say *Oden far förbi* ("Odin passes nearby") and in Skåne, the shrieking of seafowl on winter evenings is called *Odens jagt,* Odin's Hunt.

Despite various historical figures being placed at the head of this host, the Wild Huntsman himself is most often identified as Wodan. According to tales collected by Ernst Meier, he is described as handsome, proud and extraordinarily large, far superior to human size.[331] He possesses inexhaustible wealth and, like his wife, commonly gives seemingly insignificant gifts which are later transformed into gold. His train is made up of souls of the dead. As such, we occasionally find death described as "joining the old host." At the same time, we also find a woman, frequently identified as Odin's wife, at the head of the host, shepherding the souls of unbaptized children.

---

[330] Grimm, ibid., ch. 29.
[331] *Deutsche Sagen, Sitten und Gebräuche aus Schwaben* (1858).

Wotan by Arthur Rackham, 1913

While it cannot be maintained that all of this material hails from heathen times passed down to the modern era on the lips of common people, it is clear that the popular imagination further developed an existing idea, already widespread at the close of the heathen era. According to these legends, Odin hunts at the end of the year, especially in the time between Christmas and Twelfth-Night, when the winds blow their fiercest. As such, *Júlnir* or *Jölnir*, "Yule figure", occurs among Odin's names in *Snorri's Edda*. The peasants were always careful to leave the last sheaf of grain out in the fields to serve as fodder for his horse, "for the pagans believed that this same diabolical huntsman made his presence known in the fields at harvest time," according to Luthern clergyman Nicolaus Gryse, who first connected Odin's name to the Wild Hunt in 1593. The object of the hunt varies and was sometimes a spectral boar, a stag, a white-breasted maiden or some wood nymph. In the late Middle Ages, when the belief in Odin was largely forgotten, the leader of the Wild Hunt became Dietrich of Bern, Charlemagne, Frederick Barbarossa, King Arthur, King Waldemar of Denmark, or some Sabbath-breaker like Hans von Hackelberg, who, in punishment for his sin, was condemned to hunt in the air forever. In lower Germany, there are many such stories of one Hakkelberend, whose name points back to Odin, for Hakkelberend literally means "mantle-bearer" (from OHG *hakhul*; ON, *häkull* or *hekla*; AS *hacele*, drapery, mantle, armor; and *bär*, to bear).[332] Grimm was disposed to pronounce the Westphalian form Hackelberend the most ancient and genuine, suggesting that *hakolberand* was Old Saxon for a man in armor, based on Old Saxon *wâpanberand* (armiger), AS *helmberend, sweordberend*.[333] The Huntsman sometimes appears as a lone *Schimmelreiter* ("Ghostrider") on a white horse. On occasion he appears in a car drawn by four horses, cracking his whip as hunting horns blare in the distance.[334] At Ragnarök, when Heimdall blows his war-horn, Odin rides into battle with a helmet on his head (cp. *Sigurdrifumál* 14), leading valkyries and a host of fallen warriors (*Einherjar*) to face the assembled forces of evil. In the Icelandic sagas, Odin is pictured as a rider, clad in a long, dark-blue cloak and a broad-rimmed hat which shades his face. Likewise the Wild Huntsman frequently appears on horseback, clad in a broad hat and cloak. He is commonly accompanied by a train of spirits, consisting of both male and female apparitions, who are sometimes without heads or otherwise mutilated in some shocking manner. In the Norse myths, Odin himself is missing an eye (*Völuspá* 28). In *Gylfaginning* 41, we are told that for entertainment, the great troop of Einherjar residing in Odin's hall, "got dressed in war-gear every day and went out to the courtyard to fight each other and fall one upon the other," no doubt inflicting many injuries and hacking off limbs in the process which were miraculously restored each night.

---

[332] *The International Cyclopaedia*, Vol. 15 (1900), *sv* "Wild Hunt."
[333] Grimm, ibid., III, ch. 29: "helmet-bearer," "sword-bearer."
[334] Johann Wilhelm Wolf, *Beiträge zur Deutschen Mythologie*, Volume 2 (1858), p. 129.

On occasion, the horseman himself is headless. In the Harz, where the Wild Hunt thunders past the Eichelberg, the Wild Huntsman appears mounted on a headless black horse, carrying a riding crop in one hand and a bugle in the other. Between blasts of his horn, he cries "Hoho! Hoho!"

The Wild Hunt
F. W. Heine, 1882

Behind Wodan ride plenty of women, huntsmen and dogs. Sometimes, the Furious Host is made up of benign spirits, but more often of drunks, suicides and other malefactors. According to E.M.

Arndt, this eerie rabble consisted of thieves, robbers, killers and witches. Is this because Odin's original mission was to cleanse the air of evil spirits (cp. *Hávamál* 155) and rid society of unseemly elements, or perhaps simply because his role had been degraded to that of a demon in Christian times? "In the oldest Christian glosses," Jacob Grimm observes, "*wôtan* stands for *tyrannus, herus malus* (tyrant, evil master)"; he remarks that "the form *wuotunc* seems not to differ in sense. An unprinted poem of the thirteenth century has *Wüetunges her* apparently for the *wütende heer*, the host led as it were by Wuotan," now degraded to a fiendish, bloodthirsty being, whose name lives on as a form of cursing in Low German popular expressions, as in Westphalia's *O Woudan, Woudan!* and in Mecklenburg's *Wod, Wod!*[335] In this regard, it is worth noting that Johannes Geiler von Kaysersberg (1445-1510), who preached on the *wütede* or *wütische heer*, claimed that all who died a violent death "ere that God hath set it for them" joined the Furious Host.

In heathen Lappland, similar beliefs about the Wild Hunt prevailed. There, a specific sacrifice to the Furious Host is described in 1673. As in many other locations, they are conceived of as a ghostly troop that rides through the air and forests at Yuletide:

> "There are certain days which they regard with a great deal of superstition, especially the first day of Christmas, when the masters of families don't care to come to church themselves, but send only their sons, daughters and maids. The reason they allege for it is, that they dread the apparition of spirits, which they say wander about the air in great numbers on this day, and which must be appeased by certain sacrifices, of which we shall speak hereafter. ...These they call the *Juhlafolket* (Yule Folk), deriving their name from the word *Juhli* (Yule), which now signifies as much as the Feast of the Nativity of Christ, but in former Ages was used for the time of the New Year. But it being their opinion that more especially about this time the air is filled with spectres, they have given it this name. ...The day before the feast of the Juhlian Company, being Christmas eve and on Christmas day itself, they

---

335 Grimm, ibid., I, ch. 7.

offer superstitious sacrifices in honor of the Juhlian Company, the manner being thus: On Christmas eve they fast, or rather abstain from all sorts of meat; but of everything else they eat, they carefully preserve a small quantity. The same they perform on Christmas day, when they live very plentifully. All the bits they have preserved for these two days, they put in a small chest made of birch bark, in the shape of a boat, with its sails and oars; they pour also some of the fat of the broth upon it, and thus hang it on a tree, about a bowshot distant from the backside of their homes, for the use of the Juhlian Company, wandering at that time about the forests, mountains, and the air." [336]

The use of a boat sacrifice suggests a connection to the dead, often buried in ship-shaped mounds, interred within actual ships, or set adrift on such a vessel serving as a funeral pyre. Of Swedish peasants in 1870, Llewelyn Lloyd says: "the most singular and appalling superstition relating to '*Jul-night*' is the belief—one pretty generally entertained—that the dead rise from their grave."[337] Jacob Grimm (ch. 29) observes:

"With the coming of Christianity the fable could not but undergo a change. For the solemn march of gods, there now appeared a pack of horrid spectres, dashed with dark and devilish ingredients. Very likely the heathens themselves had believed that spirits of departed heroes took part in the divine procession; the Christians put into the host the unchristened dead, the drunkard, the suicide, who come before us in frightful forms of mutilation. ...Their ancient offerings too the people did not altogether drop, but limited them to the sheaf of oats for the celestial steed, as even Death (another hunter) has his bushel of oats."

Whatever its original form, by the Middle Ages the northern people dreaded the on-coming storm, declaring that it was the Wild

---

[336] Johannes Scheffer, *Lapponia* (1673), chs. 9-10, translated by Olaf Rudbeck (1704).
[337] *Peasant Life in Sweden*, p. 199.

Hunt sweeping across the sky. The sound of the Wild Hunt was frequently considered a presage of misfortune, pestilence or war. Similarly, popular superstitions held that the baying of hounds heard on a stormy night was an infallible presage of death. On rare occasions, the Wild Huntsman showed kindness toward strangers; but generally he brought harm, especially to anyone foolish enough to address him or join in his hunting cry, of which there are many stories of drunken persons having done. People considered it especially dangerous to mock the wild "Ho! Ho!" of the Huntsman, and those who did were immediately snatched up and whisked away with the Furious Host, while the few who joined the cry in good faith were rewarded. Only those who stepped aside into a tilled field, remained in the middle of the road, or threw themselves on the ground and remained silent, escaped the danger. Once when a carpenter mustered the courage to add his own "Hoho" to the Huntsman's call, a large black mass suddenly tumbled down his chimney onto the fire, scattering a spray of sparks and hot brands onto the people gathered before it. When the commotion cleared, a huge horse thigh lay on the hearth and the carpenter was dead.

At times, they say, the Huntsman shows kindness. Once a farmer in Gadendorf near Panker, while working late at night, left his door open. Suddenly, the Wild Huntsman came riding through it and took a loaf from the bread-rack. He rode out the side door, where the astonished farmer met him. "Because I have received this bread in your home," he said, "you shall never go without." From then on, the farmer never went hungry. Sometimes, the Huntsman comforts the lost. Once when a bold young girl imitated his hunting call, he suddenly stood before her and asked her why she had called him. The girl said she and her companions had lost her way and would soon starve since they had nothing to eat. She said she only wanted to ask him for some bread, salt and fat and wish him well on his way. He laughed and said it would be given to them, and at once a pot containing soup and dumplings appeared over a burning fire.[338]

---

[338] Johann Wilhelm Wolf, *Beiträge zur Deutschen Mythologie*, Volume 2 (1858), p. 132.

Odin and Brunnhilde
Ferdinand Leeke, 1890

That the Wild Huntsman is Odin is sufficiently clear in Mecklenburg legends. Often on dark nights his spectral hounds will bark on open heaths, in thickets, and at crossroads there. The local peasant knows their master Wod well, and pities the traveler who has not yet reached home; for Wod is often spiteful and seldom merciful. Only those who keep to the middle of the road will the Wild Huntsman spare. Thus he calls out: *"midden in den weg!"* as a warning to wayward travelers.

Once, a peasant was returning home drunk from a night on the town and his way led through a forest. There he heard the Wild

Hunt, the commotion of the hounds and the shouts of the huntsman above, but he did not take heed. Suddenly a tall man on a white horse dropped down from the clouds onto the road before him. "Are you strong?" he said, "Here, catch hold of this chain; we'll see who pulls harder." The peasant boldly grabbed the chain and the Wild Huntsman flew up again. The man quickly wound the end of the long chain around a nearby oak and the Huntsman tugged at it in earnest. "Did you tie your end around the oak?" demanded Wod, coming down again. "No," the peasant replied, having since unwound the chain. "See, I hold it in my hands." "Then you shall be mine!" cried the Huntsman as he bolted up into the air again. In a panic, the peasant wound the chain around the oak once more with the same result. "Surely you wrapped it around the tree," declared Wod, dropping down a third time. "No," answered the peasant, having deftly unwound it once more, "Here it is in my hands." At this, Wod flew up as fast as lightning and the peasant quickly did as he had before. The hounds barked, the wagons rumbled, and the horses snorted overhead; the tree strained at its roots and began to creak and twist around. The man's heart grew faint, but the oak held firm. At last the Huntsman cried, "Well done! Many a man, I've made mine! You are the first to hold up against me and so you shall have your reward!" On went the Hunt full tilt: "Ho, Ho, Wol, Wol!"

The peasant crept along as before when, all at once, a stag fell at his feet mortally wounded, from unseen heights above, followed by Wod, who leapt off his horse and cut up the kill. "You shall have some blood and a hindquarter!" he said, but the frightened peasant objected, "My lord, thy servant has neither pot nor pail." "Pull off your boot," shouted Wod, and the man did as he was commanded. "Now walk with blood and meat to wife and child." Initially, terror lightened his load, but it grew ever heavier, so that he hardly had strength to bear it. At length, he reached his home bent over and bathed in sweat, only to discover that the boot was laden with gold and the stag's hindquarter had become a bag full of silver. This Wod was no human huntsman, but a god of old, who had taken many men up to his cloudy abode.

The Wild Huntsman
August Malmström

Besides Woden, tradition also speaks of a woman riding at the head of the Furious Host. Holda, like Odin, can ride the wind clothed in terror. Like him, she belongs to the Wild Hunt.[339] Sometimes she is portrayed as his wife, Frau Gode (Gauden, Wode, Woden), that is "Mrs. Odin." According to one such legend preserved by Jacob Grimm, there was once a rich lady of rank named Frau Gauden who so passionately loved the chase that she sinfully declared, "Hunting is better than heaven." In time, she bore twenty-four daughters, who all held the same conviction. One day, as Frau Gauden and her daughters bounded over woods and fields in wild abandon, those

---

[339] Grimm, ibid., p. 268.

wicked words escaped her lips once more, and suddenly before their mother's eyes, her daughters' attire turned into tufts of fur, their arms into legs, and at once twenty-four hunting dogs barked around their mother's carriage —four doing duty as horses, the rest encircling the hunting-car —and away went the wild train, up into the clouds, to hunt between heaven and earth forevermore. She has long since grown weary of constant pursuit and laments her foolish words, but she must bear her guilt until the hour of redemption comes.

Frau Gauden
Ludwig Pietsch, 1860

During Yule, the only time that men can perceive her, Frau Gauden directs her chase toward human habitations. Most of all, she loves to drive through village streets on Christmas Eve or New Year's Eve, and wherever she finds an open door, she sends in a dog, who does the household no other harm than to disturb their sleep with its constant crying. It whimpers and whines the whole year through. Not until Yule comes around again is peace restored to the house. It cannot be pacified nor driven away. Those foolish enough to kill the dog bring disaster upon themselves. This is what happened to a couple in Bresegardt. From that moment on, there was no *säg und täg* (blessing and thriving) to be had, and at length their house burned down to the ground. Therefore, all must be careful during Yule to keep the house door locked after nightfall. Whoever forgets to lock up is to blame should Frau Gauden enter. Careless folk at Semmerin left their front door wide open one New Year's Eve and the next morning found a black dog lying on the hearth, who kept the household awake at night with its incessant whining. The family was at their wits' end when a wise woman told them to brew their beer through an eggshell. So they placed an eggshell in the tap-hole of the brewing-vat, and no sooner had the beer run through it, when the dog leapt up and spoke:

"ik bün so olt as Böhmen golt,	"I am as old as Bohemian gold,
äwerst dat heff ik min leder nicht truht,	And in my life have ne'er viewed,
wenn man 't bier dorch 'n eierdopp bruht."	Beer thro' an eggshell brewed."

The sight so startled the spectral dog that it fled with his tail between his legs. It disappeared and no one has seen the dog since. Better luck befalls those who do Frau Gauden a service. It happens at times, that in the dark of night she loses her way and finds herself at a crossroads, which are a stumbling block to her. Every time she strays into one, her carriage breaks down and she cannot go on. Once, while in this plight, she came dressed as a stately dame to the bedside of a laborer at Boeck, woke him, and implored his help. The man rose and followed her to the crossroads, where he found one of her carriage wheels broken off. He soon fixed the wheel and as payment she told him to fill his pockets with her dogs' dung, assuring him that his effort would not be in vain. Indignant but curious, the man reluctantly did as he was told and took some of the droppings with him. To his utter amazement, at sunrise his wages glittered and upon inspection had turned to gold. He now regretted not gathering up more and returned to the crossroads in haste, but could find no trace of her. For a man at Conow who put a new pole on her carriage and for a woman at Göhren who replaced the pivot that supports the bar,

Frau Gauden repaid their kindness with wood-shavings which fell as they worked. To their surprise, they likewise discovered that the wood-chips had turned into gold. In this she resembles Frau Holda and Berchta, who drive at Yuletide and have their vehicles repaired in the same manner. Another version of the Wild Hunt is found in Thuringia where the procession is led by Frau Holle and partially formed of children who have died unbaptized. It passes through the country on Maundy Thursday, the day marking the Last Supper before Christ's crucifixion. The people assemble to meet its arrival as if a king were coming. An old man with white hair, the faithful Eckhart, precedes the host to warn people out of the way or to go home, lest they come to harm.

In Swabia, in the sixteenth century, a spectre named Berchtold rode at the head of the Furious Host, clothed in white with a horn hanging from his neck and seated on a white horse, leading white hounds on a leash, making him a masculine counterpart of the white-robed Berchta. In the north of Switzerland, Berchteli's Day (the 2nd or 3rd of January) was once considered a day for general merrymaking and in the sixteenth century, it was still the custom of young men there to intercept each other and press one another to take wine. This was known as "conducting to Berchtold."[340] As a masculine form of Berchta, "the Bright", the name suggests a pair of divinities such as Nerthus and Njörd, Freyr and Freyja, Frigga and Fricco, etc. Nor is this phenomenon uncommon in Indo-European mythologies. In Greco-Roman sources, M.L. West notes a Phoibos and Phoibe, Hektaos and Hektate, Janus and Jana, Liber and Libera, Fauna and Faunus, among many others.[341] That the names Frau Gaue, Frau Gode, Frau Wode sprung out of her connection to a male deity is confirmed by her close association with Wodan the Wild Huntsman, who is her husband. These widespread legends thus affirm that long after the conversion to Christianity, Odin's wife was remembered as a benign goddess, the mistress of the Wild Hunt, who, appears under various names, traveling through the countryside with her spouse during the sacred times of the year.

---

[340] Grimm, ibid., p. 279.
[341] *Indo-European Poetry and Myth*, (Oxford, 2007), p. 140.

VII. Frigg, Odin's Wife

"[Bare] allusions to Frigg in the continental sources show that, since early times, Frigg had a place in the divine hierarchy comparable to that which she has in the Norse literature. Her name and eminence are shown in the name of the weekday, Friday (Old English *Frigedæg*) ...Considering Frigg's antiquity and exalted position, it is surprising how little evidence there is for her worship."
—E.O.G. Turville-Petre,
Myth and Religion of the North (1964), p. 188-89.

Frigga by Johannes Wiedewelt, 1780

Odin's wife Frigg is the oldest continually known Germanic goddess. Her name appears in the Anglo-Saxon transliteration of the Roman names of the days of the week. The modern designation of the sixth day, Friday, which corresponds to the Latin *dies Veneris*, Venus' Day, is named after her from the Anglo-Saxon *Fricg* (*Frycg*), Old Norse *Frigg*, Old Saxon *Frí*, Old High German *Frija*. That Frigg is identified with Venus, the Roman Goddess of Love, is fitting

203

considering her name is thought to derive from a proto-Germanic word, *friyo*, from the Indo-European root *priya*, "dear, beloved."[342]

Frigg is widely recorded as Odin's wife in sources dating from 750 AD onward. She and Odin have been directly linked since their first appearance together in the anonymous *Origo Gentis Langobardorum (The Origin and History of the Lombards)*. There Odin and Frigg appear as Godan and Frea, engaged in a dispute over whom to show favor, the Winnilies, Frea's favorites, or the Vandals, Godan's choice:

> "Ambri and Assi, that is the leaders of the Vandals, asked Godan to give them victory over the Winnilies. Godan answered, say thus, 'I shall give victory to those whom I first see at sunrise.' At that time Gambara, with her two sons, that is Ybor and Agjo, who were chieftains over the Winnilies, asked Frea, to be propitious to the Winnilies. Then Frea gave advice that the Winniles should come at sunrise, and that their women should also come with their husbands with their hair let down around their face like beards. When it became light as the sun was rising, Frea, the wife of Godan, turned the bed where her husband was lying, putting his face toward the east, and woke him up. And looking at them, he saw the Winnilies and their women having their hair let down around their faces; and he said: 'Who are these long-bearded ones?' And Frea said to Godan, 'Since you have given them a name, give them also the victory.' And he gave them the victory, so that they should defend themselves according to this plan and gain victory. Since that time the Winnilies were called the Longobards."[343]

Odin granted them the victory, but in practical terms, they won because their women fought alongside them. We can infer this from the text. Paul the Deacon states, "they should defend themselves *according to this plan* and gain victory." Tacitus explains why this strategy was necessary. Being few in number, they needed warriors, and so tasked their women to assist at Frigg's behest, and with Odin's blessing. Thus the Lombards were bold in battle. The

---

[342] West, ibid., p. 144.

[343] John Stanley Martin, "From Godan to Wotan: An Examination of Two Langobardic Mythological Texts", in *Old Norse Myths, Literature and Society*, Proceedings of the 11th International Saga Conference, 2000.

Lombards or Longobards ("Long-beards") are the same tribe that Tacitus knew as the Longobardi. Among the tribes listed by Tacitus as devotees of the earth-goddess Nerthus in *Germania*, chapter 40, the Longobardi play a prominent role. Of them, he says:

> "The Langobardi are distinguished by being few in number. Surrounded by many mighty peoples they have protected themselves not by submissiveness, but by battle and boldness. Next to them come the Reudigni, Aviones, Anglii, Varini, Eudoses, Suarines and Huitones protected by rivers and forests. There is nothing especially noteworthy about these states individually, but they are distinguished by a common worship of Nerthus, that is, Mother Earth, and believe she intervenes in human affairs and rides through their peoples."[344]

While it can be argued that the Longobardi are not included among the tribes who worship Nerthus, nothing prevents us from drawing this conclusion. The text is ambiguous on this point. The Longobardi may be included among the states distinguished by their worship of "*Nerthum id est Terra Mater*" depending on how the text is read. That Tacitus intended to include them becomes probable when we discover that the Longobardi (Lombards), in their earliest historical chronicle, are said to venerate a goddess who intervenes in human affairs. Instead of "Nerthus, that is, Mother Earth," their anonymous first chronicler informs us that the Lombards have long honored Odin's wife, Frea ("the beloved"), who once personally assisted their people and was instrumental in the naming of their tribe. Less than five centuries separate his testimony from that of Tacitus. Fifty years later, the first-named Lombardian chronicler, Paulus Diaconus (Paul the Deacon), retells the same tale in his *Historia Langobardorum* (*History of the Lombards*), informing us from his Christian perspective that it is a *ridicula fabla* (a silly story) told by men of old. That it was preserved in a Christian chronicle long after the conversion of the Lombards to Christianity demonstrates its age and importance to the people. Although the Longobardians had been Christians for nearly two hundred years when *Historia Langobardorum* first appeared, their long-dethroned deities, Odin and Frigg, returned

---

[344] A.R. Birley tr.

to take part in the events, not as men, but as divinities in a manner closely corresponding to their roles in eddic tales recorded much later. Paulus writes:

> "The men of old tell a silly story that the Vandals coming to Godan besought him for victory over the Winnili and that he answered that he would give the victory to those whom he saw first at sunrise; that then Gambara went to Frea, wife of Godan and asked for victory for the Winnili, and that Frea gave her counsel that the women of the Winnili should take down their hair and arrange it upon the face like a beard, and that in the early morning they should be present with their husbands and in like manner station themselves to be seen by Godan from the quarter in which he had been wont to look through his window toward the east. And so it was done. And when Godan saw them at sunrise he said: "Who are these long-beards?" And then Frea induced him to give the victory to those to whom he had given the name. And thus Godan gave the victory to the Winnili. These things are worthy of laughter and are to be held of no account."[345]

Odin and Frigg
Franz Stassen, 1920

The information in these eighth century accounts coincides with what we learn of Odin in later Icelandic sources. Here, Godan

---

[345] William Dudley Foulke tr.

and Frea already appear with the recognizable attributes and personality traits of Odin and Frigg. Godan is imagined as surveying the earth from his window. This corresponds to Odin's position in the *Prose Edda* (*Gylfaginning* 17), which informs us that from his throne Hlidskjalf, Odin can view the entire world, the traditional seat of the Indo-European Sky-Father. The events of this story are seen as an analog to the tale told in the prose prologue to the poem *Grímnismál*:

> "Odin and Frigg were sitting in Hlidskialf, looking over all the world. Odin said, 'Seest thou Agnar, thy foster-son, where he is getting children with a giantess in a cave while Geirröd, my foster-son, is a king residing in his country?' Frigg answered, 'He is so inhospitable that he tortures his guests, if he thinks too many come.' Odin replied that that was the greatest falsehood; and they wagered thereupon. Frigg sent her waiting-maid Fulla to bid Geirröd be on his guard, lest the *trollmann* [sorcerer] who was coming should do him harm, and also say that a token whereby he might be known was, that no dog, however fierce, would attack him. But that King Geirröd was not hospitable was mere idle talk. He, nevertheless, caused the man to be secured whom no dog would assail. He was clad in a blue cloak, and was named Grimnir, and would say no more concerning himself, although he was questioned. The king ordered him to be tortured to make him confess, and to be set between two fires; and there he sat for eight nights."[346]

In both sources, Odin and Frigg are depicted as a divine couple actively involved in human affairs. From his seat in heaven, Odin observes the affairs of men and assists those he favors. Frigg has favorites of her own. When Odin and his wife vie to bless them, she wins the upper hand. In the *History of the Lombards*, Frigg plays a more active part. She physically turns her husband's bed before sunrise, causing him to see her favorites first and so rename them. The Lombards revere her for this act. Among the tribes who are said to worship Nerthus, we find the Longobardi and the Anglii. As we have seen, the Anglo-Saxon *Æcerbót* contains clear evidence that the Anglii continued to worship an earth-goddess for centuries after their conversion, [See Chapter III: The Anglo-Saxon *Æcerbót*]. Likewise, less than five hundred years after Tacitus' report, the Lombards

---

[346] Benjamin Thorpe translation, 1865.

revere Odin's wife Frigg, who like Nerthus, intervenes in human affairs. This is a powerful indicator that Odin's wife, Frigg, was originally identical to Nerthus, the *Terra Mater* of the early Germanic tribes who entered history as the Lombards and the Angles.

Odin and Frigg with Fulla
E. Phillip Fleischer, 1881

We find further evidence of this divine couple in a heathen charm preserved on German soil. The *Merseburg Charms*, two verses discovered in 1841 by Dr. Georg Waitz in a theological manuscript from Fulda, a city located in Hesse, the center of the Frau Holle legends. These verses are believed to date from the tenth century and comprise the earliest record of German paganism in that language. The *Second Merseburg Charm*, which speaks of Wodan and Frija in the company of other gods, reads:

Phol ende Uuodan	Phol and Wodan
uuoron zi holza,	rode into the woods,
du uuart demo Balderes volon	There the foot of Baldur's foal
sin vuoz birenkit;	went out of joint.
thu biguolen Sinhtgunt,	It was charmed by Sinhtgunt,
Sunna era suister;	Sunna her sister;

thu biguol en Frija,	It was charmed by Frija,
Volla era suister,	Volla her sister;
thu biguolen Uuodan,	It was charmed by Wodan,
so he uuola conda:	as he well knew how.
sose benrenki,	Bone-sprain,
sose bluotrenki,	as blood-sprain,
sose lidirenki:	as limb-sprain:
ben zi bena,	Bone to bone,
bluot zi bluoda,	blood to blood,
lid zi geliden,	Limb to limb,
sose gelimida sin.	As though they were glued.

Because this verse stands alone as the sole poetic record of these gods on the continent and is separated from the Icelandic *Eddas* by more than three centuries, some scholars are reluctant to unequivocally identify the deities of this fragment with those of eddic mythology, while others do so without hesitation. The verse records an episode otherwise unknown in Old Norse mythology, nevertheless, we can easily recognize many surfaces of contact. Here we find not only Odin and Frigg (Wotan and Frija), but Fulla (Volla), also known from the Icelandic sources. In the prose introduction to *Grímnismál*, Frigg sends her handmaid Fulla to King Geirröd. In the *Prose Edda*, Fulla is said to be a handmaiden of Frigg, who keeps her casket and personal effects. In the *Second Merseburg Charm*, she is her sister, naturally explaining their close relationship. In *Gylfaginning* 35 and an older strophe by Eyvind Skaldaspillir preserved in *Skáldskaparmál* 36, Fulla is said to wear a golden band around her head (*gullband*, *höfuðband*).[347] This and her role as Frigg's casket-bearer suggest a goddess of plenty, an appropriate role for the sister and handmaiden of Mother Earth. Some scholars suggest she represents the fullness of the earth. Her golden headdress may indicate a goddess of dawn, raising her head above the horizon. In *Gylfaginning* 10, Earth is given the half-brother Dag (Day), who rides his bright horse Skinfaxi across the dome of heaven each day. Jörd herself is the daughter of Nótt (Night), who rides across the nighttime sky on her steed Hrimfaxi.

---

[347] Faulkes, *Edda*, pp. 29, 98-99, translates this as a "golden snood."

Frontispiece to Mallet's *Monumens de la Mythologie*, 1763
Frigg with sword (left) and Odin on Sleipnir (right)

Frigg next appears in Saxo's *Gesta Danorum*, Book 1, written in Denmark a generation before the work of Icelander Snorri Sturluson. As always, she is presented as the wife of Odin:

"At this time there was one Odin, who was credited over all Europe with the honour, which was false, of godhead. …The kings of the North, desiring more zealously to worship his deity, embounded his likeness in a golden image; and this statue, which betokened their homage, they transmitted with much show of worship to Byzantium, fettering even the effigied arms with a serried mass of bracelets. Odin was overjoyed at such notoriety, and greeted warmly the devotion of the senders. But his queen Frigga, desiring to go forth more beautified, called smiths, and had the gold stripped from the statue. Odin hanged them, and mounted the statue upon a pedestal, which by the marvellous skill of his art he made to speak when a mortal touched it. But still Frigga preferred the splendour of her own apparel to the divine honours of her husband, and submitted herself to the embraces of one of her servants; and it was by this man's device she broke down the image, and turned to the service of her private wantonness that gold which had been devoted to public idolatry. Little thought she of practicing unchastity, that she might the easier satisfy her greed, this woman so unworthy to be the consort of a god; but what should I here add, save that such a godhead was worthy of such a wife?"[348]

Among scholars, this episode is most frequently seen as analogous to the exchange in *Lokasenna* 26, where Loki accuses Frigg of infidelity with her husband's brothers. That strophe calls her *Fjörgynns mær.* This can be interpreted to mean that she is Fjörgynn's wife (cp. *Oðs mey*, a term for Freyja in *Völuspá* 25) or daughter, but Fjörgynn is not found as an Odin name.[349] Instead, Snorri informs us that she is Fjörgynn's daughter in *Gylfaginning* 9,[350] while at the same time, declaring *Jörð* (also known as *Fjörgynr*) to be Odin's wife and daughter. Although many translators have mistakenly taken Frigg's parent Fjörgynn to be the earth-goddess, the name *Fjörgynn* is actually a masculine version of the feminine earth-epithet *Fjörgynr.* A male Fjörgynn is otherwise unattested in the Old Norse canon. Despite this difficulty, Frigg is firmly linked to the Earth-goddess through her father's name. Considering the context of *Lokasenna* 26, the term *Fjörgynns mær* may be intended as an insult. If we take it as a double-entendre, meaning Fjörgynn's wife and daughter, then Loki, who accuses Frigg of promiscuity, may be implying she had sexual relations with her own father. This becomes probable if we understand Fjörgynn to be an epithet of one of Odin's brothers, who together raised Earth up out of the sea, (*Völuspá* 4, *Gylfaginning* 8). In that sense, they were her fathers as well as her lovers. [See Chapter X: The Mother of the Gods].

Most often, the reference is viewed as ancient, originating in an older strata of the mythology which survived into the eddic era, allowing Loki to satirize it. For example, Ursula Dronke suggests that Fjörgynn may have been the partner of Thor's mother, Fjörgyn, the earth, with the caveat that "that would have been in an older pantheon."[351] Martin L. West explains:

> "The Norse pantheon includes a god Fjörgynn and a goddess Fjörgyn. These go back to *Perk^wún(i)yos, *Perk^wuni. Apart from having a stem in –yo- instead of –o-, the masculine name corresponds exactly to that of the Baltic thundergod. Fjörgynn is

---

[348] Oliver Elton tr.
[349] Lindow, *Handbook of Norse Mythology, s.v.* Fjörgyn.
[350] Mss. T and U have *Fjörgynsdóttir*; R and W read *Fjörgvinsdóttir.*
[351] Dronke, *Poetic Edda*, Vol. II, p. 363.

an obsolescent figure, mentioned only as the father of Frigg
(*Lokasenna* 26, *Gylf.* 9, *Skáld.* 19), and we cannot tell from the
Nordic evidence what he originally stood for. ...Parjanya is called
the son of Dyaus (RV 7, 102,1), which expresses his natural
relationship with the sky. Sometimes he takes the place of Dyaus as
the consort of the Earth who fertilizes her with his seed and so
fathers living creatures (5, 83, 4; 7,101, 3; AV 12, 1, 42). He is
especially associated with the rains and *parjánya-* as a common noun
means 'rain-cloud'. He is pictured as a bellowing bull who deposits
his semen in the plants (RV 5, 83, 1; 7, 101, 6). But he is also a
thunderer (5, 83, 2-9; 10, 66, 10) and dispenser of lightning (5, 83.
4; AV 19, 30, 5, TS 3, 4. 7, 2). ...His name has long been felt to
belong in the company of Perkunas, Fjörgynn and the others."[352]

Despite her lengthy appearance in the historic record, Frigg is
best known from the Icelandic sources, where she is also depicted as
Odin's wife. Besides *Lokasenna*, she appears in the prose header of
the poem *Grímnismál*, as we have seen, where she sits beside her
husband on Hlidskjalf, looking out over the world. In *Vafþrúðnismál*,
he asks her advice before traveling to Jötunheim, to which she
replies, "I'd rather keep the Father of Hosts at home in the courts of
the gods."[353] In *Völuspá* 52, Odin is called her *angan*, a word often
defined as "joy, delight,"[354] and in strophes 31-33, she mourns the
loss of their son Baldur. In *Hrafnagaldur Óðins* 19, when the gods
receive Heimdall and the goddesses receive Loki, Odin's ill-fated
envoys to the underworld, the gathered gods salute "Hropt (Odin)
and Frigg" as they retire from the feast.[355] In a longer version of
Baldrs draumr called *Vegtamskviða* found in later paper copies, she and
her husband (designated there as *Frigg and Svafnir*) resolve to extract
oaths from all things to do their son Baldur no harm, after ominous
dreams presage his death.

The Old Norse sources certainly do not lack evidence that
Frigg is the Earth-Mother. According to *Völuspá* 33, Frigg makes her
home in *Fensalir*, the "halls of the fen." A fen is a low-lying wetland,
an odd domicile for the popularly-styled Queen of Heaven to reside.

[352] West, *Indo-European Poetry and Myth* (2007), pp. 241, 245-6.
[353] str. 2, Carolyne Larrington tr.
[354] Beatrice LaFarge and John Tucker, *Glossary to the Poetic Edda* (1992), p. 8.
[355] http://www.hi.is/~eybjorn/ugm/hrg/hrg.html str. 23; Eysteinn Björnsson and
William P. Reaves.

In ancient times, life was thought to spontaneously generate in such places. Before mankind possessed scientific knowledge of reproductive biology, insects, amphibians and other creatures were said to spring fully formed from Earth's bosom in these fertile places. Like Frau Holle who is at home in ponds and wells, Frigg takes up residence in marshland. There she weeps for her son Baldur's loss, asking all things to do the same "just as these things weep when they come out of frost and into heat," during the spring thaw. The same place is probably meant in *Grímnismál* 7, which states:

Sökkvabekkr heitir inn fjórði,	Sunken Bench a fourth is called,
en þar svalar knegu	and there cool waves
unnir yfir glymja;	can resound over;
þar þau Óðinn ok Sága	there Odin and Sága
drekka um alla daga	drink every day,
glöð ór gullnum kerum.	gladly from golden cups.

As the only poetic source for an otherwise unknown goddess named Sága, this must be Snorri's source. Although Snorri presents her as an independent goddess in *Gylfaginning* 35, saying only that she dwells in Sökkvabekkr, scholars for the most part agree that *Sága* is another name for Frigg, emphasizing her role as a seeress,[356] [See Chapter X: The Mother of the Gods]. Since she drinks with Odin every day, it stands to reason that *Sága* is his beloved bride, or else she certainly would have something to say about how he spends his time. Her role as the Lady with the Mead Cup harks back to the images of Mercury's consort Rosmerta with her pantera and strainer. Odin's wife is thus the mythic archetype for the female cup-bearer in the Germanic *comitatus*. As the constant wife of Odin, however, Frigg's most memorable role is that of his son Baldur's mourning mother. In her signature story, Frigg's character is best revealed, thus calling for a closer examination of the tale. Once the fog is lifted, her nature as the Earth-Mother becomes clear.

---

[356] John Lindow, *Handbook of Norse Mythology* (2001) *sv Sága*.

Frigga & Balder
Lorenz Frølich, 1885

VIII. Frigg, Baldur's Mother

"From the point of view of the history of religions, Frigg's role in the Baldr story deviates somewhat from her historical role, which originally was primarily that of the consort of the head of the gods. ...In most of her appearances in eddic poetry, however, Frigg is wife (*Vafþrúðnismál* 1-4) and mother (the references to Baldr in *Völuspá* and *Baldrs draumar*)."

—John Lindow,
Murder and Vengeance Among the Gods (1997), p. 49-50.

The Baldur myth is best known from Snorri's *Edda*, written in thirteenth century Iceland and verified (at least in part) by poetic sources composed up to three hundred years earlier. The eddic poems, *Völuspá, Baldrs draumar,* and *Skírnismál* provide us with details of this myth. That the Baldur myth was a pivotal episode in Old Norse mythology is evident from its central place in the *Codex Regius* manuscript of *Völuspá*, which reads:

Ek sá Baldri,	31. I saw Baldur,
blóðgom tívur,	the bloody god,
Óðins barni,	Odin's child,
ørlög fólgin:	his fate hidden.
stóð um vaxinn	There stood grown,
völlum hærri	higher than the plain,
mjór ok mjök fagr	slender and very fair,
mistilteinn.	the mistletoe.
Varð af þeim meiði,	32. From that plant
er mær sýndisk,	so slender to behold
harmflaug hættlig:	came a deadly, harmful dart,
Höðr nam skjóta.	which Hödur shot;
Baldrs bróðir var	Baldur's brother (Vali) was
of borinn snemma,	born quickly;
sá nam, Óðins sonr,	Odin's son began to fight
einnættr vega.	one night old.

Þó hann æva hendr	33. He did not wash his hands
né höfuð kembði,	nor comb his hair,
áðr á bál um bar	until to the funeral pyre
Baldrs andskota.	he brought Baldur's adversary;
En Frigg um grét	And Frigg wept
í Fensölum	in Fensalir,
vá Valhallar -	for Valhalla's woe.
vituð ér enn, eða hvat?	Understand ye yet, or what?

Modern scholars generally acknowledge Baldur's death as a central event in the Norse mythic cycle. John Lindow, for example, labels it the foremost event in the late *mythic present* which, "as the first death among the gods, changed the rules of the game. Even if it did not make Ragnarök inevitable, it made it possible."[357] Margaret Clunies Ross, who compared passages of *Völuspá, Vafþrúðnismál, Fafnismál* and *Hyndluljóð*, four eddic poems which undertake a temporal review of major mythic events providing "access to the broad outline of mythic chronology", concludes that "the picture that emerges from a comparison of the four eddic poems is one that divides elapsed time into five distinct periods whose transitions are marked by significant events."[358] All of these texts place a growing preoccupation with fate and death in the so-called *mythic present*, the period of time in which the gods live alongside other kinds of beings including humans, elves, dwarves and giants, attempting to maintain a state of order in the world. Three of the texts (excluding *Fafnismál*) indicate that the two most important events of this period were the incorporation of the Vanir into the Aesir tribe and the events leading up to the death of Baldur and its tragic consequences. But, while there is general agreement about its central importance, there remains much debate over the historical structure of the Baldur myth. Some scholars have suggested that since he is not directly implicated in *Völuspá*'s account of Baldur's demise, Loki played no part in Baldur's murder. Yet, it is probably no coincidence that the strophe describing Loki's binding follows immediately thereafter in the *Codex Regius* manuscript. The placement of the image of Loki bound after the death of Baldur suggests a causal relationship.[359] In the *Hauksbók*

---

[357] *Handbook of Old Norse Mythology* (2001), p. 42.

[358] *Prolonged Echoes* I (1994), p. 238.

[359] John S. Martin, *Ragnarök, An Investigation into Norse Concepts of the Fate of the Gods* (1972), p. 120.

manuscript, what follows is the birth of Vali, who will slay Höður for Baldur's murder and the sad fate of Sigyn, Loki's wife, who remains with him once chained. Thus, both manuscript versions of the poem place Loki's fate in close proximity to Baldur's. After admitting his role in Baldur's death, Freyja's warning to Loki in *Lokasenna* 29 that he is mad to recount his evil deeds to Frigg who knows all *örlög*, presumably including his own, probably points in the same direction.

The Death of Baldur
Franz Stassen, 1903

Sigurd Nordal observes that the available sources reveal two types of understanding of Baldur's murder: 1) that Höður is the sole killer, as supported by Saxo's *Danish History*, Book III, and the eddic poem *Baldrs draumar*, or 2) that Loki is its chief architect who uses Höður as a blind tool. Nordal concludes that "*Völuspá* belongs to the

217

second category," interpreting line 32/2 *er mær sýndisk,* "so slender to behold," as a reference to Loki handing Hödur a shaft which seemed slender and harmless, just as Odin does in *Gautrek's Saga* ch. 7 when he hands a spear disguised as a reed to Stakrad in order to sacrifice the unsuspecting King Vikar.[360] Similarly, in *Lokasenna,* once Loki confesses his role in Baldur's murder in strophe 28, he is thereafter captured and bound as described in the prose conclusion of that poem. Thus, these two events would appear inextricably linked.

The poem *Baldrs draumar* provides additional information about this myth. In it, Odin travels to Hel prior to the events described in *Völuspá* in order to consult a völva about the cause of Baldur's foreboding dreams. Through a series of cryptic questions and answers with the dead prophetess, Odin learns the essential details of his beloved son's death. In the oldest vellum manuscript of the poem (AM no. 748), most often used in modern translations, Frigg is not mentioned. However, paper copies of the poem dating from the seventeenth century provide a fuller version. This version, known as *Vegtamskviða,* contains additional lines and strophes, which may have originated in a manuscript copy of the poem, now lost. This is both possible and plausible since in October of 1728 fire destroyed a number of Icelandic manuscripts collected by the great Árni Magnússson in Copenhagen. Because Árni did not keep a catalog of his collection, no one knows what all was lost.[361] Since the extra content in *Vegtamskviða,* on the whole, agrees with the remainder of eddic poetry, there is little reason to dismiss it as a later rewrite of *Baldrs draumar.* It seems unlikely that a later scribe, who could only have been Christian considering the time and place, would have embellished the poem randomly, and if he had, it seems even less likely that he would have been able to do so without contradicting better known sources. The lines and strophes thus appear to be an original part of the poem, making *Vegtamskviða* an alternate version of *Baldrs draumar,* in much the same way that *Codex Regius* and *Hauksbók* preserve two different versions of *Völuspá.* Because there is no known vellum manuscript to "authenticate" the longer *Vegtamskviða,* more recent scholars generally ignore it. Of the English translators, only Benjamin Thorpe (1866), assisted by his

---

[360] *Völuspá,* ed. by Sigurd Nordal, tr. B.S. Benedikz and J. McKinnell, p. 67.
[361] Ólafur Halldórsson, "Árni Magnússon (1663-1730)" in *Medieval Scholarship,* Helen Damico ed. (2014), p. 41.

uncredited stepdaughter Elise C. Otté, a scholar in her own right,[362] provided the full text of the poem, which begins:

Senn váru æsir	1. Together were the Æsir
allir á þingi	all in council,
ok ásynjur	and the Asyniur
allar á máli,	all in conference,
ok um þat réðu	and they consulted,
ríkir tívar,	the mighty gods,
hví væri Baldri	why Baldur had
ballir draumar.	oppressive dreams.
Mjök var hapti	2. To that god his slumber
höfugr blundr	was most afflicting;
heillir í svefni	his auspicious dreams
horfnar sýndust;	seemed departed.
spurðu jólnar	They the Jötuns[363] questioned,
spar framvísar,	wise seers of the future,
ef þat myndi	whether this might not
angrs vita.	forebode calamity?
Fréttir sögðu,	3. The responses said
at feigr væri	that to death destined was
Ullar sefi	Ullr's kinsman,
einna þekkastr;	of all the dearest:
fékk þat angrs	that caused grief
Frigg ok Sváfni,	to Frigg and Svafnir (Odin),
rögnum öðrum:	and to the other powers
ráð sér festu.	on a course they resolved:
Út skyldi senda	4. That they would send
allar vættir	to all beings,
griða at beiða,	to solicit assurance,
granda ei Baldri;	not to harm Baldur.

---

[362] *The Athenaeum: A Journal of Literature, Science, the Fine Arts, Music, and Drama,* Jan. 2, 1904.

[363] Whereas most manuscripts read *jötnar,* "Jötuns," per Sophus Bugge, *Norroen Fornkvæði* (1867), p. 138, at least one mss. reads *jólnar* meaning "gods."

vann alls konar	All species swore
eið at vægja,	oaths to spare him;
Frigg tók allar	Frigg received all
festar ok særi.	their vows and compacts.

Charles E. Brock, 1930

Frigg soliciting oaths from all things implies she is Mother Earth. Terrestrial things are subject to her influence. In *Gylfaginning* 49-50, Snorri tells the most complete version of the Baldur story. It begins in *medias res*, where we first find Frigg bidding all earthly things to do her son Baldur no harm after dire dreams predict his death. Frigg alone excludes the most fragile of flora, the waxy mistletoe, which does not take root in earth, but grows overhead as a parasite on trees. Snorri writes:

> "The beginning of the story is this, that Baldur the Good dreamed great and perilous dreams touching his life. When he told these dreams to the Æsir, then they took counsel together: and this was their decision: to ask safety for Baldur from all kinds of dangers. And Frigg took oaths to this purport, that fire and water should spare Baldur, likewise iron and metal of all kinds, stones, earth, trees, sicknesses, beasts, birds, venom, serpents."

Noticably absent from the list are beings in human form: gods, giants, dwarves and other mythical races, as well as human beings. Only objects and animals under the purview of the Earth are named. Believing the danger averted, the gods made a game of it, taking delight at hurling weapons at Baldur, with no effect:

> "And when that was done and made known, it became a diversion for Baldur and the Æsir, that he should stand up in the Thing ("legal assembly") and all the others would shoot at him, some hew at him, some pelt him with stones; but whatever was done caused him no harm, and that seemed a very honorable thing to all."

Vexed at the success of the game, Loki disguised himself as an old woman and went to Frigg to ask her how this wonder was possible. She told him that "neither weapons nor trees" could hurt Baldur for she had taken oaths of them all. When the old woman inquired whether all things had taken the oath to spare Baldur's life, Frigg replied: "A sprout alone grows west of Valhalla: it is called Mistletoe; I thought it too tender to ask the oath of." At once Loki left, found Mistletoe and ripped it up. He made a weapon of it and returned to the court of the gods. Snorri continues:

> "Hödur stood outside the ring of men, because he was blind. Then Loki spoke to him: 'Why don't you shoot at Baldur?' He replied: 'Because I can't see where Baldur is; and also because I am

without weapon.' Then Loki said: 'Do as the other men, and show Baldur honor as other men do. I will direct you where he stands; shoot at him with this wand.' Hödur took Mistletoe and shot at Baldur, guided by Loki. The shaft pierced Baldur, and he fell dead to the earth; and that was the greatest mishap that has ever befallen gods and men."

Frigg and her Attendants
F.W. Heine, 1882

This tragedy did not deter Frigg. Again she intervenes on her son's behalf, asking who will ride to Hel to plead for her son's release. Hermod volunteers and is dispatched at once on Odin's eight-legged horse, Sleipnir. In the meantime, the gods cremate Baldur's corpse on a great pyre aboard his own ship Hringhorn. Snorri describes Baldur's funeral in great detail. The descriptions of the mourners appear to have their origin in Ulf Uggasson's poem *Húsdrápa*. If one compares Snorri's account of Baldur's funeral with the few surviving strophes of the poem preserved by him in *Skáldskaparmál*, a one-to-one correspondence emerges. The vivid visual quality of Snorri's Baldur narrative thus is likely based on the poem *Húsdrápa*, which was composed to commemorate "tales carved into the wood" of a hall, according to *Laxadaela Saga*, ch 29. The saga informs us that Ólaf Pái (Olaf the Peacock) built a magnificent hall on his farmstead in the Laxardal Valley in western Iceland, around the year AD 985, when that land was yet a heathen nation. He celebrated the wedding of his daughter there later that winter. A great number of people attended the feast. Among the guests was a poet, Ulf Uggason, who composed a poem "House Drapa" (*Húsdrápa*) about the tales carved into the wood of the hall which he recited at the feast. From surviving verses of the poem quoted by Snorri in *Skaldskaparmál*, it is clear that the carvings depicted mythological scenes such as Thor's fishing for the Midgard Serpent, Baldur's death, and Heimdall battling with Loki over Brisingamen. In *Skaldskaparmál* 12, Snorri states that "Ulf Uggason composed a long passage in *Húsdrápa* based on the story of Baldr, and an account of the events …was written above" (i.e. in *Gylfaginning* 48). That this poem was the primary source for Snorri's version of the Baldur myth is indicated by the placement of the story of Thor's fishing immediately before it in *Gylfaginning* 47.

While the eddic poem *Hymiskviða* provides the clearest account of Thor's fishing for the Midgard Serpent, there is no evidence that Snorri knew the story as it was told there. *Hymiskviða* concludes with the giant Hymir cutting Thor's fishing line and the serpent sinking back into the sea. In agreement with a surviving stanza of *Húsdrápa*, Snorri tells a much different version in *Gylfaginning* 47, which concludes, "They say that he [Thor] struck off its head …but I think in fact the contrary is correct to report that the Midgard Serpent lives still." Remarkably, the story differs enough from other accounts known to him, that Snorri pauses to reflect on it. Elsewhere in *Skáldskaparmál*, he records the *Húsdrápa* strophe in question alongside other verses detailing the same event, which confirms this view. Commonly identified as verse 56 of *Skáldskaparmál*, the *Húsdrápa* strophe stands out as the sole poetic passage, among several cited, that says Thor severed the serpent's head:

56. Víðgymnir laust Vimrar vaðs af fránum naðri hlusta grunn við hrönnum.	"Vidgymnir of Vimur's fjord [Thor, according to *Skáldskaparmál* 12] struck the

Hlaut innan svá minnum.   ear-bed [head] from the shining
snake by the waves. Within have
appeared these motifs."

The final line clearly indicates that the poet is describing images he
sees carved on the gables and rafters "within" the hall at Hjardarholt.
Since Ulf Uggason is the only poet to say that Thor dealt the serpent
a lethal blow, we should consider the context of his composition.
Ulf's purpose was not to accurately recount the events of the myth,
but rather to immortalize a carved representation of it in two-
dimensional form. One imagines a carving of Thor powerfully
striking the serpent's head, showing it separated from the snake's
body upon impact in an exaggerated fashion to emphasize Thor's
great strength, as in a modern cartoon. If the same poem was Snorri's
primary source for the Baldur myth, it may explain some of the more
fantastic features of the story.

Since *Húsdrápa* was not meant to retell the Baldur myth as it
was known in its oral form, but rather intended to describe a series of
pictorial representations of its key scenes carved into wood, wherever
the wood-carver resorted to visual symbols to represent the actual
events of the story, the poet would simply describe what he saw. In
turn, Snorri seems to have taken Ulf's descriptions of them literally,
repeating and embellishing what the poet said in his own retelling.
Thus he depicts Loki, who is responsible for planning Baldur's
murder (*raðbani*), as standing next to Höðr, the actual killer (*handbani*),
who was probably pictured with his eyes closed to show that he acted
"blindly" under Loki's influence. If Loki had actually stood beside
Höðr directing his shot as Snorri states, the gods would have
immediately recognized Loki as the culprit. As it stands, not until
Loki admits his guilt to Frigg in *Lokasenna* 28, do the gods take action
against him, seeking vengeance for this heinous deed. It is more likely
that the oral version had Loki frame Höðr (whose name means
"warrior") by slipping the "deadly, harmful dart" (*harmflaug hættlig*)
disguised to look like an ordinary arrow, into his quiver. In that case,
Höðr shot it unaware, killing his beloved brother. However, since
Húsdrápa is largely lost, this theory cannot be proven. Of the "long
passage in *Húsdrápa*" (*langt skeið í Húsdrápu*) concerning Baldur, only
five strophes remain, scattered throughout *Skáldskaparmál*, recounting
the events surrounding Baldur's funeral procession and cremation.

Tellingly, Snorri's prose account of the same events, closely follows the wording of those strophes. As shown above, other eddic poems such as *Völuspá* and *Baldrs draumar* confirm the outline of Snorri's account, as well as individual details such as the burning of the ring Draupnir on Baldur's breast, mentioned in *Skírnismál* 21. Several scholars have commented on the poetic nature of the passage describing Hermod's ride to Hel, suggesting that it too was based on a lost poem.

According to Snorri, when Hermod arrives in Hel, after riding for nine nights, he employs Sleipnir to leap the high wall surrounding the place. *Baldrs draumar* calls this place *heljar rann*, "Hel's high hall." Hermod ultimately meets Baldur, and passes the night with him and his wife there.

> "In the morning Hermod asked Hel to let Baldur ride home with him, and told her of the great sorrow and weeping among the Æsir. But Hel said that it should be put to the test, whether Baldur were so well-loved as had been said: 'If all things in the world, quick and dead, weep for him, then he shall return to the Æsir; but he will remain with Hel if anyone speaks against him or will not weep for him.' Then Hermod arose; but Baldur led him out of the hall, and took the ring Draupnir and sent it to Odin for a keepsake. And Nanna sent Frigg linen [*ripti*] and still more gifts, and to Fulla a golden finger-ring.
>
> "Then Hermod retraced his path, and rode into Asgard, and told all those things which he had seen and heard. Thereafter the Æsir sent messengers all over the world to pray that Baldur be wept out of Hel; and all men did this, and living things, and the earth, and stones, and trees, and all metals,—even as you must have seen that these things weep when they come out of frost and into the heat."

At this point in the narrative, Frigg's role as Mother Earth is self-evident. Not once, but twice, she requests all terrestrial things do her bidding. She sends messengers out all over the whole world demanding oaths of them, first to do her son no harm, then to ask all things, alive and inanimate, to weep for his return. The initial list, however, contains one large and glaring omission, beings with human form.[364] Frigg only acquires oaths of animals, plants and minerals,

---

[364] John Lindow, *Murder and Vengeance Among the Gods*, p. 48.

things clearly under the authority of Mother Earth. The second time, all living things including men are asked to weep, undercutting Snorri's statement "just as you will have seen these things weep when they come out of frost and into heat," which only applies to inanimate objects, i.e. "the earth and the stones and every metal" which thaw in the spring. The gifts Frigg receives from the underworld point in the same direction. Baldur's wife Nanna sends a linen garment from the underworld back with Hermod, to beautify Frigg along with a finger ring for her handmaiden Fulla. Both gifts carry weight as symbols, as John Lindow explains:

> "The proffered gifts are not random. First Baldr conveys Draupnir on Hermóðr, for transport to Odin. Thus the ring makes the full journey that Baldr will not make; it is burned on the funeral pyre and then returned to the world of the living. Baldr sends it to Odin as a reminder, and as such it must become part of the arsenal of weapons Odin can employ against the jötnur, another mystery, like that of Mímir's pickled head, that shares attributes of the living and the dead. Nanna sends *ripti* ('cloth', 'material', probably linen [Kuhn 1968: 168, s.v.]) or a *faldr* ('head covering'), depending on which manuscript one follows, to Frigg, and to Fulla she sends a finger ring. The gift to Frigg joins giver and receiver in traditional roles as wife and mother through the term *ripti*.[365]

According to Lindow, *ripti* is a rare word mostly limited to eddic poetry. In the poem *Rígspula*, when the freewoman Amma swaddles her newborn Karl, she does so in *ripti* (v. 21). When Karl marries, *ripti* refers to the bridal veil of Snor, his wife (v. 23). When Heimdall as Rig enters the home of the highborn Fadir and Modir who will bring the first king into the world, he finds Modir ironing *ripti*, a task appropriate to her status. Lindow continues:

> "Most proignantly, *ripti* refers to the covers of the marriage bed of Sigurðr and Guðrún, which the poet of *Siguðarkviða in skamma* has Sigurðr wrap around Guðrún while the sexually frustrated Brynhildr, outside in snow and ice, imagines the scene (stanza 8). The other word for Nanna's gift to Frigg, *faldr* ("head covering") found only in the *Codex Upsaliensis*, appears in *Rígspula* 29 in the first line following the stanza about Móðir's ironing the *ript*. It is

---

[365] Lindow, ibid., p.123-124; Mss. R, T and W read, *Nanna sendi Frigg ripti*; U reads, *Nanna sendi Frigg fald*.

the object of the rare word *keisa* which appears to mean 'to put on' (Kuhn 1968; 168, s.v.) and taken together these stanzas appear to suggest that the head covering of stanza 28 attaches to Móðir's social status."

Lindow provides further examples of the *faldr*'s significance as a symbol of marriage from *Laxadæla Saga*. As he demonstrates, the *faldr* "is unequivocally a symbol of marriage." Thus by use of the word *ripti* or *faldr,* the message is clear that Nanna's role as wife, mother, female head of household and sexual partner are at an end, since she no longer needs these accoutrements, while Frigg's role as wife and mother is reemphasized. Coming from the underworld, a covering for the earth-goddess made from flax, is best interpreted as new spring vegetation. As we have seen, Odin's wife Frau Holle — also known as Frau Goden, Frau Wode, and Frekka— in particular is associated with both spinning and the production of flax. By the same token, the linen garment Frigg receives from the underworld is reminiscent of the gift that Zas (Zeus) provides to his bride (Chthonie) in the idiosyncratic cosmology of Pherecydes of Syros (sixth century BC). In the early Greek myth, it is woven from sky, sea, etc.[366] Ursula Dronke compares this story to the courtship of Freyr and Gerd as told in *Skírnismál,* another myth widely accepted as representing the *hieros gamos.*[367] The myths are cyclical. For his father, Baldur gives Hermod the reduplicating ring Draupnir, the same gift refused by Gerd, who is generally taken to be the representative of the frozen earth. In *Skírnismál,* the ring is said to have been "burned on Baldur's breast," a direct allusion to this story. In Snorri's tale, some scholars interpret the finger ring that Hermod brings back for Fulla as a duplicate of Draupnir, and therefore also a sign of fertility.

Together, the veil and the ring are ancient symbols of marriage. As Lindow points out, a Dumézilian reading of the names of the days of the week will associate Frigg with fertility.[368] Following Tyr and Odin, who represent the first two functions of sovereignty, and Thor for the warrior function, Frigg represents the fertility function. Some placename evidence, such as *Friggjarakr* (Frigg's

---

[366] West, ibid., p. 373, cp. 182
[367] For examples, see Pierre Daniel Chantepie de la Saussaye, *The Religion of the Teutons* (1902), p. 269; Dronke, *Poetic Edda*, Vol. II (1997), p. 396-397.
[368] Lindow, ibid., p. 49-50.

cornfield) in Västergötland, supports this,[369] as does the long-standing tradition of marrying on Friday in parts of Germany.[370] Draupnir can be interpreted along other lines as well. Its very nature suggests cyclical growth and renewal. The ring which reduplicates itself every ninth night may represent the nine months of human gestation or the nine months of the agricultural cycle (spring planting, growth and harvest) followed by three harsh months of winter, just as the great outpouring of grief over Baldur's death is likened to the spring thaw, and the linen veil from the underworld for Frigg suggests the annual return of spring vegetation. In an apparent reversal of this, *Gylfaginning* 23 says that Njörd, the father of Freyr and Freyja, and his new bride, the giantess Skadi, spend nine nights (according to T, W and U) or nine years (according to the R mss) in Skadi's wintry home Thrymheim and only three nights (or years) by the sea in Njörd's more temperate home, Noatun. Unlike the union of Odin and Frigg, their marriage was short-lived. Likewise, Freyr, the Lord of Harvests, must wait nine "long nights" (a description most appropriate to the winter months when the nights are longer), before meeting his unreceptive bride, the giantess Gerd, in the wood Barri for the first time. The same concept may be present in Hermod's ride to Hel, which takes him nine nights to complete. No doubt, these myths encode ancient agricultural symbolism.

That the Baldur myth was known as early as the eighth century is evident by a detailed reference to it in the Old English poem *Beowulf* (ll. 2430-2459). Scholars have long recognized this passage as an analog to the Baldur myth.[371] In its tale of two princes, sons of a Geatish king, one brother accidentally kills the other with a misguided arrow. Their names, Herebæld and Hæðcyn, contain the primary elements —*bæld* and *Hæð*— of the names of Odin's sons, Baldur and Hödur.

---

[369] E.O.G. Turville-Petre, *Myth and Religion of the North* (1964), p. 189. Other examples include *Friggiærakær* near Gudhem, Västergötland; two examples of *Friggeråker,* one from Östergötland and another near Falköping, Skaraborgs Län, Västergötland; *Friggaskulle,* "Frigg's hillock" from Sävedals härad, Västergötland and *Fryggiosætre* in Aslak Bolts jordebok from the 1400s. Edward Smith, *Pagan and Supranormal Elements in Scandinavian Place-names*, 2011 at http://germanic.eu/heathenplace1.htm (Last Viewed 1/01/2015).
[370] Karl Helm, *Altgermanische Religionsgeschichte*, Vol. 2 (1953), pp. 270-271.
[371] Margaret Clunies Ross, *Prolonged Echoes* (1994), p. 271; John Lindow, *Murder and Vengeance Among the Gods* (1997), p. 141.

Wæs þam yldestan	For the eldest [Herebæld]
ungedefelice	undeservedly,
mæges dædum	by his brother's deed
morþorbed stred,	was a deathbed strewn,
syððan hyne Hæðcyn	when Hæthcyn
of hornbogan,	with his horn-bow,
his freawine,	his lord and friend,
flane geswencte,	with a shaft laid low;
miste mercelses	He missed his mark
ond his mæg ofscet,	and struck his kinsman,
broðor oðerne	one brother the other,
blodigan gare	with a bloody shaft.
...Swa bið geomorlic	...So bitter is it
gomelum ceorle	for an old man,
to gebidanne,	To have seen
þæt his byre ride	his son ride high,
giong on galgan,	young on the gallows;
þonne he gyd wrece,	then may he recite
sarigne sang,	a song of sorrow,
þonne his sunu hangað	when his son hangs,
hrefne to hroðre,	a joy to the raven,
ond he him helpe ne mæg,	he cannot help him,
eald ond infrod,	old and wise,
ænige gefremman.	any afford.
Gesyhð sorhcearig	...Miserable he looks
on his suna bure	on his son's dwelling,
winsele westne,	Deserted wine-hall,
windge reste	wind-swept,
reote berofene.	of joy bereft,
Ridend swefað,	then the rider sleeps,
hæleð in hoðman;	warrior in the grave;
nis þær hearpan sweg,	no harp music,
gomen in geardum,	no games in the courtyard
swylce ðær iu wæron.	as there were before.
... Swa Wedra helm	...Thus the Weder's crown [king],
æfter Herebealde	for Herebæld
heortan sorge	in his heart bore
weallende wæg.	grief overflowing.

Told at greater length than provided here, the core elements of the myth are all present.[372] Through no fault of his own, the blameless brother of Herebæld mortally wounds his brother with a projectile. Like Baldur, Herebæld's status as a rider is emphasized and the poet speaks of games played in the courtyard of Herebæld's hall, a prominent feature in the Baldur myth as told in *Gylfaginning*. The *Beowulf* poet compares their father's sorrow to that of an old man who lives to see his son hanged, becoming food for ravens. In Norse sources, Odin is the hanged god and the god of ravens. Notably, even Heremod (the Anglo-Saxon equivalent of the Norse Hermóðr) turns up later in the poem. From the viewpoint of the Icelandic evidence, what is perhaps most striking is that Heremod is directly compared to the hero Sigemund, just as Hermod appears with Sigmundr in *Hyndluljóð* 2, once again demonstrating the continuity of ideas across vast spans of time and space within the Germanic cultural sphere.[373] The presence of the essential mythic elements in *Beowulf* inspired Ursula Dronke to ask rhetorically: "if the Christian poet intended to euhemerize the myth of Baldr's death, could he have done it more effectively?"[374] In further support of early Anglo-Saxon knowledge of Baldur, we also find the name Beldeg or Beldæg as a son of Woden or Uoden in Anglo-Saxon royal genealogies.[375] Thus, we find evidence in England as early as the eighth century for Frigg's most famous role, that of mourning mother in the wake of her beloved son, Baldur's, death. That the Baldur myth is ancient should come as no surprise. Already in the *Germania* 43, Tacitus speaks of a pair of young men and brothers whom he calls the Alcis, worshiped together in a grove. He likens them to the Diskouri, Castor and Pollux, twin sons of the Sky-Father Zeus in Greco-Roman mythology. Like Baldur and Hödur, when one brother dies, the other soon follows him to the underworld. [See Appendix B: Frigg's Son, Baldur]. The story itself, which has ancient Indo-European roots, is perhaps the most tragic episode in the eddic cycle.

---

[372] Margaret Clunies Ross, *Prolonged Echoes* (1994), p. 272.

[373] John Lindow, *Murder and Vengeance Among the Gods* (1997), p. 107-108.

[374] *Beowulf and Ragnarok*, pp. 322-23 in Dronke's *Myth and Fiction in Early Norse Lands* (1996).

[375] North, ibid., p. 43.

IX. Jörd, Thor's Mother

"It is uncertain whether the names Fjörgyn, Hlóðyn, Fold and Grund (all meaning 'earth') were merely poetic synonyms for the mother of Thor created by the skalds, or whether they are various names for the old earth-goddess Jörð."[376]

—John McKinnell,
Meeting the Other in Old Norse Myth and Legend, p. 46.

Frau Holle
Franz Stassen, 1903

As we have seen, Odin's wife Frigg in her role as Baldur's mother clearly possesses characteristics of an earth goddess. Yet, in spite of this, both Frigg and Earth (Jörð) remain rather opaque figures in Old Icelandic literature. Despite her high rank, we know relatively little about Frigg. The case is much the same with Thor's mother, the Earth. Physical descriptions of Jörd are few and mainly refer to her as a personification of the land. A strophe by Hallfreðr vanræðaskald preserved by Snorri refers to Earth as "Baleyg's [Odin's] broad-faced-bride," whereas Martin L. West notes that "broad" is the most common epithet of the earth-goddess in Indo-European poetic tradition.[377] In the third strophe of Þjóðólfr

---

[376] Simek, *Dictionary of Northern Mythology*, p. 179, s.v. Jörð.
[377] West, ibid., p. 178, which notes that analogous expressions occur in Germanic verse: the Old High German poem *Muspilli* 58, speaks of *daz preita*

Árnorsson's *Sexstefja* (*Fagrskinna*, ch. 51), Earth is described as *haglfaldinni*, "hail-hooded," an allusion which compares snow-capped mountains to the white linen of a woman's *faldr* headdress. Elsewhere in Old Icelandic sources, Jörd is said to be *eiki grónu*, "grown with oak" (Guðorm Sindri's *Hákonardrápa* 5); *barrhödduð*, "fir-tressed" and *viði gróna*, "grown with woodland" (Hallfreðr vanræðaskald's *Hákonardrápa*). The expression *haddr Jarðar*, "Jörd's tresses" is a kenning for grass, just as various plants such as *galium verum* are known as *Friggjar gras*, "Frigg's grass," throughout Scandinavia.

Several scholars assume that Jörd was once a powerful goddess in her own right, but surprisingly, we learn very little of her in the sources. In *Gylfaginning* 9, Snorri states that "the Earth is Odin's wife and daughter"[378] and that with her he begot the first of his sons, Asa-Thor. Despite this, there is no evidence to support Jörd being Odin's daughter.[379] In *Gylfaginning* 10, Snorri provides additional detail:

> Norfi or Narfi was the name of a giant who lived in Jötunheim. He had a daughter named Night. She was black and dark in accordance with her ancestry. She was married to a man named Naglfari. Their son was called Aud. Next she was married to someone called Annar. Their daughter was called Jörd [Earth]. Her last husband was Delling, he was of the race of the Aesir. Their son was Day. He was bright and beautiful in accordance with his nature.

If we attempt to reconcile the statements of *Gylfaginning* 9 and 10, we must accept that Annar (or Onar, Jörd's father) is another name for Odin, yet Annar is not recorded among Odin's epithets in any of our sources, including Snorri's *Edda*. In the *Prologue* to *Gylfaginning*, we find Annar as the name of a descendant of Thor, who is portrayed as the grandson of Priam, king of Troy, and a remote ancestor of Odin, a migrant from Asia who came north with his wife Frigg to establish the Aesir dynasty in Sweden.[380] Snorri knew *Þriði* ("Third") as an Odin-name so perhaps *Annar* ("Second') designates

---

wasal, 'the broad wetland'; and Old English poetry of *widere eorþan* (*Genesis* 1348) and *Widsith* 51 of *geond ginne grund*, cp. *Judith* 2.

[378] *Jörðinn var dóttir hans ok kona hans* (Odin's).

[379] McKinnell, ibid., p. 156.

[380] See Faulkes, *Snorri Sturlusson Edda*, p. 3.

one of his two brothers. But, however one interprets them, the two statements cannot be easily reconciled. John Lindow has labeled Snorri's statements in *Gylfaginning* 9 and 10 a "confused discussion" and attempts to sort it out, explaining that "Snorri's use of the definite article in this passage (*Gylf.* 9) suggests a desire to keep separate the earth and the goddess Jörd (Earth)."[381] Even this explanation, however, does little to clear up the confusion.

Based on *Gylfaginning* 10, modern scholars often classify Jörd as a giantess, although her *ætt* is never explicitly stated in the sources. Snorri informs us that she is the granddaughter of the giant Norfi. Her mother, Night, is the giant Norfi's daughter. Because she is descended from giants, many scholars have assumed that Jörd is one too. John Lindow states: "Jörd must have been a giantess in the beginning." While this assumption sounds reasonable, upon reflection it is important to note that other beings who have giantesses as mothers are not automatically classified as giants. Although born of the giantess Bestla, Odin and his brothers are not Jötuns. Conversely, if Jörd is a giantess, her son Thor is not. Neither is her half-brother Dag, Delling's son. If we take paternity as the determining factor, we must consider that Snorri identifies Jörd as Odin's wife and daughter in *Gylfaginning* 9, and that the god Tyr's father and paternal grandmother are said to be giants in *Hymiskviða* 11 and 8. Thus we have reason to question the scholarly assumption that Jörd is a giantess. No specific source supports this supposition. Snorri himself classifies Jörd among the Asyjnes. After enumerating the primary goddesses of Asgard in *Gylfaginning* 35, he writes: "Jörd, the mother of Thor, and Rind, the mother of Vali, are tallied among the Asynjes, (*Gylf.* 36)."[382] John McKinnell remarks that "they do not really belong there,"[383] but other scholars are equally inclined to rank Jörd as a goddess. Rudolf Simek writes:

---

[381] Lindow, *Handbook of Norse Mythology*, p. 205, s.v. Jörd (Earth).

[382] *Jörð, móðir Þórs, ok Rindr, móðir Vála, eru talðar með ásynju.*

[383] McKinnell, ibid., p. 156; Her almost total lack of characterization is noticeable enough that scholars occasionally comment on it; McKinnell remarks that, even today, a young man cannot afford to acknowledge that his mother helped make him a man. Such an admission can discredit him as a 'mother's boy.' He observes: "This may explain why, although Þórr is often called the son of Jörð (or Fjörgynn or Hlöðyn), Jörð never appears as a character in the poems about Thor," p. 182. In fact, she never appears in *any* known myth.

"In the late heathen period, as recorded in our oldest literary sources, Jörð appears to have only been known as Thor's mother, and she plays no further role as an earth-goddess —as she certainly once was."[384]

Jörd is chiefly defined by her relationship to others. In a prose passage in *Skáldskaparmál* 32, Snorri provides a number of paraphrases for earth and cites some skaldic strophes as examples. Among the paraphrases for Earth provided there, Snorri lists: *móður Þórs*, "mother of Thor"; *brúði Óðins*, "bride of Odin"; *dóttur Ónars*, "daughter of Onar"; *dóttir Náttar*, "daughter of Night"; and *systir Auðs ok Dags*, "sister of Aud and Day." Notably, not all of the expressions Snorri provides find support in the given strophes. The strophes cited confirm that the heathen poets recognized Jörd as the bride of Odin, the daughter of Onar, the sister of Aud, and Thor's mother.[385] No known strophes directly support the earth-kennings "Night's daughter" and "Day's sister," although two strophes preserved in the eddic poem *Sigrdrífumál* probably point in this direction:

Heill dagr!	Hail Day!
Heilir dags synir!	Hail Day's sons!
Heil nótt ok nift!	Hail Night and *nipt*!
Óreiðum augum	With placid eyes
litið okkr þinig	behold us and
ok gefið sitjöndum sigr!	give those sitting here victory!
Heilir æsir!	Hail the Æsir!
Heilar ásynjur!	Hail the Asynjur!
Heil sjá in fjölnýta fold!	Hail to the bounteous earth!
Mál ok mannvit	Words and wisdom
gefið okkr mærum tveim	give to us noble twain,
ok læknishendr, meðan lifum.	and healing hands while we live.

If the above strophes are taken together and associated, Night and *nipt*, who appear in the third line of the first strophe, and who are associated with Day and the sons of Day there, may be

---

[384] Simek, *Dictionary of Northern Mythology*, p. 179, s.v. Jörð.

[385] In two verses by Hallfreðr the Troublesome, cited by Snorri in *Skáldskapamál* 32, Earth is called the "tree-grown only daughter of Onar [i.e. Annar]," "Baleyg's [Odin's] broad-faced-bride" and "Aud's splendid sister."

related to "the bounteous earth" which appears in the third line of the second strophe. The word *nipt* means a female relative; it can mean a sister, a daughter or a niece.[386] Here it is generally taken to mean "daughter," based on Snorri's statement that Jörd is the daughter of Night.

Day and Night
Peter Nicolai Arbo, 1874

In popular accounts of Old Norse mythology, Jörd is best known as the mother of Thor. In a strophe Snorri cites as evidence of this relationship in *Skáldskaparmál* 32, the skald Eyvind Skaldaspillir refers to Earth as "the mother of the giant's enemy." Thor is the well-known foe of giants and Earth is his mother. This designation is supported by several poetic passages, leaving no doubt that "mother of Thor" is a genuine Earth-kenning.[387] However, when examining the evidence contained in skaldic and eddic poetry, one finds that Earth is designated as the "mother of Thor" comparatively few times. Upon inspection, it becomes apparent that the skalds more often refer to Earth as "Odin's wife," typically substituting one of his many epithets for his name. At least 19 kennings of this type

---

[386] Cleasby/Vigfusson Dictionary, p. 455, s.v. *nipt*.
[387] *Haustlöng* 14, 17, *Lokasenna* 58, *Þrymskviða* 1, *Þórsdrápa* 15, *Völuspá* 56.

are found. In fact, these constitute the most common type of earth kenning, occurring about three times as often as the "Thor's mother" type:

beðja niðjar Bors, "bedmate of son of Borr" (Egill, lausvisa 21, Eg.30)
vina her-Gauts, "mistress of host-Gautr" (Bragi: *Ragnarsdrápa* 5 = *Skáldskaparmál* 156)
ekkja Svölnis, "widow of Svölnir" (Þjóðólfr, *Haustlöng* 15, *Skáldskaparmál* 66)
vára Svölnis, "wife of Svölnir" (Eyvindr: lausvisa 12, Hkr. I.102)
brúðr val-Týs, "bride of slain-Týr" (Eyvindr: *Háleygjatal* 15, Fsk. 86)
man Yggs, "maiden of Yggr" (Tindr, *Drápa* 8)
bifkván Þriðja (*barrhödduð*), "(fir-tressed) trembling wife of Þriði" (Hallfreðr, *Hákonardrápa* 3, *Skáldskaparmál* 10)
brúðr Báleygs (*breiðleit*), "(broad-faced) bride of Báleygr" (Hallfreðr: *Hákonardrápa*; *Skáldskaparmál* 119)
brúðr Yggjar, "bride of Yggr" (Eyjólfr dáðaskáld, *Bandadrápa* 3, Hkr. I.118)
víf Óska (*munlaust*), "(without doubt) wife of Óski" (Óttarr svarti, *Ólafsdrápa sænska* 2, *Skáldskaparmál* 383)
beðja Þundar, "bedmate of Þundr" (Grettir, *Ævikviða* 7, *Grettis saga* 42)
elja Rindar (*ómynd*) "rival of Rindr (without a bride-price)" (Þjóðólfr, *Sexstefja* 3, *Fsk.*186, *Skáldskaparmál* 122)
drós Þrós, "lady of Þrór" (Haukr, *Íslendingadrápa* 17)
víf Hárs, "wife of Hárr" (*Nóregskonungatal* 20)
man Yggjar, "maiden of Yggr" (*Nóregskonungatal* 47)
mála bága ulfs, "beloved of enemy of wolf" (Snorri, *Háttatal* 3)
rúna vinar Míms, "wife of friend of Mímr" (Snorri, *Háttatal* 3)
mála geir-Týs (*græn*), "(green) girlfriend of spear-Týr" (Sturla, *Hákonarkviða* 21)
beðja Svölnis,"bedmate of Svölnir" (Einarr Gilsson, *Selkolluvísur* 20)[388]

In these examples, the paraphrase "Odin's wife" is understood as a circumlocution simply meaning "earth." Poets compare a ruler's control over the land with Odin's dominance over Jörd, suggesting to some scholars that Odin took her by force.[389] In addition, a loose strophe by Þjóðólfr Árnorsson identifies her as *elja Rindar*, "Rind's rival." According to the eddic poem *Baldurs draumar*

---

[388] https://notendur.hi.is//~eybjorn/ugm/kennings/kennings.html *Lexicon of Kennings* by Eysteinn Björnsson.
[389] McKinnell, ibid., p. 154, cp. Ursula Dronke, *Poetic Edda, Vol. II*, p. 397.

11, Rind bore Odin a son named Vali, who was fated to avenge Baldur's death by killing his brother Hödur. The myth must have been well known as Rind and Vali are mentioned elsewhere in skaldic and eddic poetry,[390] as well as in the Danish histories of Saxo Grammaticus, who tells the story of their encounter in some detail.[391] Þjóðólfr informs us that "Rind's rival" (the Earth) was taken ómynda, "without a bride-price," apparently indicating that Odin took Jörd from her father by force, despite Snorri calling Earth Odin's wife and daughter in Gylfaginning 9. Likewise, much has been made of a single reference to Jörd as an "abandoned wife" of Odin, which occurs in a strophe by Hallfredr. The reading and the conclusions drawn from it, however, are tenuous, as most manuscripts read bifkván, "trembling wife" rather than bíðkvan, "waiting" or "abandoned wife." Even so, this abandonment could just as easily refer to the flight of Hakon's predecessor from Norway (cp. Ólafs saga Tryggvassonar, ch. 16).[392] In these strophes it is difficult to decide whether the reference is to the mythical Jörd or literally to the land.[393] The interpretation depends as much on the view of the scholar as it does the text. In Skáldskaparmál 32, Snorri says that Earth may be called "the rival of Frigg and Rind and Gunnlod" (elju Friggjar ok Rindar ok Gunnlaðar). But, of these, only the expression "Rind's rival" is supported by a poetic citation. We cannot independently verify whether the expressions "Frigg's rival" and "Gunnlöd's rival" are genuine poetic paraphrases for Earth or if they are back-formations created by the Christian author on the model of elja Rindar. As it stands, neither are found in existing skaldic poetry. Relevant here too, Snorri states in Skáldskaparmál 27 that Frigg can also be called "the rival of Rind," as well as "the rival of Jörd and Gunnlöd." Thus, according to Snorri, the poetic paraphrases "Rind's rival" and "Gunnlöd's rival" apply equally to Jörd and Frigg. But, since the earth-kennings "Frigg's rival" and "Gunnlod's rival" are not found in existing poetic sources,[394] it is conceivable that Snorri created them based on the genuine poetic expression "Rind's rival" (elja Rindar). Therefore we have good reason

---

[390] Grougaldur 6, Hrafnagaldr Óðins 23, Völuspá 34, Váfþrúðnismál 51and a verse by Kormak in Skáldskaparmál 55.
[391] Gesta Danorum, Book 3.
[392] McKinnell, ibid., p. 154.
[393] McKinnell, ibid., p. 155.
[394] McKinnell, ibid., p. 164.

to suspect the validity of the term "Frigg's rival" as an authentic kenning for Earth, and likewise the validity of the term "Earth's rival" as an authentic kenning for Frigg. They are otherwise unattested, and probably formed on the pattern of the genuine kenning *elja Rindar.*

While Earth is well-known as "the wife of Odin" in the poetic sources, it should be noted that Odin is never called "the husband of Earth." Instead, he is designated as the "husband of Frigg" three times and once as the "lover of Gunnlöd,"[395] corroborating what we know from other sources:

> *angan Friggjar,* "'delight of Frigg,'" *Völuspá* 56
> *faðmbyggvir Friggjar,* "dweller in Frigg's embrace," *Haraldskvæði* 12
> *frumverr Friggjar,* "foremost husband of Frigg," Hallfreðr vandræðaskald, Lv.
> *farmr arma Gunnlaðar,* "arm burden of Gunnlöd," Steinþórr

To this list, I am tempted to add *faðir Baldrs,* "Baldur's father", since Baldur is famously the son of Frigg. While Odin is known to have had other lovers than his wife Frigg, there can be little doubt that the first thing that would have occurred to a heathen audience hearing the expression "Odin's wife" would have been his constant companion since the earliest recorded sources. Godan (Odin) and Frea (Frigg) first appear as husband and wife in the eighth century *History of the Lombards.* They next appear together on German soil in the tenth century *Second Merseberg Charm* as Wotan and Frija. On Iceland, a tenth century skaldic kenning refers to the gods as *Friggjar niðja,* "Frigg's progeny."[396] In eddic poetry, she and Odin appear together as husband and wife in *Völuspá, Grimnismál, Vafþrúðnismál, Lokasenna,* and *Hrafnagaldur Oðins.* A generation before Snorri Sturlusson composed his *Edda,* the Danish historian Saxo Grammaticus also presents them as husband and wife. In contrast, Odin and Jörd are never shown together. Unlike Frigg, Jörd does not make an appearance in any known myth.

---

[395] Odin's relationship with Gunnlöd can justifiably be characterized as a marriage, cp. *Hávamál* 104-110, which alludes to a wedding, to which Odin arrives in the disguise of the expected suitor. See David A. H. Evans, *Hávamál,* pp. 120-123.
[396] *Egil's Saga,* ch. 79, *Complete Sagas of the Icelanders* I, p. 151

Franz Stassen, 1910

In skaldic poetry, we thus encounter a logical paradox without precedent. There the recurrent poetic paraphrase "Odin's wife", which means "Earth", rather than characterizing Odin's traditional spouse as the earth-goddess, is exclusively interpreted as a reference to a virtually unknown giantess! Because Snorri presents Frigg and Jörd as distinct personalities, we have been conditioned to think of them as separate entities. Thus, in skaldic poetry, we take most references to Earth literally, accepting that she is Thor's mother, Aud's sister, Dag's sister, and Annar's daughter, except in one case — the most frequently occurring— where we are supposed to take the designation figuratively. Although Loki addresses Frigg as *Viðris kvæn,* "Vidrir's (Odin's) wife" in the eddic poem *Lokasenna* (st. 26), we are expected to interpret the same kenning in skaldic verse as one, and only one, of his giantess-concubines. In skaldic poetry alone, the expressions: "Odin's wife, bride, lady, beloved, bedmate," etc. are exclusively taken to mean Earth (*Jörð*). Yet in all other poetic and prose sources, "Odin's wife" is understood to mean the goddess Frigg. This is not only illogical, but unnecessary. Following the same reasoning, we could just as easily understand the term "Odin's wife" to mean any female with whom Odin has had sexual relations. Instead of referring exclusively to Jörd, we might imagine that the kennings in question indicated Frigg, Gunnlöd or Rind, since, by this definition, they too are Odin's "wives." Yet this is clearly not the case. In the context of skaldic poetry, the expression "Odin's wife" obviously indicates the Earth. Since Frigg is recognized as Odin's wife in every other instance, it seems reasonable to conclude that Odin's wife Frigg is identical to Jörd, the Earth. Only Snorri's statements in the *Prose Edda* prevent us from drawing this conclusion with confidence.

A study of Jörd's known epithets may shed light on this matter. Thor is unquestionably the son of Odin and Earth. This is amply affirmed by poetic examples where Thor is known as "the son of Odin" (*Völuspá* 55) and more often as Earth's son. The poetic examples we have expand our knowledge of Jörd, providing us additional epithets by which she is known. They are:

> *Jarðar sunr*, Jörd's son, *Haustlöng* 14
> *Jarðar burr*, Jörd's son, *Þrymskvida* 1, *Lokasenna* 58
> *konr Jarðar*, Jörd's kinsman, *Þórsdrápa* 15
> *Hlöðynar mogr*, Hlödyn's son, *Völuspá* 56
> *Fjorgynjar burr*, Fjörgynn's son, *Völuspá* 56
> *Grundar svein*, Ground's son, *Haustlöng* 17

These epithets refer to the physical earth and the personal earth-goddess at the same time. They are indistinguishable. In *Hárbardsljóð* 56, Thor is told to meet his mother Fjörgyn in Verland, the "land of men," where she will show him the "roads of relatives (*áttunga brautir*) to Odin's land."[397] The phrase "Fjörgyn's eel" (*ál fjörgynr*) is a kenning for snake, while *á fjörgynju* simply means "on earth." The name Hlódyn first appears around 950 AD in a strophe by Völu-Steinn (*Skj* I B, 93), where the poet contrasts the dark earth with the green dress of Hlódyn, when recounting the funeral of his son.[398] Similarly, the phrase *myrk-Hlöðynjar markar*, the "dark woods

---

[397] In *Sonnatorrek* 21, the heathen skald Egill Skalla-Grímssonar describes Odin raising his dead son *upp í Goðheim* ('up into the world of the gods'). Since Thor's mother Fjörgynn-Jörd is related to Delling's son Dag, who rides his horse Skinfaxi across the sky each day, I suggest that the expression "roads of relatives" here refers to the heavens. Thor himself drives his chariot "beneath the halls of the moon" (*Haustlöng* 14).

[398] McKinnell, ibid., p. 153-54.

of Hlóðyn" in Einarr skálaglamm's *Vellekla*[399] likens the forest to the dark hair of a woman. In many Indo-European traditions, earth is characterized as "dark" or "black"[400] and plants are a common alloform of hair,[401] demonstrating the great age of these concepts.

Scholars recognize the names Fjörgynn, Hlóðyn, and Grund as synonyms of Jörd. In fact, all of the Old Norse divinities have alternate names (*heiti*). In the *Prose Edda*, Snorri Sturluson lists alternate names of Odin, Thor, and Freyja, among others. In *Gylfaginning* 3, Snorri says that Odin is known as *Alföðr, Herran or Herjan, Þriðja, Nikarr* or *Hnikarr, Nikuðr* or *Hnikuðr, Fjölnir, Óski, Ómi, Bifliði* or *Biflindi, Sviðurr, Sviðrir, Viðrir,* and *Jálg* or *Jálkr*. In the *nafnaþular*, Thor is known as *Atli, Ásabragr, Ennilangr, Eindriði, Björn, Hlórriði, Harðvéorr, Vingþórr, Sonnungr, Véudr* and *Rymr*; while Freyja is known as *Mardöll, Hörn, Gefn, Sýr, Skálf, Vanadís,* and *Þrungva.*[402] In *Gylfaginning* 27, Heimdall is known as *Hallinskíði* and *Gullintanni*. It would be a mistake to conclude that these lists were all-inclusive or complete. In addition to those listed in Snorri's *Edda*, more names can be discovered by turning to poetic sources. Numerous epithets of Odin are listed in *Grímnismál* 46-54, and in mythological poems that mention Odin we find more. In the prose introduction to *Rigsthula*, we learn that Heimdall is known as *Rígr* and in *Grímnismál* 21 he appears as *Þjóðvitnir.*[403] In *Völuspá*, Loki is called *Hveðrungr*. Oftentimes a god is called by different names in the course of a single poem. In *Hymiskviða*, Thor is known as *Hlórriði, Véurr,* as well as *Þórr* (Thor). In *Thrymskvida*, he is called *Vingþórr* and *Hlórriði*. Sometimes the meaning is not as obvious. For example, in a strophe preserved in *Skáldskparmál* 58, Freyr is called "Beli's bane" and said to ride the horse *Blóðughófi.*[404] In an adjacent strophe, the same horse bears the

---

[399] *Heimskringla, Ólafs Saga Tryggvasonar* 26.

[400] West, ibid., p. 179-80.

[401] Bruce Lincoln, as well as J.P. Mallory and D.Q. Adams (*Encyclopedia of Indo-European Culture*, s.v. *grass*) make this point.

[402] Faulkes, *Edda*, p. 156-7.

[403] *Þjóðvitnis fiskr*, "Thjodvitnir's fish," is best understood as a kenning for Bifröst in the context of this strophe. The name *Þjóðvitnir*, usually taken as "Mighty wolf," can also mean "the one with mighty senses [*vit*]" (i.e. Heimdall). His *fiskr* (fish) which stands still in the stream is the bridge Bifröst, since *spörðr*, "fishtail", designates the end of a bridge in Old Icelandic. See "When is a Fish a Bridge?" https://notendur.hi.is/eybjorn/ugm/grm21.html

[404] Compare *Völuspá* 53.

mighty *Atriði*. Thus, Atridi is probably a byname of Frey. Such polyonomy is a key characteristic of Old Icelandic poetry, as well as the conceptual basis of the *heiti* and *kenning* conventions.

In *Skáldskaparmál* 70, Snorri informs us that Earth too had many names. He cites poetic passages in support of each of the following bynames: *Jörð, Fold, Grund, Land, Fief, Hauðr, Lauð; Hlödyn, Frón* and *Fjörgyn*. By turning to poetic passages outside of Snorri's *Edda*, we can add one more: *Hlín*. In the strophe that appears in *Hávarðar saga ísfirðings*, chapter 14, lines 5-6 read:

þann vissak mér manna	"No man fell upon Hlin to a greater
mest alls á Hlín fallinn	advantage for me, than this man."

The heathen expression means that no man's death was of greater benefit to the poet than this one's. Here Hlin is used as a byname of Jörd. "To fall upon Hlin" means "to fall to the ground," "to die." Thus Hlin is a poetic synonym for Jörd, the earth. The name means "protector" from *hleina*, "to have peace and security"[405] and may be related to the word *hlein* meaning "a rock projecting like a pier into the sea" as well as a perpendicular loom used for weaving.[406] In poetic sources, where the name of a goddess can be used as the base of a kenning for woman, the name Hlin occurs frequently, indicating her divine status. As such a base, Hlin was a favorite.[407] In *Gylfaginning* 35, Snorri lists Hlin as a minor goddess, the twelfth Asynje and a servant of Frigg. Snorri portrays Hlin, Jörd and Frigg as distinct goddesses. They are all listed twice as Asynjes: once in *Gylfaginning* 35-36 and again in the *þulur* where all three names appear in a list of the Asynjur. Despite this, Hlin's status as an independent goddess is not supported by the older poetry, which is Snorri's acknowledged source. As seen above, Hlin is used as a byname of Jörd in *Hávarðar*

---

[405] Ursula Dronke, *Poetic Edda*, Volume II, p. 149.
[406] Richard Cleasby and Gudbrand Vigfusson, *An Icelandic-English Dictionary* 2nd Edition, (1957).
[407] The skald Kormak, who uses an unusual number of woman-kennings with goddess names as the base in his verse, utilizes the name *Hlín* most frequently (six times), "with the relatively unknown Eir a close runner up (five times)." "It is perhaps a meaningful coincidence" that "both names mean 'protector, protection': *eir* is used as a common noun with this meaning in Kormakr's verse (v.15)," *Mediaeval Scandinavia*, Vol. 3 (1971), p. 26.

saga ísfirðings 13, while in *Völuspá* R52, Hlin is used a byname of Frigg. The opening lines read:

Þá kømr Hlínar	Then comes Hlin's
harmr annarr fram,	second grief to pass,
er Óðinn ferr	when Odin goes
við úlf vega...	to fight the Wolf...

According to this strophe, Hlin's "second grief" occurs when Odin goes to fight the wolf. The final lines state "then 'Frigg's delight' (Odin) shall fall." The name Hlin, which means 'protector', used here for Frigg, is probably ironic since she is helpless to protect her husband. Similarly, Snorri says of *Hlín*: "she is given the function of protecting people that Frigg wishes to save from some danger," (*Gylfaginning* 35, Faulkes tr.), which "relies upon an etymological link between *Hlín* and *hlein*, 'peaceful refuge.'"[408] Snorri's identification of Hlin as an independent goddess while quoting this strophe from *Völuspá* has understandably caused some confusion among scholars. In the index to his translation of *Snorri's Edda* (1988), under *Hlin*, Anthony Faulkes writes: "...perhaps another name for Frigg; her first grief would have been the death of Baldr." Rudolf Simek (1984) states: "Presumably, Hlin is really another name for Frigg and Snorri misunderstood her to be a goddess in her own right in his reading of the *Völuspá* stanza."[409] Most translators accept the identification of Hlin and Frigg, and some go so far as to replace the name Hlin with Frigg's in this strophe. In her 1996 translation of the *Poetic Edda*, as well as her 2014 revision, Carolyne Larrington replaces Hlin with Frigg and notes that Frigg's second grief was the death of her husband Odin; her first being the death of her son Baldur. This is the most common interpretation of the strophe. The heathen skalds thus use *Hlín* as a byname of both Frigg and Jörd, but no other goddess.

At this point, the only thing that prevents us from concluding that Frigg, Jörd, and Hlin are alternate names of a single individual is Snorri's treatment of them as three distinct personalities. An attempt to explain this apparent contradiction by suggesting that the name of one of Odin's wives can be substituted for the name of any other, since in poetic kennings the name of any goddess can be used as the

---

[408] Dronke, ibid, p. 149.
[409] Simek, *Dictionary of Northern Mythology*, p. 153, s.v. Hlín.

base for a woman-kenning, is patently absurd! It would be equivalent to saying that the name of any one of Odin's sons could be substituted for the name of any other; that Thor could be used in place of Baldur and visa versa. This ill-considered supposition finds no support in the extant poetic sources. Instead, we find that Frigg and Jörd are both referred to as Odin's wife, and that the byname Hlin (as well as the poetically unattested expression "Gunnlod's rival,") can be used to designate either. As Karin Olsen notes "Unfortunately, most goddess names are so little used outside of skaldic poetry that we have to rely heavily on Snorri's interpretations of them."[410] In this case, however, we have valid reasons to doubt his explanation.

Frigga Asks All Things to Swear Oaths
Maria Klugh, 1909

It should now be obvious that the heathen poets who composed these poems knew Jörd as an alternate name of Odin's

---

[410] "*Woman Kennings in the Gísla Saga Súrssonar: A Study*" in *Studies in English Language and Literature: Doubt Wisely* (1996), edited by M. J. Toswell, E. M. Tyler, p. 269.

wife Frigg— in other words, that Frigg represents the Earth in Germanic tradition. This is immediately apparent in *Lokasenna*. When Loki first insults Frigg, she threatens him saying:

"Veiztu, ef ek inni ættak	27. "Know that if I had,
Ægis höllum i	at Ægir's halls,
Baldri líkan bur,	a son like Baldur,
út þú né kvæmir	you would not come away from
frá ása sonum,	the Æsir's sons: you would have
ok væri þá at þér vreiðum vegit."	been fiercely assailed."

When Thor finally bursts into the hall to fiercely assail Loki, after he has insulted all of the gods gathered at Aegir's for a feast, the caluminator of the gods wryly quibs:

"Jarðar burr	58. "Earth's son has now come in;
er hér nú inn kominn,	Why do you rage so, Thor?
hví þrasir þú svá, Þórr?	But you won't be so bold
En þá þorir þú ekki,	that you fight with the wolf
er þú skalt við ulfinn vega,	and he swallows Victory-father
ok svelgr hann allan Sigföður."	(Odin)[411] whole."

Thus, when Frigg (who is prescient) cries out for "a son like Baldur," *Baldri líkan bur*, to defend her against Loki's bitter accusations, *Jarðar burr*, "Earth's son," Thor, arrives to drive him from the hall. Frigg's designation of the gods as *ása sonum*, which especially applies to Thor and Baldur as sons of Odin, the father of the Æsir, corresponds to Egil Skalla-grímsson's designation of the gods as *Friggjar niðja*, "Frigg's progeny." Therefore, with this tentative conclusion in mind, let's look at what other poetic sources have to say of her.

---

[411] *Sigföður,* "Victory-father," a name of Odin, used here ironically as in *Völuspá* 53, at the moment he falls prey to Fenrir.

Frigga
The Edda Frieze by H. E. Freund, 1821

X. The Mother of the Gods

"Although the conception of a mother goddess remains a shadowy one, and Frigg in particular is an obscure figure, it is no longer customary to dismiss her as of little importance, and to explain her away as a pure literary creation. As Odin's wife and the queen of Asgard, she plays a consistent part in the poetry, and the lack of detail about her in myths and the failure to find place names named after her may be due to the fact that she was remembered under other titles."

— H.R. Ellis Davidson
Gods and Myths of the Viking Age, 1964, p.114.

Rather than a pantheon of gods, the Nordic deities are more often portrayed as an extended family, a clan. This structure can be seen in mythological as well as historic sources. In the tenth century *Second Merseburg Charm*, for example, the gods named can be identified as a husband and wife, parents and a child, and two sets of sisters. The verse begins: "Phol and Wodan rode into the woods, there the foot of Baldur's foal went out of joint." From the context, Phol appears to be the rider of Baldur's horse, i.e. Baldur himself.[412] Wodan or Odin is, of course, his father. Nearest Phol-Baldur rides Sinhtgunt and her sister Sunna, the sun goddess. Then comes Odin's wife Frija (Frigga), who is Baldur's mother, with her sister Volla, whom we recognize as Fulla, Frigg's handmaiden, in the Icelandic *Eddas*. In succession, they each attempt to heal the sprained leg of *balderes uolon*, until at last, Odin succeeds. The riding party is thus a family unit. Based on their relative positions, Sinhtgunt, being first on the scene, presumably because she rode closest to Phol-Baldur, may be Baldur's wife, Nanna, under an epithet. Her sister Sunna, the Sun, accompanies her, suggesting a celestial procession. At the very least, a minimalist reading of the charm yields two sets of sisters, Odin and his traditional wife Frigg, along with the earliest record of their son Baldur's name.[413] Likewise, in the poem *Lokasenna*, the gods gathered together for a feast are acknowledged as husbands and wives, fathers and mothers, sons and daughters. At Loki's instigation, Aegir's feast becomes a family quarrel with charges of cowardice, infidelity and

---

[412] For a full exposition of this charm, see Appendix B: Frigg's Son Baldur.
[413] Simek, *Dictionary of N. Mythology*, p. 278, s.v. *Second Merseburg Charm*.

incest until "Earth's son" arrives to drive the accuser out. Throughout eddic and skaldic poetry, we are informed of the gods' familial ties: Earth is Thor's mother, Thor is Odin's son, Frigg is Odin's wife, Baldur is their son, etc. Even relationships that are no longer understood are enumerated. In *Harbardsljóð* 9, Thor is said to be Meili's brother; in *Hymiskvíða* 5, we are told that the giant Hymir is Tyr's father; and in *Hrafnagaldur Óðins* 6, we learn that Idunn is Ivaldi's daughter.[414] Bonds of kinship were obviously important to the ancients. Poems such as *Hyndluljod* are openly concerned with the genealogy of heroic figures; members of the god clan appear liberally in their family trees. In at least two Anglo-Saxon genealogies, royal lines descend from Odin and his son Bældægg, commonly recognized as Baldur.

Some sources make this kinship plain. When the heathen king Chlodwig, the first ruler of the Franks (c. 486 AD), rebukes his Christian wife for deriding his gods as nothing but feckless bits of stone, wood and metal, he responds: "By the will of our gods all things are created and produced. Evidently your god can do nothing, nor has it yet been proven that he [Christ] belongs to the *genere* of gods."[415] The word *genere* (from *genus*) is Latin for "family, house, ancestry, race, class, noble birth," and again points to a divine hereditary monarchy, to which Jesus was an outsider. As recorded in the twenty-sixth chapter of the *Life of Anskar, The Apostle of the North* (801-865 AD), when Anskar arrived at Birka and found the congregation backsliden in grievous error, a heathen man approached him, declaring that he had attended an assembly of the gods believed to own the land, who sent him to the king with this message:

> "You, I say, have long enjoyed our goodwill, and under our protection the land in which you dwell has long been fertile and has had peace and prosperity. You have also duly sacrificed and performed the vows made to us, and your worship has been well pleasing to us. But now you are keeping back the usual sacrifices

---

[414] Meili ("the mild") is likely an alternate name of Baldur; Odin's son Týr was probably fostered by the giant Hymir in the same way Thor was fostered by the giants Vingnir and Hlóra (*Skáldskaparmál* 4), called the "Duke Loricus and his wife Lora" in the *Prologue to Gylfaginning*; and lastly Iðunn, "of elf-kind" (*álfa ættar*), who is the "youngest of Ivaldi's elder children," and thus a half-sister of Ivaldi's sons, who forge gifts for the gods (*Skaldskaparmál* 42, *Grímnismál* 43).

[415] Gregory of Tours I, 2. ch. 29: *Nee de deorum genere esse probatur.*

and are slothful in paying your freewill offerings; you are, moreover, displeasing us greatly by introducing a foreign god in order to supplant us. If you desire to enjoy our goodwill, offer the sacrifices that have been omitted and pay greater vows. And do not receive the worship of any other god, who teaches that which is opposed to our teaching, nor pay any attention to his service. Furthermore, if you desire to have more gods and we do not suffice, we will agree to summon your former King Eric to join us so that he may be one of the gods."[416]

Since gods commonly appear in royal pedigrees, we can conclude that King Eric was considered kin to them. We find an exact parallel in the case of Hakon Jarl. When the Norwegians briefly returned to paganism under his rule (c. 936-60 AD), after the efforts of his father Harald Fairhair (880-930 AD) to Christianize the country, Hakon performed sacrifices more aggressively than before, with the result that grain and herring became more plentiful and the seasons more propitious. In *Ynglingasaga* 9, a skaldic verse by Eyvindr Skáldaspillir informs us that Odin and Skadi had many sons after she divorced Njord. Snorri adds that one of them was Sæming, from whom Hakon Jarl reckoned his race. Under his reign, honoring the old gods, the earth blossomed.

According to the history of the Norwegian kings found in the *Fagrskinna* manuscript and *Heimskringla*, when Ólaf Eiríkrson's son, Jákob, whose mother was a Christian, assumed the throne, he was required to change his name by the people. According to *Heimskringla*, *Ólafs Saga Helga*, ch. 88, "his name ill-pleased the Swedes," as "no Swedish king had borne that name." At an assembly of the Uppland Swedes, one Freywith (Freyviðr) made this impassioned plea:

> "We Uppland Swedes do not wish that in our days the crown go from the line of the ancestors of our ancient kings while there is such good choice as we have. King Ólaf has two sons, and we desire one of them to be king. But there is a great difference between them. The one is born in wedlock and of Swedish races on both sides whereas the other is the son of a servant woman, herself half Wendish."

---

[416] Chapter 24, translated by Charles H. Robinson.

The text continues:

> "This opinion was received with loud acclaim and all wanted Jákob for king. ...Thereupon, the brothers Freywith and Arnvith had the king's son, Jákob, brought before the assembly and had him given the title of king."

At the same time, the Swedes renamed him *Önund*, the name he bore until his death. The rejection of the name *Jákob* by the Swedish people can be interpreted as a rejection of the new faith. The people rejected the name of the Biblical patriarch Jacob for their ruler and chose a heathen name "from the line of the ancestors" of their ancient kings instead. In *Völundarkviða* 2, Anund-Önund occurs as a byname of the elf-smith Völund. Although the name is typically emended to *Völundar* by modern editors, the *Codex Regius* manuscript at line 2/10 reads *onundar*.[417] In verses 16 and 18 of the same poem, Völund is characterized as a "prince of the elves." In *Grimnismál* 5, elves are closely associated with Freyr, who is given their realm Alfheim upon cutting his first tooth. And elves are closely associated with the gods as a whole through the alliterative formula *Æsir ok alfar*, "Aesir and elves", which appears in both Old Norse and Old English poetry.

Hermod with Frigga, Freyja, Hnoss and Gersemi
from *The Edda Frieze* by H. E. Freund, 1821

---

[417] In Saxo Grammaticus' *Gesta Danorum*, Book 7, one Anund has as his brother Toko, who like Völund, is a famed for his skill in archery.

In the mythology, the gods function as both a ruling council (*Völuspá* 6, 9, R23, R25 and R50, among others) and as an extended family or clan, whose members intermarry with both allied and enemy tribes. The divine social order reflects the Germans' own tribal structure. *Rígsthula* tells us that one of the gods, Heimdall, ordained the social order among the people, fathering the eponymous founder of each caste by sleeping between the man and wife in each of the three homes he visits. These bonds of kinship are also reflected in their temples, where we often find groups of idols representing gods among whom we can discern a family relationship where the evidence permits. In the eleventh century temple at Old Uppsala described by Adam of Bremen, we find Odin and Thor who are father and son, along with a male god named Fricco, whose name connects him to Odin's wife Frigga or Fricca. Throughout the Icelandic sagas, we discover idols gathered in such groups. *Kjalnesinga saga* ch. 2 describes a temple at Hof, 100 ft. long and 60 ft. wide with windows and wall hangings everywhere. The inner sanctuary was circular like the hull of a ship. Thor stood in the midst of it with other gods on either side. In *Eyrbyggja saga*, in the account of Thorolf Mostrarskegg's temple at Hofstaðir, idols are placed around the platform in a choir-like structure within the temple. In *Hrafnkels Saga Freysgóði*, Hrafnkel raises a great temple to Freyr at Aðalbol, where he held great sacrifices to the gods. This temple stood on a rock above a deep river pool and contained images of the gods adorned with robes and ornaments, even though Hrafnkel loved Freyr above all the others and gave him a half-share in his treasure. In *Olaf Tryggvason's saga*, Guðbrandr of the Dales, a good friend of Hakon Jarl, owned a temple dedicated to Thor, which contained figures of Thor and of Hakon's patron goddesses, Thorgerðr and Irpa. Thor was seated in his car and all were adorned with clothes and ornaments, including rings on their arms. As described, the idol of Thorgerðr stood as tall as a full-grown man and wore a hood on its head. In *Jómsvíkinga saga* and *Þorleifs þáttr jarlsskálds*, we learn that she and Irpa are sisters. This temple and Hakon Jarl's temple at Hlaðir were the two chief centers of worship. The Christian king Olaf Tryggvason systematically destroyed Hakon's temples and despoiled the idols. In his expedition to Trondhjem, Olaf desecrated the temple at Maer, which contained several fixed idols, in the midst of whom sat Thor, "an image of great size, all adorned with gold and silver," which he burned.

An eyewitness from the tenth century makes the relationship between these wooden idols plain. In the *Rusila* of Ibn Fadhlan, a firsthand account of Scandinavian merchants along the Volga river in Russia, the smaller icons surrounding the central idol, are said to represent its extended family:

> "The moment their boats reach this dock every one of them disembarks, carrying bread, meat, onions, milk and alcohol, and goes to a tall piece of wood set up <in the ground>. This piece of wood has a face like the face of a man and is surrounded by small figurines behind which are long pieces of wood set up in the ground. <When> he reaches the large figure, he prostrates himself before it and says, 'Lord, I have come from a distant land, …And I have brought this offering,' leaving what he has brought with him in front of the piece of wood, saying, 'I wish you to provide me with a merchant who has many dīnārs and dirhams and who will buy from me whatever I want <to sell> without haggling over the price I fix.' Then he departs. If he has difficulty in selling <his goods> and he has to remain too many days, he returns with a second and third offering. If his wishes prove to be impossible he brings an offering to every single one of those figurines and seeks its intercession, saying, 'These are the wives, daughters and sons of our Lord.' He goes up to each figurine in turn and questions it, begging its intercession and groveling before it." (James E. Montgomery translation).

That the gods form a family is self-evident in their leadership. Odin is the All-Father, as well as their ruler. The gods together are esteemed "Frigg's progeny" (*Friggjar niðja*) in a skaldic kenning by Egill Skalla-grímsson in *Sonatorrek* 2. As previously demonstrated, numerous poetic references designate the Earth as Odin's wife and Thor's mother, and throughout Germanic history we find traces of a powerful Earth-Mother from the earliest records to the close of the ancient heathen era and beyond. Yet, despite the diverse designations for this figure, Odin is consistently shown to have only one legal wife. Whenever he appears, Frigga most frequently stands at his side. Moreover, while evidence for Odin's wife Frigg and his wife the Earth are contemporary and congruous— occurring at the same time in the same places and genres— they are never shown together. Like Diana Prince and Wonder Woman, we apparently never see Frigg and Jörd side by side.[418] Still their common identity should come as no surprise. The conclusion is so obvious in fact that many scholars of past centuries took it for granted that Odin's wife Frigg and Mother Earth were one and the same. As early as 1771, James Macpherson writing in *An Introduction to the History of Great Britain and Ireland*, states:

> "The Angli, in the days of Tacitus, worshiped the Earth under the name of Hertha [Nerthus]; and it was the same divinity who afterwards obtained the title of Frea, the spouse of the great Odin."

In 1780, the author of *An Universal History*, Vol. 17, writes:

> "One may find a great resemblance between the ancient Germans, Suevi, Æstii, etc. and other most distant nations: such, for instance, we may reckon the worship of the goddess Hertha, …which agreed with that which the Romans and others paid to the earth under the name of *Magna Deorum Mater*; or, as their worship of Fria or Friga under that denomination."

In his *History of Great Britain* (1802), Robert Henry explains:

> "As Odin was believed to be the father, Frea [Frigga] was esteemed the mother, of all the other gods. In most ancient times, Frea was the same with the goddess Herthus, or Earth, who was so devoutly worshiped by the Angli and other German nations. But when Odin, the conqueror of the north, usurped the honours due only to the true Odin, his wife Frea usurped those which had been formerly paid to Mother Earth. She was worshiped as the goddess of love and pleasure, who bestowed on her votaries a variety of delights, particularly happy marriages and easy childbirths.."

The same explanation appears almost verbatim under the entry for *Frea* (Frigga) in the *Encyclopedia Britainnica* from at least the 7th to 10th editions (1810-1856). In 1812, François-René vicomte de Chateaubriand,[419] also speaking of "Hertha, that is Mother Earth" in *Germania* chapter 40, sees her as a universal goddess, saying:

---

[418] The same cannot be said of Frigg and Freyja who are frequently equated by scholars. They sit side-by-side in *Lokasenna* and are invoked together in *Oddrúnargrátr* 9.

[419] *The Martyrs or The Triumph of the Christian Religion*, Vol. I, pp. 241-2.

"The name of the goddess in all the northern languages signifies earth; thus in the ancient Gothic we find, *airtha*; in the Anglo-Saxon, *eorthe, ertha, hertha*; in English, *earth*. ...The earth has been worshiped as a common Mother, by most unenlightened nations. The Greeks worshiped her under the name of Ge —the Latins under that of Tellus. They considered her as the most ancient of all the gods after Chaos."

Most, however, correctly limit her range to the Germanic peoples. In *Pinnock's Improved Edition of Dr. Goldsmith's Abridgement of the History of England* (1823), the author observes, "In the most ancient times, Friga, or Frea, was the same with the goddess Hertha, or Earth," a phrase that would be repeated verbatim in numerous works until the early 20th century, frequently with its corollary, "Thor, the eldest and bravest of the sons of Woden and Friga, was, after his parents, considered as the greatest god among the Saxons and Danes."

In 1829, Finnur Magnússon wrote "[W]ith us Odin was considered the All-father, and Frigga or Earth as All-mother."[420] John Henry Brady in *Clavis Calendaria*, or *A Compendious Analysis of the Calendar* (1839) noted, "Friga was the mother, as Odin was the father, of all the pagan divinities — which, however, infringes upon the character ascribed to Herthus, or 'Mother Earth,' the reputed 'Mother of the Gods.'" William Burder in *Religious Ceremonies and Customs* (1841) affirms this view, "Frea or Friga, the consort of Odin, was the most amiable of all the Scandinavian goddesses ...and under the name of Hertha she was considered as a personification of earth." In his *Universal History from the Creation of the World to the Beginning of the 18th Century* (1847), Lord Woodhouselee echoed this sentiment,

"The next in power to Odin, was Friga or Frea, his wife. The God of heaven, says the Edda, united himself with the goddess of the earth; and from this conjunction sprang all the race of subordinate deities. ...The third divinity in power and in authority was Thor the son of Odin and of Frea."

In 1851, nearly fifteen years before publishing the first accurate English translation of the complete *Poetic Edda*, Anglo-Saxon scholar Benjamin Thorpe concurred:

[420] *Den förste November, den förste August*, p. 129.

"Odin's wife was Frigg (the earth). She occurs but rarely under the general appellation of earth, but often under other denominations, according to the several points of view from which she is considered. The supreme among all the goddesses is Frigg, the fertile summer-earth, who more than all others bewails her noble son Baldur's (the summer's) death. ... As mother of Thor, the thunder, the earth is called Fiorgyn (Fiorgvin), (Goth. Fairguni, mountain) and Hlodyn" (*Northern Mythology*, 1851)

The same concept is present in the fresco by Gustav Heidenreich in the Neues Museum, Berlin executed 1850-1852. There Odin on his throne is flanked by the earth goddess Hertha [Nerthus], as her relations Night and Day ride overhead.

Hertha, Night and Day, and Odin
Gustav Heidenreich, Neues Museum, Berlin, 1852

The *New American Cyclopaedia* (1856) *s.v. Hertha*, expands on this, stating: "The Scandinavians called her Jord; according to them she was daughter of Annar and of Night, sister of Dagur or Day by the mother's side, wife of Odin, and mother of Thor, and thought to be the same as Frigga." William Reader in *The Ruins of Kenilworth, an Historical Poem* (1856) notes, "Friga or Frea was the wife of Woden—the father and mother of all the Saxon gods. Friday derives its name from her day—Friga's daeg. Thor was the eldest son of Woden and Friga." Robert Bigby in *Irminsula, The Great Pillar* (1864), holds that "Friga or Frigga, the daughter and wife of Odin, was, in the most ancient times, the same with the goddess Hertha or Earth." Anne Fulton Hope, author of *Conversion of the Teutonic Race* (1872), writes:

"After these supreme gods may be placed the great Goddess Mother of earth, universally worshipped, though under various names, as Nerthus, Hertha, Bertha, Erce, Holda, Ostara, Cisa, Frigg, Frea, etc. The variety of her names and worship in different places, has given rise to much dispute as to the identity of the goddess. She seems to have been worshipped under the double character of the house-mother, the patroness of spinning, and all domestic duties, and of the mother, or source of all fruitfulness. Sometimes she is compared to Juno or Diana, at others to Ceres or Cybele."

The *American Cyclopædia*, Vol 12, (1874) adds:

"The goddess called Nerthus by Tacitus, which name was subsequently corrupted into Hertha, whom the Franks worshiped as Holda or Holle, the Bavarians as Perchta, and the Low Germans as Fria or Frigg, appears to have been known first to the early inhabitants of the island of Rügen in the Baltic."

In 1877, *The Condensed American Cyclopaedia*, under *"Mythology"* (p. 577) elaborates on this, stating:

"The mythology of the Germans is built upon the same foundation as that of the Scandinavians, and the principal deities are the same. Wuotan, or Wotan according to the Low Germans, is the Odin of the North. Donar, the Scandinavian Thor, is the god of storms. Fro seems to have answered to Freyr. Baldur or Phol is a youthful warrior, and somewhat connected with the blessings of the season of spring. The goddess called Nerthus by Tacitus, afterward corrupted into Hertha, was worshiped by the Franks as Holda or Holle, by the Bavarians as Perchta, and by the Low Germans as Fria or Frigg."

In his book *Dawn of History* (1878), Charles F. Keary observes: "The earth-mother of the Teutons was Frigg, the wife of Odin; but perhaps when Frigg's natural character was forgotten, Hertha (Earth) became separated into another personage." He expands on this four years later in *Outlines of Primitive Belief Among the Indo-European Races*:

"Here, as among Greeks and Romans, the great patron of the peasant folk was the earth goddess. In Tacitus the divinity appears under the name of Nerthus. ... Other German names which seem to belong more or less to the same divinity are Harke, Holda, Perchta, Bertha. We must class with these beings the Norse Frigg

(German Freka). Her I have already taken as an example of the way in which the earth goddess may lose her distinctive character and put on that of the heaven god through becoming his wife. Hera, we saw, did this in the Greek pantheon, and Frigg does the same in the Northern. She is not a conspicuous character in the Scandinavian mythology. To Frigg, Freyja bears the same relationship that Persephone bears to Demeter; wherefore we may say that Frigg, Freyr, and Freyja correspond to Demeter, Dionysus, and Persephone, and more closely still to the Ceres, Liber, and Libera of the Romans."

In 1880, M.W. MacDowall, writing in *Asgard and the Gods*, adapted from the work of Wilhelm Wägner, explains:

"The old Germanic races, therefore, knew Frea alone as Queen of Heaven, and she and her husband Wodan together ruled over the world. The name Frigga or Frick was also used for her, for in Hesse, and especially in Darmstadt, people used to say fifty years ago of any fat old woman: "*Sie ist so dick wie die alte Frick.*" (She is as thick as Old Frick.) The word *frigen* is also related to *sich freuet* (rejoice); thus Frigg was the goddess of joy (*freude*). She took the place of the Earth-goddess Nerthus (mistakenly Hertha), who, Tacitus informs us, was worshipped in a sacred grove on an island in the sea. Nerthus was probably the wife of the god of heaven, in whom we recognise Zio or Tyr."

In 1883, James Sime writing in *Histories of England, France, Germany, and Holland* published by *Encyclopaedia Britannica*, professes:

"Tacitus says that a powerful goddess called Nerthus was worshiped on the shores of the Baltic; he also mentions Isis as a goddess of the Suevic tribes. Both names evidently refer to the same divinity. On the coasts her symbol was a ship; inland, it was a waggon; in some districts she was represented with the plough. Like Donar, she presided over marriage; she also watched over the house and the fields, was the giver and protector of children, and ruled the world of the dead. At a later time she was kuown to the Saxons as Fria or Frigg, to the Franks as Holda, to the Bavarians as Perchta,— the first name indicating her freedom of manner, the second her kindness, the third her splendour. In the Scandinavian mythology Frigg is the wife of Odin; and to this day, it is said, the peasants in certain parts of Low Germany speak of Fru Fricke, the wife of the wild hunter Wod."

In 1884, Swedish scholar Viktor Rydberg in his *Investigations into Germanic Mythology*, Volume 1, (translated into English as *Teutonic Mythology* by Rasmus Anderson, 1889), concludes:

"In regard to the goddess Earth, Tacitus states (ch. 40), as a characteristic trait that she is believed to take a lively interest and active part in the affairs of men and nations (*earn intervenire rebus hominum, invehi populis arbitrantur*), and he informs us that she is especially worshiped by the Longobardians and some of their neighbours near the sea. This statement, compared with the emigration saga of the Longobardians, confirms the theory that the goddess Jord, who in the days of Tacitus was celebrated in song as the mother of Mannus' divine father, is identical with Frigg. ...Tacitus calls the goddess Jord Nerthus. Vigfusson (and before him J. Grimm) and others have seen in this name a feminine version of Njordr. Nor does any other explanation seem possible."

In 1892, Stopford A. Brooke, speaking of the Anglo-Saxon *Ǽcerbót* in his *History of Early English Literature*, writes:

"And if we wish to bind up this ancient English Earth Religion with Northern names of gods, we may think of Frigg, Woden's wife, who is the Earth goddess, and of Thor her son, the god of husbandry, 'the farmer's friend,' whose bolt cleaves the storm-clouds that threaten the grain and disperses the blighting mists, who marries Sif, the yellowhaired goddess of the cornfield."

In 1906, Thomas William Shore, author of *Origins of the Anglo-Saxon Race*, states:

"The traces that survive of a mythological or legendary kind in the counties that formed the early kingdom of Wessex find their parallels in similar survivals in Rügen and Pomerania. The most remarkable is that of Hertha, or Mother Earth, a goddess with somewhat similar attributes to the Norse Frige and the Saxon Frea. The name Frige survives in that of Freefolk in Hampshire, the Frigefolc of Domesday Book. In Wiltshire the mythological name which can be most clearly traced during the Anglo-Saxon period is that of Hertha. Latham has pointed out that there is no word beginning with 'H' in any German equivalent denoting *terra* or earth. The name Hertha, although mentioned by Tacitus, appears to have come from another source. Herkja and Herche are among its variants. Hertha is still remembered in the folk-lore of North-

Eastern Germany, the old borderland between the Teutonic and Slavonic tribes, where she goes by the name of Frau Harke, the same as our Mother Earth, but in England she has lost her personality. In the old mythology the personified Mother Earth embodied also the attributes of Ceres, and in that capacity Hertha was much honoured in the Wendish parts of Germany. Kine were yoked to her car, and her image was conducted through fields on her annual festival with much solemnity. We find that Hertha as the name for this goddess was used by the people of Rügen and the Baltic countries near it from time immemorial."

Speaking of the Indo-Europeans, Issac Taylor in *The Origin of the Aryans* (1908) writes:

"They all reverenced and personified as the supreme deity the protecting vault of Heaven, but it was worshiped under different names, by the Indians as Varuna, by the Greeks as Zeus, by the Celts as Camulos, and by the Teutons as Woden. They all reverenced Mother Earth, the spouse of Heaven, but she was called Prithivi by the Indians, Gaea or Demeter by the Greeks, and Nerthus, Frigga, or Jorð by the Teutonic nations."

In *A Guide to Mythology* (1913), Helen A. Clarke theorizes:

"The Norse earth-goddess, consort of Odin, appears in three forms—Jord, Frigg, and Rind. Jord is the original uninhabited earth, Frigg is the inhabited, cultivated earth, and Rind is the frozen earth of winter. The child of the first is Thor, the thunderer; of the second is Balder, the good or the beautiful; and of the third is Vale, who revenged the death of Balder."

The same year, Richard Ernest in *History of German Civilization* (1913) declares,

"Of goddesses we find only one with a definite character, Mother Earth, called now Nerthus or Hertha(?), now Freya or Frigg; she is always the wife of the Supreme God."

While this view may be unfamiliar to readers in the twenty-first century, the notion that Frigg represents the Germanic Earth-Mother, known under a variety of names, is certainly not a new one. Nor has it ever been disproven, and so remains a viable possibility. But more importantly, do we have any evidence that this was the way the ancients conceived of her? With this question firmly in mind, let's consider a few strophes near the end of the poem *Völuspá*. There, just before Earth sinks into the sea, some of her many names are repeated in rapid succession, one after another:

Þá kømr inn mæri	R54 Then comes the mighty
mögr Hlöðynjar,	son of Hlödyn:
gengr Óðins sonr	(Odin's son goes
við ulf vega,	to fight with the wolf);
drepr hann af móði	Midgard´s defender in his rage
Miðgarðs véor,	will slay the worm.
- munu halir allir	Nine feet will go
heimstöð ryðja -	Fjörgyn´s son,
gengr fet níu	bowed by the serpent,
Fjörgynjar burr	who feared no foe.
neppr frá naðri	All men will
niðs ókviðnum.	forsake their homes.
Sól tér sortna,	R55 The sun darkens,
sígr fold í mar,	earth sinks in the ocean,[421]
hverfa af himni	the bright stars,
heiðar stjörnur,	fall from heaven
geisar eimi	vapors assail
við aldrnara,	the all-nourishing Tree,
leikr hár hiti	towering fire plays
við himin sjálfan.	against heaven itself.

Ursula Dronke (1997) believed this repetition of Earth's names was intentional. In her commentary on *Völuspá* 53/2 (R54), she observed:

"The emphasis upon Þórr's mother, the earth, is deliberate here, as men are leaving that *heimstöð* forever. Hlöðyn is probably to be identified with Hludana, a Germanic (?earth-)-goddess of the Lower Rhine, named in five inscriptions from the second and third centuries AD. Fjörgynn's name is a (rare) *heiti* for earth."

In this, its proper context, let's reconsider a passage in *Völuspá* cited earlier in the discussion of the name *Hlín*, which the ancient heathen skalds used as a *heiti* for both Frigg and *Jörð*, the

---

[421] The word translated as "earth" here, literally means "a field of soft grass", Cleasby-Vigfusson *Dictionary*, sv. *Fold*, [AS. *folde*; cp. Engl. *field*, Germ. *feld*].

Earth [Chapter IX Jörð, Thor's Mother].[422] Not surprisingly, we again find all three names recited in close proximity to one another. Immediately before strophes R54 and R55 quoted above, the *Codex Regius* manuscript places these two thematically related verses:

Þá kømr Hlínar	R52 Then comes Hlin's
harmr annarr fram,	second grief to pass,
er Óðinn ferr	when Odin goes
við úlf vega,	to fight the Wolf
en bani Belja	and Beli's bright bane (Frey)
bjartr at Surti,	against Surt.
þá mun Friggjar	Then Frigg's
falla angan.	*angan* shall fall.[423]
Þá kemr inn mikli	R53 Then comes the mighty
mögr Sigföður,	son of Victory-father,
Víðarr, vega	Vidar, to battle
at valdýri.	the slaughter-beast.
Lætr hann megi Hveðrungs	With both hands, he stands
mundum standa	a sword in the heart
hjör til hjarta,	of Hvethrung's son.[424]
þá er hefnt föður.	Then his father is avenged.

As Ursula Dronke observed, before earth sinks into the sea, she is invoked as Hlöðyn, Miðgarð, Fjörgyn, and Fold. Since Earth is also "Odin's wife," the names Hlin and Frigg naturally expand this list. They appear together in a strophe which opens a longer thematic sequence (R52-R57) describing Ragnarok's effects on the Mother of the Gods once Surt arrives on the scene with his fiery sword (R51). One by one, everyone Earth holds dear dies. First Odin, the "one-eye in the sky" who once looked down from Hlidskjalf, is swallowed by the Wolf, the same fate that befalls the sun. Then Freyr, the Lord of Harvests, is cut down by Surt's sword. R53 describes how Vidar avenges his father's death by standing a blade in Fenrir's heart. Afterward, Earth's defender, the mighty Thor, succumbs to the

---

[422] In the strophe in *Hávarðar saga ísfirðings*, ch. 13, the phrase *á Hlín fallinn* means "to fall to Earth", "to die", while the expression *Hlínar harmr* in *Völuspá* R52 alludes to Frigg's first sorrow, the death of her son Baldur (see below).
[423] R reads *falla angan tyr*, Frigg's 'sweet-smelling', 'beloved' god; H and *Gylfaginning* [R, T, W] all read *falla angan(n)*, simply her 'sweet', 'beloved'.
[424] Here, Vidar is called *mögr Sigföður*, the son of Victory-father [Odin] and Fenrir is *megi Hveðrungs*, the son of Harsh-blast [i.e. Loki, cp. Loptr].

noxious venom of the Midgard Serpent that once wrapped itself around the whole world. In the end, the scorched earth itself sinks beneath the billows. When a fresh, green world rises anew in *Völuspá* R57, it is again called *jörð*, the name of her youth. Its unsown fields grow grain. An eagle soars overhead and fish leap in the falls. *Völuspá* R52 foreshadows these events and informs us that when Odin faces Fenrir and Freyr faces Surt, "Frigg's *angan* will fall." The word *angan*, usually translated as "joy" or "delight," is used both here and in *Völuspá* R22, where it is understood to be a figurative use of its literal sense "sweet scent," "perfume."[425] Modern scholars and translators, almost to a person, narrowly interpret the phrase *Friggjar angan*, "Frigg's delight," to mean her husband Odin, overlooking Freyr's presence in the verse. Her "second grief" is thus understood to be the death of Odin, making her implied "first grief" the death of their son Baldur described in R31-R33, which caused "Frigg to weep in Fensalir." In this limited reading, Freyr's death in the same strophe is left unexplained or simply ignored by commentators.

However, once we recognize Hlin and Frigg as alternate names of the Earth, the strophe literally blossoms with new meaning. As stated above, the word *angan* actually means "sweet scent" or "perfume"; the verb *falla*, "to fall", figuratively means "to die", as when the skald who composed the verse in *Hávarðar saga ísfirðings*, chapter 13, speaks of a mortally wounded man falling "to Hlin." There Hlin can only signify the Earth, while here Hlin is an alternate name for Frigg. So when Odin goes to meet Fenrir and Freyr goes to meet Surt, *Frigg's angan*, the "sweet scent" (*angan*) of Earth itself will die. To emphasize this point, a secondary meaning of the word *angan* is "spines" or "prickles" and is used specifically to refer to "plant fiber."[426] Thus the fall of *Friggjar angan* can also connote the conflagration of earth's fragrant flowers and trees, filling the air with the reek of smoke. *Völuspá* confirms this view in the following verse by saying that flames will play against the vault of heaven and the burnt crust of the earth will sink into the sea. Freyr's personal presence in this strophe thus is far from extraneous. Freyr himself falls under Surt's sword, called the "bane of branches" (*sviga lævi*, *Völuspá* 50), a kenning for fire. As the god of harvests (*árguð*), his

---

[425] Dronke, ibid., p. 133; see also the Cleasby/Vigfusson's *Old Icelandic Dictionary*, s.v. *angan*.
[426] Cleasby/Vigfusson Dictionary, s.v. *angan*.

fruits produce the "sweet scent" of the Earth, which will all perish when his mother, the earth, is set ablaze. As we have seen, the name *Fricco*, a masculine form of the feminine *Frigga* (*Fricca, Frekka*), is used to designate the god Freyr in the temple at Uppsala by Adam of Bremen in the eleventh century, suggesting a closer link between the two.[427] We know that *angan* can refer to Odin; as Frigg's husband, he is her "sweet scent," her "delight," but can it also refer to Freyr? The context suggests it must.

Freyr, Lord of Harvests
Detail of a Mural by Robert Müller,
Neues Museum, Berlin, 1852

The eddic poem *Lokasenna* informs us that Freyr was the offspring of an incestuous union. He is the child of Njörd and the sea-god's own unnamed sister. In strophe 36 of that poem, Loki says:

"Hættu nú, Njörðr,	"Cease now, Njörd!
haf þú á hófi þik,	contain yourself;
munk-a ek því leyna lengr:	I will no longer keep it secret:
við systur þinni	With your sister
gaztu slíkan mög,	you had such a son;
ok er-a þó vánu verr."	and he is hardly worse than you."

---

[427] In the surviving myths, besides Odin and Frigg, only Freyr sits in Odin's highseat Hlidskjalf.

Ynglingasaga ch. 4 affirms this relationship, stating that "while Njörd lived with the Vanir he had his sister as wife, because that was the custom among them. Their children were Freyr and Freyja. But among the Aesir it was forbidden to marry so close akin." Thus, when Njörd came to live among the Aesir, he could no longer keep his sister as his wife. Unfortunately, Njörd's sister remains unnamed in our fragmentary sources, although the original audience must have known who she was. Possible candidates have been suggested, including *Njärð*, a feminine form of the name found only in the East Nordic area under such place-names as *Närlunda*,[428] and *Njörun*, a "goddess-name" used as a base in some kennings and so included in a list of *ásynjur* in the *þular* attached to Snorri's *Edda*.[429] But, among scholars who have hazarded a guess historically, most have identified Njörd's unnamed sister as Nerthus, "that is, Mother Earth", since the two names are etymologically related. Edgar Polomé (1999) sought to reject the connection between Nerthus and Njǫrðr on linguistic grounds, but his conclusions were not generally accepted.[430] As we have seen, the comparison runs much deeper than just linguistic correspondence. Even if the etymological link is rejected, continuity may be argued on the grounds of their associations with bodies of water, wagons, and fertility.[431] In the available sources, the religious wagon procession is most closely connected with Nerthus and Njörd's son Freyr, and a wide range of evidence supports the veneration of a male-female divine pair associated with fertility across northern Europe. While we cannot determine the name of Njörd's sister with certainty, we do discover a brother of the earth-goddess whose name may prove relevant to our investigation. In *Gylfaginning* 10, Snorri informs us that Jörd's brother was called *Auðr*, a name that means "wealth." As a mythic personality, *Auðr* is likewise unknown.

---

[428] E.O.G. Turville-Petre in "Fertility of Beast and Soil," *Old Norse Literature and Mythology*, ed. Edgar Polemé, 1969.

[429] Joseph S. Hopkins, "Goddesses Unknown I: Njǫrun and the Sister-Wife of Njǫrðr," *RMN Newsletter* 5, 2012:39-44. Examples include: *öldu eld-Njörun,* "gold-Njörun" in strophes by Gísli Súrsson and Björn Breiðvíkingakappi; *Njörun steina,* "Njörun of stones," Lausavísur, *Third Grammatical Treatise* 28; *Njörun vínkers,* "Njörun of the wine-vessel," *Krákumál,* 20; *hrannblakks hól-Njörun,* "ship-Njörun," a dubious kenning by Björn hítdælakappi; and *Draum-Njörun,* "Dream-Njörun", for Night, *Alvíssmál* 30

[430] "Nerthus/Njorðr and Georges Dumézil," *Mankind Quarterly*, p 143-154.

[431] See Chapter II: Nerthus, who is, Mother Earth.

However, we find *auðr* as a characteristic attribute of Njörd. In a proverbial expression from *Vatsdaela Saga* 47, a wealthy man is said to be *auðigr sem Njörðr*:

Þá mælti Þróttólfr: "Eigi skiptir þat högum til, at Húnrøðr, góðr drengr, skal vera félauss orðinn ok hlotit þat mest af okkr, en þræll hans, Skúmr, skal orðinn auðigr sem Njörðr.	Then Throttolf said, 'It is not as it should be that Hunrod, a good man, should have become penniless, mostly on our account, while his slave Skum grows as rich as Njörd.'

In her commentary on *Lokasenna*, Ursula Dronke (1997) observed: "The sea is a rich giver, and Njörðr, its god, is proverbially wealthy."[432] In *Gylfaginning* 23, Snorri informs us that Njörd "rules over the motion of the wind and moderates the sea and fire. Men pray to him for good voyages and fishing. He is so rich and wealthy that he can grant wealth of land or possessions to those that pray to him."[433] In addition, the *Codex Regius* manuscript of *Gylfaginning* 10 contains a significant variant.[434] There the name *Auðr* reads *Uðr*, a proper name equivalent to *Unnr*, which means "wave."[435] Richard North (1997) has pointed out that in the *Codex Regius*, *Codex Trajectinus*, and *Codex Wormianus* manuscripts of *Snorri's Edda*, the name Idunn is spelled *iðvðr*, in which *–vðr* is a fourteenth century spelling of *–unnr* ('wave').[436] Thus the name of Jörd's brother may be interpreted as either "wealth" or "wave," names which apply equally to Njörd as a god of rich coastal harbors. So, although the name of Njörd's sister is lost to us, we have strong circumstantial evidence that Njörd (aka *Auðr, Uðr, Unnr*) was Jörd's brother. Since we have discovered that Jörd is also a byname of Frigg, we can surmise that Njörd and Frigg are siblings.[437] At once this explains the apparent relationship between the names Njörd and Nerthus. Indeed they are

---

[432] *Poetic Edda*, Vol. II, p. 360.

[433] *Hann ræðr fyrir göngu vinds ok stillir sjá ok eld. Á hann skal heita til sæfara ok til veiða. er svá auðigr ok féscæll at hann má gefa þeim auð landa eða lausafjár er á hann heita til þess*; http://www.hi.is/~eybjorn/gg/ggrpar23.html

[434] *Uðr*] *Auðr* WTU, http://www.hi.is/~eybjorn/gg/ggrnot01.html#10.

[435] Cleasby/Vigfusson *Dictionary*, s.v. *Uðr*; Egilsson's *Lex. Poeticum* s.v. *Uðr*

[436] *The Haustlöng of Þjóðólfr of Hvinir* (1997), p. 42.

[437] Of interest, Kormak the skald uses *auð-Frigg*, as a kenning for woman, in a lausvisa found in *Kormák's Saga*, ch. 19, one of the oldest sagas.

a pair as many scholars have theorized, not unlike their own children, Freyr and Freyja. As Njörd's sister, Frigg is not only the mother of Freyr and Freyja, but also the mother of Odin's sons, Baldur and Thor. Thus, she is truly the Mother of the Gods.

Njörd Longs for the Sea
W.G. Collingwood, 1908

The revelation of these relationships allows us to plumb the depths of *Völuspá* R52 further. As the beloved son of Frigg and her brother Njörd, Freyr can also be designated as *Friggjar angan*, "Frigg's sweet scent," evoking the tender image of a mother and child. The same imagery is evoked in the opening line of the strophe, which alludes to Hlin's first grief, the death of her beloved son Baldur. Thus Frigg's second grief entails not only the loss of her husband, but also the loss of a second son, as well as her own fragrant verdure, and ultimately her own life. The Earth Mother loses everything dear to her. Even her most powerful son, *Miðgarðs véor* ("Midgard's defender"), who once came to drive Loki, the Midgard Serpent's father, from Aegir's hall, will be powerless to protect her. Her own name *Hlín*, which means "safe refuge" is thus used ironically, since she cannot protect those she loves anymore than they can save her from sinking beneath the waves once the fires of Ragnarök have been kindled. That the name *Hlín* comes first in the recitation of Earth's many names is undoubtedly significant. Ursula Dronke adds, "There is probably a tragic irony implied in the use of *Hlín* for Frigg, in that she was unable to protect either son or husband," (*Poetic Edda* II, p. 149). While she clearly meant Baldur and Odin, Professor Dronke's insight becomes even more significant when we realize that the broader passage describes the death of Earth's sons Freyr and Thor too. By the same token, Odin is called *Sigföðr*, the Father of Victory, in the jaws of defeat —at the very moment he is swallowed by the Fenris wolf (*Völuspá* R53). At last, the poet's brilliance in the selection of the single word *angan* is brought to light. This strophe is certainly one of *Völuspá*'s most poignant and most tragic.

With the understanding that Frigg is the sister of Njörd, and the mother of Freyr and Freyja, another episode in *Lokasenna* becomes deeper and more comic. In that poem, Loki bursts into the divine feast held in Aegir's hall uninvited and begins hurling insults at the gathered gods, each in turn. In one sequence, Loki exchanges barbs with Odin until his wife Frigg intervenes. Both the earth and the world of men are invoked immediately before she speaks. Odin reminds Loki that once he was *fyr jörð nedan*, "down below earth," shamefully acting the part of a milkmaid (st. 23). Loki retorts that Odin moved *yfir verþjóð*, "through mankind" i.e. "through the world"[438] dressed as a völva (prophetess, st. 24). Frigg advises Loki that the fates (*örlögom*) they met in times past should never be spoken of before men. When Loki lashes out at her, admitting that he is the reason she no longer sees her beloved son Baldur riding to halls (st. 28), Freyja rises to her defense. In strophe 29, she reinforces Frigg's words stating that Frigg knows all fate (*örlög*), but remains silent regarding it. When Loki turns his venom toward Freyja, her father Njörd rises to her defense. Frigg, Freyja and Njörd, therefore, act as a family unit: Frigg rises to assist her husband Odin, Freyja rises to aid her mother Frigg, and Njörd stands to defend their daughter. The poet emphasizes their relationship through the structure of the surrounding stanzas. At the beginning of the exchange (st. 24), Loki mentions Baldur, the son of Odin and Frigg; while, at the end, Loki mentions Freyr, the son of Frigg and Njörd (st. 36). Freyja, the daughter of Frigg and Njörd, is placed directly between them. Against the three of them, Loki levels charges of sexual misconduct of the kind common among the Vanir. First he accuses Frigg of sleeping with her husband's brothers (st. 26):

---

[438] Beatrice LaFarge and John Tucker, *Glossary to the Poetic Edda*, p. 302, cp. *Verland, Hárbarðsljóð* 56.

"Þegi þú, Frigg,	"Shut up Frigg,
þú ert Fjörgyns mær	You are Fjörgynn's girl
ok hefr æ vergjörn verit,	and have ever been eager for men,
er þá Véa ok Vilja	when you, Vidrir's (Odin's) wife,
léztu þér, Viðris kvæn,	embraced Vili and Ve
báða i baðm of tekit."	both in your bosom."

Loki at Aegir's Feast
Carl Emil Doepler Jr., 1905

Ynglingasaga 3 informs us that once, during a particularly long absence, Odin's brothers thought he would not return and thus began to share his wealth and his wife between them, a relationship that John McKinnell characterizes as a "semi-incestuous betrayal of her husband."[439] When Freyja rises to defend her, she too is hit with a similar accusation. Knowing what we do of the Vanir's sexual mores, the insertion of Frigg's father here may be more than a simple genealogical notice. From the context, it probably implies an added insult, suggesting that she had sexual relations with him too. The word *mær* (from the stem *mey-*), meaning a young woman, could

---

[439] *Essays on Eddic Poetry* (2014), p. 182.

indicate that she is Fjörgynn's daughter, as in the expression *Billings mær* in *Hávamál* 97, typically taken to mean "Billing's daughter"; or his lover, as in *Völuspá* 25, where Freyja is called *Óðs mey*, "Odr's wife." The only reason *Fjörgyns mær* is narrowly defined as "Fjörgynn's daughter" is because Snorri, in *Gylfaginning* 9, designates Frigg as *Fjörgvinsdóttir*, a term not found outside his work. The *Lokasenna* poet, however, probably chose this ambiguous term intentionally. His heathen audience would have been expected to know their relationship and need not have it spelled out for them— as some today insist must be done before they can accept it. The accusation would be implicit if Frigg's father was one of Odin's brothers.

In *Gylfaginning* 6, Odin and his brothers Vili and Ve are said to be born from the union of the giantess Bestla and the god-man Borr, the son of Burr, whom the primeval cow Audhumbla licked from the ice at the dawn of time. Snorri probably found the names of Odin's brothers in *Lokasenna* 26, where Odin is called Vidrir, making for an alliterative fraternal trio: Vidrir, Vili and Ve. In *Gylfaginning* 7 and 8, the sons of Borr sacrifice the primordial giant Ymir and create the upper worlds from his body, an act which finds parallels across the Indo-European spectrum.[440] In *Gylfaginning* 9, the sons of Borr, having completed their creation, walk along the seastrand, where they find two trees from which they fashion the first human beings, Askur and Embla. *Völuspá* 17-18, which Snorri does not cite here despite quoting the poem extensively throughout *Gylfaginning*, attributes this same event to Odin, Hönir and Lodur. Each endows the newly created human beings, male and female, with equal gifts. Thus, we can reasonably conclude that in a poetic tradition well known for its use of polyonomy, Hönir and Lodur are alternate names of Ve and Vili. The sons of Borr are three of the first beings in existence, and as such constitute the third generation from chaos. Odin is clearly the father and founder of the Æsir. Besides the Æsir, the Nordic mythology knows two more divine tribes: the Vanir and the Alfar (elves). Like Borr's sons, the divine *ættar* are three in number. Snorri groups Odin's brothers among the Æsir, but it is more likely they were clan founders in their own right, just as Zeus' brothers, Poseidon and Hades, had kingdoms of their own. If so, it stands to

---

[440] Mallory and Adams, *The Oxford Introduction to PIE and the PIE World*, pp. 435-436.

reason that Hönir and Lodur founded the other two divine clans, the Vanir and Alfar, just as Odin founded the ruling god-clan, the Æsir.

As stated above, *Lokasenna* 26 informs us that Frigg is *Fjörgyns mær*, which can mean his daughter or wife. The name is a masculine form of Fjörgynr, a byname of Thor's mother, leaving no doubt that Fjörgynn is male. In *Gylfaginning* 10, Snorri informs us that Jörd's father was named Annar, but in *Gylfaginning* 9 makes the curious statement that Jörd was the wife and daughter of Odin. Despite this, Annar is not found as a name for Odin, least of all in Snorri's own text, and there is no evidence to support Jörd being Odin's daughter.[441] We cannot now know who Annar or Fjörgynn was, but since Odin was also called *Þriði*, "Third," the name *Annar*, meaning "Second," would be an appropriate designation for one of his two brothers. Since the number of beings at this stage of creation is very limited, Odin's brothers are both strong candidates for Annar or Fjörgynn, the father and/or lover of Odin's wife. Because Loki describes Frigg as *æ vergjörn*, "ever eager for men," and directly states that Frigg slept with both of Odin's brothers in the same verse which Fjörgynn is named, this seems all the more likely. In other words, Loki makes the same accusation in two different ways in both halves of the strophe: Frigg, who is Fjörgynn's daughter, took her own father, who is one of Odin's brothers, into her bed.

According to *Völuspá* 4, because Odin and his brothers[442] together raised the ground (*bjöðum*, referred to as *jörð* in verse 3) out of the sea and created Midgard, they could jointly be referred to as her father, metaphorically speaking. This mythic circumstance is probably the conceptual basis of the information provided by Snorri in *Ynglingasaga* 3 and his "confused discussion" (as John Lindow terms it) in *Gylfaginning* 10 that earth is Odin's wife and daughter. Therefore, Loki's innuendo that Frigg as "Fjörgynn's girl", is his wife and daughter, is confirmed from a mythological perspective, assuming Fjörgynn is an alternate name of one of Odin's brothers. Annar and Fjörgynn are not recorded as names of Odin, particularly by Snorri, demonstrating that he did not make this connection, but the heathen poet and his intended audience, well-versed in their native myths, certainly would have. To underscore this point, Loki

---

[441] McKinnell, ibid., p. 156.
[442] *Burs synir* [R]; *Bors synir* [H].

follows up by making the very same accusation against Freyja in *Lokasenna* 30:

"Þegi þú, Freyja,	"Shut up, Freyja
þik kann ek fullgörva,	I know all about you
er-a þér vamma vant:	You are not without fault;
ása ok alfa,	The Æsir and Alfar
er hér inni eru,	who are herein,
hverr hefir þinn hór verit."	each have been your lover."

The implications of this accusation are apparent when we realize that Freyja's father and brother are both seated in the hall. To make this plain, in strophe 32 Loki adds that when the gods surprised Freyja astride her own brother, she farted. Her father Njörd intervenes on her behalf, not disputing the charge as untrue, but justifying it, stating that there is no harm in a woman finding herself a husband, a lover, or both! Instead, he counterattacks Loki calling him *ragr* ("sexually perverse") for having borne children.[443] Loki retaliates, reminding Njörd that he was sent to the Aesir as a hostage, and that the giantesses' known as Hymir's daughters used his mouth as a urinal.[444] He ends by stating that Njörd begot his son with his own sister in strophe 36. Not only is Frigg closely associated with the Vanir in this passage, but, according to Loki, she shares their morality. Our recognition of her role as Mother Earth and sister of the sea-god Njörd only deepens our understanding of this well-constructed *flyting* (insult poem).

Other poets also seem to be aware of the family ties between Frigg and Njörd, Freyr and Freyja. In the late eddic poem *Solarljóð* 77-79, which mingles Christian and heathen imagery, "Odin's wife" is once again associated with Njörd and his famous children:

---

[443] LaFarge/Tucker *Glossary*, p. 211; Cleasby/Vigfusson, *Dictionary*, p. 481: "*ragr*, adj. [*rög, ragt* (q.v.), by way of metathesis from *argr*] :— craven, cowardly; ...2. = *argr*, q.v.; e.g. to say that a man is a woman (*blauðr*) is the gravest abuse in the language."
[444] This crude statement is explained if we accept that Njörd, as a god of coastal harbors, represents the sea and that Hymir's daughters represent raging mountain streams, who flow into the ocean at the river's 'mouth,' (see further in this chapter).

Óðins kván	77. Odin's wife
rær á jarðar skipi,	rows in earth's ship,
móðug á munað;	eager after pleasures;
seglum hennar	her sails are
verðr síð hlaðit,	are loaded late,
þeim er á þráreipum þruma.	on the ropes of desire hung.
Arfi, faðir	78. Heir! your father
einn þér ráðit hefi	and Solkatla's sons
ok þeir Sólkötlu synir	alone have obtained for you
hjartar horn,	that hart's horn,
þat er ór haugi bar	which the wise Vigdvalin
inn vitri Vigdvalinn.	bore out of the gravemound.
Hér eru rúnar,	79. Here are runes
sem ristit hafa	which were cut by
Njarðar dætr níu:	Njörd´s daughters nine,
Böðveig hin elzta	Radvör the eldest,
ok Kreppvör hin yngsta	and the youngest Kreppvör,
ok þeira systr sjau.	and their seven sisters.

Here Odin's wife (*Óðins kván*, cp. *Viðris kvæn* in *Lokasenna* 24) is said to sail in *jarðar skipi*, "earth's ship," perhaps a reference to the religious processions that made their way through the heathen countryside in wagons or ships. Although the references are obscure, in the next two strophes, we can discern poetic allusions to both Freyr and Freyja, followed by a direct reference to Njörd. The allusion to Freyr, addressed as *Arfi* meaning "heir" or "son" in verse 78, is not immediately apparent, until we remember that Freyr is said to have slain the giant Beli with a "hart's horn" (*hjartarhorni*, *Gylfaginning* 37). In *Völuspá* R52, the poet invokes Freyr as *bani Belja*, "Beli's bane," at the moment of his death at Surt's hand, evoking this scene. Just before the Ragnarök sequence in the R manuscript of *Völuspá*, when Surt sets the whole world ablaze with his fiery sword, the poet speaks of the "old one in the Iron-wood" (*aldna í Járnviði*, R39), a giantess breeding Fenrir's kin, and her herdsman, who sits on a gravemound strumming a harp, happy about what is to come (*sat þar á haugi...gýgjar hirðir*). Freyr's servant Skirnir, who carries Freyr's sword, encounters the same figure, a herder sitting on a gravemound (*hirðir... á haugi sitr*), outside the giantess Gerd's dwelling, as told in

Skírnismál 11-12 and the preceding prose. In *Völuspá* the herdsman's name is *Eggþér* which means "the blade-servant" or "sword-watcher." *Þiðreks Saga af Bern* ch. 193, knows him by the name Edgeir, who watches over a subterranean treasure chamber in *Ísung's wood* (cp. *Jarnviðr*, Iron-wood). In *Solarljóð*, a "hart's horn" (i.e. Freyr's weapon against the giant Beli, "the howler," who is Gerd's brother) is taken from just such a chamber by one Vigdvalinn ("War-Dvalin"). Like Freyr's sword, it too is engraved with runes (cp. *Skírnismál* 23, 25). *Lokasenna* 42 informs us that Freyr exchanged his sword for Gymir's daughter, who is Gerd according to *Skírnismál* 6 and *Hyndluljóð* 30, thus placing Freyr's sword in the hands of the giants, adding that he will regret this loss when he goes to meet Surt. In *Gylfaginning* 4, Snorri says that Surt wields a flaming sword with which he will defeat all of the gods and set the whole world ablaze.[445] It is likely that Surt wields the same sword that Freyr forfeited. In regard to this, Sigurd Nordal (1923) concluded:

> "It would have been pointless if Freyr had merely given his sword to Skirnir, his page. Of course it came into giant hands, and the tale becomes more impressive of all if it is precisely Freyr's own sword which Surt bears."[446]

Ursula Dronke (1997), in her commentary on *Völuspá*, concurs:

> "The sword is a symbol of Freyr's power to defeat the giant forces of death…That this sword is now wielded by Surt implies that the *heill* of the gods has left them, they are vulnerable to death. That *sól valtíva* shines from this sword identifies it as Freyr's sword."[447]

Völuspá R51 informs us that Surt yields *sviga lævi*, "the bane of branches," a kenning for fire, which shines like *sól valtíva*, "the sun of the god (*or* gods) of the slain."[448] If Freyr is the *val-tíva* in question, the term "hart's horn" may be nothing more than a poetic designation for his magnificent sword. Surt sets the world ablaze with Freyr's own weapon, the "sun" whose warmth plants require to grow,

---

[445] *Hann hefir loganda sverð, ok í enda veraldar mun hann fara ok herja ok sigra öll goðin ok brenna allan heim með eldi.*

[446] Nordal, ibid., pp. 103-104.

[447] *Poetic Edda*, Vol. II, p. 147

[448] *valtíva* can be either singular or plural; Nordal, ibid., p. 104.

but which can be scorched by its heat. *Solarljóð* 78 cryptically says that Vigdvalinn bore a "hart's horn" out of a gravemound. In *Þiðreks Saga af Bern*, ch. 40, we find a parallel story about a dwarf named Alfrekkr, who bore a sword from a gravemound to give to a king (compare ch. 16). In a possible connection with this, *Sörla þáttur*, the late *Fornaldarsaga*, informs us that Dvalin (cp. Vig-dvalinn) and Alfrigg (cp. Alfrekkr) were two of the smiths that forged Freyja's necklace Brisingamen.

The *Solarljóð* poet next invokes Njörd's nine daughters, who cut runes on the hart's horn. As daughters of the sea-god, they are probably intended to represent the nine waves, akin to Aegir's daughters, known from *Skáldskaparmál* and Heimdall's mothers from *Hyndluljóð* 37. In skaldic poetry, the phrase "Njörd's daughter" is a kenning for Freyja. Except for her, no other daughters of Njörd are named outside of this poem. Here they are nine in number, the same as Menglad and her attending maids in *Fjölsvinnsmál* (st. 38).[449] There *Menglad*, "the necklace lover" (an allusion to Freyja's necklace, *Brisinga-men*) sits surrounded by eight handmaidens, one of whom is Eir, the goddess of healing, and another named Aurboda, the mother of Freyr's wife Gerd, according to *Hyndluljóð* 30.[450] That Menglad is a goddess is made clear in strophes 36, 39 and 40 of *Fjölsvinnsmál*: any woman who climbs her hill will be cured, even if she has a year's sickness upon her, and her maidens will protect those who worship at her holy altar. That she is one of the highest goddesses is indicated by the subordinate position that Eir, the goddess of healing (*Gylfaginning* 35), takes at her feet. Jacob Grimm and others have long identified Menglad as Freyja. We might reasonably suspect that she was either the youngest or the oldest daughter of Njörd, named Kreppvör and Radvör respectively in *Solarljóð*, but neither is found among the surviving names of Freyja. Nevertheless, Odin's wife, who sails in earth's ship, and Njörd are mentioned here in close proximity, along with poetic allusions to both of their children, Freyja and Freyr, just as in *Lokasenna*, suggesting the poet was cognizant of a connection between them. Thus, this late eddic poem, freely mixed with

---

[449] *Hlíf heitir, önnur Hlífþrasa, þriðja Þjóðvarta, Björt og Blíð, Blíður, Fríð, Eir, Aurboða*; "Hlif is one, a second one Hlifthrasa, Thiodvar is the third; Bright and Look, Happy and Peaceful, Eir and Aurboda," (C. Larrington tr., 2014).
[450] "Freyr gained Gerd, she was Gymir's daughter, of the giant race and Aurboda's," (C. Larrington translation, 2014).

Christian imagery, seems to convey a half-muddled memory of Njörd and Jörd's union.

Freyr and Freyja
Donn T. Crane, 1920

As Njörd's sister-wife, Jörd bore his children, Freyr and Freyja, before becoming Odin's wife, Frigg (the "Beloved"). That Freyja is Frigg's daughter makes perfect sense in the context of Norse mythology, where Frigg is the foremost goddess and Freyja, a close second. Because of their similar names and attributes, scholars have sometimes "confused and conflated" them, suggesting that they were once one figure.[451] There is no question that Frigg and Freyja are depicted in similar fashion. Both goddesses are said to own a falcon guise. In *Skáldskaparmál*, Loki borrows Frigg's falcon form to journey to the giant Geirröd. In the poem *Þrymskviða*, Loki borrows Freyja's to fly to the giant Thrym in search of Thor's stolen hammer. Frigg and Freyja are both depicted weeping—Frigg for the loss of her son Baldur and Freyja for her lost husband Odr. The names of their spouses also form an obvious parallel. Whereas Frigg is Odin's wife, Freyja is known as *Oðs mey* (Od's girl) in *Völuspá* 25 and a few skaldic passages, understandably causing several scholars to conclude that

---

[451] Andy Orchard, *Dictionary of Norse Myth and Legend*, (1998), p. 121

Freyja was Odin's wife.[452] In support of this, both Frigg and Freyja seem to share a similar attitude toward Odin. Like Frigga the wife of Othinus in Saxo's *Danish History* Book 1, Odin's wife Frigg in the prose introduction to *Grímnismál* and Frea, the wife of Godan, in the seventh century account of how the Lombards (*Longobardi*) got their name, Freyja is set at odds with Odin in the late *Fornaldarsaga, Sörla þáttur*. There Odin, a human king, objects to his mistress Freyja prostituting herself to four dwarf-smiths in exchange for a necklace and so sends his man Loki to steal it from her. In Saxo's *Danish History*, Book 1, Frigg with the aid of some "smiths" strips gold and bracelets from a statue of Odin incurring his wrath. Margaret Clunies Ross suggests that these narratives are "essentially the same."[453] The name of Wodan's wife, Frija, in the *Second Merseburg Charm* and Frigg's equation with Venus, the Roman goddess of love, in the Anglo-Saxon transliteration of the weekday Friday are frequently offered as evidence for their identity. Noticeably, scholars most often cite non-eddic material in support of this theory. Yet, for all of this, Snorri keeps both goddesses, Frigg and Freyja, and their husbands, Odin and Odr respectively, distinct from one another. The same holds true in eddic poetry, where one goddess is named and the other either directly named or alluded to in *Völuspá* and *Grímnismál*, while both appear together in *Lokasenna*. In *Oddrunargratr* 9, they are both invoked in the same strophe:

"Svá hjalpi þér
hollar véttir,
Frigg ok Freyja
ok fleiri goð,
sem þú feldir mér
fár af höndum."

"May the kind powers,
Frigg and Freyja
and the other gods,
Help you
as you have saved me
from dangerous distress." [454]

Certainly the Icelandic poets were able to and did distinguish them from one another. Evidence from other times and regions is simply too sparse to determine if this was the case elsewhere, and the *Fornaldarsögur*, composed at least a century after Snorri's *Edda*, are too late to be of value on this point. In this regard, it is worth noting that, while Frigg was known in England from the names of the weekdays

---

[452] Näsström, ibid., p. 81, among others. See above.

[453] Clunies Ross, ibid., p. 98.

[454] Näsström, ibid., p. 80.

and Freyja is seemingly unattested there, her necklace Brisingamen (*Brósinga mene*) is named in the poem *Beowulf* at line 1199, suggesting knowledge of Freyja herself. Tacitus' distinction between the pan-Germanic goddesses: "Nerthus, that is, Mother Earth", and Isis, known by her emblem the light warship, suggest the same. Like the Egyptian Isis, known to the Romans, Freyja wanders the world weeping for her lost husband and can be identified with a light warship by association with her brother Freyr, the owner of the ship Skidbladnir, which is large enough to hold all the gods equipped for war, and be folded up like a napkin when not in use. Thus, rather than explaining the parallels between Frigg and Freyja as a shared identity or common origin, it is just as plausible to conclude that their similarities derive from their relationship as mother and daughter. Among Frigg's many sons, Freyja appears to be her only daughter, making their relationship that much closer. The similarity between the names of Frigg's and Freyja's husbands is probably intentional on the part of the poets. In *Gylfaginning* 35, Snorri identifies her husband as "the man called Odr" and says that she long went in search of him, travelling through many lands. That the story of Freyja's husband appears to be lost, despite a number of poetic references to him, suggests that Odr may be an epithet of a better known figure, and that Freyja's husband should be sought under other names. In *Hyndluljóð*, her lover is called Ottar, which several scholars recognize as Odr. In Book 7 of his histories, Saxo Grammaticus tells the tale of Otharus and Syritha (Ottar and Sýr), widely seen as a reference to Odr and Sýr, a known name of Freyja. In *Fjölsvinnsmál*, the young hero Svipdag seeks *Menglad*, the "necklace-lover" frequently identified as Freyja, the owner of Brisinga-men. After a perilous journey, the hero arrives at her castle, shaded by "Mimir's Tree," widely recognized as Yggdrassil (st. 20) and is met by the watchman *Fjölsviðr*, a name of Odin in *Grímnismál* 47, who brags that he made the place himself from the giant Lier-brimir's limbs (st. 12) just as Odin and his brothers fashioned the world from the corpse of Ymir, called Brimir in *Völuspá* 9. Two guard dogs, one of which shares the name of Odin's wolfhound Geri, stand guard at the gate (st. 14). Like Odr, Svipdag has travelled through many lands. Like Freyja, Menglad has met and lost track of him before. She sits in a languid stupor awaiting his return, as if enchanted.[455] The poet calls her his "fated wife" (st.

---

[455] Compare Freyr's love-sick state for Gerd, most likely caused by sorcery.

42, *kvon of kveðin*) and she welcomes him "back" with a kiss (st. 49), once he reveals his identity.

The available evidence suggests that Svipdag is an Odinic hero and a warrior destined for Valhalla, like Freyja's lover Ottar in *Hyndluljóð* (see further). He is probably identical to Odin's messenger Hermod (*Herm-óðr*), who along with Bragi welcomes kings into Odin's hall. From the context of the poem, it appears that he has travelled to the underworld and retrieved a sword kept there, "below the gates of death" (st. 26 *fyr nágrindur neðan*). This sword is the only weapon which can subdue the golden cock at the top of the tree (cp. *Gullinkambi* in *Völuspá*), whose wings conceal the twin delicacies the watch-dogs will accept allowing the stranger to pass (sts 17-32).[456] Since the gates swing open for him and the dogs rush to greet him, it is safe to surmise that he arrives with the weapon from the underworld. Having achieved this singular feat, the young warrior is welcomed by Odin (Fjölsviðr) himself, and wins Freyja for his wife. Freyja's husband *Óðr* is thus portrayed as an exemplory Odinic hero who joins the ranks of the *Einherjar* as Hermod, *Herm-óðr*, the foremost hero. As Svipdag ("Swift-day"), he delivers the sword to Asgard and exchanges it for a wife. As Freyr's man Skirnir ("Shining"), he will deliver the same sword to the giants on behalf of his brother-in-law, again as a bride-price, this time in exchange for the giantess Gerd (*Lokasenna* 42). Called *sól valtíva*, "sun of the god (or gods) of the slain" in *Völuspá* R51, this weapon, once hidden in the underworld and brought up to heaven, can be interpreted as a symbol of the sun, coveted by both gods and giants alike. The parallel imagery of a raised sword entering a walled city, symbolizing the sexual union of a man and woman, is almost too obvious to mention.

Frigg is best interpreted as one of the Vanir. Hilda Ellis Davidson, in *Gods and Myths of the Northern Europe* (1964) observes:

Freyr's mother-in-law, the giantess Aurboda, appears as one of the maidens at Menglad's feet (st. 38), suggesting she may be the culprit.

[456] Here, Odin's wolfhounds, one of which sleeps by day and the other by night, are figuratively compared to the wolves Sköll and Hati who are destined to consume the sun and moon, "the twin delicacies" under the golden cock's wings. This subtle allusion to Ragnarök is another indication that the sword Svipdag carries is the same one that Surt will wield to destroy the earth and heavens.

"There is little doubt that Frigg and Freyja are closely connected. As weeping mother, the goddess associated with childbirth and linked to the benevolent Mothers, Frigg appears to have her roots in the Vanir cult."[457]

Like the Vanir, Frigg is prescient. *Þrymskviða* 15 says that "all the Vanir" know the future (*vissi ...vel fram sem vanir aðrir*). When Loki admits to Frigg that he is the reason she no longer sees Baldur riding to halls in *Lokasenna* 24, thereby admitting his role in Baldur's murder, Freyja calls Loki insane for recounting his evil deeds, since Frigg knows "all fate", presumably including Loki's own. In verse 41, Freyr predicts that Loki will soon be bound beside the wolf. This implies that Freyja and Freyr, like their mother Frigg, are prescient and know that, because of his misdeeds, Loki will soon lie in chains next to his monstrous son Fenrir. Freyja adds that, while Frigg knows *öll örlög*, she never speaks of it (*Lokasenna* 29). In practical terms, the earth sees everything and remains silent. In *Germania* 7, Tacitus notes that the Germanic people "believe that there is something holy, and an element of the prophetic in women, hence they neither scorn their advice nor ignore their predictions."[458] In the eddic poems *Helgakviða Hundingsbani* I and *Fafnismál*, birds also display this gift. Tacitus affirms the age of this concept in *Germania* 10, speaking of the widespread practice among the Germans "of seeking an answer from the call or flight of birds." In prehistoric Germanic iconography, bird-headed and winged figures sometimes appear in ritual settings, perhaps representing divine figures.[459] Several human figures with beaks and wings are found on the petroglyphs from Bohuslän. On the Oseberg tapestry, we find a horned man leading a wagon procession, a valkyrie with a boar headdress, and another figure depicting a woman dressed as a bird with beak and wings. In later German folk tradition, costumed women with beaks known as *Schnabelperchten,* sometimes represent Frau Percht, in whom we have previously recognized Odin's wife.

In this light, we should reconsider Frigg and Freyja's falcon-guises. Both goddesses are associated with Valhalla. Frigg sits with Odin on his throne Hlidskjalf, presumably located in Valhalla. As the queen of Asgard, she would have fulfilled the ceremonial role of the

---

[457] p. 123.
[458] A.R.Birley tr.
[459] Gunnell, *Origins of Drama in Scandinavia*, pp. 47 and 51.

"lady with the mead cup", widely represented in Germanic iconography, which Michael Enright has identified as a key figure in the Celtic and Germanic *Comitatus*. *Grímnismál* 7 informs us that the goddess *Sága*, whom many scholars identify as Frigg, drinks daily from golden cups with Odin in her watery home. The second strophe of the Valhalla sequence in the same poem (*Grímnismál* 18-26) informs us that Odin imbibes "one wine" (*vín eitt*), but feeds his portion of meat to Geri and Freki —illustrating the kenning "food of wolves", designating warriors slain on the battlefield. As the head of the Furious Host, Odin himself will become "food" for the wolf Fenrir at Ragnarök. *Grímnismál* 14 says that Freyja selects half of the battle-slain. Poetically *Hermóðr*, the foremost of the Einherjar, appears to be Freyja's "other half," *Óðr*. In *Skáldskaparmál*, she is the only one who dares to serve the giant Hrungnir mead when he arrives in Valhalla, a function normally carried out by valkyries (*Grímnismál* 36, *Gylfaginning* 36). In one of the oldest Old English poems, *Exodus* line 164, a bird of prey is called *wonn wælceaqsega*, "dark slaughter-picker," a play on the traditional *wælcyrige* (valkyrie), found in an Old English gloss for the Roman Bellona, Furies, etc.[460] In *Helgakviða Hundingsbana* I, strophe 15, a troop of valkyries with byrnies soaked in blood and luminescent spears are described as *dísir suðrænar*, "southern goddesses," the same term used in *Völundarkviða* 1 (cp *drósir suðrænar*). In *Helgakviða Hundingsbana* II, Sigrun, who is the valkyrie Sváfa reborn, rides through the air to haunt Helgi's battles. When she embraces his lifeless body, she identifies with carrion birds, rejoicing like "Odin's hawks" when they smell fresh slaughter (*HH* II, 43). Helgi characterizes her as "sun-bright," *sólbjört*, and "southern," *suðræn* (str. 45), the same direction from which the sun first rises (*Völuspá* 5). In Snorri's *Edda*, we learn that Urd's well also lies to the south,[461] and that swans swim in its waters, (*Gylf.* 16). In *Völundarkviða* 1, three winged swan-maidens fly "from the south":

Meyjar flugu sunnan	"Maidens flew from the south
myrkvið í gögnum,	through Mirkwood,
Alvitr unga,	foreign beings, young,
örlög drýgja;	their *fate* to fulfil.

---

[460] Ursula Dronke, *Poetic Edda*, Vol. II (1997), p. 301.

[461] *Skáldskaparmál* 65 in a verse by Eilif Gudrunarson: "He [Christ] is said to have his throne in the south, at Weird's well." A. Faulkes tr.

þær á sævarströnd	They on the lakeshore
settusk at hvílask	settled to rest,
drósir suðrænar,	southern damsels,
dýrt lín spunnu.	precious linen they spun."[462]

They weave as do Frau Holle and Frigg, whose spindle forms the constellation known as Orion's Belt, also called "the Three Sisters." Their description evokes the norns, the weavers of fate. Like the norns, these "southern damsels," three in number, set about spinning. They are driven by fate. Like Frigg and Freyja, the swan-maidens are able to transform into birds by means of a feather garment. In the German Berchta legends, she appears as a radiantly white woman with one webbed foot, like a swan's, as a sign of this transformation. These ladies rush to meet their husbands who are designated as "elf princes," *alfa ljóði* and *vísi alfa*. Völund, "the elf-prince," himself takes flight at the end of that poem in a feathered guise of his own device. The elves are closely associated with the gods, primarily through the common eddic expression *Æsir ok alfar*, a formula which also occurs in Old English.[463] *Grímnismál* 5 says that the Van-god Freyr was given Alfheim as a tooth-gift, and in Germanic legend, Frau Holle (Frigg herself) is sometimes seen as the queen of the elves and *hulde*-folk. As shown above, the three divine tribes— Aesir, Vanir and Alfar, were probably founded by Odin and his brothers, Hönir and Lodur, and as such were intimately connected through ties of blood and marriage. In support of this, *Lokasenna* 30, speaks of the *ása ok alfa* (Aesir and elves) seated in the hall, stating that the Vana-dis Freyja has been with them all.

As shown above, the gift of prophecy among the gods is especially associated with the Vanir. In *Völuspá* 24, the Vanir conquer the Aesir during the war between them through *víg-spa*. Despite many unclear translations over the years, we can still arrive at the meaning of this rare word if we look at its component parts. The Cleasby-Vigfusson *Dictionary of Old Icelandic* defines *víg-spá* as "war-spells" or "war news," but that definition can be further refined if we take *spá* in its common sense as meaning "to prophecy, foretell" and *víg-* as "a

---

[462] *Völundarkviða* 1: Ursula Dronke tr.
[463] *Hávamál* 159, 160; *Lokasenna* 2, 13, 30; *Völuspá* 48; *Þrymskviða* 7; *Grímnismál* 4; *Sigrdrífumál* 18, and the Old English metrical Charm 4, line 23: *esa gescot* and *ylfa gescot*.

fight, battle." By employing *víg-spá*, the Vanir use the power of prophecy in battle to conquer the more powerful Aesir:

Fleygði Óðinn	Odin cast (his spear),
ok í folk of skaut,	And shot into the folk:
þat var enn folkvíg	that was the first
fyrst í heimi;	folk-war in the world.
brotinn var borðveggr	Broken was the boardwall
borgar ása,	of the Aesir´s burgh.
knáttu vanir vígspá	The Vanir, with battle-prophecy,
völlu sporna.	marched over the plains.

The identification of Jörd and Frigg provides us a natural explanation of why the Aesir could not defeat the Vanir in war. Their opponents need not have been numerous. The Vanir represent powerful natural forces: earth and sea, as well as the fertility and fecundity of the land and the loin. The Aesir could not hope to defeat such powers. Their sacred duty is to protect them from the powers of frost and decay. In terms of simple symbolism, the earth (Frigg-Jörd) first weds her brother the sea (Njörd), who were created together when the Sons of Borr sacrificed Ymir and made the world from his corpse. His flesh became the land and his blood became the sea. Together, earth and sea produce fertility and fecundity (Freyr and Freyja). In turn, the earth (Frigg-Jörd) marries the sky (Odin), producing the thunderbolt (Thor). This is not to reduce the gods to mere personifications of nature, but only to show one level of symbolism inherent in a mythology very much concerned with the cycles of nature. Snorri himself in the Prologue to *Gylfaginning* argues that pre-Christian deities arose because people worshiped natural forces and because human rulers elevated themselves to divine status.[464] Modern scholars such as Thomas DuBois[465] express similar views:

> "The arrival of agriculture in the Nordic region brought with it distinct and revolutionary religious concepts. Celestial bodies— stars, the moon, the sun— rose as favored motifs in rock paintings dating from the second millennium B.C. and after, coincident with the spread of agricultural practices in the region. As the coital act

---

[464] McKinnell, *Meeting the Other in Old Norse Myth and Legend*, p. 44.
[465] *Nordic Relgions in the Viking Age*, p. 54.

emerged as the prime metaphor for the mystery of agricultural fecundity, the gods responsible for the seasonal cycle, sunshine, rain, and plants took on the characteristics of human sexuality: gender, reproductive organs and appetites. Although anthropomorphic in many respects, these gods are often marked by sexual ambiguities, theriomorphic elements of physique (such as antlers of the Celtic god Cernunnos), and appetites akin to animals in rut. The deities of the earth—the Vanir of Scandinavian texts—were on the whole a passionate, lascivious lot."

While some have suggested that the heathen gods may have developed in this fashion, once personified, these forces naturally would have taken on personalities and relationships of their own, outgrowing their narrow meteorological origins. Frigg's relationship as mother to Freyr and Freyja naturally explains their overlapping functions and why they so frequently have been associated and conflated. The confusion between Frigg and Freyja is well-established, however, as we have already seen, Frigg and Freyr were also conflated. In Adam of Bremen's account of the temple at Old Uppsala, he clearly described a male deity named Fricco with an erect phallus. By the mid-1500s, Olaus Magnus identified the same idol as Frigga, whom he depicts carrying a sword and bow, stating, "her image also shamelessly flaunted its sex and for this reason was worshiped among the Goths as Venus was among the Romans." After 1605, with the publication of Richard Verstegan's *Restitution of Decayed Intelligence in Antiquities*, this image of Frigga became the standard, whenever Saxon gods representing the days of the week were pictured. Apparently aware of the gender disparity between the descriptions of the idol by Adam of Bremen and Olaus Magnus, Verstegan wrote:

> "This Idoll represented both sexes, as well man as woman, and as an Hemophrodite is said to have had both the members of a man, and the members of a woman. ... Some honoured her for a God and some for a Goddess, but she was ordinarily taken rather for a Goddesse than a God, and was reputed the giver of peace, and plenty, as also the causer, and maker of love, and amity, and of the day. Of her especiall adoration we yet retaine the name of Friday."

Frigg, the Idol of Friday, 1838
After Richard Verstegan, 1605

In the same spirit, some scholars of the 1960s and 1970s, recognizing the similarity of the names Nerthus and Njörðr, suggested that the female idol described by Tacitus was actually male, transgendered or had switched sex over time. The apparent similarities between the Vanir deities were undoubtedly exploited by heathen skalds whom understood and juxtaposed their relationship in poems such as *Völuspá*, *Lokasenna* and later *Solarljóð*. This understanding not only allows us to appreciate the well-chosen words of the ancient skalds, but also helps us recognize a continuous thread of evidence running throughout the Germanic historical record for a native Earth-Mother, known by a number of names as all Germanic deities are.

As we have seen, Frigg's children rank among the highest gods: Thor, the twins Baldur and Höður, and the twins Freyr and Freyja all spring from her womb. This naturally explains the kenning *Friggjar niðja*, "Frigg's progeny" used of the gods by the heathen skald Egill Skalla-grímsson in his poem *Sonatorrek*.[466] Just as Odin is known

---

[466] Bernard Scudder translation, *Egil's Saga*, ch. 79; *Complete Sagas of the Icelanders*, Vol. I, p. 151. The noun *niðr* means "son," and in the plural commonly refers to "relatives," "members of the same family."

as *Alföðr*, "All-father," Frigg is the All-Mother of Asgard. As Odin's only lawful wife, she is the mother of his most prominent sons: Thor, Baldur and Höður.[467] As the former sister-wife of Njörd, Frigg is the mother of his famous children: Freyr and Freyja. In effect, Frigg has two husbands: her lawful husband and her brother, both of whom father children by her. With these close connections, Frigg is the epicenter of the divine family dynamic. She is Odin's equal in all respects, surpassing him in practical power as shown by the outcome of their disputes in *Grímnismál* and *Historia Langobardorum*. She is truly the power behind the throne, not even Odin can oppose her. Frigg's powerful position beside Odin on his throne *Hliðskjalf* should not come as a surprise. While men and women had separate roles in Old Norse society, the gods gave the sexes equal gifts. The sons of Borr bestowed senses, wit and spirit on Ask and Embla alike. Women are not subordinate to men. The sources, both religious and historical, are rife with strong, independent women. Both men and women appear on the battlefield, as mythological, historical and archaeological evidence affirms. Equality of the sexes was a Germanic reality, long before modern times. This equality also may be seen in the reflexive nature of the names of Vanir deities: Njörd and Nerthus/Jörd, Fjörgynr and Fjörgynn, Freyr and Freyja, Fricco and Frigga. In the archaeological record, we also find pairs of male and female idols, confirming the widespread incorporation of the *hieros gamos* motif in Germanic religion. No fewer than four sets of these have been recovered from Oberdorla in Thuringia, the Braak Bog from Schleswig-Holstein, and the Wittemoor Timber Trackway in Berne, Lower Saxony.

In *Germania* 45, near the end of the second half of the work, discussing the customs of individual tribes, Tacitus mentions a divine figure he designates as the "Mother of the Gods", worshipped among the Aestii on the eastern shores of the Baltic Sea. Although a majority of scholars identify the Aestii with the ancient Balts, J.B. Rives notes there is room for doubt. Tacitus may have erroneously applied Germanic practices to neighboring peoples, since the boar played little role in the Baltic religion, and the Aestii called amber

---

[467] It occurs to me that Thor and Týr may be perceived as twin sons of the Earth-Mother by Odin. Both appear to have been fostered by giants: Thor by the giants Vingnir and Hlora, and Tyr by the giant Hymir and his wife. Perhaps Frigg, who was a twin herself, always bore sets of twins.

glesum, which is in fact a Germanic word. Tacitus never travelled to
these parts and so passed along what little information he could
obtain about these remote tribes. Thus, the latter portion of the work
provides brief sketches of limited scope.[468] Of the Aestii and their
religion, he writes:

> "The right shore of the Suebic sea washes the tribes of the
> Aestii, whose rites and fashions are those of the Suebi, although
> their language is closer to the British. They worship the mother of
> the gods, and wear images of the boar as an emblem of her cult; it
> is this, instead of the arms and protection of mortals that renders
> the goddess' votary safe, even amidst enemies. The use of iron
> weapons is rare, but that of cudgels common. They cultivate grain
> and other crops more patiently than one might expect from the
> indolence typical of Germani. But they also search over the sea and
> are the only ones in the world to gather amber in the shallows and
> on the shore itself."[469]

Notably, among them the use of iron weapons is rare", just as
during the Nerthus procession "all objects of iron are locked away."
From what little information Tacitus provides, we discover that the
Aestii, who cultivate crops more patiently than the other Germanic tribes,
adore a deity known as "Mother of the Gods" whose emblem was a
boar. The association of this ancient symbol with the Mother of the
Gods further supports the conclusion that Odin's wife, the mother of
the most powerful Germanic gods, belonged to the Vanir tribe, since
the boar is closely associated with their cult. Freyr and Freyja, the
consummate Vanir deities, both possess boars. Freyr owns the
golden boar Gullinbursti, forged for him by dwarves. Snorri says: "it
could run across sky and sea by night and by day faster than any
horse, and it never got so dark from night or in worlds of darkness
that it was not bright enough wherever it went, there was so much
light shed from its bristles."[470] Freyr rides to Baldur's funeral in a
chariot pulled by Gullinbursti, also called Slidrugtanni.[471] *Hervarar
Saga* refers to a boar sacrifice performed in the name of Freyr at Yule.
In the poem *Hyndluljóð*, Freyja rides a boar named *Hildsvini*, "battle-
swine," made for her by the dwarves Dainn and Nabbi (v. 7). The

---

[468] J.B. Rives, Tacitus *Germania*, p. 49, also 317-320.
[469] Rives, ibid., p. 95.
[470] *Skáldskaparmál* 35, Anthony Faulkes tr.
[471] *Gylfaginning* 49.

witch Hyndla perceives that it is actually her lover Ottar (*Óðr*) transformed, "on the way of the slain," (v. 6, 7, 8). Freyja confirms that they are on the road to Valhalla (v. 1). Since one of Freyja's many names is *Sýr* (Sow), riding her lover in the shape of a boar has overt sexual connotations.

Overall, the pig seems to be an ancient Germanic fertility symbol. As such, it seems to have been a symbol of resurrection itself. *Grímnismál* 18 cryptically alludes to this. There we learn that the heroes of Valhalla, the singular *einherjar*, are fed on the meat of an ever-renewing boar, *Sæhrimnir* (*Grímnismál* 18). It is "the best of meats" (*fleska bezt*) which shall ever feed the Einherjar. The poetic allusion appears to refer to human flesh, "the best of meats," which ever "feeds" (i.e. increases the numbers of) the Einherjar. In other words, human men slain on the battlefield enter Valhalla as Einherjar. Odin, who feeds this meat to his wolves, choses half of their number, Freyja selects the other half. As a goddess of love, Freyja is directly responsible for their continuous creation by promoting human procreation, a point underscored by her role as wife to "the man called *Óðr*". *Gylfaginning* 41 says that every day these warriors put on their armor and go out into the courtyard to fight and fell each other, but when evening draws near, they return to Valhalla and sit down together again to drink. Like the boar Saehrimnir, they are slain and dismembered daily, but return to the table whole each night. Similarly the Einherjar drink the ever-flowing milk of the goat, Heiðrun (v. 25), who stands on the roof of Valhalla feeding on the leaves of Yggdrassil. Hyndla, speaking of Freyja, likens her burning passion for Ottar, the boar she rides, to Heiðrun "ever running out at night, hot among the he-goats," (v. 48). So again, Freyja is directly linked to the food-source in Valhalla, this time as a lactating goat.

Like the renewing boar, the mythology also knows of a renewing pair of he-goats, Tanngrisnir and Tanngnjóstr (Tooth-grinder and Tooth-gnasher), who pull Thor's chariot. They too can be slain, eaten, and resurrected so long as their bones are laid back in their hides unbroken. Thor then hallows the pile with his hammer, and the bucks spring back to life. The procreative symbolism of this act is clear, when we remember that Thor's hammer (a phallic symbol) is laid in the lap of a newly-wed bride, most likely to insure the fertility of the wedded couple. No such ritual is prescribed for Sæhrimnir. That the skalds were conscious of this symbolism is evident from the close connection between Thor and Freyja. In *Skáldskaparmál*, Thor possesses the largest drinking horn in heaven. Freyja herself serves the giant Hrungnir from it. In *Völuspá*, when "Óðs mey" is given to the giants, it is Thor who swells in rage (*þrunginn móði*). In *Þórsdrapa* 17, Thor is designated as an "old friend of Thröng" (*langvinr Þröngvar*), where the name *Þröng* is recognized as an epithet of Freyja.[472] In *Lokasenna*, when Loki accuses Freyja of having taken all of the gods and elves assembled in Ægir's hall as her lover, Thor is not in the house. He bursts in at the end and puts Loki to flight, proving that he is more powerful than the rest. In *Þrymskviða*, when Thor's hammer is stolen, he must dress as Freyja, his sexual counterpart, to retrieve the symbol of his virility. Together, their power preserves the chain of generations unbroken. That this symbolism is ancient is made clear by an image on the rock-carvings at Bohuslän, depicting a god-like figure wielding an axe above a couple locked in an intimate embrace. As stated earlier, the probable purpose of consecrating the couple with a weapon at that moment would be to keep malignant spirits who might blight the union at bay.

Clearly, there is a close connection between the Vanir gods, procreation, war, and the symbol of the boar. In the *Nafnaþular*, among the names of swine, we find *val-glitnir* (slaughter-shiner) and *val-bassi* (slaughter-bear), as well as *vigrir* (war-like) and *vaningi* (Van-child).[473] In *Hrolf Kraki's Saga*, *Hildsvín* (battle-swine) and *Hildigöltr* (battle-boar) are the names of helmets. In Anglo-Saxon art, boars are frequently depicted on helmets and other battle-gear. In twelfth century England, the poet Cynewulf speaks of *eoforcumble*, "boar-crested," helmets (Elene 76, 260). Similarly, the *Beowulf* poet refers to "boar figures" which "gleamed over plated check-guards, inlaid with gold," (*eoforlic scionon ofer hleorberan gehroden gold*e, 303-305), "the boar's head standard, high-crowned helmet" (*het ða in beran eafor-heafodsegn, heaðosteapne helm*, 2152-2155), "the pig atop the helmet" (*swin ofer helme*, 1286), and a magnificent helmet with its "boar-plates" (*swinlicum*, 1453).[474] Among the armor placed on Hnaef's funeral pyre is "a pig all-golden, an iron-hard boar," *swyn ealgylden, eofer irenheard*.[475] The

---

[472] Sveinbjörn Egilsson, *Lexicon Poeticum* (1932), p. 650. Þrungva is found as a name of Freyja in the *Þular*.
[473] All translations by Anthony Faulkes, *Edda*, p. 164.
[474] Howell Chickering translations.
[475] North, *Heathen Gods in Old English Literature*, p. 71

Beowulf poet unequivocally says that the boar images on the helm prevent penetration by point or edge (ll. 1448-1454).[476] According to Tacitus, the sea-faring Aestii, whose "language is closer to the British", carry the emblem of their goddess, the Mother of the Gods, into battle; it is this emblem, the boar, and not their arms or gear, which keeps her devotees safe amidst enemies. When not at war, he remarks, they cultivate grain more patiently than one might expect from a Germanic tribe.

Öland Bronze plates depicting boar-crested helmets (left) and helmet with horns ending in bird-terminals (right)

Pigs are not only fertile, producing many young, but are fierce fighters which bear tusks, likened to weapons of war, making them appropriate symbols of the Vanir, who once defeated the more powerful Aesir in war (*Völuspá* 23-24). They too are rooting animals, which conceptually connects them with the ard and plow. Ulf Uggasson depicts Freyr in a chariot pulled by a boar. In *Ögmundar þáttr dytts ok Gunnars helmings*, the idol of Freyr, conveyed through the countryside, is said to provide *arbót* (help with the crops), as it travels the land. Freyr himself is called *árguð* (harvest-god) in *Skáldskaparmál* 14. This connection naturally explains Freyr's close association with the earth goddess Frigg via the name Fricco for his idol in the temple of Uppsala and his designation as Frigg's *angan* (beloved) in *Völuspá*. The mystery of the boar symbol, so prevalent throughout ancient Germanic culture, makes perfect sense in this light. It is closely

---

[476] Sam Newton, *The Origins of Beowulf: And the Pre-Viking Kingdom of East Anglia* (2004), p. 41.

connected with the Vanir cult, who like the Germanic Earth-Mother, are intimately associated with the fertility of the land and the loin.

As noted above, the Vanir gods are closely associated with natural forces. Other poems consciously play on this imagery. In *Lokasenna* 34, Loki says:

Þegi þú, Njörðr,	Shut up, Njörd!
þú vart austr heðan	you were sent from the east
gíls of sendr at goðum;	as a hostage to the gods:
Hymis meyjar	Hymir's daughters
höfðu þik at hlandtrogi	used you as a urine-trough,
ok þér í munn migu.	and pissed in your mouth.

In *Hymiskviða*, Hymir is a giant who lives beyond the Elivogar, the icy-waves at the end of the world, where the Midgard Serpent dwells. Thor contends with him in fishing, and wins from him a giant brewing kettle big enough for the gods. In *Þórsdrápa*, Thor must wade through a raging river, which proves to be caused by a giantess standing over the stream. Thor launches a rock at her saying "a river must be stopped at its source." Hymir's daughters are undoubtedly giantesses of the same kind.[477] As a river meets the sea at its mouth, Loki says that Hymir's daughters flow into the sea-god's mouth. Without an understanding of the natural allusion behind this crude poetic conceit, the comic insult would be meaningless. Hymir's daughters represent the raging mountain-streams which flow into the sea. In contrast to the happy union of Njörd and his sister Jörd, who represent the sea and fertile earth, the marriage of Njörd and the giantess Skadi represents the unhappy union of the sea and the mountains. He cannot stand the howling of wolves in her father's hall Thrymheim, while she cannot stand the shrieking of sea-fowl in his home Noatun. Jörd is a goddess of arable lands and forests near bodies of water, while Skadi is inherently a giantess of wild mountain tracts. She inherits her father Thjassi's halls and, like Völund and his brothers in *Völundarkviða*, hunts with a bow on skis.[478] She is known as the snow-shoe goddess. Njörd's marriage to her may be seen as a reversal of his marriage to his sister, the earth. Odin's marriage to Jörd leaves Njörd without a partner. As a replacement for Jörd, the

---

[477] Dronke, Lindow and others agree.
[478] *Lexicon Poeticum* s.v. *brunni. Völundarkviða* 9, "is undoubtedly distorted."

myths present him with Skadi, an austere mountain giantess. The Old Norse poets were fond of these kinds of juxtapositions.[479] She first arrives in Asgard to avenge the death of her father Thjazi, like a son would. As a condition of peace, she is allowed to choose a husband from among the gods, but only if they can make her laugh. As part of the bargain, Skadi is forced to select a husband from among the veiled gods by their feet alone. She desires Baldur and so selects the loveliest, whitest feet. When the veil is lifted, she has chosen Njörd. To emphasize the dissonance between them, the sexual roles are reversed. The bride choses her groom and he is the one wearing the veil. The other gods stand like bridesmaids beside him. Instead of choosing her spouse by the beauty of his face, as a man would chose a woman, Skadi must select a spouse by the comeliness of his feet. To underscore this reversal, Loki makes her laugh by emasculating himself. He ties a cord around his testicles and secures the other end to the beard of a nanny goat— a female beast with a distinctly masculine facial feature. He falls into her lap, causing Skadi to laugh at his antics. The same scenario is repeated in *Þrymskviða*. There Thor must don a wedding gown and present himself as a bride to the giant Thrym in order to retrieve his stolen hammer, a symbol of his manhood. Loki accompanies him there, comically comfortable in drag. Order is restored when the natural roles are set right.

These natural associations were probably already established by the first century AD. As we have seen, the name Nerthus in Tacitus' *Germania* is an etymon of Njörd, the wealthy (*auðigur*) sea-god, and *Auðr* or *Unnr* is Earth's brother in *Gylfaginning* 10. Nerthus may be linked to *Oceanus* by Tacitus in the same manner; he speaks of her sacred grove on an island located in the Ocean (*in insula Oceani*). In Latin, Oceanus (*Okeanos*) can be understood as a proper name.[480] The designation of Frigg's home *Fensalir* (Fen-halls) may also indicate that she was thought to reside in or near water, even as Midgard (Earth) is conceived of as an island in the ocean.[481] In Snorri's *Edda*, Sælund is an island dislodged from mainland by Gefjun, the goddess with a plow, and placed in the ocean. The spot from which it came is now Lake Mälar in Sweden. Might this disjointed myth have once

---

[479] Eleazar Meletinskij, "*Scandinavian Mythology as a System of Oppositions*" (1974).
[480] North, ibid., p. 23.
[481] Näsström, ibid., p. 110.

referred to the island of Nerthus, that is, Mother Earth? If so, they were already distinct figures by the Viking Age, as Gefjun and Frigg appear separately in *Lokasenna*.

Gejfon, the Goddess with the Plow
by Lorenz Frølich, 1882

In late German folklore, Odin's wife Frau Holle is depicted as a goddess not only with a wagon, but a plow as well. She emerges from lakes, wells, and ponds, considered sacred to her. Such pools were seen as an entryway to her hall. In connection with this, the goddess *Sága*, who is said to reside in *Sökkvabekkr*, the "Sunken-bench" or "Sunken-brook"[482] while "cool waves resound above" (*Grimnismál* 7) is often identified as Frigg, a goddess not otherwise mentioned in the poem, although she figures prominently in its prose introduction. Regarding the halls *Fensalir* and *Sökkvabekkr*, Sigurd Nordal (1923) concludes: "both names have the same meaning, 'hall in the deep (of the sea)' and *Sága* is doubtless only one of Frigg's names."[483] Ursula Dronke believes that Frigg's *Fensalir* is "a subterranean water-palace like the submarine *Sökkvabekkr*." She suggests that "*Fen*, 'quagmire,' might imply great pools leading down into marshes, such as those into which the poet Egill cast his treasure

---

[482] *Bekkjar* means either 'bench' or 'brook'; Richard North, *Haustlöng*, p. 38.
[483] *Völuspá* ed. by Sigurður Nordal, tr. by B.S. Benedikz and John McKinnell (1978), p. 69. Despite this, Snorri identifies her as second among Asynjes, after Frigg, in *Gylfaginning* 35.

and slaughtered his slaves as an offering to Odin (*Egils saga* 297-8)."[484] Similarly at the conclusion of Nerthus' circuit, the idol was bathed in a lake and the slaves who accompanied her were drowned. We find this close connection between earth and sea repeated throughout Old Norse mythology. Earth emerges from the sea. In *Völuspá* 4, Odin and his brothers— Borr's sons— lift her up out of it. At Ragnarök, she sinks into the same waters and emerges renewed. Dronke interprets *Skírnismál* as a late reflection of this mytheme, writing:

> "We know that the emergence of earth from the ocean was a well established pattern in Norse mythology. ...Gerð is the only partner I know in a 'sacred marriage', who represents an earth that still resides in the sea when the sky woos her. ...It is no doubt the poet's representation of the god's bride as the rich girl from the sea that has prevented general acceptance of the 'sacred marriage' of Sky and Earth as the basic plot of *Skírnismál*."[485]

This well may be an ancient cosmic legend.[486] We find evidence of it throughout the Indo-European diaspora. In Greek mythology, evidence suggests that Hera, besides being the "wife and sister of Zeus," was a cyclical earth-goddess.[487] The three principal sources of knowledge regarding her early worship are the *Illiad* and her two earliest sanctuaries at Argos and on Samos off the coast of Turkey. As in Tacitus' account of the Nerthus cult in northern Europe, the sacred bath of the goddess or her idol was apparently an important element in her worship. That a majority of her sanctuaries are placed in marshy areas (Kroton, Metapontum and Samos), often near the confluence of waters, supports this. Several myths associate her with rivers and streams. Hera herself comes from such a place:

> "I go on my way to the bourne of Earth, to see Okeanos, from whom the gods arose, and Mother Tethys. In their

---

[484] Dronke, *Poetic Edda*, Vol. II, p. 140.
[485] Dronke, ibid., pp. 396-397.
[486] Dronke, ibid., p. 396, marking the sixth century tale of Zas and Chthonie by Pherecydes as an analog.
[487] *The Transformation of Hera: A Study in Ritual, Hero and the Goddess in the Illiad* by Joan V. O'Brien, (1993) p. 4.

distant hall they nourished me and cared for me in childhood."
(*Illiad* 14.200-301).[488]

Both Hera and Okeanos (Ocean) share the epithet "origin of
all things."[489] Like Nerthus, Hera's archaic association was primarily
with cattle. Her most common Homeric epithet βοῶπις is translated
"cow-faced"[490] or more traditionally "cow-eyed." To hide an illicit
affair from her, Zeus transformed his lover, Io, into a white heifer.
When Hera asked for it, Zeus granted her wish. She accepted the gift
not knowing that it was actually Io, one of her own priestesses. As
the daughter of Inachus, a river god, Io once judged a dispute
between Hera and Poseidon over the island Argos. Because modern
scholars question the boundaries that Greek and Roman authors
assigned to the people of northern Europe,[491] Herodotus statements
regarding the Scythians may be relevant here. He reports (7, 64) "The
Persians call all the Scythians Sakai," a group some scholars have
identified as ancestors of the Saxons. According to him (4, 59), they
"propitiate by worship …Hestia most of all, then Zeus and the
Earth, supposing that Earth is the wife of Zeus, and after these
Apollo, and Aphrodite Urania, and Heracles, and Ares. Of these all
the Scythians have established worship, and the so-called royal
Scythians sacrifice also to Poseidon."[492] Like Nerthus and Njörd in
the Germanic realm, Earth and Sea in Greek mythology appear to be
intimately related, a natural connection for sea-faring peoples. In
Greek sources, Poseidon and Hera vie for the possession of the
island Argos, where she ultimately establishes her cult. In the *Illiad*,
Hera and Poseidon conspire together to thwart the will of Zeus
(Book 8). Like Njörd, Poseidon and Okeanos are powerful sea-gods
with a close relationship to the earth. In Germanic mythology, Njörd
is the Earth-Mother's own brother and her first husband. No doubt,
these ties have very deep and ancient Indo-European roots.

---

[488] Joan O'Brien tr.
[489] *Illiad* 14.201 Okeanos is *genesis pantessi*; and Hera is *genethlê pantôn*
(Alcaeus 129) cited from O'Brien.
[490] West, ibid., p. 185.
[491] Peter Wells, *Beyond Celts, Germans, and Scythians*, (2001).
[492] My gratitude to Carla O'Harris for pointing this out.

CONCLUSION

"It has always been the problem of the student of primitive Germanic religion to distill the religiously significant out of the mash of documentation—a process often leading to divided opinion. Each of us is almost forced to develop some sort of overall attitude towards the material, based on patterns which seem to repeat themselves in certain texts, and then to subject further material to the results of these observations to see if our key will open the door. If it does, this supports the basic premise— if it does not we must either assume that the theoretic principle with which we are working is false, or that the sample under present investigation is at fault. No key has been discovered to date which opens every door— and external evidence assures us that our materials are not beyond suspicion. So we do not have to apologize for using this method— it remains the standard tool of the trade."

— Jere Fleck,
"The 'Knowledge-Criterion' in the Grímnismál," (1971).

Since the middle of the twentieth century, much has been done to broaden the research into individual goddesses, yet this research has tended to reduce their individual characters, interpreting them all as aspects of a single Great Mother Goddess.[493] In the Germanic pantheon Frigg and Freyja, the two chief goddesses, have frequently been treated as one amalgam entity and most of the other named goddesses have been regarded as aspects of this united figure. Since archaeologist Marija Gimbutas first presented evidence for the veneration of a prehistoric Great Mother Goddess, other scholars have followed her lead, reducing a number of named goddesses into this prehistoric figure. In *Freyja, Great Goddess of the North* (1988), Britt-Mari Näsström defines this Great Goddess as "sometimes divided into two goddesses who are apprehended as mother-daughter or as two sisters," (p. 73). She concludes that there was only "one Great Goddess" in the Indo-European sphere, Freyja, from which all other goddesses derive, (p. 103). Hilda Ellis Davidson follows suit in her book *Roles of the Northern Goddess* (1998), stating,

---

[493] According to Ingunn Ásdísardóttir, "Frigg and Freyja: One Great Goddess or Two?," (2006).

"It seems likely that Idun, who guarded the golden apples which ensured perpetual youth to the gods, may be identical with Freyja, since she like Freyja is carried off on more than one occasion by the giants and has to be rescued by Loki. Moreover, the maiden Gerd, who may also represent Freyja, is offered golden apples when wooed by Freyr in the poem *Skírnismál*" (p. 85).

Ultimately she reduces all the northern goddesses into one great Northern Goddess, a conclusion self-evident in the title of her book. Richard North also does this when he speaks of Idunn "who is probably a hypostatis of Freyja, the owner of Brisingamen," because Loki is designated "the thief of Brisingamen" in the poem *Haustlöng*, which recounts the tale of Idunn's theft by Thjazi.[494] We should not be quick to identify goddesses based on superficial similarities. Ingunn Ásdísardóttir, in her perceptive presentation at the 2006 *Medieval Saga Conference*, notes that the hypothesis of one Great Goddess, although understandable for its time as a means of uniting the international women's movement, must now be seen as somewhat simplistic and overgeneralized. Even though female deities from different societies may share similar aspects and attributes, this need not be due to monogenesis, but can be attributed to common human psychology and aspiration more so than to supposed shared roots. She writes:

"When looking through the relevant archaeological finds concerning the existence of goddesses and goddess-worship in Scandinavia, there are two things especially that catch the attention: One is that feminine deities seem to have been worshiped over a very long period of time – since the earliest references to such divinities seem to reach all the way back to the Stone- and Bronze-Age rock carvings in Norway and Sweden. The other is that there are certain recurrent strands and characteristics in these finds that seem to point to little or no change in concept over almost as long a period of time."[495]

When dealing with archaeological finds from a non-literate culture, we have no way of knowing whether these deities had names

---

[494] Richard North, *The Haustlöng of Þjóðólfr of Hvinir* (1997), p. 41 cp. p. 86, "The name *Gefn* denotes the giving for which Iðunn, as an aspect of Freyja, is invaluable."
[495] Ingunn Ásdísardóttir, ibid., p. 2

and, if so, what they were. Despite this, the same scholar notes that many of these archaeological finds, especially the earlier ones, appear to be connected with water, (i.e. were found in or near water), and seem to be associated with war and sacrifice. Therefore, it seems quite likely that the deities associated with them were of the kind that later came to be defined as Vanir gods. As we have seen in the foregoing chapters, a strong tradition flows from ancient times regarding the marriage of earth and sky, most often depicted as a wedded couple united in sacred marriage (*heiros gamos*). Several sources preserve the basic mytheme of a masculine sky impregnating a feminine earth. Within the Indo-European sphere, *Dyeus Pater* or Sky-Father is the oldest god whose name can be traced over a vast area.[496] Lexically, he is the most secure deity and heads the pantheons of Greece and Rome.[497] He serves as the father of several other Indo-European deities and unites with "Mother Earth" in some traditions, including the Germanic.[498] This relationship is exemplified in the Hindu *Rigveda,* the oldest Indo-European religious text, where Dyaus appears with his companion Prthivi, the Earth. In the sixth century BC, Pherecydes of Syros describes a wedding between two primal deities, Zas (Zeus) and Chthonie (the Earth spirit). Zas clothes his bride in a veil embroidered with land and sea to honor her.[499] Several of Zeus' consorts in later Greek mythology have names which can be traced to words meaning earth, including Demeter (from *Ge-meter,* Earth-Mother; or *Deus Mater,* the Divine Mother), Plataia, and Semele.[500] The same holds true in northern Europe. According to Herodotus (4, 59), the Scythians of northeastern Europe, "propitiate by worship ... Zeus and the Earth, supposing that Earth is the wife of Zeus." Whereas the sky is known as Father among the Indo-Europeans, earth is widely celebrated under the title Mother.[501] The Vedic Prthivi often carries the epithet "Mother" especially when she is invoked with Dyaus the Father. In Hittite, Mother Earth (*annas*

---

[496] M.L. West, *Indo-European Poetry and Myth,* (Oxford, 2007), p. 166.

[497] J.P. Mallory and D.Q. Adams, *Oxford Companion to Proto-Indo-European and the Proto-Indo-European World* (2006), p. 431.

[498] Mallory and Adams, ibid., p. 432.

[499] Ursula Dronke, *The Poetic Edda Volume II: The Mythological Poems* (1997), p. 396. See also, West, ibid., p. 182.

[500] West, ibid., p. 182.

[501] West, ibid., p. 175.

Daganzipas) is paired with the storm-god.[502] In ancient Greece, Ge was known as "the mother of all," "mother of the gods," the "all-mother," or simply as "the mother."[503] While in the late Celtic and early Germanic periods, a goddess of agricultural plenty is often paired with the Roman Mercury, who has long been identified with Odin the All-Father in the North.

In Germanic sources, Mother Earth holds a prominent position. The evidence, as compiled in the previous chapters, is overwhelming. She is present from the beginning of the record. In *Germania*, chapter 2, Tacitus informs us that the Germanic tribes in common claim descent from an earth-born god.[504] In chapter 40, he says that no less than seven tribes worshiped Nerthus, who is *Terra Mater*, Mother Earth. As the first named Germanic goddess, Nerthus takes interest in human affairs and rides among her people in a wagon procession to a lake where her idol is bathed. She is worshiped across a broad geographical area dominated by seven northern tribes.[505] Among them, Tacitus names the Anglii and Langobardi who enter history as the Angles and the Lombards. Among both, we later find evidence of her worship. The descendents of the Anglii in the Anglo-Saxon *Æcerbót* record a charm to restore fertility to blighted land, in which earth is addressed as *Erce*, which may be a proper name; e*orþan modor*, Mother of Earth; and *fira modor*, the mother of men. She is exhorted to become fertile, i.e. pregnant, "in God's embrace." There the Christian God takes the place of the old sky-god.[506] In the eighth century, the now Christian Lombards speak of a "ridulous fable" or "silly tale" told by old men in which Godan's (Odin's) wife, Frea, once assisted them in their time of need. Odin's wife instructed them to have their women appear on the horizon at sunrise with their hair arranged like beards. Frea turned her husband's bed around so that he would see them first upon rising.

---

[502] West, ibid., p. 176.
[503] Hes. *Op.* 563, Hymn. Hom. 30, 1, 17, Solon fr. 36, 4, Aesch. *Sept*, 16, [Aesch.] *Prom.* 90, Soph. fr. 269a, Eur. *Hipp.* 601, *Hel*, 40, fr. 182a, 839.7 etc. (after West, ibid., p. 176).
[504] "In ancient lays, their only type of historical tradition, they celebrate Tuisto, a god brought forth from the earth. They attribute to him a son, Mannus, the source and founder of their people." Translated by J. B. Rives, *Tacitus Germania* (1999).
[505] North, *Heathen Gods in Old English Literature*, p. 20.
[506] Davidson, *Roles of the Northern Goddess*, p. 62; West, ibid., p. 177.

Taken with this strange sight, he asked: "Who are these long-beards (Langobardi)?" Having given them a new name, he was compelled by force of custom to also grant them victory over their enemies, just as Frea had planned. For this act they revered her, as recorded a century after their conversion to Christianity. The story has a direct analog in the eddic poem *Grímnismál* more than four hundred years later. Likewise, in skaldic poetry, among the oldest known compositions of Scandinavia, we find the kenning "Odin's wife" frequently used to exclusively designate the Earth. In Snorri Sturluson's fictive account of the development of religion in the *Prologue* to *Gylfaginning*, he writes that the generations after the Biblical flood forgot the name of God and knew nothing of their Creator. They reasoned that the earth was alive, gave it a name, and traced their ancestry to it, mirroring Tacitius' statements a thousand years earlier. In *Skáldskaparmál*, Snorri informs us that earth was known as *Folde*, *Jörð*, *Hlóðyn* and *Fjörgynr*, demonstrating that the Earth-Mother was known by many names, although she plays no role in the mythology he expounds. The heathen skalds call her "Odin's wife" most often, but in our mythological and historical sources, the position of Odin's wife and queen is always occupied by Frigg, who, not surprisingly, exhibits clear characteristics of being the Indo-European Earth-Mother.

All across northern Europe, throughout the Middle Ages and into modern times, folktales tell of a matronly figure who makes the snow and rain fall. She dwells in ponds and wells from which babies are born. Women and children are often seen in her train. Closely associated with agriculture, spinning and domestic affairs, she visits homes at Yule along with her husband Wodan (Odin), richly bestowing blessings on the industrious and punishing the lazy. She is Mother Nature herself, the old heathen Earth-Mother. In Christian times, her teaching remains; Earth rewards those who work hard, and deals harshly with those that do not. The people call her Frau Holle, Frau Holda (cognates of the name *Hlóðyn*, an epithet of Jörd), Herke, Perchta, and Berchta (cognates of Erce in the Anglo-Saxon *Æcerbót*). The further north one travels, she is known as Frau Wode, Frau Gode (both meaning Mrs. Odin) and Frekka, a designation which corresponds to Odin's wife, the "beloved" Frigg, whose name first occurs as Frea in the same region. Along with her husband Wodan, she leads the Wild Hunt, sometimes appearing among the people in a wagon, like Nerthus. In the tenth century, in Merseburg at the very heart of the Frau Holle legends, a heathen charm records the names Wodan, Frija and Volla, an Old High German form of the name Fulla, Frigg's handmaiden in the *Prose Edda* three centuries later. These divinities work together to cure *balderes volon,* "Baldur's foal," widely recognized as the first literary mention of Baldur, Odin and Frigg's famous son. A similar scene is depicted on fifth and sixth century bracteates, where the head of a god, probably Wodan, frequently appears above a horse with quite obviously dislocated forelegs.[507] A brachteate of the same type from southwest Germany, depicts a female with a weaving implement of the same type found in the Oseberg ship burial, suggesting a pre-Christian goddess associated with weaving.[508]

Welschingen-B Bracteate (IK 389)
"The Goddess Who Weaves"

Also, in tenth century Germany, farther north, a historian from Bremen records the names of a trio of gods in a temple at Old Uppsala in Sweden. They are Wodan, Thor and Fricco, the latter being a masculine version of the names Frigga and Frekka. The recognition of a divine pair, Fricco and Frigga, adds to an existing pattern of such god names: Freyr and Freyja, Njörð and Nerthus,

---

[507] Rudolf Simek, *Dictionary of Northern Mythology* (1984), p. 278.
[508] Davidson, ibid., p. 116, citing Michael Enright (1990).

Fjörgynn and Fjörgynr, Bercht and Berchtold—a phenomenon reflected in the ancient pairs of male and female wooden idols found throughout the same area, and not uncommon in the Indo-European sphere. In thirteenth century Denmark, Saxo names Frigg once again as the wife of Odin. A generation later on Iceland, Snorri Sturluson names two wives of Odin: Frigg, the mother of Baldur and Jörd (Earth), the mother of Thor. He also provides a list of minor goddesses, including Hlín, "who protects people that Frigg wishes to save from danger," (*Gylfaginning* 35). Despite this, we find the name Hlín used as an epithet of Frigg in the eddic poem *Völuspá* and of *Jörd*, the earth, in a skaldic verse recorded in *Hávarðar saga Ísfirðing* ch. 14, suggesting that the heathen poets whose works Snorri relied on knew the names Frigg, Jörd and Hlín as epithets of one goddess. In the same sources, only Frigg plays an active role. Nowhere do Jörd and Hlín appear as distinct figures in their own right. In contrast, other minor goddesses, such as Fulla and Eir do appear individually. The fact that Frigg is Odin's traditional wife in a broad range of historical sources and that the common skaldic kenning "Odin's wife" refers exclusively to the earth, suggests the same, that Frigg and Jörd (Earth) are one. Taken together, the evidence converges on a single conclusion. A goddess representing the earth, known as the queen of heaven and mother of the gods, firmly rooted in Indo-European tradition, is attested across Germania from the first records for over a millennium.

In no way is this meant to suggest that all Norse goddesses are one "Great Goddess," quite the opposite. Freyja, Idunn, Gerd, Skadi and other Nordic goddesses are clearly independent figures with their own associated myths. Nevertheless, a preponderance of evidence supports the conclusion that Odin's wife, Frigg, is the Germanic Earth-Mother, who like all other Germanic deities was known by a number of names. An unbroken chain of evidence demonstrates that Odin and Frigg are the Germanic analogs of the ancient Indo-European Sky-Father and Earth-Mother, consistently occurring since the beginning of the historical record. Distorted images of this divine couple have even survived into modern times in the form of the Wild Huntsman and Frau Holle, attesting to the powerful hold these figures have on the Germanic psyche. Nothing bars this conclusion other than the learned belief that Frigg and Jörd are separate entities, an erroneous notion originating in and perpetuated by Snorri Sturluson's *Gylfaginning*. To accept that Frigg and Jörd were indeed viewed as one, we must acknowledge that Snorri's opinion differed from that of the ancient heathen skalds' on this point. Understandably, this is not easy for some to accept. When considering this conclusion, we must remember that Snorri was a Christian author writing two hundred and twenty years after the Christian conversion of Iceland, for a Christian audience that was openly opposed to pagan worship.[509] The generally accepted view of Icelandic scholars in the twelfth and thirteenth centuries was that the old heathen gods were long dead kings, who were well-versed in sorcery.[510] They were mortal men who had deceived their subjects and allowed themselves to be worshiped. By then heathen practices were outlawed in both public and private, but their active distortion and suppression by adherents of the new worldview did not result in a sudden disappearance of traditional Norse poetry from the native conscience.[511] It lingered on for some time as a cultural, although no longer religious, phenomenon as the new religion took hold and began to flourish. Even so, by Snorri's time, it too was in imminent danger of being lost altogether. During the thirteenth century, oral poetry which had been Scandinavian culture's principal means of expression and preservation from the time of Tacitus, was being rapidly supplanted by written prose.[512]

The most casual reader will notice that Snorri openly mixes Christian theology with the narratives about the old gods.[513] The *Prologue* to *Gylfaginning* places his account of Scandinavian myth in "the universal context of Christian cosmology."[514] He opens his work with the Christian creation story, calls the old gods men, and no where deviates from this view. He locates their home in the Classical city of Troy, which he re-christens Old Asgard, and attributes their migration northward to the outcome of the Trojan War, using folk-etymology to explain that the Æsir had actually derived their name from their supposed origin in Asia. When the heathen view is

---

[509] Jónas Kristjánsson, *Icelandic Manuscripts* (1996), p. 27
[510] Simek, *Dictionary of Northern Mythology*, p. 241.
[511] Abram, ibid., p. 180.
[512] Anthony Faulkes, *Edda*, p. xii.
[513] Näsström, ibid., p. 13.
[514] Margaret Clunies Ross, *Skáldskaparmál*, 10., cited in Guðrún Nordal's *Tools of Literacy* (2001), p. 43.

subsequently introduced, it is a deception practiced by the migrant Æsir on a native Swedish king.[515] *Gylfaginning* clearly reflects Christian and Classical motifs derived from the Roman Catholic Church. Although the usual demonization of the old gods, so common in early Christian texts, is largely absent, heathenism on the whole is presented as an unacceptable, but blameless deception—blameless, because the northern people had been deceived by a band of powerful foreign sorcerers posing as gods! Nowhere does Snorri stray from his core premise. This conceit extends from the introduction to the conclusion of *Gylfaginning* and continues into *Skaldskaparmál,* as well as his *Ynglingasaga,* albeit inconsistently. Snorri's unique method of mixing Christian motifs with heathen myths naturally has caused some scholars to pause and question Snorri's credibility as a source of heathen mythology, pointing out apparent misunderstandings and contradictions in his text, suggesting that some elements and even entire narratives were of his own device. The value of Snorri's learned explanations, including those seemingly supported with citations of eddic verse, are frequently questioned by modern scholars, but only to a limited degree. Roberta Frank with the University of Toronto (1981) observes:

> "Ever since the pioneering work of Eugen Mogk in the 1920s and 30s, Old Norse scholarship has been forced to consider the possibility that some of the myths related in the *Prose Edda* were devised by Snorri himself. The notion that the master of Reykjaholt may have more or less continuously created and elaborated the stories of Old Norse paganism no longer shocks us, but we do not really believe it either."

This observation is not intended to diminish the value of Snorri's work in any way, but merely to properly assess its authority as a source of heathen belief against the older poetic material that he used as his source. Rather than a primary source of Old Norse mythology, a place properly reserved for the eddic and skaldic poetry which are widely regarded as genuine products of the heathen era, we must recognize that Snorri's *Edda* is actually the first scholarly work on the subject. Even though the manuscripts of eddic poetry we have are slightly younger than manuscripts of *Snorri's Edda,* it is clear that their content predates his work. Snorri himself most likely used a

---

[515] McKinnell, *Both One and Many,* p. 13.

written collection of poems such as those found in the *Codex Regius* manuscript of the *Poetic Edda* when writing for his work. He quotes or paraphrases large tracts of poems we have for study, including *Völuspá*, *Vafþrúðnismál*, *Grímnismál* and *Lokasenna*, and others we do not, such as *Heimdallsgaldr* and *Húsdrapa*. Still we must remember that Snorri was a member of a universally Christian society, and there is no reason to think he had any desire to present the mythology as truth.[516] He wrote his *Edda* as a treatise on traditional skaldic verse in an attempt to keep interest in it alive. The form of the work itself is highly literary and owes much to the recently introduced tradition of learned Latin treatises.[517] His purpose was to preserve the ancient skaldic art, already in an advanced state of decay, as a source of cultural pride. His interests were antiquarian and not theological. He wrote primarily for the benefit of aspiring poets, who could only appreciate and emulate the art of their predecessors if they understood the myths alluded to in their works. Almost all of the recommended types of kennings listed for the gods in *Skáldskaparmál* refer to myths that Snorri sets forth in *Gylfaginning*. Thus, he only provided a brief account of those myths and legends which were exemplified in the poetic authorities he cites, akin to those that accompanied Classic Greek and Latin literature in the medieval classroom.[518] That he had to explain them at all, suggests that the myths were no longer common currency. As further evidence of this, almost no mythology is preserved in contemporary sagas that mention the old gods, apart from poetic citations. Snorri was the only medieval Icelandic author to provide a systematic overview of the pagan myths of Scandinavia alongside an analysis of poetic diction and verse forms. Carolyn Larrington observes:

> "His selection was no doubt affected by his primary purpose of clarifying poetic allusions, and it is probable, as Anthony Faulkes suggests, that the pagan religion was never systematically understood by those who practiced it."[519]

---

[516] McKinnell, ibid., p. 14.
[517] Faulkes, ibid., p. xiii.
[518] M. Clunies Ross, *A History of Old Norse Poetry and Poetics* (2005) p. 173.
[519] *The Poetic Edda* (1996), p. xii.

This does not mean, however, that we can dismiss it as primitive or incomplete.[520] The longevity and conservatism of pagan religious iconography in northern Europe over great expanses of space and time indicates otherwise.[521] The fact that scholars can trace specific narratives found in ancient Scandinavian poetry, such as Thor's fishing for the Midgard Serpent, in both Scandinavian literature and art over at least four centuries, as well as identify ancient Indo-European parallels in them, demonstrates a conservative continuity of ideas over time, whenever the fragmentary records allow us to know. That the oral mythology had an underlying epic structure, as any history would, is evident from the many temporal and causal references in eddic poetry, as well as the chronological arrangement of events in poems like *Völuspá*. Scholars such as Viktor Rydberg, and more recently John Lindow and Margaret Clunies Ross, have used these references to reconstruct chronological outlines of the epic "mythic timeline" inherent in the eddic poems.[522] Snorri's mythic overview, derived from his understanding of the old poetry he knew, is largely achieved in *Gylfaginning*, but augmented in *Skáldskaparmál*.[523] Today, we owe our knowledge of many ancient poems to Snorri's citations of them. Without his *Edda* many eddic and skaldic poems would not have survived, and few of those that did would be comprehensible.[524] In skaldic, as well as eddic poetry, the referential meaning of a verse is intentionally veiled and understanding largely depends on the audience's knowledge of certain facts that were part of the common cultural knowledge, like the events and personages of Norse myth or the military campaigns of a Norwegian king.[525] By Snorri's day, this knowledge was already distorted, accelerated by the advance of Latin learning and literature. Without his work, our understanding of the often cryptic references in both eddic and skaldic poetry, especially in

---

[520] Jónas Kristjánsson, *Icelandic Manuscripts* (1996), p. 27.
[521] Gunnell, ibid., p. 49.
[522] V. Rydberg, *Investigations into Germanic Mythology*, Volume 2 (1889), "An Overview of the Germanic Mythology's Epic Order" pp. 375-426 (Translated into English, 2007); Margaret Clunies Ross, *Prolonged Echoes* (1994), pp. 234-238; John Lindow, "The Nature of Mythic Time" in *Handbook of Norse Mythology* (2001), pp. 39-43.
[523] M. Clunies Ross, *A History of Old Norse Poetry and Poetics* (2005) p. 177.
[524] McKinnell, *Meeting the Other in Norse Myth and Legend*, p. 45.
[525] Margaret Clunies Ross, ibid., p. 76.

the kennings of the latter, would be severely impacted. Snorri's efforts even sparked a brief revival of skaldic poetry, but as Christopher Abrams observes, "The flowering of mythological literature in the thirteenth century was glorious, but short-lived."[526]

Within Iceland, *Skáldskaparmál* was arguably the most important, most copied and most imitated part of Snorri's *Edda* in the late Middle Ages and well into the Renaissance.[527] However, it was not regarded as a historical work or a book of old heathen mythology. His *Edda,* especially *Skáldskaparmál,* handed down in copies and abridgments through the Middle Ages, set the standard and ideal of poetry.[528] As evidence of this, the word *Edda* was synonymous with "poetic technique" throughout the Middle Ages. Known from the *Codex Wormianus* manuscript which contains the complete *Prose Edda* and a number of additional grammatical treatises called *Skálda,* it seems to have kept alive the very remembrance of old court-poetry, which would have otherwise perished. Constant allusions to it appear from 1340 to 1640 using *Edda* as a synonym for the technical laws of court-meter. In his *Lilia,* verse 97, Eysteinn Ásgrímsson (c. 1310–1360) wrote: "In all speech the substance is the thing, though the obscure rules of *Edda* may here and there have to give way; so I shall write plainly." Around 1380, Abbot Ami wrote: "The great masters of the Eddic Art, who cherish the precepts of learned books, may think this poem too plain, but the plain words of Scripture are better suited in my opinion to the lives of saints, than the dark likenings which give neither strength nor pleasure to any one." Numerous similar examples occur in the *Rimur* from 1450-1550 as well as prose sources afterward, down to the beginning of the seventeenth century.[529]

---

[526] Abrams, ibid., p. 230.

[527] Margaret Clunies Ross, ibid., p. 170.

[528] Gudbrand Vigfusson, *Corpus Poeticum Boreale* (1883), p. xxvi.

[529] Vigfusson, ibid., p. xxvii. From the *Rimur*: "I have never heard or seen Edda", i. e. I have never learned poet-craft. "There is no pleasure in speaking in riddles, according to the dark rules of Edda", "I am tired of Edda." "I send my poem forth though I have not learnt my words or art from Edda!"; "I have never learnt any of Edda's figures"; "No help of Edda have I got, she is thought hard to master, and she has never got into my brains!" After 1550: "The crooks or gambits of Edda"; "Many sing though they know little of Edda"; "I shall not fix my mind on Edda, the meaning is the important thing"; "The laws of the poets and the rules of Edda"; "The similes or figures of Edda", and so on.

The fact that Norse mythology sprang up in new forms in thirteenth century Iceland suggests that pagan myth, as a cultural rather than a religious phenomenon, never entirely died out.[530] While it is sometimes taken for granted that Icelanders preserved the old poems and myths of their forefathers in an unbroken chain, in reality, interest in the *Eddas* and *Sagas* waned throughout the Middle Ages, almost to the point of extinction. After the fall of the Icelandic Commonwealth in 1281, great activity in collecting and copying historical literature ensued during the following century, as the descendants of the old families were moved to protect their heritage. By far, the greatest portion of Icelandic sagas have come down to modern times in fourteenth century manuscripts. By the fifteenth century, however, popular tastes had changed and, although the number of vellums produced did not change significantly, their subjects were now mostly foreign and fictitious romances.[531] The sudden disinterest in skaldic poetry by 1400, after a long period of active revisions, coincides with a decline in the practice of skaldic verse-making.[532] The last skaldic poems were composed in the fourteenth century, raising the spectre that at least some of the verses found in the sagas may be contemporary compositions. No independent redaction of Snorri's *Edda* is found from about 1400 until the Reformation. By the dawn of the sixteenth century, *Rímur* and Saint's lives dominated the public taste. While poems in *drótt-kvætt*-related meters, such as *Lilja*, were composed in the fifteenth and sixteenth centuries, the diction is clearer and simpler, and clearly divorced from *regla eddu*, "the rules of *Edda*." From 1530 to 1630, hardly any Saga manuscripts, no copies of *Landnamabók* (*Book of Settlements*), and almost no copies of Snorri's *Edda* were produced. About 1595 *Codex Trajectinus*, a single paper copy of Snorri's *Edda*, was written in the West Fjords by Páll Jónsson from a late thirteenth century manuscript now lost.[533]

Signs of a Renaissance emerged about the last ten years of the sixteenth century, but the impulse came from overseas. About 1550, a vellum manuscript of kings' lives in Old Icelandic was found at Bergen, Norway. Translated and published in Copenhagen in 1594,

---

[530] Abrams, ibid., 181.
[531] Primarily *Fornaldarsögur, Riddarsögur and Rimur*.
[532] Guðrún Nordal, *Tools of Literacy* (2001), p. 45.
[533] Guðrún Nordal, ibid.,

the collection sparked royal interest which led to the employment of Icelanders to find and interpret such documents. From the influential position conferred upon him by the Danish crown, Arngrímur Jónsson (1568-1648) was able to acquire no less than twenty-six manuscripts during his professional life. As a result of this renewed interest in antiquities in the late 1500s, Snorri's *Edda* was first published in early modern times as the popular *Laufás Edda* (1609), presenting *Gylfaginning* from the *Wormianus* manuscript rearranged into sixty-eight short prose tales along with the kennings of *Skáldskaparmál* organized alphabetically. Produced by the Icelandic priest Ólafur Magnússon at the request of Arngrímur Jónsson, the purpose was to make available a systematic version of the *Prose Edda*. This distorted version of Snorri's work quickly became a popular reference work for poets and antiquarians. *Codex Wormianus*, however, does not contain an ascription to Snorri, and although there are many references to *Edda*'s rules prior to 1609, there are none to its rule-maker, which is, as Vigfusson says, "a thing most strange, but which may fairly be taken as evidence that Snorri was clean forgotten in the popular mind." In his *Crymogaea* (1609), Arngrímur was the first to acknowledge Snorri's authorship of the *Prose Edda*, probably on the authority of some copy such as *Codex Upsalensis,* one of two manuscripts which contains an ascription to the author.[534] Arngrímur's contemporary Björn Jónsson of Skardsa, on the contrary, assigned the authorship of Snorri's *Edda* and the *Skálda* to Sæmund the Wise, based on a reference to him in Gunlaug's *Jóns Saga helga*. Faced with Arngrímur's confident statement of the *Edda*'s true authorship, Björn later revised his theory saying that Sæmund had begun the *Edda*, which Snorri finished. Arngrímur, perhaps in a desire to appear consistent, agreed with this statement in a letter to Ole Worm in 1637 when asked about the apparent discrepancy. Because of this, when Bishop Brynjólfur Sveinsson of Skálholt discovered the first copy of eddic poetry now known as the *Codex Regius* manuscript, he erroneously dubbed the collection the *Sæmundar Edda* or Sæmund's *"Edda,"* a title exclusively applied for Snorri's book of poetics before 1642.[535] Brynjólfur had a copy made on vellum, which he inscribed *Edda Sæmundi multiscii* and sent abroad. From the undeserved authority of its inscription, this misnomer

---

[534] Gudbrand Vigfusson, *Corpus Poeticum Boreale* (1883), pp. xxi.
[535] Vigfusson, ibid., p. xxx.

became spread on the continent. This vellum copy came with the rest of Thormod Torfæus' manuscripts into the possession of Árni Magnusson, who would later complain that scholars accepted the superscription as an oracle not to be doubted. It has since disappeared, probably burnt in the great Copenhagen fire of 1728.

The theory of an older archetypical *Edda* upon which Snorri based his own, first proposed by Magnus Ólafsson in 1629, paved the way for accepting the newly found *Codex Regius* manuscript (GKS no. 2365 4to.) as another *Edda*. Magnus held that the *Codex Wormianus* manuscript of Snorri's *Edda* was merely a compendium of an archetypical *Edda*, an encyclopedic store of ancient wisdom composed by the Aesir themselves, i.e. the men who migrated from Asia led by Odin, as described by Snorri, or their grandsons. Bishop Brynólfur, apparently then unaware of the *Codex Regius* manuscript, in a letter dated 1641, writes:

> "Where be those mighty treasuries of all human knowledge, written down by Sæmund the Wise, and in especial that most noble Edda, of which beside the name, we have but a thousandth part; yea, and that which we have had been altogether destroyed had not the compendium of Snorri Sturluson, which we have, preserved to us what I would call a bare shadow and footprint of that ancient Edda."

The first reference to the eddic poems preserved in the *Codex Regius* manuscript appears in an essay on runes by Björn Jónsson of Skardsa in 1642, which contains the name *Hávamál* for the first time and quotations which could only have been drawn from that manuscript. He speaks of the songs contained therein as "dim, obscure and difficult, needing interpretation, as of immense age," and as being composed by the Aesir themselves.[536] He accounts for this book by referring to it as a second, older *Edda*, the archetype written down by Sæmund the Wise, a theory by then widely accepted among the learned men of Iceland. In another passage, alluding to *Völuspá,* he refers to "that obscure prophecy which Sæmund places first in his book and which is named after the *Völsu.*" Björn concludes: "All that I have just stated comes from the *Sæmundar Edda* and its extremely old poems, prophecies and proverbs of wisdom, which are too long to insert here." In 1662, Bishop Brynjólfur gave the same

---

[536] Vigfusson, ibid., p. xxxiv.

manuscript, along with several others, to Torfæus, an agent of King Frederick III of Denmark, who was then in Iceland in search of old vellums for the the king's new library. The now elderly Brynjólfur sent this precious treasure along with other manuscripts as a gift to the king, probably as a conciliatory present in hope of a Letter of Rehabilitation for his beloved daughter Ragnhild, who had been seduced and left pregnant by a young man the bishop had taken in. Unfortunately the girl died a short time later, and Brynjólfur died childless in 1675, his only son also having died young. It was thus most fortunate that Bishop Brynjólfur sent some of his best manuscripts to Denmark. Without an heir, the remainder of his collection was dispersed upon his death, so that Árni Magnússon, the great collector of Icelandic manuscripts could find little trace of them in the early years of the eighteenth century. All except one of his gifts to the king have come down to our time, while the vellums left in Iceland, known from copies made by Jón Erlendsson, somehow perished in the thirty year interval between Brynjólfur's death and Árni Magnússon's arrival.

In addition to *Codex Regius*, other manuscripts containing eddic songs have surfaced. The first of these was *Rigspula* in *Codex Wormianus*, which was known before 1609, when Magnús Ólafsson first mentioned it. A second MS. of *Snorri's Edda* (*r*) purchased by Bishop Brynjólfur in 1641 preserves the *Grotta-söngr*. Within a few years of the discovery of *Codex Regius*, a fragmentary MS designated AM no. 748, yielded the previously unknown *Baldrs Draumar*, also called *Vegtamskviða* in later, extended paper versions. *Hyndluljóð* came to light with the *Flateyjarbók* in 1643. Besides these, a few more old poems composed in eddic meters, whose date and authenticity remain in question today, were recognized in late paper manuscripts including *Grougaldur*, *Fjölsvinnsmál*, *Sólarljóð* and *Hrafnagaldur Óðins*; and at least one new poem, *Gunnarslagr*, was composed in imitation of the ancient style during this period by clergyman Gunnar Pálsson (1714-1791), who made no attempt to conceal its authorship. Yet, outside of a small group of scholars, the influence of the newly-discovered *Poetic Edda* was not great. As evidence of this, the first edition of the mythic poems was not published until 1787. Few pieces saw print prior to that time. *Hávamál* and *Völuspá* were the first to be published, along with a new edition of Snorri's *Edda*, titled *Edda Islandorum* by Peder Hansen Resen in 1665. A few eddic poems (primarily *Völuspá, Hávamál,* and *Vegtamskviða*) were translated into Latin, German, Swedish and Danish prior to 1779. Collections of mythic poetry began to first appear in the 1780s and the earliest edition of the heroic poems saw print in 1814. The first complete edition of the eddic corpus was that of Rasmus Rask in 1818.

As soon as these volumes reached a mass audience, eddic studies, heavily dependent on Snorri's *Edda* for guidance, began in earnest. Since that time, our understanding of the poems has slowly evolved. Early modern scholarship in this field began sporadically in the late eighteenth century, primarily concerned with establishing and translating the source texts and developing reference material. As eddic scholarship found its footing in the mid-nineteenth century, many excellent investigations were conducted by such luminaries as Finnur Magnússon, Jakob Grimm, Karl Simrock, Gudbrandr Vigfússon, Sophus Bugge, Frederich Bergmann, Viktor Rydberg and others. In the early 1800's and throughout most of the century the poems were loosely regarded as derived from the true history of the Bible, often using Snorri's Christianized account as support. Another school held that the gods were best interpreted as personifications of natural phenomena. By the third quarter of the nineteenth century, these widely accepted views began to be seriously challenged by a growing number of scholars who instead proposed an Indo-European (also called Indo-Germanic or Aryan at that time) origin for the mythology, independent of Biblical roots. They also argued that the Norse myths were much more sophisticated than simple expressions of nature. By centuries end, they had won their case, culminating in the great debate by A.C. Bang, Sophus Bugge and Viktor Rydberg over the true origin of the eddic mythology, whether it was to be regarded as native or foreign. Having thrown off the yoke of a foreign origin, eddic scholarship began to flourish as a science. Yet, despite this burden having been lifted, eddic studies advanced slowly for several years. With the popularity of Richard Wagner's Ring Cycle of operas beginning in 1876, eddic scholarship was blessed with a wealth of new works, then suffered a marked decline during and after the First and Second World Wars, when the rest of the world shunned all things Germanic. It was nearly two decades before eddic scholarship would once again became fashionable.

Throughout much of the nineteenth and twentieth centuries, the Icelandic texts remained the primary source for the study of Scandinavian pre-history and religion. The eddic poems were looked upon as literary creations and often analyzed as written works, sometimes deconstructed to the point of absurdity, particularly during the first post-war revival in the 1960s and '70s. Many translators felt free to revise, edit and emend the material as they saw fit. Archaeology was typically treated passively as a means to confirm texts. As a result, the Icelandic textual sources were taken as a starting point, sometimes supplemented with additional written resources, and used to retroactively describe religious practices in the Viking Age and times before. The obvious distances between time and space were commonly overlooked. Elaborate theories were sometimes developed to support an individual point of view, based on little more than the theories of previous scholars and selective passages from the source material. During this period, many prominent scholars such as Hilda Ellis Davidson saw the Norse divinities as aspects of a single Great Mother goddess and a universal Sky-Father figure, but, despite popular trends, the true light of scholarship remained, producing many valuable studies, translations and reference works throughout the century.

Since the mid-1990s, the world has experienced a Renaissance in eddic studies with more books and articles published on the subject than at any time in history. This is due primarily to technological advances in the various fields within the study of ancient Germanic religion, resulting in an increasingly interdisciplinary approach, combining expertise from different departments such as archaeology, comparative mythology, folkloristics, the history of religion, linguistics, literary criticism, philosophy, and place-name studies. Today, scholars no longer approach ethnic religions, such as the Germanic, from the standpoint of universal, scripture-based religions intended to apply to all people regardless of origin, such as the Abrahamic religions for example. Instead, ethnic religions are understood as traditional community-based beliefs and practices, which develop organically within a specific society, typically defined by a specific timeframe and geographical region, despite later mobility. Ethnic religions, which clearly include the pre-Christian heathen religions of Northern Europe, have existed among all people and can still be observed among the indigenous people of Africa, the Americas, Australia, and on the Pacific. As a result, the old Heathen religion has ceased to be treated as theology and more as a series of rituals, traditions and symbols, extending across overlapping social and geographic spheres over a broad expanse of time. Both textual and physical remains, analyzed in their proper contexts, are now equally regarded as vehicles which serve to create and define social relationships through ritual. Catherine Bell, author of *Ritual Theory, Ritual Practice* (2009), notes that once created, such traditions are not then left to their own momentum. Rather, they are constantly reinforced through rituals, both public and private, which continuously incorporate new practices and discard old ones, even if those who participate in them do not perceive them as changing. Therefore, of necessity, the myths associated with them must also evolve through time and place, a fact abundantly clear in the study of comparative Indo-European mythology which applies equally to research within its various branches, including the Germanic. As Joshua Rood observes:

> "While the writings of a thirteenth-century Icelander may well reflect a great deal of truth about his personal perceptions of the past, or even the preceptions that other members of his society had of the past, they do not necessarily reflect a past reality itself or the perceptions of other areas or people."[537]

Today, scholars recognize that Snorri may have invented whole mythic episodes from poetic passages he struggled to understand (such as Odin's theft of the mead of poetry from Gunnlod, alluded to in *Havamál* 13-14, 104-110), and simply ignored those that he did not (for example, the Gullveig verses in *Völuspá* 21-22). Terry Gunnell summarizes this belief, stating "the views increasingly expressed over the last twenty years or so [demonstrate] that there is good reason for students and scholars to be highly wary of trusting the image of Old Norse cosmology and mythology presented in Snorri Sturluson's *Prose Edda*."[538] Indeed, modern research shows that many of the apparent contradictions we find in the mythology originate with Snorri, either directly or through scholarly interpretations of the *Poetic Edda* using his work as a guide.

---

[537] *Ascending the Steps to Hliðskálf,* p. 12.
[538] Terry Gunnell, "Pantheon? What Pantheon? Concepts of a Family of Gods in Pre-Christian Scandinavian Religions," in *Scripta Islandica* 66/2015.

In places, Snorri's explanation of a strophe overtly contradicts the words of the passage he quotes, and in some cases the strophe he quotes varies significantly from the same strophe recorded elsewhere. Therefore, a closer examination is warranted in these cases. Unfortunately, however, the recognition of such contradictions has led to a new interpretation at the dawn of the twenty-first century, which understands the poems and other sources of our knowledge as only loosely related, but *wholly* independent of one another. John Lindow expresses it this way:

> "Such evidence as we have suggests that, with no canonical scriptures and no organization to enforce orthodoxy, Germanic heathenism was constantly shifting and might contain differing traditions even within the same culture and period. *Snorra Edda* gives it a more unified appearance, but that is a work of the Christian Middle Ages and sometimes reveals its author's orthodox Christian faith."[539]

Christopher Abram, Thomas Dubois, Terry Gunnell, Carolyne Larrington, John McKinnell, Jens Peter Schjødt and many others have expressed similar views, not seeing the *Poetic Edda* as a mythic corpus, but viewing each eddic poem as an independent creation, composed by different skalds, in different regions, for different purposes, despite being largely preserved together in one language, in a single manuscript. Scholars today tend to see the eddic poems as less cohesive than their counterparts did in the past. In a recent work, Professor Gunnell for example suggests that one eddic poem cannot be used to explain another. He questions "whether all of these myths come from the same cultural environment, or whether, like the later folk legends, they were actually collected in different places, and never actually belonged together as a corpus."[540] Still, many scholars recognize a remarkable amount of iconographic and narrative consistency over several centuries across the region, as demonstrated in the preceding chapters, which warrants a re-evaluation of this emerging trend.

Throughout the history of eddic studies Snorri's *Edda* has been used as a guide to illuminate the often obscure and allusive eddic poetry. Modern readers commonly take Snorri's *Edda* as their

---

[539] *Meeting the Other in Norse Myth and Legend*, p. 13
[540] Gunnell, ibid., (2015)

starting point since no other text presents this material in such a comprehensive and comprehensible manner. But for all that, *Snorri's Edda* is unquestionably a late, post-heathen reconstruction of Old Norse mythology by an author who emphasizes that the pagan world has passed.[541] We must remember his *Edda* was not intended as a book of mythology as we know it today, but expressly composed as a book of poetics. Snorri's primary purpose was not to revive the old religion, but to keep alive the traditional skaldic art which was rapidly losing ground to new genres of imported romance, courtly love poems, and popular ballads flooding in from Norway and Christian Europe under the patronage of King Hákon and his successors.[542] While Snorri had no reason to deliberately distort the material he inherited, he received it as a Christian from Christian informants and his understanding of it is inevitably limited by this fact.[543] Today, more than any other time in history, scholars are questioning the authority of Snorri's *Edda*. They recognize that he gave an account of the mythology only as a means to illuminate and demonstrate techniques for composing Christian verse using the complex system of metaphorical comparisons characteristic of the skaldic art. Snorri's account, based largely upon his personal understanding of the traditional literature, was written long after heathen practices had died out in Iceland, and so represent a learned rationalization of his cultural inheritance. Scholars agree that he certainly embellished and may have even created some of it himself. Yet there is no need to reject it outright, particularly when it does not contradict other primary sources of evidence.[544] The less dominant clerical culture in Iceland held a more tolerant attitude to pre-Christian material than was the case elsewhere in Europe. In the *Prologue* to his *Edda* and *Ynglingasaga*, Snorri attempts to reconcile the pagan past with contemporary Christianity. Alongside his own prose, he quotes passages of old poetry unknown elsewhere. Snorri's *Edda* is thus simultaneously a source and a commentary on the sources, even if the dividing line is not always clear. Still, we must never take its statements as "a Nordic Bible, reflecting a pan-Nordic or even

---

[541] Abram, ibid., p. 27.
[542] McKinnell, *Meeting the Other in Norse Myth and Legend*, p. 44.
[543] McKinnell, *Both One and Many*, p. 14.
[544] Abram, ibid., p. 75.

Germanic pre-Christian worldview."[545] That said, the importance of Snorri's *Edda* as a source cannot be overstated. Without it, many eddic and skaldic poems would be lost and the late thirteenth century anthologies of eddic verse may never have been compiled.[546] Even so, we must recognize that Snorri's account of Norse mythology is selective and highly dependent on his poetic sources.

The framing device of his narrative allows Snorri to closely control its content. In *Gylfaginning,* which means the "Deceiving of Gylfi," the native King Gylfi arrives in Asgard under an assumed name to question three shadowy Æsir, who are identified as men, not gods. From the onset, the reader thus understands all is not what it seems. In the end, the hall and all its inhabitants suddenly vanish, leaving the real possibility that everything therein was a delusion. In addition, the narrative frame supports fictional dialogue, one of most common educational techniques of the Middle Ages, reminding the audience that *Edda* was intended as a Classical textbook on poetics, nothing more. There is strong evidence that the account of pagan myth that he presents in *Gylfaginning* in particular is slanted in such a way to make it a slightly distorted version of Christianity. In other words, as Margaret Clunies Ross says, Snorri may have "*massaged* his sources for evidence" and "made up a line or two."[547] There are many examples in *Gylfaginning* of attempts to include concepts familiar to Christians. For example, the Swedish king Gylfi finds himself confronted with a counterpart to the Christian trinity in the form of a trio of Æsir who answer all his questions, and the narrative is concerned with building up Odin not just as the chief of the pagan gods, but as a supreme and omnipotent god, who lives throughout all ages, rules all kingdoms, and governs all things great and small,[548] a concept appropriate to the Christian God, but foreign to Odin as far as one can tell from the old poetic sources.

Although Snorri clearly had skaldic sources attributed to known poets for at least some of the individual myths he relates— the Baldur myth in particular— his exclusive use of anonymous eddic poetry to support his narrative in *Gylfaginning* suggests that he wanted to lend the mythology an air of antique authority. Yet, the strophes

---

[545] Gunnell (2015), ibid.,
[546] McKinnell, *Meeting the Other in Norse Myth and Legend*, p 45.
[547] M. Clunies Ross, *A History of Old Norse Poetry and Poetics* (2005) p. 180
[548] Ross, ibid., p. 180.

he cites are sometimes different from the same ones found in *Codex Regius*, arousing suspicion that he chose versions favorable to his Christian interpretation or, more plausibly, emended or invented a line here and there as Professor Ross suggests. For example, in *Gylfaginning* 4, when quoting *Völuspá* 3/2, Snorri says that before the creation of the world, *þat er ekki var*, "there was nothing then," whereas both extant manuscripts of *Völuspá* read *þar er Ymir bygði*, "when Ymir made his dwelling." While Snorri certainly knew the myth of Ymir and used it later in *Gylfaginning*, it would not have fit his *interpretatio Christiana* to have a primeval giant present at the beginning of time, given the Christian concept of a creation *ex nihlio* ("from nothing").[549] Clearly, he was concerned with providing an explanation for the Norse gods that fell in line with Christian orthodoxy.[550] Since *Völuspá*'s apocalyptic vision suggests that the world of the old gods was coming to an end with the promise of being replaced with something better —the obvious candidate for this 'better' world to a post-conversion author such as Snorri would be the one offered by Christianity.[551] In this regard, he portrays Surt and his men as angels of light, descending from above to annihilate the pagan gods. In *Gylfaginning*, he has Surt's forces descend from a crack in the heavens, as opposed to riding up over Bifröst, as told in *Fafnismál* 14-15, from their subterranean home in *Surts sökkdölum* ("Surt's deep dales"), an expression preserved within a poetic passage by the skald Eyvind in *Skáldskaparmál* 9. Logically, the world of fire inhabited by Surt which already existed at the beginning of time, sits lower than the earth and heavens built over them. Yet for all this, scholars remain dependent on Snorri's text. As John McKinnell, quoted earlier, states: "Many modern descriptions rely heavily on the *Prose Edda* of Snorri Sturluson, and especially on the fluent and persuasive account of the gods in *Gylfaginning*, its first major section." Carolyne Larrington concurs, stating: "Just as Snorri could not help but be influenced by his Christian beliefs in his account ...so we cannot now read the *Poetic Edda* without using Snorri to clarify and explain," even though she herself acknowledges "the picture given is misleading in its coherence and clarity."[552]

---

[549] Ross, ibid., p. 181-2.
[550] Carolyne Larrington, *Poetic Edda* (2014), p. xii.
[551] Abram, ibid., p. 166.
[552] *Poetic Edda* (1996), p. xiii.

Throughout the history of eddic scholarship, Snorri's work, being both accessible and informative, has consistently been used to interpret the older, more allusive eddic poems. No one has seriously questioned the overall authority of Snorri's interpretations, although many scholars have taken issue with individual points. Inconsistencies between the poems and Snorri's text are often explained as variants, and scholars are understandably reluctant to dismiss any of his statements even when faced with hard evidence. It is my hope that a clearer understanding of Snorri's purpose will assist readers in their use of his *Edda* as an interpretive aid, realizing that he did not necessarily understand the eddic poems in the same manner as the heathen poets who composed them did. Considering Snorri was an educated man in a universally Christian society, it's unlikely he could have. Therefore, the traditionally oral eddic and skaldic poems which Snorri used as his source should be regarded as a more reliable record of heathen thought, particularly when they contradict him, rather than the other way around. Snorri's main sources in *Gylfaginning* are *Völuspá*, *Vafþrúðnismál*, *Grímnismál* and *Lokasenna*, with references and citations to *Fáfnismál* and *Álvismál*. His Baldur myth is most likely based on the skaldic poem *Húsdrápa*, which according to *Laxadæla Saga* ch. 29, was intended to describe a visual representation of the Baldur myth carved on the walls of a hall, rather than serving as a direct retelling of the tale.[553] This knowledge can help us understand why they vary from those found in other sources.

While internal evidence indicates that Snorri had access to more eddic poems than we have today, we cannot assume that he had sources for everything he writes, nor that his sources were any less cryptic or allusive than the ones we possess today. Remarkably, internal and external evidence also indicates that we possess poems that Snorri did not know, and that he sometimes ignored passages he must have known. His treatment of *Völuspá*, a poem he cites extensively throughout *Gylfaginning*, best illustrates these points. Both manuscript copies of *Völuspá* refer to mankind as "Heimdall's sons" in the opening strophe, a kenning naturally explained by the contents of *Rigspula*, a poem which explains how Heimdall fathered and sanctified each strata of old Norse society. Although that poem is preserved in a manuscript of Snorri's *Edda*, Snorri himself makes no reference to it, despite its status as a foundational myth with ancient

---

[553] Christopher Abram, *Myths of the Pagan North* (2011), pp. 185-6.

Indo-European parallels. From this, one can reasonably conclude he was unfamiliar with *Rigspula*. Similarly, Snorri does not seem to be aware that Lodur and Hönir are alternate names for Odin's brothers Vili and Ve, eventhough they are named as co-creators of Askur and Embla in *Völuspá* 17. He also says nothing of the witch Gullveig-Heid who features prominently in *Völuspá* 21-24, despite linking verses 25-26 to the myth of the giant builder contracted to construct Asgard's wall. Snorri either did not know or did not understand these strophes, but since they all appear in both manuscript copies of *Völuspá*, the latter seems more probable. On occasion, he also contradicts information in verses he cites as support. In *Gylfaginning* 51, for example, Snorri says that, "the giant Hrym, who captains Naglfari," the ship made of of deadmen's nails, will come to the battle of Ragnarök "with all the frost-giants" (*Hrymr heitir jötunn er stýrir Naglfara …með honum allir hrímpursa*). He adds that Loki will arrive "with all Hel's people. But Muspel's sons will have their own battle array," (*Loka fylgja allir Heljarsinnar. En Muspellssynir hafa yfir sér fylking*). "The sky will open and from it will ride the sons of Muspell. Surt will ride in front," (*klofnar himinninn ok ríða paðan Muspellssynir. Surtr ríðr first*). He then cites *Völuspá* 50 and 51 [R48 and 49; H42 and H43] which state that: "Hrym drives from the east holding his shield before him, …Naglfari is loosed" (*Hrymr ekr austan, hefisk lind fyrir… Naglfar losnar*) and "A ship fares from the east, across the sea will come Muspell's sons, with Loki at the helm." (*Kjóll ferr austan, koma munu Muspells um lög lýðir, en Loki stýrir*). Surt on the other hand, "fares from the south," (*Surtr ferr sunnan*; R51, H44). Thus, according to *Völuspá*, the giant Hrym who steers Naglfari, and Loki with the Sons of Muspel in a second ship, will sail in from the east, while Surt will arrive from the south. According to the eddic poem *Fafnismál*, which Snorri also cites, when Surt and his men ride together over Bifröst that span will break forcing his horses to swim in the currents of air. This begs the question whether Surt's men and Muspell's sons are even the same group of people. We have come to believe they are, based on Snorri's work, but a study of the eddic poems suggests otherwise. While the "sons of Muspell" are always associated with Ragnarök, it's important to note that they arrive with Loki from the east, and that the designation of the southern world of fire as *Muspellsheim* or *Muspelli* is unique to Snorri's text.

Today, roughly thirty-five eddic poems survive. These compositions when studied independently from *Snorri's Edda*, form a cohesive, if incomplete, picture of the heathen worldview. Recognizing this will help the researcher obtain more meaning from the poems than would be possible if he or she accepts Snorri's quasi-historical and fictional presentation of Old Norse mythology as a valid variant or worse, as a more reliable source of information than his own poetic sources. A more fruitful approach, in my opinion, is to study the eddic poems independently, and then compare the findings obtained in this manner to Snorri's text, paying close attention to where they correspond or compliment one another, and where they diverge. While there is no reason to reject Snorri's statements when they do not conflict with the poetic sources, there is certainly no reason to accept them as viable variants when they do. Overall, we should recognize that all of our sources are not of equal weight. The surviving evidence for the Norse gods is fragmentary and from different periods, some closer to or within the heathen period and some further from it both chronologically and conceptually. The purpose and perspective of the author, when known, must also be taken into account objectively. Nor can we assume that the poetic sources have come down to us directly and unadulterated even if they hail from the heathen era. The rewriting, elaboration and transformation which inevitably accompanies the recording of oral material is well known.[554] The process of editing oral texts for print commonly requires one to sample it, rather than reproduce it in full,[555] thus there is often much more to it than initially meets the eye. Jónas Kristjánsson, the former head of the Árni Magnússon Institute in Reykjavik,[556] observes:

> "The most ancient poems in the [Poetic] Edda also show various signs of abridgement and alteration – some of which of course may be due to editing or error in the written stage. On the other hand, it seems an inescapable conclusion that stories told in prose must always have existed alongside stories told in verse. Many of the heroic lays are shaped in such a way that it is evident the poets assumed more knowledge of the subject-matter on the

---

[554] O'Donoghue, ibid., p. 5.
[555] Margaret Clunies Ross in *The Editorial Gaze* (2014), p. 178.
[556] *Icelandic Manuscripts: Sagas, History, and Art* (1996); tr. by Jeffrey Cosser.

audience's part than the poems themselves encompass: a whole legend is there as a backdrop to the verse."

All of this must be taken into consideration when weighing the value and reliability of the available evidence. The major literary sources of Norse myth are of four kinds: eddic poems, skaldic stanzas, Snorri Sturluson's *Prose Edda,* and the sagas. What unites this body of literature is that it provides us with a picture of the pre-Christian past, either, because the material itself originated in the pre-Christian period and was recorded later, or because its authors were re-creating a pre-Christian past from their own contemporary understanding. Either way, the surviving representations of Norse myth almost entirely derive from literary texts written down in Iceland by Christians, long after the heathen era had passed. These texts encompass different literary genres and vary widely in how authentically they transmit heathen material or convey reliable information concerning heathen beliefs and practices.[557]

According to John McKinnell,[558] when we look for genuine heathen voices, there are three or perhaps four principle sources:

a) Mythological eddic poems
b) Skaldic verse
c) Viking Age Picture stones
d) Contemporary Christian views of Norse heathenism

Dating the material is problematic. While some of the eddic poems and skaldic verses may have been composed after the conversion of Iceland, in particular those poems preserved only in late paper manuscripts and skaldic verses incorporated into later sagas, there is little debate that on the whole, the bulk of eddic and skaldic poetry contain authentic heathen material. If the physical texts of the eddic poems can only be dated to the thirteenth century, that is not to say that the poems themselves did not originate much earlier.[559] Eddic poetry bears all the hallmarks of oral-traditional verse, including alliteration, repetition and formulaic construction, with direct analogs in both Old English and Old High German

[557] Heather O'Donoghue, *English Poetry and Old Norse Myth: A History* (2014), p. 5-6.
[558] *Both One and Many*, p. 1.
[559] Abram, ibid., p. 19

poetry. Evidence indicates that the eddic songs are the last vestiges of the ancient oral histories of the Germanic people which Tacitus, writing in the first century AD, says "form the only record of their past,"(*Germania* 2), and which the Gothic historian Jordanes, writing in the sixth century, confirms, stating that "in the earliest times, they sang of the deeds of their ancestors," (*Getica*, ch. 5)."[560] In contrast, Snorri's *Edda*, composed pen in hand, is a learned work based on his personal understanding and interpretation of those poetic sources. There is no reason to suspect that Snorri did not give an accurate account of the heathen religion as it was understood in his time. However, that is not to say that he understood the old poetry in the manner his heathen forebears did. Snorri clearly places the whole of his cultural heritage firmly within the confines of Christian and Classical learning, presenting it as an error from start to finish. Thus, one cannot simply remove the overtly foreign material in his work and assume what's left is wholly heathen. Since the eddic poems themselves are older than Snorri, and composed by actual heathen skalds, they naturally contain a more accurate reflection of the ancient heathen worldview, being conceptually closest to the source. Thus, when Snorri's statements conflict with the older poetic sources which are his acknowledged source, the older poems along with historical and archaeological information should be taken as a more reliable record of heathen belief, as I have sought to do here, within this investigation of Mother Earth in Germanic mythology. It is my belief that the preponderance of available evidence, weighted accordingly, clearly demonstrates that during the pagan period the names Frigg, Jörd and Hlin were regarded as belonging to one goddess representing the Earth, best known as Odin's wife and the Mother of the Gods, whose existence can be traced from the beginning of Germanic history to the present day. Snorri Sturluson alone suggests otherwise. The reader, of course, must be the judge which view offers a more accurate reflection of ancient heathen belief.

---

[560] Jordanes makes it clear that these songs were a history of the people in such statements as "for so the story is generally told in their early songs, in almost historic fashion," (ch. 4); "They retain it to this day in their songs," (ch. 11).

Appendix A:

Erce, Erce, Erce, eorþan modor
The Text of the Anglo-Saxon *Æcerbót*

The *Æcerbót* or "Field-remedy" is found in the British Library MS Cotton Caligula A. vii, fol. 176a-178a, dating to the late tenth or early eleventh century. The same manuscript contains the C version of the *Heliand* or Saxon Gospel. The full text of the charm reads:

Her ys seo bot, hu ðu meaht þine æceras betan gif hi nellaþ wel wexan oþþe þær hwilc ungedefe þing on gedon bið on dry oððe on lyblace.

Here is the remedy, how you may amend your fields, if they will not wax well, or if therein anything improper has been done, by sorcery or poison.

*Genim þonne on niht, ær hyt dagige, feower tyrf on feower healfa þæs landes and gemearca hu hy ær stodon. Nim þonne ele and hunig and beorman and ælces feos meolc þe on þæm lande sy and ælces treowcynnes dæl þe on þæm lande sy gewexen, butan heardan beaman and ælcre nam cuþre wyrte dæl butan glappan anon and do þonne haligwæter ðær on and drype þonne þriwa on þone staðol þara turfa and cweþe ðonne ðas word:
Crescite, wexe et multiplicamini and gemænigfealda et replete and gefylle terre þas eorðan In nomine patris et filii et spiritus sancti sit benedicti.*

Take then at night, ere it dawn, four turfs from the four quarters of the land, and mark how they ere stood. Then take oil and honey and barm and milk of all cattle on the land, and part of every kind of tree which grows on the land but hardwoods, and part of every wort known by name, but only burr [*glappan*], and on them pour holy water, and drip it thrice upon the underside of the turfs, and then say these words:

Crescite, grow; *et multiplicamini*, and multiply; *et replete*, and fill; *terram*, this earth. In the name of the Father and of the Son and of the Holy Spirit be blessed.

And Pater Noster swa oft swa þæt oðer

And say *Our Father* [The Lord's Prayer], as often.

And bere siþþan ða turf to circean and mæssepreost asinge feower mæssan ofer

And thereafter bear the turfs to church and let a mass-priest sing

323

þan turfon and wende man þæt grene to ðan weofode and siþþan gebringe man þa turf þær hi ær wæron ær sunnan setlgange

four masses over the turfs, and turn the green side to the altar, and then bring the turfs back to where they were before, ere the sun sets.

And hæbbe him gæworht of cwicbeame feower Cristes mælo and awrite on ælcon ende: Matheus and Marcus, Lucas and Iohannes.

And have him fashion of quick-wood [green-wood] four crosses, and let him write upon each end: Matthew and Mark, Luke and John.

Lege þæt Cristes mæl on þone pyt neopeweardne cweðe ðonne: Crux Matheus crux Marcus crux Lucas crux sanctus Iohannes.

Lay the marked crosses upon the floor of each pit, then say: Matthew's Cross, Mark's Cross, Luke's Cross, Saint John's Cross.

Nim ðonne þa turf and sete ðær ufon on and cwepe ðonne nigon siþon þas word Crescite and swa oft Pater Noster and wende þe þonne eastweard and onlut nigon siðon eadmodlice, and cweð þonne þas word:

Then take the turfs and set them on there, and then say nine times this word: *Crescite* and as often *Our Father* [The Lord's Prayer], and then turn eastward, and bow humbly nine times, and then say these words:

Eastweard ic stande,
arena ic me bidde
bidde ic þone mæran domine
bidde ðone miclan drihten
bidde ic ðone haligan heofonrices weard
eorðan ic bidde and upheofon
and ða soþan sancta Marian
and heofones meaht and heahreced
þæt ic mote þis gealdor mid gife
drihtnes toðum ontynan
þurh trumne geþanc
aweccan þas wæstmas us to woruldnytte
gefyllan þas foldan mid fæste geleafan
whitigigan þas wangturf swa se witega cwæð
þæt se hæfde are on eorþrice se þe ælmyssan
dælde domlice drihtnes þances

Eastward I stand
For mercies I ask (i.e. "pray")
I ask the powerful ruler,
I ask the mighty Lord
I ask the Holy Ward of Heavens' kingdom
Earth I ask and Heaven above
And the true Saint Mary
And Heaven's might and high hall
that through this *galdor*, I may, with the Lord's grace,
open my teeth (i.e "speak")
through firm intent,
awaken these plants for our worldly use,
fill these fields with steadfast faith
beautify this grassy turf, as the wiseman said, he would have riches on earth who gives alms
justly as the Lord intends.

Wende þe þonne III sunganges astrece þonne on andlang and arim þær letanias and cweð þonne: Sanctus, sanctus, sanctus oþ ende.

Then turn yourself thrice sunwise, and then stretch lengthwise and there count the litanies, and then say *Holy, Holy, Holy* to the end;

Sing þonne Benedicite aþenedon earmon and Magnificat and Pater Noster III and bebeod hit Criste and sancta Marian and þære halgan rode to lofe and to weorþinga and to are þam þe þæt land age and eallon þam þe him underðeodde synt ðonne þæt eall sie gedon þonne nime man uncuþ sæd æt ælmesmannum and selle him twa swylc, swylce man æt him nime and gegaderie ealle his sulhgeteogo togædere borige þonne on þam beame stor and finol and gehalgode sapan and gehalgod sealt. Nim þonne þæt sæd, sete on þæs sules bodig, cweð þonne:

Sing then *Benedicite* with arms extended, and *Magnificat*, and *Our Father*, thrice, and commend it to Christ and to Saint Mary and to the Holy Rood, for love, and for worthiness of the land-owner, and all those who are subject to him. When all that is done, then let a man take unfamiliar seed from almsmen, and give them twice as much as was taken, and gather all his plowing gear together; then bore a hole in the plow beam and therein put storax (frankincense) and fennel and hallowed soap and hallowed salt, then take that seed, and set it on the plow's frame, then say:

Erce, Erce, Erce eorþan modor
geunne þe se alwalda, ece drihten
æcera wexendra and wridendra
eacniendra and elniendra
sceafta hehra, scirra wæstma
and þæra bradan berewæstma
and þæra hwitan hwætewæstma
and ealra eorþan wæstma
Geunne him ece drihten
and his halige, þe on heofonum synt
þæt hys yrþ si gefriþod wið ealra feonda gehwæne
and heo si geborgen wið ealra bealwa gehwylc
þara lyblaca geond land sawen
Nu ic bidde ðone waldend,
se ðe ðas woruld gesceop

Erce, Erce, Erce, Mother of Earth!
May the Almighty, eternal Lord
grant you,
fields growing and flourishing,
increasing and strengthening,
high shafts, bright crops
and there, broad barley crops
and there, white wheat crops
and all earth's crops.
Grant him, eternal God
and his holy ones, who are in heaven,
that his farm be fortified against all fiends, every one,
and protected against all evils, each one
from curses sown round the land.
Now I ask the Master,
H who created this world

325

þæt ne sy nan to þæs cwidol wif
ne to þæs cræftig man
þæt awendan ne mæge
word þus gecwedene

that there be no wife so cunning,
no man so crafty man,
that can unravel
words so deftly spoken.

þonne man þa sulh forð drife and þa
forman furh onsceote, cweð þonne:

Then drive forth the plow and cut
the first furrow. Say then:

Hal wes þu, folde, fira modor
Beo þu growende on godes fæþme
fodre gefylled firum to nytte

Hail to you, *Folde*, mother of men
grow fertile in God's embrace
food-filled for mankind's use.

Nim þonne ælces cynnes melo and
abacæ man innewerdre handa bradnæ
hlaf and gecned hine mid meolce and
mid haligwætere and lecge under þa
forman furh. Cweþe þonne:

Then take every kind of meal and
bake a loaf as broad as the palm of a
man's hand, and knead it with milk
and with holy water, and lay it under
the first furrow. Then say:

Ful æcer fodres fira cinne
beorhtblowende   þu   gebletsod
weorþ
þæs haligan noman þe ðas heofon
gesceop
and ðas eorþan þe we on lifiaþ
se god, se þas grundas geworhte
geunne us growende gife
þæt us corna gehwylc cume to
nytte

Fill fields with food to feed men
bright-blooming,   your   blessed
worth
the holy name of Him who created
heaven,
and this earth on which we live,
may God who wrought these
grounds
grant us growing gifts,
that grain comes to us to use

Cweð þonne III
Crescite   in   nomine   patris,   sit
benedicti
Amen and Pater Noster þriwa

Say then thrice *Crescite in nomine
patris, sit benedicti* [Grow in the
name of the Father, be blessed].
Amen and *Our Father* thrice.

APPENDIX B:
Frigg's Son, Baldur

"The various sources which touch on an aspect of the Baldr myth present contradictory images of the god. Baldr has never failed to evoke an æsthetic response: the craftsman who depicted scenes from Baldr's death in a frieze on Ólafur pái's hall, the poet Ulf Uggason who found inspiration in these carvings, the unknown poet of *Völuspá*, the Icelander Snorri Sturluson and his Danish contemporary Saxo Grammaticus— all were inspired by the sublimity of the theme. For this reason research into the mythological content of Baldr stories is made more difficult."
—John S. Martin, *Ragnarök , An Investigation* (1972).

Few mythological themes are as consistent or as widespread among Indo-European groups as that of the Divine Twins.[561] Although there is no convincing lexical set designating a pair of twins, who are sons of the sky-god, they are abundantly represented on every level (myth, history, and folklore) in the various Indo-European traditions. There we find a regular association between two sons of the Sky-Father, depicted as young men closely connected to horses, who share a consort related to the sun or other sky-god.[562]

Despite being twins, they are often differentiated. One is represented as a healer and the other as a young warrior. Since the middle of the nineteenth century, scholars have been struck by the similarities between the Vedic Asvins, the Greek Diskouroi, and the 'Sons of God' who appear in Lithuanian and Latvian songs, recognizing a distinct pair of brothers from the Proto-Indo-European era. There is rare consensus among comparative mythologists on this.[563] That these brothers had analogs in the Germanic sphere is evident. Timaeus (332-256 BC) says that the Celts who lived near the ocean worshiped the Diskourai above all other gods, and Tacitus describes a native Germanic pair of divinities known as the Alci, who

---

[561] J.P. Mallory and D.Q. Adams, *Encyclopedia of Indo-European Culture* (1997), p. 161.
[562] J.P Mallory and D.Q. Adams, *The Oxford Introduction to Proto-European and the Proto-Indo-European World* (2006), p. 432.
[563] M.L. West, *Indo-European Poetry and Myth* (2007), p. 187.

are worshiped as young men and brothers, which he compares directly to the Diskourai (*Germania*, ch. 43). Although scholars have sought to identify a pair of divine twins in Germanic mythology — often suggesting Freyr and Freyja, Hengst and Horsa (Bede, HE I, 15), Ibor and Ajo of the Longobardi (Paulus Diaconus, *Hist. Lang.* I, 3), as well as Baldur and Hödur—the latter are an obvious choice. Odin's sons Baldur and Hödur fit the pattern on almost every account. They are young men and brothers, sons of the Germanic Sky-Father. Like the Diskourai, Castor and Pollux, when one brother dies, the other follows him to the underworld.

Alcis or Twins Horse Collar
Fogdarp, Scania in Sweden, Late Bronze Age

Whereas Baldur is described as a peacemaker, the name *Höðr* means "battle" (OE *heaðu-*, OHG *hadu-*, OS *hathu-*) and he is most often depicted shooting (*skjóta*) a weapon which kills his brother. In Saxo's version of the tale, Baldur and Hödur compete as warriors for the love of the same woman, who probably has close connections with the sun and moon, as shall be shown below. Saxo paints a rich portrait of Hotherus, in contrast to Snorri's sparsely defined Hödur.[564] Yet, even in Snorri's version, the brothers are as different

---

[564] Lindow, *Vengance and Murder Among the Gods*, p. 62.

as night and day. In the *Prose Edda, Skáldskaparmál* 22 expressly states that Baldur is the son of Odin and Frigg. As his brother, Hödur must share at least one parent with Baldur. Although the gods are collectively called "Frigg's progeny,"[565] Baldur is her only named child. According to *Gylfaginning* 22, "the second son of Odin is Baldur." His first, of course, is Thor, the son of Jörð (earth). In the *Prologue to Gylfaginning*, we read: "Odin's second son was named Beldeg, whom we call Baldur; he had the country now called Westphalia; his son was Brand." Anglo-Saxon royal genealogies also call Woden's son Bældæg and provide him with the son Brand. The name Bældæg is not unusual. Anglo-Saxon and Old High German have plenty of proper names compounded with the word *dæg* and *tac,* whereas even the ON has *Svipdagr.* This suffix semantically associates Baldur with day (*dag, dæg, tac*), indicating a god of light, much like the words *tyr, tivar, dies* express a "shining one," a "white one," a god. This is confirmed in *Gylfaginning* 22: "He is best, and all praise him; he is so fair of feature, and so bright, that light shines from him." In accord with this, both Snorri and the Anglo-Saxon genealogy assign him a son Brand, signifying "beam," "torch," "brand." The name Bældæg therefore agrees with *Berchta,* "the Bright one," found as an epithet for Odin's wife in German legend. Knowledge of Baldur was widespread. Over the whole of the Germanic region, certain flowers were named after him. *Gylfaginning* 22 continues, "A certain herb is so white that it is likened to Baldr's brow; of all grasses it is whitest, and by it you may judge his beauty, both in hair and in body." The flower-name *Baldrsbrá* for Scentless Mayweed (*Matricaria perforata*) and Sea Mayweed (*Matricaria maritima*), in particular, still occurs in southern Sweden, Denmark, Norway, Iceland, the Faeroes, and northern England. Placename evidence occurs sporadically all over Scandinavia.[566] In Sweden, we find *Baldersberg* in Småland and *Baldersnäs* in Långvik near Stockholm.; *Ballesager* from Jylland, recorded in 1566 as *Boldersagger,* which corresponds to Old Norse *Baldrs-akr; Baldirs æng* in Nørrejylland, recorded in 1387; *Bollershøwe* (ON *Baldrshøgh*) in Hassing Herred from 1485; and *Boldershøj* "Balder's hill" in Sønderjylland, recorded as *Boldershøy* in the 1700s. In Norway, we find *Baldrsberg* in Vestfold, *Baldersheim* in Hordaland from

---

[565] *Egil's Saga,* ch. 79; *Complete Sagas of the Icelanders* I, p. 151.
[566] Edward Smith, *Pagan and Supranormal Elements in Scandinavian Place-names* (2011) at http://germanic.eu/heathenplace1.htm (Last Viewed 1/01/2015).

the 1300s; *Ballheim* (ON *Baldrsheimr*) and *Balleshol* (ON *Baldrshóll*) in Hedmark. On Iceland, we find *Ballesheim* (ON *Baldrsheimr*) in north Hordaland and *Baldursheimur* in Hörgárdalur, Eyjafjarðarsýsla and Mývatnssveit. The latter two had churches built on their sites. Since the suffix *-heimur* is not common there, they may have been brought from Norway. Such places are likely named after the figure from Norse mythology since Baldur is not recorded as a personal name until the 1850s according to Halldór Halldórsson.

The earliest reference to Odin and Frigg's son, Baldur, occurs in the tenth century verse known as the *Second Merseburg Charm*, which reads in full:

Phol ende Uuodan	Phol and Wodan
uuoron zi holza,	rode into the woods,
du uuart demo Balderes volon	There the foot of Baldur's foal
sin vuoz birenkit;	went out of joint.
thu biguolen Sinhtgunt,	It was charmed by Sinhtgunt,
Sunna era suister;	Sunna her sister;
thu biguol en Frija,	It was charmed by Frija,
Volla era suister,	Volla her sister;
thu biguolen Uuodan,	It was charmed by Wodan,
so he uuola conda:	as he well knew how.
sose benrenki,	Bone-sprain,
sose bluotrenki,	as blood-sprain,
sose lidirenki:	as limb-sprain:
ben zi bena,	Bone to bone,
bluot zi bluoda,	blood to blood,
lid zi geliden,	Limb to limb,
sose gelimida sin.	As though they were glued.

Scholars have long debated the meaning of the name Phol and the word *balderes* in this verse. Phol is sometimes interpreted as the male half of an otherwise unattested couple: Phol and Volla. Likewise scholars have argued that the word *balderes* should be understood as a simple appellation meaning "lord," also otherwise unattested in German. Today, this is a minority view. Rudolf Simek clearly states that "this is difficult to prove, and therefore the *Second Merseburg Charm* should continue to be regarded as the first recording of the name Baldr."[567] John Lindow agrees, stating that "Frija, the Old

---

[567] Simek, *Dictionary of Northern Mythology*, p. 278, s.v. *Second Merseburg Charm*.

High German equivalent of Frigg, participates in the curing of Baldere's (Baldur's) horse."[568] Not surprisingly then, in the *Second Merseburg Charm*, we find Odin and Frigg associated with Baldur, their famous son, whose death is a central storyline in later Scandinavian sources. The verse speaks of an otherwise unknown episode in Old Norse mythology, the laming of Baldur's horse. Baldur's role as a rider is emphasized in the *Second Merseberg Charm*, in Saxo's *Danish History*, and in the eddic poem *Lokasenna*, where Loki says:

"Enn vill þú, Frigg,
at ek fleiri telja
mína meinstafi:
ek því réð,
er þú ríða sér-at
síðan Baldr at sölum."

28. "Do you, Frigg,
want me to recount
more of my mischief?
I am the cause
that you do not see
Baldur *riding* to the halls."

Odin Heals Balder's Horse
Carl Emil Doepler Jr., 1905

In the *Second Merseburg Charm*, *balderes* horse is injured when Odin and Phol ride into the wood. According to Book 3 of Saxo's *Gesta Danorum*, Baldur himself, before his death, was lamed and conveyed about in a carriage. In the same narrative, he is said to open a freshwater well for his men. This ability is closely associated with Baldur's demise:

---

[568] *Handbook of Norse Mythology*, p. 128.

"The conquering Baldur, in order to slake his soldiers, who were parched with thirst, with the blessing of a timely draught, pierced the earth deep and disclosed a fresh spring. The thirsty ranks made with gaping lips for the water that gushed forth everywhere. The traces of these springs, eternised by the name, are thought not quite to have dried up yet, though they have ceased to well so freely as of old. Baldur was continually harassed by night phantoms feigning the likeness of Nanna, and fell into such ill health that *he could not so much as walk*, and began the habit of going his journeys in a two horse car or a four-wheeled carriage."[569]

This passage may aid our understanding of the name Phol. Saxo informs us that Baldur had the power to open springs, which were called by his name. In Denmark there is *Baldersbrønde,* "Baldur's spring," in Sjælland, recorded as *Baldorpsbrynnæ* in 1321. Benjamin Thorpe states that "on the right hand side of the road leading from Copenhagen to Roeskilde there is a spring called Baldur's Brönd. ...The tradition among the country people is that it was produced by a stroke of the hoof of Baldur's horse."[570] In Germany, we frequently find references to "Phol's"— or "Fal's spring." In the province of Thuringia, a *Pholesbrunnen* is reported. Not far from the Saale river lies a village named *Phulsborn.* In the Franconian Steigerwald, we find a *Falsbrunn.* Similarly, we find a *Baldersbrunno* in the Eifel mountains and in the Rhineland Palatinate, the very regions we discover widespread legends of Frau Holle, Frau Percht, and Frau Goden, who is the wife of Godan or Wodan (Odin). Of the original name of the German village Pfalsau, recorded between 774 and 778 as *Pholesauwa* or *Pholesouwa,* Jacob Grimm writes:

"Its composition with *aue* (*auwa*) quite fits in with the supposition of an old heathen worship. The gods were worshiped not only on mountains, but on '*eas*' enclosed by brooks and rivers, where fertile meadows yielded pasture, and forests shade. Such was the *castum nemus* (sacred grove) of Nerthus in an *insula Oceani.*"

Evidence of such enclosed sanctuaries is found in several Old Norse sources as *Oðinsey, Thorsey, Hlessey,* etc. *Pholesouwa* is an Old High

[569] Oliver Elton translation.
[570] *Northern Mythology* (1878, reprinted by the Folklore Society 2001) p. 26, citing P.E. Müller's edition of Saxo and J.M.Thiele's *Danmarks folkesagn.*

German equivalent of names of this type, which means Phol's sanctuary.[571] Thus Phol or Fal is best interpreted as the name of a god. In early Christian times, partial to euhemerism, Baldur was sometimes transformed into a king in Vestphal. According to the *Prologue to Gylfaginning*, "Odin's second son was called Beldegg, whom we call Baldr; he had the country that is now called Westphalia."[572] According to ancient belief, nearly all countries and peoples took their names from some ancient ruler: The Franks from Francio, the Angles from Angul, Denmark from Dan, etc. The names Phalen, and Vestphal or Westphalia can be logically explained in the same manner if Baldur was also known as Phol or Fal, and his name was said to have given rise to these districts. As far as Jacob Grimm could determine, the name Phol was used chiefly by the Thuringians and the Bavarians, although they knew the god by the names Palter or Baldur. The same initial sound shift occurs in the names Perchta and Berchta for Frau Holle. Among the Saxons and Westphalians the names Baldag and Bældæg prevailed.[573] If Phol can be identified with Baldur in the *Second Merseburg Charm* as the foregoing evidence suggests, then we have a natural explanation of its contents. The events may be seen as a presage of Baldur's death: One day, Phol (Baldur) and his father are out riding with members of their family. The foot of Baldur's horse is sprained, and each family member comes to his aid in order of proximity. Closest is a female rider named Sinhtgunt, probably representing Baldur's wife Nanna, and her sister Sunna (see further). Next comes Frigg, his mother, and her sister, Volla, known as Fulla in the later Icelandic sources. Last comes Odin, Baldur's father, whose superior magic cures the sprain no doubt caused by witchcraft. Thus Baldur appears by two names, *Phol* and *Baldere*, in a single verse— a not uncommon phenomenon in old Germanic poetry where, for example, Odin's wife is called Hlin and Frigg in the space of a single strophe, *Völuspá* 53 [See Chapter IX: Jörd, Thor's Mother].

Adalbert Kuhn identified a much older parallel to the *Second Merseburg Charm* in the Hindu *Atharvaveda*, demonstrating that its formulaic pattern was traditional in Indo-European healing

---

[571] Grimm, ibid., p.225.
[572] A. Faulkes' tr.
[573] Grimm, ibid., p. 229.

incantations.[574] Many later versions of this spell have been recorded from Scandinavia and Great Britian (in English and Gaelic) as well as one from Latvia and another from Russia. In these, the narrative opening is often retained with pagan or Christian subjects. Most persistent is the formula: bone to bone, blood to blood, etc, although the actual substance may vary. These verses are not considered to be variants retelling the same myth, but simply products of an Indo-European poetic-rhetorical style. That Phol is Baldur, however, finds confirmation in later Christian charms of the same type. Axel Kock[575] cites a Swedish charm against sprains recorded in the Court Record of Sörbygden (*Sörbygdens dombok*) for 1672, which reads:

Vår herre Jesus Kristus och S. Peder de gingo eller rede öfver Brattebro. S. Peders häst fick vre eller skre. Vår herre steg af sin häst med, signa S. Peders häst vre eller skre: blod vid blod, led vid led. Så fick S. Peders häst bot i 3 name o.s.v.

"Our Lord Jesus Christ and Saint Peter walked or rode over Brattebro. St. Peter's horse got a twist or sprain. Our Lord dismounted, blessed St. Peter's horse's twist or sprain: blood to blood, joint to joint. So St. Peter's horse was cured in three names [Father, Son and Holy Spirit], etc."

In content, this verse presents a direct parallel to the *Second Merseburg Charm*. The traveling companions Wodan and Phol correspond to Christ and St. Peter in the Sörbygden charm. Whoever Phol was, Odin must have been the more prestigious of the two, just as Christ was more prestigious than St. Peter. Wodan is the healer of the horse in the *Second Merseburg Charm*, while Christ is the healer in the Sörbygden charm. A similar agreement exists between Odin and Christ in other medieval formulas against sprains. In a charm from Småland, Odin, out riding alone, heals his own horse, and, in a charm recorded in *Kungelf's dombok* (1629), Christ, riding alone in the same manner, is said to cure his. Besides the motif of an injured horse ridden by a divine figure, these charms all contain the formula: joint with joint, blood with blood, sinew with sinew, bone with bone, demonstrating their origin lies in a common tradition. Jacob Grimm

---

[574] West, ibid., pp. 337-338.
[575] *Svenska Landsmålen* 5/1887, citing Carl Ohlson Arcadius, *Om Bohusläns införlivande med Sverige*, University of Lund dissertation, pg. 118, (1883).

records Danish and Scottish variants.[576] He provides an additional charm in Latin, which also points to Phol's identity with Baldur. In it, three persons ride together: St. Peter, St. Michael and St. Stephan. When Stephan' horse is injured, the archangel Michael is called upon to heal it.[577] The war-god Odin's place is occupied by the warrior angel St. Michael, while Phol-Baldere's place is occupied by Stephan.

The legend of St. Stephan as told in the Bollandist work *Acta Sanctorum*, contains features which indicate that elements of the Baldur myth were incorporated into it after the Christian conversion of the Germanic tribes. Baldur's story, which is uniquely suited to that of Stephen the first martyr, probably invited the assimilation. The *New Testament* (*Acts* 7:59) says that Stephen was stoned to death by a crowd surrounding him. When Baldur dies, he stands within a circle of men (*mannhringr*) who "shoot and cast stones at him."[578] *Gylfaginning* informs us that Baldur's death caused the world great sorrow, while *Acta Sanctorum* says of one *beatus Stephanus*,[579] an abbot in a Frankish Monastery, that

> "when he died, a grief arose in which the heavens and the entire earth took part. All activity ceased; no one was in a condition to do anything. Rumbles and whimpers were heard among the constellations. Multitudes of lamentation streamed together. It was as if the whole world emitted a moaning cry."

This universal despair has its parallel in what is said of Baldur's death. The Aesir are paralyzed with grief. They do not speak or move but simply burst into tears. The entire world shares their sorrow. Everything weeps: *menninir ok kykvendin ok jörðin ok steinarir ok tré ok allr málmr* ["people and animals and earth and stones and trees and all metals"]. Their tears are said to flow like water from frozen things melting in Spring. Baldur's death was preceded by ominous dreams that disrupted his sleep, causing those around him great anxiety. Saxo says that phantoms troubled him at night and that *Persepina* (Persephone), the queen of the underworld revealed herself

---

[576] Grimm, ibid., ch 33; and 38, citing Robert Chamber's *Popular Rhymes, Fireside Stories, and Amusements of Scotland*, 1842, p. 37.
[577] *Petrus, Michael et Stephanus ambulabant per viam. Sic dixit Michahel: Stephani equus infusus, signet illum Deus, signet illum Christus, et herbam comedat et aquam bibat.*
[578] *Gylfaginning* 49.
[579] *Beatus*, "beatified", the stage before becoming a saint.

to him while he slept (Book 3). Of *beatus Stephanus,* it is said that before his death he was afflicted by fiends with such persistence that he could not rest at night. The monks, awakened by his cries, held all-night vigils, saying prayers over him as he slept. Baldur's dreams moved Frigg to request that all nature take oaths not to harm her son. Because of her actions, he was impervious to weapons. Saxo says that iron could not pierce Baldur's "sacred bodily strength," but this invulnerability must have failed, since Hotherus was able to inflict a wound that killed him. Similarly *beatus Stephanus* wore a heavy mail-coat, which finally fell asunder by supernatural intercession.

Baldur's Death
Carl Emil Doepler Jr., 1905

Additional clues aid the identification of St. Stephen and Phol. A saint after his death typically becomes the healer of the sicknesses that he suffered. Saint Stephen cures leg pain and diseases of the foot. The feast day of St. Stephen, like Phol's Day, falls at the beginning of May. A Swedish folk-ballad concerning St. Steffan has him lead five horses of different colors to water.[580] In the *Second Merseburg Charm,* Phol is accompanied by five riders on horseback, Odin and two pairs of sisters. Variants of the ballad, describing St. Steffan as a rider, who *"leder de Foler i Vand alt ved den ljuse Stærne"* ("led the foals to water, all by the bright star"), are recorded in Denmark. In Helsingland, a story is related that "he made his journey following the sun's path."[581] Like the Latin charms mentioned above, the *Ballad of Steffan* makes St. Stephen a rider without having the

---

[580] R. Bergström's and L. Höijer's edition of Geijer's and Afzelius' *"Svenska folkvisor."*
[581] Bergström and Höijer II, p. 354.

slightest basis in the *Book of Acts* or the Catholic tradition of the first martyr. This is easily explained if we recognize a Germanic god clothed as a Christian saint.

The legend of St. Stephen, the first Christian martyr, was particularly popular in Scandinavia, where he appeared in costumed Christmas traditions as Staffan or Helm-staffan, one of the figures who accompanies the Julbock from house to house during Yuletide processions. Like Baldur, he is associated with death and resurrection.[582] In a sixteenth century translation of a Norwegian poem dealing with the Nativity, *Stephanus* allows himself to be hacked into three pieces before returning to life, an image that contradicts the traditional account of the saint's martyrdom by stoning.[583] Two versions of Norwegian folk-plays involving the Three Kings and Staffan contain directions stating that "the skin-clad figure lies down" and "the skin-clad figure gets up," referring to the Julbock. In the second play, Staffan himself boasts how he had fought with the "great jul-bock." In an 1860 variant from Bergen, as well as those from Blekinge, Öland, and Bohuslän, the goat is systematically covered after its death by a series of colored cloaks, before returning to life. Both motifs originate in the mythology. Thor's goats, once slaughtered and eaten, spring back to life when the hide and unbroken bones are hallowed by Thor's hammer. Baldur and Hödr return after Ragnarök, according to *Völuspá*.

Carla O'Harris suggests that the content of the *Second Merseberg Charm* describes a ritual procession led by Baldur.[584] In his train, we find his father Odin, rider of the eight-legged horse Sleipnir, whom we have previously recognized as Wodan, leader of the Wild Hunt. Here, he is the powerful "father of galdur" who alone can cure the foot of Baldur's horse. In *Hávamál* 155, he professes to know spells that cleanse the air of evil spirits. Near him rides his wife, Frigg (Frau Frekka, Frau Gode), who accompanies her husband through the air in the Furious Host [See Chapter VI: The Wild Hunt]. Sunna, a representative of the Sun rides with them. In the *Second Merseburg Charm*, just as Odin's wife Frigg is accompanied by her sister Volla who later appears as her handmaiden Fulla, Sunna is accompanied by

---

[582] Gunnell, *The Origins of Drama in Scandiavia*, p. 119.
[583] Gunnell, ibid.
[584] Carla O'Harris with Siegfried Goodfellow, *"When Did the Events in the Merseburg Charm Occur in the Mythic Cycle?"* (2014).

her sister Sinhtgunt. Since Sinhtgunt rides closest to Phol-Baldur, indicated by her being the first on the scene to assist him, she probably represents his wife, Nanna. The name Sinhtgunt, if one sticks to the manuscript reading, means "the night-walking one."[585] Her role as Sunna's sister suggests a moon-goddess. The primary objection to this has been that the Moon, Mani, is masculine in the North. This does not bar Sinhtgunt from representing the Moon. In *Vafþrúðnismál* 47, Sol is said to bear a daughter, who shall ride after her. Sunna's sister, Sinhtgunt, thus may be a child of the moon-god. Two of the names given for Nanna's father suggest as much. In Saxo's *Danish History*, he is named Gevar (*Gevari*), which could mean "the ward of the weather" from *gæ*, a synonym for "weather" found in the *Nafnaþulur* (*veðra heiti*). In *Hyndluljóð* 20, she is the daughter of *Nökkvi* meaning "boat." Taken together, these names suggest that Nanna's father was a mythic person operating in the atmosphere in connection with a boat. The crescent moon certainly could be imagined as a boat sailing across the sky. In *Gylfaginning* 32, Nanna is called *Nefs dóttur* [R and U mss.]. In *Beowulf*, which refers to the Baldur myth and knows Hermod, one Hnæf is attacked and burnt by a vassal, the same fate shared by Nanna's father Gevar in Saxo's version, who is attacked and burnt at night by his vassal (perhaps intended as a mythic illustration of the Harvest Moon, which appears large and orange-colored on the horizon). Although this evidence is merely suggestive, considering that Baldur is most often conceived of as a solar god, it would not be unusual for his wife to be associated with the moon. Sunna and Nanna thus appear to be the daughters of Sol and Mani.

Seen in this light, the *Second Merseburg Charm* clearly refers to a celestial procession in which Baldur and his family accompany representations of the Sun and Moon across the sky. Such a procession is commonplace in Norse mythology. *Grímnismál* 37 informs us that the horses Árvakr and Alsviðr draw the sun across the sky, and strophe 30 names ten horses that the gods ride across the Bifröst bridge daily. According to *Vafþrúðnismál*, Night and Day traverse the heavens on horses of their own. The presence of such high ranking deities with the sun and her sister was perhaps intended to protect these luminaries from the monsters which pursue them across the sky. According to *Grímnismál* 39:

[585] Simek, ibid., p. 285, citing Erik Brate and Folke Ström.

Sköll heitir úlfr,	Sköll is the name of the wolf,
er fylgir inu skírleita goði	who follows the fair-faced goddess
til varna viðar,	to *varna viðar,*
en annarr Hati,	while another called Hati
hann er Hróðvitnis sonr,	—he is Hróðvitnir's son—
sá skal fyr heiða brúði himins.	Shall precede the bright bride of heaven.

The phrase *varna viðar* can be read in two ways: 1) as the "wardens' wood" or "protectors' wood" if *varna* is understood as an adjective, or 2) as the "Varns' wood," if *varna* is taken as a proper name. The Varns must be "protectors," as their name implies. The presence of Sunna in the *Second Merseberg Charm* indicates that the procession leads to *varna viða*r in the west. This finds support in the text, where the riders are said to enter the "wood" when Baldur's horse is lamed. His companions rush to his aid, no doubt in the order they were riding. Baldur leads his wife and her sister, Sihntgunt and Sunna, followed by his mother and her sister, Frigg and Fulla. Odin takes up the rear until they are all safely "in the wood."

Sol and Day
Karl Ehrenberg, 1882

The Baldur myth easily lends itself to solar interpretations.[586] Baldur's burning funeral pyre aboard a ship pushed out to sea may represent the setting sun. Along the same lines, *Gylfaginning* 50 says that the mistletoe which causes Baldur's death grew "west of Valhalla." Similarly, in *Baldrs draumar* 10-11, when Odin asks who will avenge Baldur, the völva states, *Rindr berr Vála í vestrsölum*, "Rind shall bear Vali in western halls." His tale is told most fully by Saxo (*Gesta Danorum*, Book III). There Odin is rebuffed by Rind three times, before touching her with a piece of bark upon which he had cut runes. At once she fell ill. He returns shortly thereafter dressed as a woman, pretending to be a physician offering to cure the girl, but once alone with her, he ravishes Rind. This is confirmed in a poetic passage by the skald Kormak in *Skáldskaparmál* 68, which states that "Ygg [Odin] worked *seið* on Rind." That this is a shameful episode in Odin's history is made apparent in *Lokasenna* 24, where Loki mocks Odin for going about dressed as a völva, practicing *seið*. In Saxo's Danish History, Book 3, Odin is dethroned and exiled for ten years for committing this vile act. *Hávamál* 96-102, which describes Odin's conquest of Billing's daughter, appears to refer to the same myth. That passage too is steeped in solar imagery, making it probable that Billing's girl, the *sól-hvíta* "sun-white" maiden whom Odin seeks (v. 97), is Sol herself. Odin first arrives in the evening to find her well-guarded by warriors with burning torches, a picture of the western sky at sunset. He returns early the next morning to discover she is gone. In her stead, he finds a bitch tied to the bed, perhaps alluding to the wolf who persues her. Billing's name occurs in the dwarf-list of *Völuspá*. It is also found in the Anglo-Saxon poem *Widsith* (*Exeter Book* 320, 7), which states: *Billing veold Vernum*, "Billing ruled the Varns," immediately recalling the *varna viðar* associated with the setting sun in *Grímnismál* 39. If this is correct, Billing appears to be a counterpart of Delling, the elf who guards the sunrise in the east (*Hávamál* 160). Delling is the father of Dag (day) who accompanies the sun across the sky on his own horse Skinfaxi ("Shining-mane"), according to *Gylfaginning* 10 and *Vafþrúðnismál* 11-12. It appears that Billing resides on the western horizon with a contingent of warriors who protect the sun after her journey across the sky, by burning

---

[586] In *Murder and Vengeance among the Gods*, p. 79, John McKinnell, when speaking of interpretations of the Baldur myth notes "a surprisingly large number of fairly recent attempts rely on solar mythology."

torches in the west. The road is frought with danger, for not only do the wolves Sköll and Hati lurk, but according to *Völuspá* 40-41, an old giantess sits in the east, the beginning of their path each day, nurturing the offspring of Fenrir, one of whom will snatch the moon and dye the gods' citadel red with blood. This mythic scenario seems to lie behind the *Second Merseburg Charm*. On one of these occasions, as he accompanies his wife and her sister Sunna across the sky, keeping them safe from harm, Baldur's horse is lamed. This fateful injury must presage his own demise.

According to Scandinavian tradition, Baldur's death occurred at Midsummer. In Sweden in the nineteenth century, Midsummer fires were known as Baldur's balefires (*Balders bålar*), a tradition followed by the Swedish poet Elias Tegner in the thirteenth song of his *Fridthjof's Saga*, which places Baldur's death at Midsummer, during the time of the midnight sun. In the 1870s, Llewlyn Lloyd, author of *Peasant Life in Sweden*, writes:

> "St Han's (St. John's) eve is, in Sweden, the most joyous night of the whole year. In parts of the country, more especially in the provinces of Bohus and Scania, and in the districts bordering Norway, in which country Balder was worshiped, it is celebrated by the frequent discharge of firearms, and also by huge bonfires, formerly called '*Balder's Bålar*', symbols of the obsequies of that god, whose body was consumed on an immense funeral pyre,—which are kindled at dusk on hills and eminences, and throw a glare over the face of the surrounding country. It is remarkable that it is still the custom to dance around and jump over and through, these fires reminding one of the ancient feast of Baal."

Jacob Grimm wondered if this could be the true origin of such fires. Although this attribution may be due to the recent revival of Scandinavian mythology beginning in the late 1700s, several aspects of the Midsummer traditions seem to reflect elements of the Baldur myth and so may have their root there. The most obvious is the ritual gathering of mistletoe, the plant responsible for Baldur's death. As such, it has elicited considerable discussion in the scholarly literature.[587] Rembert Dodoens in the sixth book of his *A Niewe Herball, or Historie of Plantes* (1578) describes Mistletoe as a "plante with many slender branches," leaves "of a darke or browne greene

---

[587] Lindow, ibid., p. 60.

colour" and small yellow flowers, which appear at the end of May. Its berries "small rounde and white," ripen by the end of September and remain all winter. Mistletoe does not grow in earth, but is found rooted on apple trees, pear trees, as well as the linden, birch and other species in the more temperate regions of Northern Europe and Scandinavia. Dodoens concludes that "the best mistletoe, of greatest estimation, is that which grows upon the oak." In France and Sweden special virtues are ascribed to mistletoe gathered at Midsummer. In Sweden, where the people "believing it to be, in a high degree, possessed of mystic qualities"[588] held that "mistletoe must be cut on the night of Midsummer Eve when sun and moon stand in the sign of their might."[589] The most precious virtue of mistletoe is that it affords sure protection against sorcery and witchcraft. In Sweden, "if a sprig of it be attached to the ceiling of the dwelling, the horse's stall, or the cow's crib, the Troll will then be powerless to injure either man or beast."[590]

That these beliefs date back to heathen times seems certain, as mistletoe has been revered in Northern Europe for centuries. Fragments of mistletoe have been found among the remains of the ancient lake dwellings in Switzerland (c. 5000 to 500 BC), some of the earliest agricultural settlements in Europe. The stomach contents of Lindow Man, a second century BC victim of sacrifice recovered from a peat bog in Cheshire, England in 1984, revealed traces of mistletoe pollen among a last meal consisting of burnt wheat, bran, and barley, indicating a grain offering rather than a common supper. Analysis of the pollen suggests it had collected on the stigmas of flowering cereals, stored and eaten with the grain. The manner of Lindow Man's death — a "triple death" from blows to the head, an incision and a cord wrapped around the neck— is consistent with the sacrifice of the slave girl described by Ibn Fadlan among the Scandinavian Rus in the tenth century. Based on the available evidence, scholars such as Anne Ross have suggested that Lindow Man was sacrificed at Beltain, after a symbolically burnt meal of bread made from many types of grain, reminiscent of the loaves of mixed grain associated with Germanic plowing rituals [See Chapters I: The Prehistoric Context and III: The Anglo-Saxon *Æcerbót*]. Some

---

[588] Lloyd, ibid., p. 269.
[589] Grimm, ibid., III, p. 353 after Richard Dybeck, *Runa* (1844), p. 22.
[590] Lloyd, ibid., p. 269.

have suggested that Lindow man enacted the role of a dying fertility god, such as the "Green Man." Celtic tradition taught that mistletoe was a safeguard against poison and a remedy for disease. The Roman writer Pliny the Elder (23-79 AD) states: "While on this subject we also must not omit the respect shown to this plant by the Gallic provinces. The Druids—that is what they call their magicians—hold nothing more sacred than mistletoe and a tree on which it is growing, provided it is a hard-oak," (*Natural History*, XVI, 95). He further describes the ritual associated with its gathering:

> "The mistletoe, which they term all-healing, is not commonly met with, but when found is gathered with great solemnity, and especially on the sixth day of the moon (which they reckon as the beginning of their months and years) …they prepare a ritual sacrifice and banquet beneath a tree and bring up two white bulls, whose horns are bound for the first time on this occasion. A priest arrayed in white vestments climbs the tree and with a golden sickle cuts down the mistletoe, which is caught in a white cloak. Then finally they kill the victims, praying to God to render his gift propitious to those on whom he has bestowed it. They believe that mistletoe given in drink will impart fertility to any animal that is barren, and that it is an antidote for all poisons."[591]

In the Scotch shires of Elgin and Moray, down to the second half of the eighteenth century, people would cut mistletoe and ivy at the full moon of March, make circles of it and keep them all year, professing to cure persistent fever and other afflictions by means of them. In Sweden, a sprig of mistletoe is hung round a patient's neck or a ring of it is worn on the finger to cure complaints. In Wales it was believed that a sprig of mistletoe gathered on Midsummer Eve, or at any time before the berries appeared, would induce dreams of omen, both good and bad, if it were placed under the pillow of the sleeper. In Austria a twig of mistletoe was laid on the threshold of the bedroom for the prevention of nightmares. Baldur, of course, is well known to have suffered crippling nightmares before his death and subsequent journey to Hel. Can it be a coincidence that an ancient Roman poet states that just such a plant is necessary to enter into and

---

[591] Harvard edition, Rackham. Jones & Eichholz translation, 10 Volumes (1949-54).

return from the underworld? In his *Aeneid* (VI, ll. 133-143), Virgil places these words on the lips of a Sibyl:

> "But if such desire is in your mind, such a longing
> to sail the Stygian lake twice, and twice see Tartarus,
> and if it delights you to indulge in insane effort,
> listen to what you must first undertake. Hidden in a dark tree
> is a golden bough, golden in leaves and pliant stem,
> sacred to Persephone, the underworld's Juno, all the groves
> shroud it, and shadows enclose the secret valleys.
> But only one who's taken a gold-leaved fruit from the tree
> is allowed to enter earth's hidden places.
> This lovely Proserpine has commanded to be brought to her
> as a gift."[592]

When the titular hero of the tale first finds this plant, it is expressly compared to mistletoe (VI, ll. 202-208):

> "Just as mistletoe, that does not form a tree of its own,
> grows in the woods in the cold of winter, with a foreign leaf,
> and surrounds a smooth trunk with yellow berries:
> such was the vision of this leafy gold in the dark oak-tree."

Like Baldur, Demeter's daughter Persephone (Proserpine) is associated with the underworld realm and its ruler. She too is held in the realm of death, despite the best efforts of her mother to free her. Her myth personifies the annual agricultural cycle of life, death and renewal— the same themes present in the Baldur myth. According to Virgil, all she asks of travelers is to bring her the fruit of the mistletoe in exchange for their safe return. Pliny states that its small round berries, gathered at harvest time while still unripe, can be dried and pounded and placed in water, where "in about twelve days they turn rotten," adding that "this is the only case of a thing that becomes attractive by rotting." When processed in this manner, the berries "become viscous in their inner flesh. After being kneaded with oil it becomes bird-lime, a substance used for entangling birds' wings by contact with it when one wants to snare them," (*Natural History* XVI, 94). It goes without saying that this process forms a parallel to the stories of Persephone and Baldur, who are trapped and held against

---

[592] *The Aeneid*, A. S. Kline translation (2002) with thanks to Carla O'Harris for bringing this to my attention.

their will in the land of the dead. The twelve days required to complete this process may be symbolic of Yule.

Mistletoe is one of the many plants whose magical or medicinal qualities were believed to peak with the sun on the longest day of the year if gathered on Midsummer Eve before sunrise. Another favorite was St. John's Wort, which, like mistletoe bears yellow flowers, resembling a little copy of the sun itself. According to Sophus Bugge, the plants in the North designated *Baldrsbrá,* (Baldur's brow) resemble each other in that they are composed of a yellow disc with white rays.[593] The petals of St. John's Wort, which are marked with dark purple spots, when squeezed yield an essential oil, red in color. German peasants believed that this red oil was the blood of St. John and healed all sorts of wounds. In Mecklenburg they say that if you pull up St. John's wort at noon on Midsummer Day you will find a bead of red juice called St. John's blood at the root; smear this blood over your heart and no dog will bite you. In the Mark of Brandenburg, the same blood rubbed on the barrel of a gun will make every shot hit its mark. Another tradition in Mecklenburg says a burning coal can be found beneath the same plant at noon on Midsummer's day, which if found and carried off in silence while the church bells ring will prove a remedy for all sorts of maladies. According to another German superstition, the same coal will turn to gold. In Sweden, people gathered nine kinds of flowers including *Johannes-gras* on St. John's Eve in strict silence to fashion Midsummer bouquets called *Qvasts*. Fathers hung them in the house, one for each of his family; whosever withered first, indicated who would be first to die. A *Qvast* was also hung in the barn as protection against witchcraft and said to retain this virtue the whole year until it was replaced the next with a fresh one.[594]

In ancient times, the most festive season of the year was known as *Sunewende,* "sun's wending," referring to the summer solstice when the sun had reached its highest point and from there would begin its annual decline, reaching its lowest point at Yule. The term was commonly stated in the plural *sunewenden,* because this high position of the sun lasts several days. In Christian times, this Midsummer season coincided with St. John's day (June 24), explicitly expressed in the OHG phrase: *sant Johans sunewenden tac.* Charlemagne

[593] Bugge, *Studier* I, 283.
[594] Lloyd, ibid., p. 268.

(d. 814 AD) kept this festival at Eporediarea and Louis the Pious of Aquataine held assemblies on the same day in 824 and 831. That these practices had heathen roots is made evident in *The Life of St. Eligius* (588-660 AD), who worked for twenty years to convert the pagan population of Flanders. He warned, "No Christian on the feast of Saint John or the solemnity of any other saint performs *solestitia* [solstice rites?] or dancing or leaping or diabolical chants. ...None should presume to make lustrations or incantations with herbs, or to pass cattle through a hollow tree or ditch because this is to consecrate them to the devil." During this season great numbers of people gathered to celebrate around ritually kindled bonfires. The Solstice was celebrated in this manner by the Germans, the Romans and the Slavs. In 1593 in Rostock, Germany, Nicolaus Gryse mentions as a regular practice on St. John's day:

> "Toward nightfall they warmed them by St. John's blaze and needfire (*nodfür*) that they sawed out of wood, kindling the same not in God's name but St. John's; leapt and ran and drove the cattle therethrough, and were fulfilled of a thousand joys whereas they had passed the night in great sins, shames and harms."

In German documents of the fourteenth and fifteenth centuries, these fires were called *sunwentfeuer* or *sunwentfewr;* and *sunäwetsfoir* or *sunwentsfeur* among the Austrian and Bavarian peasantry of the nineteenth century. Throughout northern Europe we find evidence of such fire festivals at Easter and Midsummer. A common feature of these festivals is a burning wagon-wheel, which indicates that the original rites were most likely held at Midsummer when the sun reached its highest point in the sky. In 1823 at Konz, a German village on the Moselle near Sierk, a huge wheel was wrapped with straw, so that none of the wood was left showing. A pole was passed through it so it could be carried. At the signal of the Mayor (who, according to long-standing custom received a basket of cherries for his service), the wheel was set ablaze to the cheers of the crowd and sent rolling downhill into the Moselle. Inhabitants of neighboring villages flocked to the river side to join in the rejoicing. In his *Weltbuch* (1534), Sebastian Franck reported the following Shrovetide custom in Franconia, the home of Nürnberg:

> "They draw a fiery plow kindled by a fire cunningly made thereon, until it falls to pieces. They wrap a wagon wheel all round

in straw, drag it up a high steep mountain, and hold thereon a merrymaking all the day, as they may for the cold, with many sorts of pastime, as singing, leaping, dancing, odd or even, and other pranks. About the time of vespers they set the wheel afire, and let it run into the vale at full speed, which to look upon is like as the sun were running from the sky."[595]

On St. Vitus's Day (June 15th, near Midsummer) at Obermedlingen in Swabia, a cart-wheel covered with pitch and plaited straw was hoisted atop a 12 foot pole inserted in the nave of the wheel and ignited. This blaze, called the "fire of heaven", was kindled on the summit of the mountain and, as the flame ascended, the people recited a set formula with eyes and arms raised heavenward. A German *Weisthümer* (2, 615-6. 693-7) speaks of a custom in which "at the great yearly assize, a cartwheel that has lain soaking in water for six weeks and three days was placed in a fire kindled." A great banquet lasted until the nave of the wheel, which must not be turned or poked, was consumed. Such fires are attested in France as early as the twelfth and thirteenth centuries by John Beleth, a Parisian priest writing about 1162, and William Durantis (1237- 1296). Beleth, the author of *Summa de divinis officiis*, printed in 1572 at Dillingen describes the ritual in Christian terms:

> "Brands of their lighted torches are also brought (on the feast of John the Baptist) and they become the fires which signify St. John, who was burning like the light of a lamp, preceding and the precursor of the true light of the world; The wheel turns in some places, in order to signify, that just as the sun can reach no higher in its own circle, he (St. John) cannot march forward to a higher level, but just as the sun must descend in its circle, thus the fame of John, who was thought to be the Christ, must descend, a fact that he bore witness to, saying: I must decrease, so that he may increase." (ch. 137, p. 256)

That these festivals were long considered heathen in origin is evident by a number of edicts concerning them. The Council of Constantinople in Trullo in 680 AD expressly forbid kindling need-fires, as did the Synod of Rome in Leptina in the year 743. Older, but more specific, is the testimony of Eligius (d. 660 AD) who writes

---

[595] That these activities, as well as their association with the plow and the wagon, mirror the Yule rites held at the winter solstice, should not escape notice.

"'No one at the feast of St. John or any of the holy feasts of the summer solstice may dance or recite songs of the devil." Throughout the Roman Empire, certain popular pastimes were forbidden to lay people and clergy alike under pain of excommunication, including the consultation of soothsayers, the use of incantations, public dancing, men dressed as women and vice versa, the use of masks, the invocation of Bacchus at vintage time, and jumping over bonfires lit at new moon. Such folk customs, however, were too deeply ingrained to be rooted out by conciliar decree and thus long survived.[596] On June 20, 1653, the Nürnberg town-council issued the following order:

> "Whereas experience heretofore hath shown, that after the old heathenish use, on John's day in every year, in the country, as well in towns as villages, money and wood hath been gathered by young folk, and thereupon the so-called sonnenwendt fire kindled, and thereat winebibbing, dancing about the said fire, leaping over the same, with burning of sundry herbs and flowers, and setting of brands from the said fire in the fields, and all manner of superstitious work carried out---Therefore the Honorable Council of Nürnberg town neither can nor ought to forbear to do away with all such unbecoming superstition, paganism, and peril of fire on this coming day of St. John."

In 1682, Gustavus Adolphus, Duke of Mecklenburg, forbid the kindling of need-fires and as late as 1850, Sunwend fires were forbidden in Austria. In the north of Germany these festivals took place at Easter where they marked the entrance of spring (the vernal equinox). In the south, they occurred at Midsummer where they marked the longest day of the year. The time depended on whether the people were Saxons or Franks. All Lower Saxony, Westphalia, Lower Hesse, Gelders, Holland, Frisia, Jutland and Zealand had Easter fires, although England has no trace of them. While up the Rhine in Franconia, Thuringia, Swabia, Bavaria, Austria, and Silesia, Midsummer fires burned. Some countries, such as Denmark and Carthinia did both. Olaus Magnus (1555) holds that Midsummer fires were burned in Scandinavia. Llewellyn Lloyd reports bonfires at Midsummer and on May Day in nineteenth century Sweden. Of the May Day fires, he says:

---

[596] J. M. Hussey, *The Orthodox Church in the Byzantine Empire* (2010), p. xxxiv.

"Huge bonfires, which should be lighted by striking two flint stones together, then blaze on all the hills and knolls. Every large hamlet has its own fire, so that one may at times see from twenty to thirty in the same parish. The youth of both sexes assemble from all parts of the country at these fires, when forming a ring (two or three rings, one within the other, it may be, if the company is numerous), they dance round them until the night is well advanced. Whilst the young are thus enjoying themselves, the old people take note and carefully mark if their number be odd or even; as also if the flames incline to the north or south. In the former case, they believe the spring will be cold and backward, but in the latter, genial and mild."

The grand high time of the spring festivals occurred on May Day, mostly falling on May 1st, but sometimes on the 2nd or 3rd. In the Rhine districts, a Pfultag, Pulletag (Phol's day) fell precisely on the 2nd of May (*Weistheimer* 2, 8. 3, 748), corresponding to Phol's day in the Rhineland, nearly midway between Easter and Midsummer, but closer to Easter when it fell late. In Irish and Gaelic, this day is known as *la Bealteine* or *Beltaine*, also spelt *Beltein*, from *teine* or *taine* meaning fire, and *Beal, Bel*, understood to be the name of a deity of light peculiar to the Celts. A *Pholmânôt* [Phol's month] which ended on the autumn-equinox, may also be relevant here, as Phol-Baldur is typically interpreted as a god of light and summer.

Closely related to the Midsummer fires are the so-called need-fires, not kindled at fixed periods, but on occasions of distress, particularly at the outbreak of an infectious disease affecting cattle or other animals, commonly in spring and summer. Need-fire is always produced by friction and frequently by the revolution of a wheel; in Mull, where a heifer was sacrificed, it was made by turning an oak wheel over nine oak spindles from east to west, in the direction of the sun. Livestock were typically driven through the need-fire, just as they are sometimes driven through the Midsummer fires. In the first historic mention of Beltain, made by Cormac, Archbishop of Cashel (d. 908), two fires were made near one another, for men and cattle to pass through unharmed. This practice survived the centuries. When a deadly cattle-plague raged at Neustadt near Marburg in 1598, a man by the name of Johan Kohler induced the authorities to adopt the following remedy: He instructed them to take a new wagon-wheel and spin it around an axle, which had never been used before, until it burst into flame, then to kindle a bonfire with it between the gates of the town and drive all the cattle through it. Moreover, every homeowner must rekindle his hearth fire with a brand lit from it. So it was done. This measure, however, had no effect on the plague, and seven years later Kohler was burnt as a witch. According to a book published nine years after Kohler's death, many Germans, especially those in the Wassgaw mountains, confidently believed that driving sick animals through a need-fire kindled by the friction of a pole on dry oak could cure such a murrain; but only if all fires in the village had previously been extinguished with water.

At Gandersheim down to about the beginning of the nineteenth century, need-fire was commonly lit by causing a cross-bar to revolve rapidly on its axis between two upright posts. The rope which produced the revolution of the bar had to be new and if possible woven of threads from a gallows-rope. On the lower Rhine, need-fire is said to have been kindled by the friction of oak-wood on fir. In Germany, need-fires were popular down to the second half of the nineteenth century. The bonfire itself had to be kindled before sunrise, often beginning at two a.m., and made up of straw and wood contributed by every household. In some places, nine different types of word were required. Anyone who failed to put out his own hearth fire before the need-fire was kindled was punished. Searches were conducted through the houses and any flame discovered was extinguished, so that not even a spark remained alight in the whole village. If in spite of every precaution, no flame could be elicited by the friction, the failure was attributed to witchcraft. If the efforts were successful, a bonfire was lit from it at the gates of the city and when the flames had died down, the animals were driven through the glowing embers three times, amid a great commotion of people shouting and shrieking and cracking whips. Comparing accounts, swine were driven through first, then cattle, followed by other animals such as horses and geese. As soon as all the beasts passed through, the youth of the village would rush wildly into the ashes, blackening each other with them, then march in triumphal procession behind the cattle into the village. That this custom is old is evident from the writing of Evinus, abbot of Rosmic-Treon and author of *Vita sexta St. Patricii*, who says of the Beltaine fires: "it was provided by a rigorous law that all fires should be extinguished in every district on that night, and that no one should be at liberty to rekindle fire before the pile of sacrifice had been raised. Whoever transgressed this law in any respect was visited for the offence with nothing less than capital punishment." John Colgan's *Acta Triadis Thaumaturgae* (1647), which presents seven lives of St. Patrick including Evinus' work, states that priests strictly supervised the sacrifice.

Although the majority of the available accounts limit the use of needfire to an outbreak of murrain, some expressly inform us that it was resorted to at stated times of the year, especially Midsummer, and that cattle were driven through the flames to protect them against future illnesses. The fire itself was thought to avert the harmful effects of witchcraft. In Sweden, need-fire was called either *vrid-eld*, "turned fire" or *gnid-eld*, "rubbed fire" after its means of production. Down to the end of the eighteenth century need-fire there, as in Germany, was kindled by rubbing two pieces of wood together. Sometimes, nine different kinds of wood were used. The smoke of the fire was considered beneficial. As in Germany, cattle were driven through its smoke. In addition, fruit-trees were fumigated with it, so that they might bear fruit, and nets, so that they might catch fish. In the second half of the nineteenth century an old man in Sundal, Norway who made his living setting salmon-traps in the Driva river, kindled *naueld* ("need-fire") or *gnideld* when his yield fell, in order to counteract the witchcraft, which he believed to be the cause of it. For this purpose, he set up two planks of wood, boring a hole in each, then through the holes inserted a pointed rod, around which he had wound a long cord. He used the cord to make the rod revolve rapidly, thereby creating much friction. Thus he drew fire from the wood in the belief that it would render the witchcraft powerless. In Denmark, Baldur's death was attributed to witchcraft. In Saxo's account, Hotherus (Höðr) meets three witches from whom he learns the secret of Baldur's strength and obtains a magic belt that insures him victory over that god. Need-fire also plays a role in Snorri's account of Baldur's death. When the gods cannot launch Baldur's ship laden with grave goods, they summon the giantess Hyrrokin to accomplish this task. She shoves the ship so hard that the wooden rollers beneath it burst into flame, igniting the funeral pyre built aboard the boat. Thor (who represents lightning) is so enraged, he raised his hammer to strike Hyrokkin dead, but the gods restrain him. Hyrrokin means the "fire-smoked" and may refer to the enigmatic witch Gullveig-Heid mentioned in *Völuspá* 21-24, whom the gods burn three times in Odin's hall in an effort to kill her. Their efforts are in vain. Thrice burnt and thrice reborn, she yet lives. No matter how hot the flame, her cold heart remained. Loki found it and ate it each time, giving birth to a series of three terrible monsters, beginning with the Fenris Wolf (*Hyndluljóð* 41). According to *Völuspá*, wherever Gullveig went men called her Heid. The Codex Regius version says she was ever the delight of evil people, (*illrar þioðar*); the *Hauksbók* manuscript reads *illrar bruðar* ("evil women") and places the strophe (H 25) concerning "the old one in the Iron wood" who breeds Fenrir's kin (*aldna í Járnviði ..ok fœddi þar Fenris kindir*) immediately before those concerning Gullveig-Heid (H26-27), suggesting a link between her and the mother of Fenrir's children. In *Baldurs draumar* 13, Odin calls the dead völva he summons to learn details of Baldur's death, "the mother of three monsters," (*þriggja þursa móðir*). Thus, she must be the same as Angrboda, the mother of Loki's terrible children. Like Baldur, she too is associated with death and resurrection, but all the usual symbols are reversed. In the Icelandic sources, the mistletoe, which elsewhere protected the wearer from injury, becomes an instrument of death, and friction fire normally used to repel witchcraft is kindled by the arch-witch herself, as she pushes the innocent Baldur's pyre out to sea. Such reversals often found in Norse myth,[597] commonly indicate an imbalance in the natural order, appropriate for the occasion in which they occur—in this instance, the death of the Earth Mother's beloved son.

Other curious traditions suggest that the Midsummer fires originally had their root in the Baldur myth. Both Tacitus and Ibn Fadhlan speak of different kinds of woods being used by the Germans to raise a funeral pyre. The same seems to be true of curative need-fires. In Austrian Silesia in the early twentieth century, need-fires produced by the friction of nine kinds of wood were employed for the purpose of curing or preventing the spread of murrain. Cattle, both sick and sound, were driven through these fires with the expectation that the sick would be healed and the sound saved. When plague broke out among the cattle at Dobischwald in Silesia a half century earlier, a splinter of wood was chipped from the threshold of every house and the cattle were driven to a cross-road where a pair of twin brothers had felled a tree. The splinters and the tree were burnt together in a bonfire, kindled by rubbing two pieces

---

[597] Eleazar Meletinskij, "Scandinavian Mythology as a System of Oppositions",. *Patterns in Oral Literature*, ed. Dimitri Segal and Heda Jason, (1977).

of wood together. Once the bonfire blazed, the horns of the cattle were trimmed and the parings thrown into the flames, before the animals themselves were driven through the fire to guard the herd against the plague. Among the Germans of Western Bohemia, the persons who kindle the need-fire must also be brothers or share the same first name. In the Halberstadt district, the rope used to wind the wood in the socket had to be pulled by two chaste young men. In June of 1868 a traveller in Mecklenburg saw a couple of peasants pulling a rope back and forth in silence to make a roller revolve with great speed in the socket of an upright post. When he inquired what they were up to, an old woman confided to the stranger that because her pigs were sick, her two sons were busy extracting a need-fire from the post in order to ignite a bonfire through which the ailing swine would be driven. She explained that two brothers or at least two men who bore the same name must be employed for this task. Just like the association of Midsummer fires with mistletoe and Baldur's pyre, the kindling of curative need-fires by two brothers may point back to the myth of Baldur and Höður. The evidence is simply too far removed from the source to draw any firm conclusions.

Nothing Could Harm Baldur
Charles E. Brock, 1930

Sports and games associated with Midsummer festivities may provide yet another link to the Baldur myth. Both *Snorri's Edda* and *Beowulf*'s account of Herebeald inform us that games were being played at the time of his death. Because all things had sworn to do Baldur no harm, he was in effect was invulnerable. The gods made a sport of this circumstance, standing in a circle (*mannhringr*) and shooting weapons at him. This practice finds an analog in historical practice. In the *Germania* ch. 24, Tacitus speaks of just such a game among the early Germanic tribes:

> "They have only one kind of public show and it is the same at every gathering; naked youths whose sport this is to fling themselves about in a dance between swords and spears leveled at them. Training produces skill, and skill grace, but they do it not for gain or any payment. However daring their abandon, their sole reward is the spectators' pleasure."

Sporting events and games are closely associated with Midsummer, although traditions vary widely. Olaus Magnus (Book 15, ch. 23-25) describes sword and hoop dances taking place in Sweden as late as the sixteenth century. Violet Alford notes that the sword dance described by Olaus Magnus is typical of European dances of the same type.[598] It is found all over Germany, in Sweden, Scotland, England and the Hebrides. Other reports of Scandinavian sword dances occur in Börgo, Finland; Copenhagen (1554) and Aalborg (1431), where the dance was already regarded as an old custom. The hoop dance which involved more circus-like acrobatics is in the same genre.[599] The most characteristic feature across the board in the recorded examples is one in which the swords are interlaced around the neck of one of the dancers, kneeling in the center of the circle, suggesting a ritual sacrifice. At the climax of the dance, each dancer withdrew his sword from the lock with a clash of steel, which would have injured the kneeling figure if performed in earnest. According to Benjamin Thorpe (1851), "in the neighborhood of Dent in Yorkshire, the country people, at certain seasons, particularly in Autumn, have a procession, and perform old dances, one of which they call the giants' dance. The principal giant they call Woden, and his wife Frigga. The chief feature of the spectacle is, that two swords are swung round the neck of a boy and struck together without hurting him."[600] Sword dances and Morris dances, which probably derived from them, are designed primarily for young, active

---

[598] *Sword Dance and Drama* (1962), p. 115.
[599] Terry Gunnell, *Origins of Drama in Scandinavia*, p. 130, fn.
[600] *Northern Mythology* Vol. I, p. 276 "from a communication by Kemble. Müller, p. 121."

men and require bodily strength and agility. The sword dance is typically the privilege of certain guilds or closed societies, generally of young unmarried men. That it is limited to men only indicates its ritualistic character.[601] In the early decades of the twentieth century, Cecil Sharp observed: "Out of the debris of ancient faith and cult have issued three forms of folk-art", the Morris Dance, the Sword Dance, and the Mummer's Play.[602] These sword dances may be related to circle dances, such as the masked Gothikon, war-dances accompanied by lutes, performed by Varangians in Constantinople on the ninth day of Christmas, most likely intended to symbolize the seasonal drama as a cycle of death and rebirth, the same elements present in the Baldur myth.

The Sword-Dance
F.W. Heine, 1882

Scattered reports of a dramatic annual battle between Summer and Winter occur all over the north, where occasionally, the same battle is enacted against Death, embodied by the Grim Reaper. Since ancient times, acrobatics and leaping have been associated with ritual processions. In Bohuslän, Sweden and elsewhere in

---

[601] Kris Kershaw, *The One-Eyed-God* (2000), p. 88.
[602] Roger Savage, *Masques, Mayings and Music-Dramas* (2014), p. 329.

Scandinavia, Bronze Age rock-carvings depict human figures leaping off of ships, laden with people, some playing instruments or carrying banners and "sun-wheel" emblems. Four Bronze Age figures found at Grevensvænge, Zealand in 1779 depict three men in a kneeling position wielding axes, and a fourth in an acrobatic position, as if throwing himself over a pole. Such leaping is frequently associated with the Midsummer fires. In the nineteenth century at Marseille, France, early in the morning on St. John's day, the country folk would bring flowers into town to sell, ascribing a healing virtue to those picked before sunrise. Great bonfires were lit and some of the plants were thrown into the flames. The young people jumped over it and played jokes on passers-by with hidden fireworks, or dowsed them from windows with water. Jacob Grimm provides a number of references to such activity. He notes: Reiske said "the fire is made under the open sky, the youth and the meaner folk leap over it, and all manner of herbs are cast into it: like these, may all their troubles go off in fire and smoke!"; Denis, recalling his younger days recollects, "Everywhere on St. John's eve there was merry leaping over the *sonnenwendefeuer*, and mead was drunk over it." In Donauländchen on St. John's eve, the townspeople lit fires on the hill, boys and girls competed jumping over the flames amid the joyful cries and songs of the spectators. At Nürnberg the lads went about begging billets of wood, carted them to Bleacher's pond by the Spital-gate, made a fire of them, and jumped over it; this kept them in health the whole year. At Gernsheim in Mentz, the fire was blessed by a priest, and there was singing and prayer so long as it burned; when the flames died out, children jumped over the glowing embers, just as grown-ups did in days past.[603]

While nothing conclusive can be drawn from these scattered traditions, the death of Frigg's beloved son at Midsummer completes the annual cycle of seasonal rituals, which as previously shown, forge connecting links between Harvest, Yuletide, and Spring planting. The association of the Baldur myth with Midsummer completes the annual circle, ever turning in a ring of seasons revolving around the Germanic Earth-Mother and her family. From ancient times, the Northmen divided the year into two seasons, winter and summer, and reckoned the passage of time in winters.[604] After the conversion,

---

[603] Grimm, ibid., II, p. 617 ff, Stalleybrass tr.
[604] Jónas Kristjánsson, *Eddas and Sagas* (1988), p. 133.

Christian time-reckoning was introduced, though it was far from unified in European practice. According to Icelandic law, at the end of the Althing each summer, the lawspeaker would announce the calendar and feast-days to be observed in the coming year. In the oldest Germanic calendars, the year is split into two halves, marked by the summer and winter solstices. In Germanic tradition, Frigg and her husband ride through the air at Yule cleansing the air of malignant spirits and blessing their followers, when the sun is at its lowest point in the sky and the days are shortest. At Midsummer their beloved son —a god of light—is murdered, when the days are longest and the sun begins its annual decline. On first blush, the celebration of the birth of Jesus Christ in winter and his subsequent death in spring appear to be the antithesis of the heathen religion, which is widely believed to reflect the cycles of Nature. Birth in the winter and death in the spring are an apparent contradiction to the observable course of nature, which welcomes new life in the spring, which withers and dies at the onset of winter. Nevertheless, in the Germanic tradition, Baldur dies at the height of summer seemingly in conflict with the natural order of things. This is best explained by celestial events. At midsummer the days begin to gradually shorten until the winter solstice, when they begin to gradually grow longer once more. Most often interpreted as a god of light, Baldur's life mirrors that of the sun, which begins its annual descent at the height of summer. This is not to identify Baldur as a "sun god," or suggest that his sole purpose was as a representation of the sun. Baldur's father, as the inheritor of the mantle of the Indo-European Sky-Father, is also steeped in solar imagery. Odin is the "one eye in the sky" so to speak, who surveys all of the created worlds from his throne at the apex of heaven. Such natural imagery is inherent in Norse mythology. The Germanic Earth-Mother, who is described as "hail-hooded" (likening her white snood to snow-capped mountains) and "fir-tressed", is spoken of in the same manner, directly identifying the goddess with the earth itself [See Chapter IX: Jörð, Thor's Mother]. This leaves little doubt that in ancient times, Odin's wife, the Earth-Mother in Germanic Mythology, was conceived of as Mother Nature.

Mother Earth
in *Atalanta Fugiens*, 1617

ABOUT THE AUTHOR

William P. Reaves is the webmaster of GermanicMythology.com; as well as the translator of Viktor Rydberg's *Our Fathers' Godsaga* (2003), Viktor Rydberg's *Investigations into Germanic Mythology*, Volume II: Parts 1 and 2 (2004-2007), *The Heroic Saga on the Rök Stone* (2007), and *The Sword of Victory: The 2ⁿᵈ Epic* (2013). The author resides near Clearwater, Florida and may be reached at asvinr@yahoo.com.

www.GermanicMythology.com
Texts, Translations and Scholarship
A Resource for Researchers

www.ingramcontent.com/pod-product-compliance
Lightning Source LLC
Chambersburg PA
CBHW021959090426
42811CB00001B/84